Race and British Colonialism in South-East Asia, 1770–1870

The idea of 'race' played an increasing role in nineteenth-century British colonial thought. For most of the nineteenth century, John Crawfurd towered over British colonial policy in South-East Asia, being not only a colonial administrator, journalist and professional lobbyist, but also one of the key racial theorists in the British Empire. He approached colonialism as a Radical liberal, proposing universal voting for all races in British colonies and believing all races should have equal legal rights. Yet at the same time, he also believed that races represented distinct species of people, who were unrelated. This book charts the development of Crawfurd's ideas, from the brief but dramatic period of British rule in Java, to his political campaigns against James Brooke and British rule in Borneo. Central to Crawfurd's political battles were the debates he had with his contemporaries, such as Stamford Raffles and William Marsden, over the importance of race and his broader challenge to universal ideas of history, which questioned the racial unity of humanity. The book taps into little-explored manuscripts, newspapers and writings to uncover the complexity of a leading nineteenth-century political and racial thinker whose actions and ideas provide a new view of British liberal, colonial and racial thought.

Gareth Knapman is a researcher at the Australian National University.

Empires in Perspective

Series Editor
Jayeeta Sharma
University of Toronto

This important series examines a diverse range of imperial histories from the early modern period to the twentieth century. Drawing on works of political, social, economic and cultural history, the history of science and political theory, the series encourages methodological pluralism and does not impose any particular conception of historical scholarship. While focused on particular aspects of empire, works published also seek to address wider questions on the study of imperial history.

Missionary Education and Empire in Late Colonial India, 1860–1920
Hayden J A Bellenoit

Natural Science and the Origins of the British Empire
Sarah Irving

Race and Identity in the Tasman World, 1769–1840
Rachel Standfield

Secularism, Islam and Education in India, 1830–1910
Robert Ivermee

Slaveholders in Jamaica: Colonial Society and Culture during the Era
    of Abolition
Christer Petley

The English Empire in America, 1602–1658: Beyond Jamestown
L H Roper

The Theatre of Empire: Frontier Performances in America, 1750–1860
Douglas S Harvey

Transoceanic Radical: William Duane: National Identity and Empire,
    1760–1835
Nigel Little

Race and British Colonialism in South-East Asia, 1770–1870: John
    Crawfurd and the Politics of Equality
Gareth Knapman

Race and British Colonialism in South-East Asia, 1770–1870

John Crawfurd and the Politics of Equality

Gareth Knapman

Routledge
Taylor & Francis Group

NEW YORK AND LONDON

First published 2017
by Routledge
711 Third Avenue, New York, NY 10017

and by Routledge
2 Park Square, Milton Park, Abingdon, Oxon OX14 4RN

First issued in paperback 2018

Routledge is an imprint of the Taylor & Francis Group, an informa business

Library of Congress Cataloging-in-Publication Data
Names: Knapman, Gareth, author.
Title: Race and British colonialism in Southeast Asia, 1770–1870 :
    John Crawfurd and the politics of equality / by Gareth Knapman.
Description: New York : Routledge, 2017. | Series: Empires in
    perspective | Includes bibliographical references and index.
Identifiers: LCCN 2016030681 (print) | LCCN 2016031103
    (ebook) | ISBN 9781138211766 (hardcover : alk. paper) |
    ISBN 9781315452173 (ebk) | ISBN 9781315452173
Subjects: LCSH: Southeast Asia—History—19th century. | Southeast
    Asia—Civilization—Political aspects. | Great Britain—Colonies—
    Asia—History—19th century. | Crawfurd, John, 1783–1868. |
    Race relations—History—19th century. | Imperialism—History—
    19th century | Orientalism—History—19th century.
Classification: LCC DS526.4 .K63 2017 (print) | LCC DS526.4
    (ebook) | DDC 325.01—dc23
LC record available at https://lccn.loc.gov/2016030681

ISBN 13: 978-1-138-32981-2 (pbk)
ISBN 13: 978-1-138-21176-6 (hbk)

Typeset in Sabon
by Apex CoVantage, LLC

MIX
Paper from
responsible sources
FSC
www.fsc.org   FSC™ C013985

Printed in the United Kingdom
by Henry Ling Limited

Contents

List of Figures   vii
Preface   ix

Introduction   1

1   The East India Company's Scottish Critic of Empire in Asia   12

2   Land, History and the Source of Civilisation   42

3   Searching for the Aboriginal Pre-History of the Savage   71

4   Race and the Natural History of the Savage   98

5   Singapore and Competing Visions of Colonialism   125

6   Protecting and Civilising Savages in Sarawak   154

7   Resisting Colonialism in Sarawak   179

8   Civilisation, the Savage and Equality   209

Conclusion   233

Appendix: Identifying John Crawfurd's Writings
    in The Examiner   241
Bibliography   253
Index   273

Figures

1 John Crawfurd by unknown photographer, c. 1860
  ©National Portrait Gallery, London   146
2 'The large temple at Brambánan, Thomas Stamford Raffles,
  History of Java (London : Black, Parbury, and Allen : and
  John Murray, 1817) Vol. 2, p. 18. Note Raffles's image of
  the temple at Brambánan is indicative of his argument that
  Java originated as a Hindu colony. The architectural
  grandeur was a statement of Indian civilisation, and all
  achievements towards civilisation in Java were therefore a
  consequence of foreign colonisers. The decay of the temple
  in the modern era also represented the decay of civilisation
  in Java and was a subtle message to Raffles's readers that
  Java need a new colonising force from British India.   147
3 'A Family in Dusk Bay, New Zealand' drawn by William
  Hodges from George W. Anderson, *A New, Authentic
  and Complete Account of Voyages Round the World,
  Undertaken and Performed by Royal Authority. Containing
  an Authentic, Entertaining, Full and Complete History of
  Captain Cook's First, Second, Third & Last Voyages*
  (London: Printed for the proprietors, and published
  by Alex. Hogg, 1784). Note the detail in the material
  culture and fauna. In comparison, the people have
  a very European complexion.   148
4 'A Magindano Marriage', Thomas Forrest, *Voyage to New
  Guinea and the Moluccas* (London: G. Scott, 1779). Note
  the Grecian appearance of the subjects and the material
  culture in the background.   149
5 'A Javanese Ronggeng' ©The Trustees of the British
  Museum. Anthony Forge has identified this image as the
  original source illustration used in the production of
  'A Ronggeng or Dancing Girl' in Raffles's *History of Java*.
  See Figure 5.   150

6 'A Ronggeng or Dancing Girl' in Thomas Stamford Raffles,
   History of Java (London : Black, Parbury, and Allen : and
   John Murray, 1817) Vol. 1, p. 342. Compare with Figure 6.   151

7 'A Malay, native of Bencoolen', from William Marsden's
   History of Sumatra (London: The Author, 1810–1811),
   p. 44. This is the only ethnographic image of a person in
   Marsden's history. It is one of the first racial images in
   South-East Asia published in English.   152

8 'A Papua or Negro of the Indian Islands' and 'Kutut a
   Native of Bali one of the Brown complexioned Race',
   John Crawfurd, *History of the Indian Archipelago*, 1820,
   p. 17. Crawfurd used these images to illustrate the 'two
   aboriginal races of human beings inhabiting the Indian
   islands'. The image of the Papuan was a reproduction
   of Dick from Thomas Stamford Raffles's *History of Java*.   153

Preface

The origins of this book began 10 years ago, when I first read John Crawfurd's *History of the Indian Archipelago* in the rare books reading room at Monash University. I was perplexed by what appeared to me at that time to be a strange conglomerate of ideas. Crawfurd appeared to represent the worst aspects of nineteenth-century racism, but at the same time, he clearly asserted democratic ideas that were universal in scope and not limited to Europeans. I soon realised that very little of the secondary literature on racial thought in South-East Asia explained the complexity of Crawfurd's ideas. This search for an explanation into what appeared to be inconsistencies between Crawfurd's ideas grew into a study of nineteenth-century racial and liberal thought in colonial South-East Asia. As I read through Crawfurd's writings and biographical details, I discovered that Crawfurd was not only an important figure for South-East Asian history, but nineteenth-century history more broadly.

The process was a long one and stood idle until 2013, when I decided a comprehensive account of colonial thought on race and liberalism in South-East Asia needed to be written. Central to the story of this book is the fact that Crawfurd's long life meant he participated in debates on colonial policy and scholarship that crossed generations of historian administrators. I am particularly grateful to John Walker, whose expertise on the life and archive of James Brooke enabled me to verify Crawfurd's important role in organising resistance to James Brook's program of colonisation in Sarawak and Borneo amongst British humanitarians.

The preparation of any manuscript for publication involves saying thank you to numerous people. This book would not have made it to publication without the persistence of the *Empires in Perspective* series editor, Jayeeta Sharma, and Max Novick, the editor at Routledge. I would particularly like to thank Robert Cribb, Anthony Milner, Anthony Reid, Mary Quilty, David Rosenberg, John Conner and Lynette Russell for looking at earlier manuscript versions of this book. Their comments, along with the engaging dialogues and exchanges I had with Martin Müller, Tze Shiung and Nadia Wright, helped me refine my interpretation of racial and liberal thought in colonial South-East Asia.

I also thank the following libraries and archives: British Library, National Archives (United Kingdom), National Library of Australia's collection of East India Company archives on microfilm, the Menzies Asian Studies Research Library at the Australian National University, West Sussex Regional Archive, the Royal Geographical Society Archive, the Royal Anthropological Society Archive. Most of all, I need to thank technological change in the last 10 years.

John Crawfurd went out of his way to make tracking his involvement in political debates difficult. Many of the links made in this book were not easy to establish before the existence of digitisation and word searchability. This technology greatly reduces the amount of time involved in shifting through sources. It also means that the type of research is different. Historians traditionally built their research around government archives and therefore narrated the extant debates that were already present in the archive. Thanks to the wonderful work of previous generations of scholars, the colonial-era archives have been extensively researched. Although new insights can certainly be ascertained, it is now a process of diminishing returns.

One of the themes that I demonstrate in this book is that the colonial archive is only one source of authority that provides a disproportionate view of events. There are many actions that officials and lobbyists did not want in the government archive. Much of Crawfurd's activity fell into this sphere. Whether it be his reliance on the Chinese community for internal security in Singapore or his involvement in lobbying against the designs of James Brooke in Sarawak, Crawfurd wanted to limit the information extant in the colonial archive. That does not mean the information is not there, but rather, it is held in a multitude of places. Computing power means that these connections are visible in ways that they were not in the past.

Research that looks at connections between people, power and the archive can change our view of figures of importance. For example, James Mill and his son John Stuart Mill have both been extensively studied as purveyors of a particular form of colonial liberalism. However, they are also the easiest to study, and as a consequence, their ideas can be taken as disproportionately important. This book presents a different view of the relationship between racial thought, liberalism and colonialism in the nineteenth century—one that demonstrates that liberal ideas deriving from the colonial environment of Asia were radical in scope and looked to a unified humanity, based on individual legal equality as a means of overcoming diversity, parochialism and entrenched inequality.

In the final stages of preparation of this book, I was glad of the extra proofreading by Sebastian Clark and Erica Fisher. Finally, I would like to thank my parents Denis and Pamela Knapman and my partner Shobha Varkey, who all supported me through the writing of this book.

Canberra, February 2016

Introduction

In 1820, John Crawfurd (1783–1868) pondered the cause of human conflict across the globe. He wrote that the '[d]ifferences of colour and language are the great obstacles to happiness, improvement, and civilisation of mankind'.[1] He was reflecting on his colonial experience in India and Java, where he witnessed the interaction between Europeans and Asian ethnicities. He subsequently devoted much of his life first to understanding the role of race in human history and secondly, to the promotion of democracy, universal suffrage, free trade and the limiting of European colonialism, as solutions to the problems he identified in 1820.

Crawfurd was a colonial administrator, historian, journalist and orientalist. He was also a constant critic of colonial expansion and argued for the continued independence of native states in South-East Asia.[2] Throughout his careers, first as a colonial administrator and then as a journalist and lobbyist, Crawfurd fought, as a warrior in the battle of ideas, and succeeded in containing British colonial expansion in South-East Asia until his death. Through his activism, scholarship and anonymous writings, he argued for the equality of all peoples.

Crawfurd was one of a number of historian-administrators who used historical writing to debate the morality of colonial rule in South-East Asia. The historian-administrators were late eighteenth century and early nineteenth century colonial administrators who wrote histories of the peoples of Asia as a response to their administrative duties. In South-East Asia, the historian-administrator contemporaries of Crawfurd included William Marsden (1754–1836), John Leyden (1775–1811), Thomas Stamford Raffles (1781–1826) and later the adventurer James Brooke (1803–1868) and his 'Sarawak historian'[3] followers, such as Henry Keppel (1809–1904), Rodney Mundy (1805–1884), Edward Belcher (1799–1877) and the St. John family, James August St. John (1795–1875) and his two sons, Horace (1830–1888) and Spencer (1826–1910). These men wrote about the peoples of South-East Asia with the view to advancing commercial interests in Asia, but in doing so, these histories also debated British colonial policy towards Asia. As part of their plans to advance commercial interests, these historian-administrators also documented the manners, customs and stages of civilisation of the people in Asia.

Their writings shared a strong tradition of internal criticism of colonialism, the British East India Company and the actions of Europeans generally in South-East Asia. A constant theme in the writings of these historian-administrators was the criticism of previous colonial practices of Europeans as being rapacious towards South-East Asians. All the historian-administrators called for a more caring form of colonialism which helped the colonised peoples as well as profiting from them—although the nature of this more caring form of colonialism varied from advocates of individual rights, racial equality and respect for native states, such as Crawfurd, to proposals for aggressive paternalism and racial hierarchies, such as the St. John family.

In writing about the manners, customs and civilisation of South-East Asian peoples, the historian-administrators sought to place the people within a comparative schema of civilisation known as conjectural or stadial history. Stadial history assumed that all societies followed the same broad schema of social development. This schema was a theory of staged social development that explained the pathway to civilisation via the stages of savagery and barbarism. Stadial history could inform both the historian as well as the colonial administrator.

Implicit in the colonial administrator's use of stadial history was a belief that he was helping the colonised society advance through the stages of social development. Europeans believed all peoples shared a common history back to the common biblical ancestor of Adam and that all societies shared a similar path towards civilisation. Europeans could point to their own savage and barbarian past—which, in the case of the British, was not that long ago. In the mid-eighteenth century, the parts of Scotland where Crawfurd grew up were still seen as domains of barbarism. In 1775, just prior to Crawfurd's birth, the English essayist Samuel Johnson published an account of his tour through the Highlands and western islands of Scotland. In his account of the Scottish Highlands, Johnson wrote of the barbarism of the Highlanders, comparing them to the Ancient 'Greeks in their unpolished state' and believed them to be a secluded, 'unaltered and discriminated race'.[4] Johnson's interpretation of the Highlanders as barbarians was common amongst British thinkers. Global comparisons between the barbarians of European history and the savages that Europeans encountered in Asia made possible a unified global history, connecting the historical experience of Europe with Asia. A unified global history placed European colonialism and Asian indigenous[5] development within a grand narrative of development, now called universal history.

The grand narrative of development advocated by the historian-administrators also made a moral claim about the savage, barbarian and semi-civilised peoples in Asia, often labelled liberal imperialism.[6] Raffles chose to dedicate his history to the Prince Regent, and advised him that the duties of the British Empire were to 'uphold the weak, to put down lawless force, to lighten the chain of the slave, to sustain the honour of the British arms and British good faith; to promote the arts, sciences, and literature, [and] to establish humane institutions' and that in 'preside[ing] over a mild and simple people, it has been my pride and my ambition to make known to them the justice and benevolence of my Prince'.[7] Raffles's dedication was a blatant attempt to gain the patronage of the Regent, but he was also making a claim that the British Empire had a mandate to civilise people. Raffle's civilising objectives were interconnected with a sense of history. First, his dedication is in the opening pages of his history of Java; secondly, he identifies civilisation as a process of advancement, by which the British Empire trains a 'mild and simple people'. There is a belief that British colonial policy in South-East Asia during the late Enlightenment period involved a series of debates about moral claims derived from that particular stadial historical understanding of the past and how that past shaped the future.

Because we still speak English and Enlightenment ideas still play an important role in our current society, we can easily fall into the trap of believing that Enlightenment thinkers approached issues from the same perspective that we do today. That was not the case. Reflecting on modern readings of Enlightenment writings, Emma Rothschild observed that 'our sense of the familiarity of eighteenth-century thought is an illusion'.[8] Similar comments can be found in the works of most historians writing on the eighteenth and early nineteenth centuries. The people of the Enlightenment period possessed a different historical understanding from that which we have today.

Our distance from the eighteenth-century mindset is particular when we consider how eighteenth- and nineteenth-century people thought about historical change. At the beginning of the twenty-first century, we can measure time (and therefore track historical change) to fractions of a second[9] after the Big Bang, or in other words, to nearly the beginning of the creation of the Universe. The advancement of science and therefore historical understanding has meant we live in a world where most events can be explained as change over time, or, if they cannot be explained, we believe that science will eventually explain them. The people who lived in the early nineteenth century did not have that insight. They could track history back 3,000 years reasonably accurately and after that, they were into the realms of myth and the idea of God's creation.

Many of the intellectual debates of the Enlightenment focused on extending the parameters of history. Martin Rudwick described the Enlightenment debates on natural history as 'bursting the limits of time'.[10] The nineteenth century saw people challenge the boundaries of what was seen as historical time in many ways. First, Enlightenment intellectuals questioned the Bible's account of human migration and creation. Secondly, they used fossils to propose the existence of time before human existence, what we now call deep time. Thirdly, they used reason to theorise about the social structure of past societies with very little written (or recorded) history to support such theorising. The chapters in this book demonstrate how these developments in the historical understanding shaped the attitudes of Crawfurd and his fellow historian-administrators towards colonial policy and the peoples being colonised.

I maintain throughout this book that John Crawfurd and the colonial historian-administrators of the Enlightenment and early nineteenth century are as exotic to twenty-first century eyes as Asia was to an Enlightenment European traveller or reader in the early nineteenth century. They are exotic because the examination of their writings pushes against the limitations of our late-Enlightenment stereotypes. For example, the historian Fairish Noor in a recent interview observed that the language that the historian-administrators used to describe peoples in South-East Asia are 'full of biases that we hardly encounter today'.[11] Noor is correct in the observation that descriptions in politics change and what also changes is the meaning, style and implications of those words. Although we understand the words written by the historian-administrators from the late eighteenth and early nineteenth centuries, their meaning and preoccupations are often more elusive than we realise.

Today, the dominant view of nineteenth-century British colonial thought is that South-East Asian colonial subjects were seen as an exotic 'other' that needed to be ordered and controlled. However, this book contends that Crawfurd and many British colonial historian-administrators saw themselves as the civilised descendants of European barbarians. They believed that this shared past put them in a unique position to bring 'freedom' to the people and cultures of South-East Asia, even though they argued about how best to achieve this. This historical understanding of a shared barbaric past affected British colonial policy in South-East Asia in areas such as land tax, racial thought and the morality of colonisation.

Yet, what this shared past meant could change considerably from person to person, based on their differing ideas of historical change. As part of these debates, Crawfurd proposed radical ideas of democratisation. He argued against colonial attitudes that presented some colonised peoples as inferiors who should be treated as children by the colonial state, who needed protection rather than freedom. In comparison, Raffles and James Brooke argued that increased colonial control and authority were necessary to introduce civilisation. As I will demonstrate throughout this book, these different ideas also correspond to different ideas of history, with Crawfurd adopting a polygenic view of human creation. His polygenic view was highly critical of universal history, with Crawfurd believing that universal history gave undue weight to the importance of colonialism and imperialism in shaping human history.

The approach I use here is contrary to many contemporary interpretations of colonial thought. I argue that British colonialism in the early nineteenth century occurred in the context of a series of interconnected debates on the morality of colonialism and the unity of human history. The answers to these debates were not given at that time and the content was rapidly changing. This meant that people like Crawfurd could argue that all races of humans are separate species, believe in the equality of democratic rights to those separate species, but still describe some peoples as more civilised. The idea that the Europeans debate their barbarian heritage and existence of a unified history and saw themselves as carrying aspects of a barbarian heritage into Asia is in direct opposition to one of the dominant interpretations of colonial thought: Edward Said's Orientalism thesis. Said's argument was that European colonialism was beset by a sense of its own superiority gained through civilisation. The belief in progressive development towards civilisation, for Said, meant that Europeans saw themselves as distinctly different from all other peoples of the world. For Said, Europeans saw Asia as the barbarous oriental 'other' whom Europeans could objectify, describe and rule over because Europeans were civilised. In the 36 years since Said wrote Orientalism, his critique of European colonialism and its ideas of progressive development and ordering the exotic, it has manifested into a growing body of literature that addresses the idea of European universal history as a legitimisation of colonialism.

The line of argument of this book begins with the role of colonialism in shaping British thought on history. It was through colonialism that the histories of Asia and Europe were united into the same narrative of commercial exchange. The historian-administrators of the late eighteenth and early nineteenth centuries generally agreed that their guiding principle as administrators of empire was the introduction of freedom into South-East Asia, or as Raffles said, a 'spirit of liberality'. Their focus on freedom made their tomes appear highly critical of European colonialism. Their idea of freedom demonstrated a tension between individual and collective freedoms, with empire providing individual freedom of property, whilst the promise of collective freedom was held as a distant possibility. Such statements of freedom were not legitimisations of colonial rule in Asia, but rather, they were an attempt to connect their colonising actions to broader historical themes as they saw them.

The development of freedom was a fixation of British historiography in the Enlightenment. Historians wrote about the development of freedom and liberty within the historical narrative of the evolution of the British state. Central to this narrative of freedom was the belief that barbarians introduced freedom into decadent societies. The barbarian invaded the decadent and corrupt society of the civilised. Through barbarian invasions and then settlement (on the remnants of the old, decayed civilisation), the barbarian introduced a new government built on tribal freedom, thereby reinvigorating civilisation. The historian-administrators saw colonialism as a new form of barbarian invasion, reinvigorating a decadent Asian society.

Crawfurd and the historian-administrators wanted to introduce liberal ideals of free trade, rule of law and private property to South-East Asia. These policy themes interconnected with the preoccupation of Enlightenment historiography to describe the evolution of individual liberty as a product of barbarism. Therefore, when writing their histories, the historian-administrators focused on the development of freedom in South-East Asia and the role of colonialism—as a new form of barbarian invasion—in achieving this end.

Historiography has labelled concerns of freedom as the liberal face of the British Empire and has explored the relationship between the pursuit of empire and liberalism.[12] Eric Stokes first identified a connection between liberal thinkers and colonial practice, leading to liberals arguing for different applications of liberty in Europe to Asia. This argument has been more forcefully presented by Bhikhu Parekh, Javed Majeed, Uday Singh Metha and Thomas McCarthy, who have all identified inherent authoritarian practices within 'liberal imperialism'.[13] Yet, these writers also draw on a limited range of liberal thinkers, in particular, John Locke, Jeremy Bentham, James Mill and John Stuart Mill—none of whom ever went to Asia.

In their analyses of metropolitan eighteenth-century Enlightenment thinkers, Jennifer Pitts and Sankar Muthu both argued that Enlightenment thought was inherently against imperial expansion.[14] They cite key liberal thinkers such as Jeremy Bentham, who spoke out against colonialism. In his speech 'let go of your colonies', Bentham pointed to the moral contradiction of advocating freedom within Europe but enslaving colonial peoples, and therefore advocated an end to colonialism.[15] Another leader of eighteenth-century liberal thought, the pioneering economist and philosopher Adam Smith, concluded that colonialism was a product of mercantilism, and in his arguments for free trade provided strong reasons why European colonialism was ineffective.

In arguing that Enlightenment thought was against imperialism, Pitts and Muthu were merely pushing forward the time frame for liberalism's adoption of a paternalist approach towards colonised peoples. Both writers argued that a change occurred in the early nineteenth century. To use Pitts's phraseology, liberalism made a 'turn towards empire'.

Pitts concluded that the move to empire in liberal thought was a response to calls for democratisation within Europe. Pitts's proposal follows from Emma Rothschild's study of Adam Smith. Rothschild argued that liberal thinkers in Britain had to narrow their idea of freedom to economic freedom in the wake of the French revolution. Therefore, Rothschild argued, Smith was reinterpreted as a 'conservative philosopher' supporting established institutions through property rights in a political environment highly critical of liberal revolutionaries.[16] In her broader study, Pitts made the argument that as liberal thinkers extended rights to the working class within Europe, these same liberal thinkers reacted by increasingly seeing Asians as an 'other' that needed controlling and were incapable of behaving as adults when given democratic freedoms.[17] Such an argument has a long pedigree, going back to Marxist interpretations of European colonialism via postcolonial studies.

Mehta, Muthu and Pitts's studies rely on major metropolitan thinkers. As Catherine Hall reminded us, writings on liberalism are both a metropolitan and a colonial phenomenon, and we cannot separate the two.[18] If we limit our understanding of liberalism's relationship to empire to mere metropolitan thinkers, all we are doing is analysing the obsessions and fears of people who had no actual experience of Asia. These metropolitan thinkers would naturally find Asia exotic because they had never been there. To understand the relationship between liberalism and empire, we need to explore the liberal writings of officials within the East India Company who had the real experience of empire.

This book takes a different interpretation to Pitts and Muthu, arguing that the historian-administrators working for the East India Company developed ideas of legal equality of people within the empire, widespread democratisation and an argument to limit colonial expansion. The gaping omission within recent studies on liberalism and empire is any serious attention to the liberal ideas by officials within the East India Company. Michael J. Turner's writings on Independent radicals, such as Thomas Perronet Thompson and Joseph Hume, suggests that some returned East India Company officials were actually more radical than their metropolitan liberal contemporaries. Thompson, Turner notes, rejected 'Anglo-Saxon superiority' and maintained that '[i]f peace, liberty, and equal rights were not forthcoming, British rule in India might be "most unpleasantly put down"'.[19] Crawfurd worked with both Thompson and Hume and, like them, Crawfurd responded to British colonial expansion by arguing for equal rights for the Asian colonised peoples and called to limit and prevent further colonial expansion in Asia.

The tradition of critical historical writing practiced by the historian-administrators was pushed to its extremes by Crawfurd, whose life spanned the end of the eighteenth century and two-thirds of the nineteenth century. He is a link between the world of the philosophies of the Enlightenment and the racial thinking of the nineteenth century. Throughout Crawfurd's long life, he theorised and pondered the origins of humans and why different societies appeared to develop whilst others stagnated. His attention to race has seen him dismissed as a 'racist' today, but a closer look shows that many of his racial theories were used to oppose colonial expansion and argue against injustices which he believed were being perpetuated against South-East Asian peoples.

Crawfurd was born in the Scottish Highlands in 1783 to a mixed English and Gaelic family. He attended medical school in Edinburgh in 1801 and joined the British East India Company as a doctor in 1803. He rose up the British East India Company ranks, moving from medicine to the diplomatic corps, gaining the sought-after post of Resident of Yogyakarta in Java (1811), followed by the position of envoy to the Kingdom of Siam (Thailand) in 1821 and Resident of Singapore (1823–6) and finally, as an envoy to the Kingdom of Ava (Myanmar/Burma) in 1826.

After retiring from the East India Company in 1827, he made four failed attempts at being elected to the House of Commons.[20] His second career was as a journalist and lobbyist for commercial interests in South-East Asia, advocating for free trade and the breakup of the East India Company commercial monopoly of the Asian trade. Much of his work was conducted under a cloak of anonymity—a normal practice for nineteenth-century British journalists and reviewers. Crawfurd regularly wrote anonymous articles that were published in *The Examiner* newspaper. His lobbying work consisted largely of private communications with leading politicians. Much of this work was conducted whilst he lived on his farm in Monmouth, Wales.

Throughout his careers as a colonial administrator, journalist and political lobbyist, he also maintained an active interest as a scholar. From 1813, when he published his first article with the *Edinburgh Review*, until his death in 1868, Crawfurd was a consummate writer, publishing works on history, ethnology, linguistics, philology and economics. He served as the President of the Ethnological Society of London from 1861–1868 and as Vice President for the Royal Geographical Society from 1864–1866. The geologist and long-time President of the Royal Geographical Society, Roderick Murchison, said, 'Mr. Crawfurd has perhaps written more than it has been given to any one author of this century to accomplish'.[21]

Crawfurd brought to debates on colonisation and race relations the hands-on experience of a colonial administrator and the mind of an economist, ethnographer and racial philosopher. He gave nineteenth-century arguments over the colonisation of Borneo a sophistication and complexity that we do not easily appreciate today.

The following chapter outlines Crawfurd's place amongst the historian administrators writing about colonialism in Asia after the British return of Java to Dutch colonial rule. The historian-administrators researched the history of Javanese land tenure and culture to determine how Java had diverted from what these historians believed was the natural path of history. Chapter 2 explores the opposing colonial administrative ideas of Raffles and Crawfurd. These ideas were based on opposing interpretations of the history. Raffles believed in universal history and that civilisation was because of earlier colonial invasions; however, Crawfurd concluded that Javanese civilisation was indigenous and that colonialism played very little role in shaping societies.

Chapters 3 and 4 expand on Crawfurd's ideas of indigenous sources of civilisaiton by explaining how his thinking on sources of civilisaiton in South-East Asia developed into a polygenic interpretation of race. Chapter 5 examines the creation of Singapore and how Crawfurd attempted to apply his ideas of liberal equality between the races in the governance of Singapore and establish a pattern of colonialism in South-East Asia that would limit further colonial expansion.

Crawfurd's ideas of limited colonial expansion dominated British thinking towards South-East Asia until the 1840s, when James Brooke, inspired by Raffles, advocated the broad colonisation of Borneo as a process of ending piracy and civilising the region from barbarism. Chapter 6 outlines the nature of Brooke's new form of empire, and Chapter 7 reveals how Crawfurd worked with other Radicals and humanitarians to oppose Brooke's colonising plans and prevent the further expansion of the British Empire in South-East Asia.

Crawfurd fought a 20-year battle with Brooke and his supporters. The campaign changed Crawfurd's thinking on ideas of civilisation, savagery and barbarism. Chapter 8 argues that by the late 1850s, Crawfurd distanced himself from many of the stadial or conjectural history approaches of his youth. Instead, he favoured addressing the opposition he was witnessing between the savage and the civilised world. This opposition, he believed, brought out the barbarism of the civilised and resulted in the immoral destruction of the savage. Throughout the 1860s, Crawfurd avoided the use of universal history, choosing instead an alternative in the examination of indigenous conditions that were increasingly relative to other societies. Finally, his belief in the equality of individuals (be they savage or civilised) forced him to reject Darwinian theory and evolution. Crawfurd believed it supported a hierarchy of races and, therefore, this ideology was against his principles of equality.

This study of Crawfurd's intellectual thinking on race and equality demonstrates the diversity of nineteenth-century liberal thinking. Crawfurd brought to nineteenth-century British liberalism his personal experience in the colonies. Faced with racial and cultural diversity, Crawfurd argued for inclusiveness based on democratic values and rejected colonial hierarchy and servitude. He questioned and researched how humans were connected to each other, but this knowledge was not merely a means to gain power over Asians. It was, rather, a search for the basis of an inclusive society in the new colonial world that was democratic and based on individual equality, whilst also recognising the cultural integrity and equality of all societies.

Notes

1 John Crawfurd, *History of the Indian Archipelago: Containing an Account of the Manners, Arts, Languages, Religions, Institutions, and Commerce of its Inhabitants*, (Edinburgh: Archibald Constable and Co., 1820), vol. 1, p. 63. Hereafter HIA.

2 I have chosen to use the geographic term South-East Asia rather than Southeast Asia. The reason for this decision is that Southeast Asia only came into use in the 1960s. The geographical term of the nineteenth century was either the 'Indian archipelago', the 'Malay archipelago', the 'Asiatic archipelago' or, even earlier, the 'East Indies'.

3 John Crawfurd*, 'A Vist to the Indian Archipelago in H.M.S. Maeander, with Portions of the Private Journal of Sir James Brooke, K.C.B. By Captain the Hon. Henry Keppel, R.N. Two Vols. Bentley', *The Examiner*, 2351 (19 February, 1853).

4 Samuel Johnson, *A Journey to the Western Islands of Scotland*, (London: Everyman Publishers, 2002 [1775]), p. 36.

5 Throughout this book, I use the word indigenous to mean endogenous. John Crawfurd used the term 'indigenous civilisation', meaning that the source of development derived from local and internal factors.

6 Eric Stokes, *English Utilitarians in India*, (Oxford: Clarendon Press, 1959); Javed Majeed, *Ungoverned Imaginings : James Mill's the History of British India and Orientalism*, (Oxford: Clarendon Press, 1992); Bhikhu Parekh, 'Liberalism and Colonialism: A Critique of Locke and Mill', in *The Decolonization of Imagination: Culture, Knowledge and Power*, ed. by Jan Nederveen Pieterse and Bhikhu Parekh (London: Zed Books, 1995); Uday Sing Mehta, *Liberalism and Empire: A Study In Nineteenth-Century British Liberal Thought*, (Chicago: University of Chicago Press, 1999). These accounts fall under the category of post-colonial studies and present a very critical role of liberalism in supporting colonial empire. For a response to this post-colonial literature, see Jennifer Pitts, *A Turn to Empire : The Rise of Imperial Liberalism in Britain and France*, (Princeton: Princeton Unversity Press, 2005); Thomas McCarthy, *Race, Empire, and the Idea of Human Development*, (Cambridge, UK; New York: Cambridge University Press, 2009); Theodore Koditschek, *Liberalism, Imperialism and the Historical Imagination: Nineteenth Century Visions of Great Britain*, (Cambridge: Cambridge University Press, 2011).

7 Thomas Stamford Raffles, *The History of Java*, (Kuala Lumpur: Oxford University Press, 1965 [1817]), vol. i, p. iv.

8 Emma Rothschild, *Economic Sentiments : Adam Smith, Condorcet, and the Enlightenment*, (Cambridge: Harvard University Press, 2001), p. 44.

9 Steven Hawking's work *A Brief History of Time* lists it as 0.000 000 000 000 000 000 000 000 000 000 0001 seconds.

10 Martin J.S. Rudwick, *Bursting the Limits of Time: The Reconstruction of Geohistory in the Age of Revolution*, (Chicago: University of Chicago Press, 2005).

11 Farish A. Noor, 'Know our People', S. Rajaratnam School of International Relations, Nanyang Technological University, <https://www.rsis.edu.sg/profile/farishbadrol-hisham-ahmad-noor/#.Vpgsmvl97IV> date accessed 15 January, 2016.

12 For a focus on the early nineteenth century, see Homi K Bhabha, *The Location of Culture*, (London: Routledge, 2004), p. 29; Bhikhu Parekh, 'Liberalism and Colonialism: A Critique of Locke and Mill'; Uday Sing Mehta, *Liberalism and Empire*. These accounts fall under the category of post-colonial studies and present a very critical role of liberalism in supporting colonial empire. For a response to this post-colonial literature, see Jennifer Pitts, *A Turn to Empire*; Theodore Koditschek, *Liberalism, Imperialism and the Historical Imagination*. Whilst for the impact of the second half of the nineteenth century, see B. Porter, *Critics of Empire: British Radical Attitudes to Colonialism in Africa, 1895–1914*, (London: Macmillan, 1968); G. Claeys, *Imperial Sceptics: British Critics of Empire, 1850–1920*, (Cambridge: Cambridge University Press, 2010). For an examination of non-European responses to colonial thought, see Anthony Milner, *The Invention of Politics in Colonial Malaya*, (Cambridge: Cambridge University Press, 2002). and more recently C.A. Bayly, *Recovering Liberties: Indian Thought in the Age of Liberalism and Empire*, (Cambridge: Cambridge University Press, 2011).

13 Bhikhu Parekh, 'Liberalism and Colonialism: A Critique of Locke and Mill'; Uday Sing Mehta, *Liberalism and Empire*; Javed Majeed, *Ungoverned Imaginings*; Thomas McCarthy, *Race, Empire, and the Idea of Human Development*.

14 Sankar Muthu, *Enlightenment against Empire*, (Princeton, NJ; Oxford: Princeton University Press, 2003); Pitts, *A Turn to Empire*.

15 Jeremy Bentham, *Emancipate Your Colonies!* (London: Robert Heward, 1830).

16 Rothschild, *Economic Sentiments: Adam Smith, Condorcet, and the Enlightenment*, p. 52.

17 Pitts, *A Turn to Empire*, p. 254.

18 Catherine Hall, *Civilising Subjects: Metropole and Colony in the English Imagination, 1830–1867*, (Oxford: Polity, 2002).
19 Michal J Turner, *Independent Radicalism in Early Victorian Britian*, (Westport: Praeger, 2004), p. 181, 184.
20 Glasgow in 1832, Paisley in 1834, Stirling Burghs in 1835, and Preston in 1837.
21 Roderick Murchison, 'Address to the Royal Geographical Society', *Journal of the Royal Geographical Society of London*, 38 (1868), p. cli.

1 The East India Company's Scottish Critic of Empire in Asia

Perhaps paradoxically, colonial history in the late eighteenth and early nineteenth centuries was highly critical about the practices of European colonial expansion. Much of this criticism was written either by Scottish philosophers and historians observing the European colonial experience from Britain or Scottish orientalists who worked within the British East India Company. These Scottish writers included Adam Smith, William Robertson, Adam Ferguson, Walter Scott and James Mill, to name a few, but also East India Company officials such as Colin Mackenzie, John Malcolm, John Leyden, Mountstuart Elphinstone, Joseph Hume and John Crawfurd as well as many others.[1] Yet, despite the centrality of critical philosophers and historians, the criticism of colonial practice also presented a moral contradiction between the control necessary for empire and the ideal of advancing freedom.

Early nineteenth century historians romanticised the barbarian and advocated advancing the cause of freedom in Asia. Theodore Koditschek has recently argued that the romanticism of the barbarian was particularly strong with Scottish orientalists, who compared tribal groups in Asia to freedom-loving Scottish Highlanders, whose freedom was also suppressed by the British Empire.[2] For Koditschek, the East India Company officials Elphinstone, Leyden and Malcolm all shared a personal friendship with Walter Scott. Each of these Company writers extended Scott's romanticised view of Scottish Highlanders to various war-like tribal groups in India, Afghanistan and South-East Asia. In romanticising the warlike groups in Asia, these writers looked on these warlike peoples as analogous to the early stages of human society, in which individual freedom was a guiding principle of social interaction.

As colonial administrators, the historian-administrators of the late eighteenth and early nineteenth centuries also believed that aspects of individual freedom were important for colonial settlements to flourish. Their focus on freedom made their tomes appear highly critical of European colonialism for suppressing freedom in Asia, whilst at the same time, these same writers advocated the continuation of colonial regimes. Their idea of freedom demonstrated a tension within their writings between colonial suppression and individual freedom.

The tension within colonial histories can be viewed as a distinction between individual and collective freedoms, with empire providing individual freedom of property, whilst the promise of collective freedom was held as a distant possibility. For Scottish historians, distinction between individual and collective also corresponded to their personal narratives, where their Scottish nation has been subsumed within the broader British Empire. Such statements of freedom were not legitimisations of colonial rule in Asia, but rather, they were an attempt to connect their colonising actions to broader historical themes as they saw them.

The development of freedom was a fixation of British historiography in the Enlightenment. Historians wrote about the development of freedom and liberty within the historical narrative of the evolution of the British state. Central to this narrative of freedom was the belief that barbarians introduced freedom into decadent societies. The barbarian invaded the decadent and corrupt society of the civilised. Through barbarian invasions and then settlement (on the remnants of the old, decayed civilisation), the barbarian introduced a new government built on tribal freedom, thereby reinvigorating civilisation. The historian-administrators saw colonialism as a new form of barbarian invasion reinvigorating a decadent Asian society.

Crawfurd and the historian-administrators wanted to introduce liberal ideals of free trade, rule of law and private property to South-East Asia. These policy themes interconnected with the preoccupation of Enlightenment historiography to describe the evolution of individual liberty. Therefore, when writing their histories, the historian-administrators focused on the development of freedom in South-East Asia and the role of colonialism— as a new form of barbarian invasion—in achieving this end.

This chapter demonstrates how Crawfurd and the historian-administrators used the barbarian past of Europe to present colonialism as a new form of barbarism which would bring individual liberty to a decadent Asia. Although they acknowledged colonialism was at times immoral and filled with self-serving vice, the historian-administrators maintained that colonialism was also a force for good. Despite the contradiction between their language of freedom and their practice of administration, some of these Scottish colonial critics produced radical ideas of individual freedom through democratisation and developed the first ideas of national independence for colonised peoples.

Freedom and Empire

In 1811, the Governor-General of India, Lord Minto, led a British East India Company expeditionary force from India to conquer the Dutch colony of Java. This expedition was part of the strategic posturing of the Napoleonic wars, which had seen the British take possession of many Dutch colonies.

Minto was a product of the Scottish Enlightenment. As a child, he was tutored by the philosopher-historian David Hume before going on to study law at the University of Edinburgh. Minto's family were immersed in the East India Company. He was a shareholder and his younger brother had moved up through the ranks of the East India Company. Minto quickly went into parliament and became a member of the Commons select committee on the Bengal judiciary and managed the House of Commons' impeachment of the Governor-General Warren Hastings in 1788. With his experience in overseeing the Company, Minto was made Governor-General of India in 1806.[3]

The orders that Minto received from the Court of Directors in London for the invasion of Java stipulated that he was to 'expel the Dutch Power, to destroy the fortifications, and to distribute the arms and stores among the natives' and restore power back to the traditional Javanese elites.[4]

Minto chose to disregard his orders and instead took possession of Java for the East India Company and gave Lieutenant Governor Thomas Stamford Raffles the job of establishing a permanent British authority in the island. Five years later, Charles Assey, Raffles's secretary in Java, wrote the first history of the occupation and justified Minto's decision to disregard his orders in the following terms:

> It appeared to the enlightened mind of Lord Minto, that the opportunity should not be lost of bestowing on a whole nation [of Java] the freedom which is everywhere the boast of British subjects: perhaps he also contemplated the prospect, thus offered, of establishing a new empire to Great Britain.[5]

In reasoning why Minto chose to disregard his orders, Assey is actually explaining why Minto did not give the Javanese their independence and instead extended to the Javanese the liberal freedoms of British law. In writing the history of the British occupation of Java, Assey made Minto the agent of the European Enlightenment extending freedom to the people of Java.

In Assey's narrative, Minto becomes a liberal reformer who was introducing morality into an empire that in the eighteenth century was, at best, amoral. Assey presented the idea that it was commercially beneficial to take possession of Java almost as an afterthought. Implicit in his statement was a belief that the Javanese were better off and should be grateful for Minto for not giving them independence. Herein lies the contradiction and problem that existed throughout British historical writing in Asia in the early nineteenth century: historians wanted to bestow a moral cause to British expansion but, at the same time, these historians were describing the enslavement of Asians under the imperial yoke.

Assey's account of Minto presents a contradiction in the moral logic of freedom. Assey's contradiction extends to most early nineteenth century British historical writing on South-East Asia. Many of the historians were equally aware of the contradictions. In 1830, Basil Hall also reflected on Minto's decision as part of a reflection on the life of Stamford Raffles. Hall concluded that if independence were immediately given, it would cause 'the most calamitous consequences to all parties concerned'.[6] In protecting the 'parties concerned', Hall supported individual freedoms guaranteed by law rather than national freedoms. For Basil—and for many others—the contradiction was overcome by the idea that colonial government prepared the natives for independence. Therefore, how to teach individual freedom became a focus of colonial administration.

By the early nineteenth century Britain was a liberal society, with a growing consensus around freedoms encompassing trade, labour, association, the press and some formal equality before the law. These freedoms were not egalitarian rights of freedom to achieve, but they were negative rights of freedom from oppression.[7]

Individual and national freedom are two related yet different concepts in liberal thought. National freedom is the right for a nation to exist independently from others, and there was broad support for this idea within British liberal thinking in the early nineteenth century. Minto chose to reject this collective national freedom when he disregarded the objective of Javanese self-determination in 1811. The idea of national freedoms for people outside of Europe was a fraught area. As we will see in this chapter, many historian-administrators grappled with this issue. Accepting the right to national independence meant rejecting their own actions as administrators in removing the independence of colonised peoples.

The alternative idea of freedom was individual freedom, that is, the freedom to be protected by law and the freedom from invasive government. The idea of individual freedom did not pose so many contradictions. The British Empire could easily guarantee individual freedoms under the law. Therefore, when faced with the issue of national freedom or individual freedom, the historian-administrators supported extending the British Empire to support individual freedom, with the vague idea of national freedom being delivered at a later date.

In favouring individual rights over collective rights, the historian-administrators were disregarding South-East Asian collective rights in favour of their own system and culture of individual rights. When talking about freedom, the historian-administrators assumed the universality of their British system of rights. In his study of liberalism and empire, Uday Singh Mehta concluded that the contradiction between liberal rhetoric and colonial reality occurred because of the British universalist ideas of history.[8] He argued that the British liberal tradition made claims about rights and responsibilities as being innate and therefore universal, when in actual fact, those rights and responsibilities were historical constructions that evolved into a British national narrative and assumed certain norms of behaviour. Liberal colonial officials then took these ideas—which they believed were natural—to Asia, and found that the rights that they assumed to be natural often did not exist, and that the people did not necessarily want them in the form being offered.

Faced with resistance to what they saw as the natural order, liberal thinkers such as James Mill often branded Asian people as lazy and consequently proposed character-reforming mechanisms. Eric Stokes's 1949 study of the influence of liberal thought in India is a classic example, in which utilitarian philosophers saw India as a blank slate to enact and try out their disciplining mechanisms of reform. Metha and Stokes both argued that Asia became the laboratory which liberal thinkers used to test their ideas.

Theodore Koditschek has extended the study of the liberalism and empire to the East India Company. Exploring the writings of John Leyden, John Malcolm, Mountstuart Elphinstone and James Mill, Koditschek noted the centrality of the romantic ideal of the barbarian within British ideas of liberalism in India. British liberal thinkers remarked on the similarity between the Scottish Highlanders and barbarian rebels in India, but unlike the Highlanders of Scotland, who had been displaced by the forces of capitalism, the barbarians of Asia were a real threat.[9] These liberal thinkers advocated empire as a means of controlling the barbarian desire for freedom and considered that Britain's role was to create the conditions for eventual independence in the distant future.

Freedom therefore became the negative freedom of British laws and not the freedom of independence. Although Koditschek focused on the transition from liberal orientalist romanticism to the hardnosed liberal reforms of the nineteenth century, he did not, however, address the traditions of colonial critique within the East India Company or how this contributed to developing a belief in national freedom.

Enlightenment Critique and the East India Company

John Crawfurd's *History of the Indian Archipelago* is a story of global history, written in what he believed was the Scottish style of history, pioneered by David Hume and William Robertson.[10] Through his narrative, Crawfurd linked the social development of European nations to the social development of Asian nations. The impetus behind this connection was the 'the search for the spiceries of the East'.[11] Since ancient times, a few spices had reached the Mediterranean world, flavouring foods and providing medicinal remedies. The quantities were small and the prices astronomical. They were the luxury goods of the ancient, medieval and early modern periods in Europe—fit only for kings. The discovery of Asia in the European imagination was a search for the source of the spices: because Europeans only received the end product, nobody in Europe knew where spices came from nor what the original plants looked like.

The European search for spices was a search of discovery that, Crawfurd argued, transformed the history of humanity, giving 'rise to the two greatest events in the history of our species, the discovery of a new world and that [sic] of a maritime route to India'. He contended that the latter 'open[ed] another new world, richer and more interesting than America'.[12]

He suggested these events set the scene for charting a history of South-East Asia. It meant that events in South-East Asia were of global importance and that the events he was considering were above all products of economic interactions. Such a global view of history was in keeping with late Enlightenment scholarly trends, when the act of writing history was increasingly a global affair. This was the story of Europe's relationship with archipelagic South-East Asia, and, for Crawfurd, the story was not a tale to invoke pride; rather, a critique of European expansion into South-East Asia was necessary.

Crawfurd's criticisms were reasonably common amongst East India Company officials, even though empire ran through the veins of these men. Their lives were all shaped by the imperial structures of the British Empire and the expansion of that empire into Asia. Yet their own pathways to wealth were through a career in the colonial service of India and Asia. These tirades against the colonial practices of the East India Company used the emerging techniques of global historical writing to prosecute internal political arguments within the East India Company.

Although national historical writing dated back to the Renaissance, eighteenth-century historians such as Edward Gibbon, William Robertson, Abbé Guillaume-Thomas-François Raynal, Denis Diderot and Montesquieu all chose to locate the history of Europe on both a continental and a global stage.[13] Renaissance historical writings had established the purpose of historical writing as narrating the development of 'civil government' and the formation of European nations. These histories were confined to the story of the state or the city. By the eighteenth century, historians realised that European institutions did not exist in isolation, but changed by virtue of the expansion of European society. William Robertson's *The History of the Reign of the Emperor Charles V*, published in 1769, was a watershed and is often labelled the first modern work of history in English.[14] Robertson's work broke away from the mould of national history and addressed Charles V's empire in Europe and described the European system of power. His second work, *History of America* (1777), moved the focal point across the Atlantic and charted Europe's interaction with America.

In his 1777 *History of America*, William Robertson castigated the Spanish for cruelty in their conquest of America. Likewise, in 1811, the influential German liberal philosopher Alexander von Humboldt attacked the Spanish for the cruelty in his *Political Essay of New Spain*. The Scottish philosopher and economic theorist Adam Smith claimed that the evil of colonialism, such as slavery and the 'oppression' of the indigenous peoples, was attributable to the processes of monopoly by colonial companies.[15] Monopoly did not, in Smith's mind, lead to an expansion of trade, but rather to corrupt practices to protect that monopoly. Therefore, he concluded that the holders of company stock would not curtail the venality and corruption of its servants in Asia because returns derived not from the 'plunder of India, but the appointment of the plunderers of India'.[16] The Company ceased being a mechanism for distribution of Indian produce and instead became a tool of its self-interested directors who could be legitimately corrupt for their own personal benefit.

Smith's critique of mercantilism and the East India Company was part of a general eighteenth-century trend in anti-East India Company writing. These criticisms resulted in British Prime Minister William Pitt's 1784 *India Act*, which placed parliamentary control over the Company and, through clause 34, attempted to prevent the further expansion of territorial control in India. In the words of Pitt's act: 'to pursue schemes of conquest, and extension of domination in India, are measures repugnant to the wishes, the honour, and policy of the nation'.[17] During the impeachment of the Governor-General of British India, Warren Hastings, Edmund Burke and other Whig politicians[18] (one of whom was the later Governor-General of India, Lord Minto) castigated the East India Company's policy in India for enslaving the natives and destroying the rights of natives. Therefore, throughout the late eighteenth century, parliamentarians became increasingly strident in demanding information on the activities of the East India Company.[19]

Despite the language of colonial criticism within the *India Act*, the overwhelming response of critics was to suggest reforms to the East India Company, rather than propose its abolition. Although the British parliamentarian Edmund Burke mounted a passionate campaign against Warren Hastings for abuses of power in India, Burke, however, saw the remedy to these abuses as extending the rights of freeborn Englishmen to India, creating a 'magna carta for Hindustan' by continuing to include India within the British Empire. Similarly, the senior and Scottish Company official Charles Grant wrote an influential pamphlet 'Observations on the State of Society among the Asiatic Subjects of Great Britain' in 1792.[20] The paper was a scathing criticism of the Company for producing merchant 'adventurers' who were 'suddenly raised to power' and had 'little concern for the lasting prosperity' of India. These characters, Grant argued, were 'suspicious and rapacious' and had no other goal than pursuing their self-interest.[21] Grant stated these charges merely to gain support for his proposals for transforming Company policy, to make the Company provide more 'civilising' services such as education and Christian proselytisation. In most cases, colonial criticism from the late eighteenth and early nineteenth centuries constituted an attempt to reform the institutions of empire, not to end them.

Crawfurd certainly positioned himself within the anti-Company critics, writing his first criticism in 1813.[22] His citations demonstrate he had read Smith, Robinson and Humboldt, but he would have equally been aware of the wider anti-Company literature and arguments.[23] In his narrative, Crawfurd compared the colonial practices of the Portuguese to those of the Dutch and English. These practices, he maintained, shaped the 'commercial destinies of the nations of the Indian Archipelago'.[24] He argued that the mercantilist structures of the European companies monopolised trade and destroyed competition, creating a quasi-state and suppressing indigenous political development, using violence as a means to gain access to markets.

Crawfurd argued that all Europeans in Asia were equally bad in this regard. Living a generation after Crawfurd, John Turnbull Thompson commented that it was common to find European 'servants of the late East India Company' who had been openly critical of the Company for its 'intemperance', 'avarice', 'rapacity', 'violence' and 'injustice'.[25] Such criticism was not just tolerated, but tacitly promoted by the shifting and competing factional rivalries within the East India Company.

Parliamentary oversight of the East India Company meant there were ample channels for returning Company officials to vent their frustrations. Many of them published internal memos to demonstrate their frustrations, and such criticisms of the Company's direction could always find a supportive voice in the Company hierarchy. Indeed, internal criticism was often rewarded. The Company was an extensive patronage network; therefore, critical memos could act as a means of gaining the attention of likeminded patrons.[26] James Mill's *History of British India* is an example of a highly critical series of tomes that demolished the previous politics of the East India Company. Mill was an unemployed outsider when he wrote his history, and one interpretation of his history is that it was a gigantic job application.[27] For instead of being rejected for his criticism, he was rewarded with a career in the East India Company's London offices. Importantly, however, Mill's work was an attempt to set a new direction for colonialism. Similarly, John Malcolm's critical histories of India also advanced his career in the Company.[28] There was a great deal of tolerance within the company for intellectual dissent provided the dissenters focused on reform of the East India Company.

From Islay to Java and the Experience of Empire

Large numbers of Scots were attracted to careers in the East India Company. Once in the East India Company, Scottish patronage networks continued to support the recruitment of the Scottish nobility and Edinburgh University graduates into the political, military and medical services of the East India Company. George McGivary, in his study of the Scottish patronage networks within the East India Company, has gone so far as to argue the capital flows from the Company developed Scotland and made possible the Scottish Enlightenment.[29]

The Scottish Enlightenment, like the Scots in the East India Company, is inseparable from the British Enlightenment and the English and Irish who also served in the Company. Nevertheless, the Scottish Enlightenment and the Scottish experience in the eighteenth and early nineteenth centuries is different from the broader British Enlightenment. The Scots lost their political independence from England in 1807 with the Act of Union. This act replaced the Scottish Parliament with Scottish seats in the British Parliament. Therefore, Scotland was a country/nation subsumed within a larger empire.[30] It was also a country in which clear vestiges of feudalism and tribalism survived in the Scottish Highlands.[31] Much of the political writings of the Scottish Enlightenment focused on the course of civilisation, the role of commerce in creating civilisation and the idea of freedom and how commercial society fulfilled the freedoms lost with the creation of imperial government.

Crawfurd ventured to India in 1803 as one of these Scots looking to make a fortune in the service of the East India Company. He was 20 years old and fresh out of medical school. Although a passage to Asia directly confronted him with the mechanisms of empire, his experience with empire began with this childhood in the Scottish Highlands. He was born in the newly founded fishing port of Bowmore on Island of Islay, in the Inner Hebrides. Raised speaking Gaelic and English, Crawfurd's family story reflected the social changes engulfing the Highlands, as the region was integrated into the broader British Empire, creating economic transformation for the people of Islay in the Scottish Highlands, but also the destruction of the feudal society of the Highland Clans.[32] Crawfurd saw it as an economic transformation, but he would later recount to people that his understandings of the world were shaped by what he learnt in Bowmore.[33] His proposals for colonial reform in Asia mirrored many of the reforms he witnessed as a child in Bowmore and Islay.

Islay and the Hebrides were impoverished regions of Scotland in the late eighteenth century but were slowly undergoing an economic transformation.[34] The Glasgow merchant and member of parliament Daniel Campbell, who bought the Lairdship of the island in 1726 from John Campbell, began the modernisation of the economy and society. His reforms were followed by his two grandsons, who both followed as Lairds: Daniel Campbell (the younger) and Walter Campbell.

As part of the transformation, Daniel Campbell the younger founded the town of Bowmore in 1768 as a new model village, commercial fishing port and centre of local government for the island.[35] Daniel Campbell and his sons embraced capitalist transformation of landownership in the Highlands by demanding that tenants improve their land as a condition of their lease—these were very similar to the conditions that Crawfurd would impose in Java and later in Singapore. Unlike many of his contemporary Lairds in the Scottish Highlands, Daniel Campbell and the subsequent Lairds Daniel Campbell (the younger) and Walter Campbell did not clear tenant farmers off the land. Islay was underpopulated in the eighteenth century, with large swathes of the island not cultivated. Hence, the Lairds' strategy was to attract new settlers from the English-speaking Scottish lowlands.[36] Walter Campbell introduced long leases of land to tenants and allowed subleasing of fields to encourage investment in land improvement—an idea that Crawfurd would also replicate in Java and Singapore.[37] During the period of Walter Campbell's Lairdship, which coincided with Crawfurd's time on the island, the population of the Island grew by 50 percent.

Crawfurd grew up in a divided society. The Campbells had only gained control of the island from the McDonalds in 1614 and lacked a clan connection with many of the inhabitants of the island. The division was made worse when the English-speaking Daniel Campbell bought the island. Campbell and the subsequent Lairds could not communicate with many of their Gaelic-speaking subjects. Many of the new settlers that the Campbells attracted were also English speaking; therefore, many of the old tenants saw the newcomers and the Campbells as foreign overlords of the common Gaelic-speaking folk, with little appreciation of Gaelic or Highland culture.[38]

Three distinct class groups developed: the English-speaking Laird and his family, followed by a bilingual or creole class of tenants and merchants who had 'absorbed Gaelic at their mothers' knee but had been educated in English and the ordinary people.[39] Crawfurd was one of those bilingual or creoles whose Highland heritage came from his maternal side. His mother's family had been, for several generations, small freehold farmers in Islay.[40] The social divisions were still present in the 1830s, when Baron Teignmouth travelled through the island and remarked: 'The farmers in Islay are chiefly natives of the island, or from the adjacent countries: there are among them few Lowlanders'; 'I visited some poor hovels, and found among the inmates only two who could speak English: they had a singularly wild appearance, and stared at me like savages'.[41]

Crawfurd's father, Samuel Crawfurd, was one of these Lowland English-speaking settlers in Islay. He originally came as a doctor, but after marrying Margret Campbell, he took ownership of her family's freehold lands. The Laird wanted to encourage improvement and noted that Crawfurd's father had 'carried on [land] improvements with vigour and success'.[42] Samuel Crawfurd also became the Laird's 'factor' or land agent as well as the Collector of Cess (Tax) and therefore the young John Crawfurd's own father was part of the colonising forces from the south that imposed an economic transformation, but at the same time naturalised into the local population through marriage.[43]

As the Laird's 'factor', Crawfurd's father was a member of the 'Stent Committee' or 'parliament of Islay'. The Stent Committee was established by Daniel Campbell soon after he took ownership of Islay and included in its membership all the principle landholders and large tenant farmers. It was the duty of the committee to decide taxes, finance the government and set regulations within the island. These powers were the prerogative of the Laird, but Daniel Campbell chose to cede the powers to body of locals. One interpretation of the Laird's actions was that he was trying to mitigate the effects of what would have appeared as colonial rule by a non-Gaelic-speaking interloper.[44] Most certainly the Laird was attempting to increase the involvement of his subjects in the economic transformation of Islay.

Crawfurd was at once a child of internal colonialism and a Highlander who saw throughout his childhood a society undergoing social and economic change. Later, when faced with introducing land reforms in Java, he used highland terms such as 'factor' and 'crofter' as analogies in his reports and proposed a system similar to what he witnessed as a child.[45] Crawfurd's arguments for representative government in Asian colonies shares a strong similarity to Daniel Campbell's introduction of the Stent Committee to mitigate the effects of colonial foreign rule in Islay, in which local landowners and tenants collectively decided the taxing powers of government and collectively made government decisions.

Crawfurd's experiences with the ideas of the Scottish Enlightenment began in Islay. Before becoming Laird, Walter Campbell had been the rector of Glasgow University, following on from Adam Smith in 1789. When Crawfurd was 18, his father sent him for medical studies at the University of Edinburgh, at the time when Edinburgh was still the centre of Enlightenment learning. He more than likely attended Dugwald Stewart's lessons on Adam Smith's political economy and probably met his future patron in the East India Company: Lord Minto, the future Governor-General of India, who at the time was attending Stewart's lectures and attending some medical classes at Edinburgh.[46] Although Crawfurd did not finish his degree, he saw himself as a product of the Scottish Enlightenment, and the Scottish ideas of progressive development were the starting point of Crawfurd's own thinking on the spread and development of civilisation.

Crawfurd began his service in the East India Company in 1803 as a medical officer in North-West India. In 1805, he became the sole doctor in the besieged fortress of Rampoora, looking after approximately 1,120 malnourished solders. Contemporary accounts describe the garrison as being 'deprived of nearly every necessity of life' and in 'sickly state'.[47] Although a doctor, Crawfurd probably coveted a profitable position in the political office of the Company. In pursuing a transfer from medical officer to resident, Crawfurd followed a well-trodden path that connected medicine to colonial power, as the senior Company official and colonial historian Sir John Malcolm made clear: 'There are two side-gates in the East to the Great Park of English Diplomacy. The one is Commerce. The other is Medicine. We owe, indeed, our Indian Empire to them'.[48] To become a political officer, Crawfurd would have needed to acquire and demonstrate an extensive understanding of Indian languages and courtly culture, or as Richard Jenkins, a senior resident, advised a prospective political officer that 'knowledge of the languages, and an acquaintance with the manners and habits of the Natives, [are] highly necessary for a diplomatic man'.[49]

Crawfurd was posted to Penang in 1808 and threw himself into acquiring 'knowledge of the language and manners of the native tribes'. After three years of dedication, Lord Minto recognised Crawfurd's ability and employed him in the public service as a translator, and he became resident of Yogyakarta in 1811.[50] At the time, Yogyakarta was the centre of Javanese power in Java, and capable of presenting a major challenge to the British rule of Java. Residents were often isolated from British military support and relied on diplomatic and intellectual capacity to carry out their work. Crawfurd's previous experiences with isolation in a remote garrison of Rampoora probably also recommended him to the task.

With his interest in ethnology, Crawfurd excelled as a resident. He befriended a Javanese aristocrat, Běndara Pangéran Arya Panula, who wrote a traditional Javanese *babad* about Crawfurd's time as resident of Yogyakarta. Panula represented him as a fair-minded man with an accomplished knowledge of Javanese custom (*adat*) and traditional lore (*ngelmi Jawi*).[51] In the account, Panula describes Crawfurd as having a good command of spoken Javanese, especially the courtly 'High' Javanese (*Krama*), and as using this ability to negotiate with the Javanese elite and even conduct interviews with local villagers in Kedhu about their experience in the customs of land tenure. Crawfurd's experiences with the Javanese elite and peasant society contributed to his writing of the *History of the Indian Archipelago*.

The Historic Role of Colonial Barbarism

Crawfurd wrote his criticism of the East India Company policy in 1820 on his return from Java, when he was 37 years old. His ideas began life not as an all-encompassing history of South-East Asia, but instead as a pamphlet on colonial reform originally penned out in a series of Edinburgh Review articles, which he then expanded into a historical narrative.[52] An important part of Crawfurd's criticisms of colonialism was the idea of the barbarian. Crawfurd depicted the barbarian as an historical agent who had delivered a cleansing shock to Europe and would now do the same in South-East Asia. In both cases, societies that had got stuck or too settled in their historical stage would be unsettled by the barbarians and impelled on up to the next stage of social advancement. The difference in Crawfurd's South-East Asia was that now the barbarians were the civilised Europeans and that European barbarism in Asia should cease.

He developed his argument around the idea of barbarism in European and world history. The central problem of colonialism for Crawfurd was the legacies of barbarism: 'how institutions, having their origin in the barbarism of the early part of the seventeenth century, have been prolonged to more enlightened ages'.[53] The reference to 'barbarism' situated European colonialism in a pre-Enlightenment era characterised by the raw desire to pillage. Crawfurd was not alone in his belief that colonialism was a form of barbarism, for example, in 1813, James Mill used the reference to barbarism to claim that the East India Company belonged to 'an unenlightened and semi-barbarous age' of British civilisational development.[54]

In his narrative, Crawfurd painted the Europeans of the sixteenth and early seventeenth centuries as 'barbarians' and the Asians as civilised or semi-civilised. These comments fed into a narrative about order and progress based on the freedom of barbarian nations. The narrative of freedom and barbarism runs through most British political and historical writing in the eighteenth century. It is best characterised however, by the then leading historian Edward Gibbon in his *Decline and Fall of the Roman Empire*:

> The Roman world was indeed peopled by a race of pygmies; when the fierce giants of the north broke in, and mended the puny breed. They restored a manly spirit of freedom; and after the revolution of ten centuries, freedom became the happy parent of taste and science.[55]

In encapsulating the idea of the barbarian in eighteenth-century thought, the modern historian J. G. A. Pocock asked the question, 'who were the Barbarians?' He ultimately responded to this question by stating that 'they are ourselves'.[56] The story of Europe was therefore the story of the curtailment of primeval liberty as it was confronted and then reconciled with the traditions of Roman law of the state.

Crawfurd had certainly read Gibbon's *Decline and Fall*, citing his theoretical approach on numerous occasions, and Crawfurd's argument about Asian history attempted to follow Gibbon's pattern of rise, decline, fall and rising again.[57] Gibbon's 'manly barbarians from the north' became Crawfurd's colonising 'barbarian nations of the north of Europe'.[58] For Gibbon, the barbarian invasions destroyed a decadent corrupt Roman Empire and over a process of a thousand years, the barbarians re-created a civilisation with renewed vigour and freedom. Crawfurd plays on this same idea. Although he castigates the Company as 'barbaric', a usurper of 'native rights' and a destroyer of 'native nations', he still perceived European involvement in Asia as a positive cultural force. In Gibbon's narrative, the barbarians of the north created the nations of modern Europe. Likewise, in Crawfurd's writing, the nations of modern Europe would reinvigorate the nations of archipelagic South-East Asia. Thus, according to Crawfurd, the barbarian was central to producing a national culture.

Crawfurd's argument begins by focusing on the example of the Portuguese. In general, British historical tradition of the nineteenth century, writers disparaged the Portuguese and Spanish conquistadors as being 'cruel', 'despotic' and only interested in souls and gold.[59] Crawfurd supported this view, but to many of his contemporaries' dismay, he also argued that under the Portuguese, a 'degree of freedom prevailed' and their influence was limited to 'emporium' cities like Malacca, which Crawfurd argued (wrongly) 'lost none' of their previous 'reputation' as centres for trade 'under' Portuguese rule.[60] He underlined the barbarism of the various East India Companies (English, French, Dutch, Danish), depicting their modern Dutch and British administrators as even more barbaric than the famously barbaric Portuguese.

In developing his criticisms of the East India Company policy in South-East Asia, Crawfurd presented the history of European involvement in South-East Asia as being akin to a barbarian invasion. His argument was that the Company's monopolies necessitated a European land grab, which created the conditions ripe for barbarism.

In comparison to the Portuguese, Crawfurd maintained that 'commerce' made 'considerable advances' when the Dutch and British ventured into Asia, using the collected 'wealth of individuals' in the guise of 'joint-stock companies' to trade in Asia.[61] He declared that 'no military navy existed to protect their distant adventures from the hostility of European and native enemies'.[62] Importantly, he argued, these adventures were not supported by the British or Dutch state, and consequently, the state granted the company a monopoly 'with a portion of sovereign authority' so that the nationals could look after themselves—making the merchant company a quasi-state.[63] With their private quest for riches, the East India Companies acted like the freebooting barbarians that founded Europe after the fall of the Roman Empire. These companies unleashed a 'barbarism' in Asia which—as the 'private capital of the nation'—was much worse and rapacious than the 'barbarism' of the Portuguese state.[64]

The need for 'monopoly' and 'sovereign authority' resided in the difficulty of long-distance trade in the seventeenth and eighteenth centuries. Extensive logistical planning and practice were required to transport goods to faraway regions. The journey and the transportation of goods were made more precarious by the treacherous waters, the slowness of vessels and the continual threat of piracy. The India trade required the establishment of outposts that were self-sufficient enough to cover the long periods between trading voyages. This meant that the East India Company had to develop a military capacity as a means of defence and an overarching system of governance to arrange the logistics and military support necessary for its survival and growth.

As a mercantilist enterprise with exclusive rights to British trade in Asia, the East India Company was governed, Crawfurd believed, more by the 'spirit of gambling than by views of fair trade'.[65] Importantly, he saw the lack of 'fair trade' as the source of conflict between European and local peoples. Initially, he argued, 'the Dutch and the English appeared in the simple character of traders, committing occasional acts of piracy, but, upon the whole, maintaining a tolerably fair reputation with the natives'.[66] Once the companies superseded the Portuguese, he believed 'they lost' their 'reputation' as traders and 'entered upon the system of coercion'. Transforming from individual traders into companies of 'armed traders', Crawfurd surmised, 'they did not fail to use the power which they had in their hands to possess themselves . . . of the produce or property of the native states with which they traded'.[67]

He argued that 'the treaties which' European companies

> entered into with these governments had for their object to exclude all rivalry or competition, to obtain the staple products of industry at their own prices, and to possess the exclusive monopoly of the native market for their own imagined advantage.[68]

These mercantilist treaties were commercial in their nature, but the context meant that these treaties were also political, 'subverting' the 'independence of most of the natives of the Archipelago'. The treaties Crawfurd declared were not negotiated on equal terms, as they were 'violently or surreptitiously obtained'; the result of this was that native states attempted to 'evade the flagrant injustices, as well as absurdity, which an adherence [to these treaties] implied'.[69] As the treaties were political, however, the European traders 'exercised sovereign authority' to defend the 'perfidious violation of their rights', punishing perceived native transgressions 'to the utmost of their power'.[70]

Crawfurd recognised the natural independence of the South-East Asian states. He believed that the Company's treaties establishing trading relations which did not stipulate free trade (which he refers to as 'fair trade') and hence effectively removed the independence of native states.[71] As pseudo-states, the companies enforced their rights with military power. Crawfurd maintained the result of this use of military power was that 'the independence of most of the natives of the Archipelago was subdued, and their commerce and industry subjected to the will of the monopolists'.[72]

The companies built strategic ports as isolated territorial strongholds inside native states. These company strongholds challenged native independence when they became 'an independent authority within . . . [a] kingdom'.[73] As independent authorities, they existed in a matrix of other territorial-political entities. Although they were fortified, the security of these strongholds was not just dependent on defences. More importantly, their security was maintained by the company's relationship with surrounding native polities.

These machinations led Crawfurd to comment that 'the animosity of the European nations against each other, and their machinations against the native . . . [was] impossible to read without disgust'.[74] Crawfurd's annoyance was aimed at the damage these conflicts inflicted on the native states, which were forced to take sides; as a result, many suffered internal civil wars and were further weakened by their interaction with Europeans.[75] Crawfurd understood these destabilising wars as detrimental to the people and economy of the region.[76] With 'the country depopulated and exhausted by wars', the 'incentives to industry and production' were 'removed'.[77]

He believed that truly independent indigenous states in South-East Asia were in everybody's interest, creating 'incentive to industry and production'. Faced with territorial control of a socially and economically depleted land, however, 'the monopolist' responded by 'converting the population of each particular country into predial[78] slaves . . . to cultivate the most favoured products of their soil, and deliver these exclusively to the monopolist, at such prices as the latter might be pleased to grant'.[79] Crawfurd accused the East India Company of numerous crimes (although he did not give details); he concluded that these crimes led the natives to develop a 'hatred' of 'the whole English nation'.[80]

Crawfurd saw mercantilism as a ruthless pursuit of profit that belonged to an earlier barbarous age. Mercantilism unleashed the European barbarian into Asia. This process destroyed the native economy and created an exploitative empire. Crawfurd considered this a disaster for all parties involved. For the local economy to thrive, he believed that Asian nations needed their independence. At the same time, he also saw that barbarism was a creative force bringing change and new forms of individual freedoms into Asia. His critique was that European barbarism had served its purpose and needed to end.

Colonial Reform in South-East Asia

Crawfurd was a liberal Radical[81] who expressed deep concern at the plight of people suffering under colonialism in South-East Asia. Yet his position on the future of the East India Company was for reform, not abolition, and resembled the characteristics of colonial rule in Islay. At first glance, it seems that although he advanced a harsh criticism of previous British practices, his solution followed the tradition of East India Company critics in merely proposing reform.

Closer inspection of his reforms, however, reveals that, if followed, they could totally transform the nature of colonial relations. Crawfurd maintained an Enlightenment disdain for empire, but he also radically argued for the equality of all subjects under the law and widespread suffrage in the colonies as early as 1820—therefore giving substantial voting rights to Asian subjects.[82] Extending suffrage to Asian subjects was a radical idea, particularly when voting rights were still limited in metropolitan Britain only to men owning land.

As we have seen, the eighteenth-century critique of empire was contradictory. Eighteenth-century historians and critics may have been strident in chastising the East India Company, but their conclusions were timid, centring on ways to reform the company or the practices of colonialism. By the 1820s, the mood turned against colonialism, and the nature of the critique went further than previously suggested reforms. Crawfurd's views contributed to this turning. They were not only circulated within the company; they also affected public opinion. In the 1820s, Crawfurd contributed to a growing critique of colonialism, which in many ways was more substantial than anything in the late eighteenth century. An anonymous reviewer of Crawfurd's *History of the Indian Archipelago* in the *Asiatic Journal* described how in tune it was with the changing attitudes:

> There is every reason to expect that it [Crawfurd's book] will be popular. There exists at the present time such a general prejudice against all monopolies, without regard to equity or right, that the subject itself will recommend the book, independently of the consideration that it is the production of a servant of one of those very Companies whose awarded rights he questions, and whose conduct he publicly arraigns.[83]

The mood at the time was decidedly moving against colonial territories to such an extent that James Macqueen penned a book in 1823 called *The*

Colonial Controversy, containing a refutation of the calumnies of the anti-colonists. The book was an appeal against the humanitarians who, in Macqueen's opinion, were attempting to destroy the colonial establishments. The book was responding to the vibrant debate in the various review journals: *Edinburgh Review, Quarterly Review* and *Westminster Review.* Macqueen overstated the anticolonists' position, presenting them as advocates of decolonisation.[84] In reality, few of the critics of colonialism could conceive of a world without colonies.

Part of the reason for their inability to think of abolishing the colonial system was that most critics saw colonialism as a historically normal phenomenon that had ancient Greek and Roman antecedents.[85] As a consequence, they also used the word in practical terms, which is hard for post-colonial twenty-first-century readers to grasp fully. For example, they used the word 'colony' to convey the practicalities of establishing trading establishments in foreign lands that today would resemble a small gated community of foreigners, living with consular protection. However, the word colony could also relate to large, expansive colonial settlements at the same time.

People in the early nineteenth century were equally confused by the use of the word colony. Only a month after he published his *History of the Indian Archipelago*, Crawfurd was called before the House of Lords to give evidence into trade in the East Indies and China.[86] His use of the world colony confused his House of Lords inquisitors. When Crawfurd was asked the question, 'can you state any circumstances or arrangements which might contribute to promote the trade between China and those islands, by means of European vessels?', he responded by exclaiming, 'the formation of European stations or colonies, or emporium, in those islands, would materially contribute to increase the commercial intercourse'.[87] At this point, the contradictory evidence Crawfurd was giving on colonies clearly confused his inquisitor. In frustration, the inquisitor asked Crawfurd to clarify what appeared to be a contradictory position on the importance of colonies:

> In the early part of your evidence, you state, that you considered our commerce with the East India islands might be considerably extended by means of colonies and establishments, and you have just stated, that the success of the Americans had, in a considerable degree, resulted from their having abstained from making conquests and forming military establishments; how do you reconcile these statements?[88]

Crawfurd believed in colonies; however, he was advocating small colonies that could be territorially contained and would have a minimal effect on Asian states and societies. He was trying to explain that the Americans' trade was increasing in South-East Asia, and his answer to the committee was simple: 'one good reason, because they have never formed commercial monopolies, nor attempted conquest, or to form any military establishment in the country'.[89] If British colonies could be kept small, Crawfurd proposed, people and goods could come and go freely and this trade would benefit everyone: 'Colonies formed in the manner to which I have alluded, ought to be established upon the liberal principles of free trade, and for the mutual advantages of the natives of the country and those who establish them'.[90]

Crawfurd connected these two streams of thought through what he called 'fair trade', which meant allowing individual Europeans to trade directly and openly with native traders in Asia and exclude the Company from trade in Asia.[91] The problem was that it was not realistic to 'expect that the distant and inexperienced trader of Europe should be able to directly conduct commerce' in Asia.[92] Consequently, he argued that an 'intermediate class' is necessary to mediate between the 'European trader' and the 'native trader' for 'convenience and security'.[93] He considered 'a colonial establishment' to be 'the only means' of achieving this goal.[94]

Although he favoured the creation of colonies, Crawfurd distinguished between the notion of 'colonies' and what we call colonialism.[95] A 'colony', he argued, would be separate and distinct from the Asian states. No 'control ought to be attempted over . . . independent governments' in Asia, with whom a 'friendly and equal correspondence [should be] maintained'.[96] Implicit in his logic is a territorial distinction between the location of the old Company factories, which existed inside Asian communities, and Crawfurd's new colonial establishment.[97] The new colonial system would not reside in existing Asian polities; rather, it would exist in a separate and independent space and allow for settlers.

A 'colony', he argued, should be established on one of the 'innumerable islands of the vast archipelago' which were 'still unappropriated' and constituted a 'moral duty'.[98] The establishment of a colony on 'unappropriated' land is a contentious, recurring and usually an erroneous concept in British colonial thought. The idea of 'unoccupied' land in Crawfurd's thought derives from a pre-existing British cultural preference for the rights of farmers over fishermen, pastoralists and hunter-gatherers.[99] The idea that there were 'unoccupied' islands in archipelagic South-East Asia is a common theme in colonial dispatches from South-East Asia.

In 1784, the East India Company had held public consultations over the creation of a new colony in South-East Asia. In a similar vein to Crawfurd, Thomas Forrest, who surveyed for locations for the new colony, argued that there was 'moral certainty' that an 'uninhabited island' should be 'selected' to 'settle'.[100] Despite Forrest's assurances, few of these islands were really unoccupied—including all the ones he recommended. In most cases, people actually lived on the islands.

For example, the island of Penang was called 'unoccupied' prior to British settlement, but actually had a number of fishing villages on the island when the British arrived. It appears Forrest meant Penang was 'unoccupied' in that it had no established community that farmed the land. Therefore, British descriptions of Asian lands as 'uninhabited' in the late eighteenth and early nineteenth centuries focus on the type of land management as well as relative state of occupation. Crawfurd's idea of an 'uninhabited' island is therefore a relative concept that denoted a lesser degree of land management and occupation compared to more densely settled areas rather than literal occupation of the land.

Crawfurd envisioned the island settlement to become a 'great emporia' attracting 'the native trader[s]', who 'would find' in such a settlement 'the best and safest market'. This freedom from fear would mean all the 'scattered productions of the archipelago' would be 'accumulated' in one place and give the 'inexperienced trader[s] of Europe' and the world 'immunity' from the 'risks' of dealing directly with native states.[101] In his vision, small colonial settlements on islands were about the alleviation of risk for all people.

The role of island colonies was also strategic. Crawfurd argued his proposed island colonies could stop the spread of territorial control over mainland South-East Asia or over the larger islands such as Sumatra and Borneo. He held that colonial expansion occurred because of European insecurity and a need for protection. This insecurity resulted in Europeans getting involved in local territorial disputes. Islands meant that Europeans had protection from such uncertainty, and this, in Crawfurd's view, would prevent territorial expansion.

Inside these colonies, Crawfurd foresaw a cosmopolitan mix of cultures. 'We discover', he wrote in 1817, 'in the Asiatic group of isles, the only great theatre where the varied population of Asia and Europe, even of Africa and America, meet none of the bigotry and intolerance which belong to most of them in their own country'.[102]

He returned to this vision in 1820, that 'differences of colour and language are the great obstacles to the happiness, improvement, and civilization of mankind'. In outlining his model colony, Crawfurd maintained that racially mixed spaces would be beneficial to a society and that necessitated the need for democratic governance of the colony, possibly drawing on experience with the Stent Committee in Islay. The colony's government, he maintained, 'should make no distinction' between Europeans, Chinese, and the 'mixed mass of native inhabitants' but rather treat all equally, for 'the dark-coloured races should not be looked upon as minors under the guardianship of the state'.[103]

Crawfurd saw the racial diversity and pluralism of old Portuguese colonies as one of their strengths. The racial intermixing of Portuguese and Asians, he concluded, had resulted in the 'benefits' of an 'unfettered influence of European manners and institutions' and more lasting cultural impact than 'those who succeeded them'.[104] Crawfurd repeatedly pointed to intermixed communities as one of the success stories of colonialism. He was not an advocate of racial purity.

It was clear from Crawfurd's references to mixed populations and his later advocacy of blended racial communities that Crawfurd expected the sexual mixing of the population. He saw the creation of Eurasian populations under democratic governments in positive terms, believing it must 'create a race of men more improved, more intelligent, and more virtuous, than either the existing native or European population'.[105]

Crawfurd's ideas on mixed colonial populations were in opposition to the emerging prevailing opinions of the time that focused on racial purity. In the nineteenth century, degeneracy of the European through contact with Asian people was a consistent concern of colonial officials. Sir James Mackintosh, chief justice in the Court of Vice Admiralty in Bombay, wrote to his officers of the court, 'In your intercourse with each other, as well as with the natives of India, you will keep unspotted the ancient character of the British nation'.[106]

Crawfurd proposed voting for all races in his proposed mixed-race Asian colonies. In this, he was more radical than many other liberal metropolitan thinkers, as was his idea of a democratic legislature. He advocated an extension of voting to all naturalised residents of the colony, who would then have the right to represent themselves. Anticipating objections to this form of colonial citizenship, he argued that a mixed-race population, if it had lived in a place long enough or owned enough of it, could rule itself:

> To establish, in all respects, a free government on a representative system, will be found, perhaps, impracticable with the motley population, of which such a colony would consist. To a representative body, however, the right of imposing taxes must be left, and, if the representatives are chosen alike from all the classes of inhabitants—if the elective franchise be confined to those who, by long residence, have acquired the right of naturalization, and to persons of considerable estate, no danger from turbulence or anarchy can be apprehended.[107]

Crawfurd's ideas on racial equality in his *History of the Indian Archipelago* were not a mere aberration. He restated them in 1833 in his pamphlet on the future of British India, maintaining that 'all classes should be equally admissible' in the colonial legislature.[108] He again argued for equality of all and the need for a colonial legislature in India in which all subjects voted for their representatives. In 1833, however, he was advocating for a permanent British settlement in India, not in the enclaves he espoused in the *History of the Indian Archipelago*, but for a more widespread migration. The British would settle in India in the same way the Moguls had settled and been integrated into Indian society.[109] In 1834, when Crawfurd ran for the House of Commons, he proposed extending voting rights to all classes without any reference to wealth: 'the extension of the suffrage to every Inhabitant Householder, without making the payment of rates or taxes a condition of franchise; the introduction of secret voting for the protection of the honest Elector'.[110] And in 1837, he was chairman of the Radical Club and organised a petition to the House of Commons for 'Universal Suffrage'.[111]

Crawfurd's colonialism in both theory and practice saw the blending and mixing peoples as a good thing. He saw such colonies as a means of granting rights and equality to people throughout the world. Crawfurd's ideas on extending the franchise to Asian and African peoples contrasts with Uday Singh Mehta's and Jennifer Pitts's arguments that liberal thinkers retracted with systems of authority when faced with difference.[112] In Crawfurd's case, experience in the real colonial world of South-East Asia led to an embracing of difference and the promotion of equal legal and political rights for all peoples in the colonies.

Crawfurd's ideas in the 1820s were a product of his cyclical theory of barbarism and rejuvenation. In his *History of the Indian Archipelago*, he is presenting his idea of small emporia-like colonies as the future, a logical next step for the British Empire as a means of ending barbarism. This logic only makes sense in the context of his argument that earlier Europeans in South-East Asia were barbarian hordes reinvigorating Asia in the same way as Edward Gibbon's barbarian hordes reinvigorated Europe after the decay of the Roman Empire. Gibbon had argued that barbarians reintroduced the spirit of liberty to Europe and eventually, after ten centuries, democratic institutions. Crawfurd, building on Gibbon, argued that after earlier exploitive destructive barbarism, the British needed to settle and blend with the vibrant indigenous cultures of South-East Asia (similar to what his father had done in Islay). In settling within Asian colonies, the British would reintroduce liberty through what, in effect, would be colonial republics.

The Response to Crawfurd's Critique of Colonialism

Compared to the Dutch, who had controlled parts of Java since 1602, British colonial involvement in South-East Asia was minimal. Nevertheless, the idea of providing 'protection' to Asian peoples was a constant theme among British advocates of greater colonial engagement. Early nineteenth-century writing on South-East Asia was part of a wider discourse on the protective benefits of British colonial rule in South-East Asia. A generation before Crawfurd, William Marsden, Thomas Forrest and Francis Light had all argued that the natives received social benefits through the colonial occupation of territory in South-East Asia. Each of them saw the practice of European governance as leading by example.

Marsden, who was stationed in the East India Company of Sumatra, argued in his *History of Sumatra* in 1783 that the 'Company' had a moral duty to 'extend' its 'power' to create 'peace' between warring 'chiefs' and that the 'Resident'[113] was a 'protector of the people from the injustice and oppression of the chiefs'.[114] Forrest wrote in a report a year later that if a British settlement were established, 'natives' would 'flee' to British 'protection'.[115] At the same time as Forrest was proposing a new British settlement, Francis Light (who a few years later founded Penang as a British settlement) wrote a letter to the government in Bengal requesting support to build a settlement in Junk Ceylon (Phuket). He also commented on the attraction that British protection: 'I have observed every year the People to grow more desponding', and that 'the People have often hinted to me that I ought to take the Government of Junk Ceylon to myself', for if the 'island become an English colony, the inhabitants will be relieved from their slavery'.[116] In each instance, these writers invoked the idea of protection to justify to the East India Company why the Company should extend British power to South-East Asia.

Crawfurd's 1820 account of the Indian Archipelago came in the wake of a raft of books and articles by soldiers and East India Company officials returning from Java.[117] Those published after 1815, when the British decided to hand Java back to the Netherlands, proposed that the Dutch colonial government was illegitimate for monopolising trade and enslaving the populations of Java through monopolistic activities and corvée labour. These works, therefore, were highly critical of the British decision to return the colony. Charles Assey asked in his brief history of the occupation of Java, 'ought such a nation to be again given up to the servitude from which they have been released?'[118] Each of these writers castigated the Dutch colonial regime for rapacious conduct towards the peoples of Java and South-East Asia, yet they were less confident in criticising the East India Company's legitimacy in Asia. Raffles made some vague criticisms of the British generally in Asia, maintaining:

> It must be admitted, that the line of conduct pursued by the English towards the Malayan nations, had by no means been of a conciliatory or prepossessing character. Our intercourse with them had been carried on almost exclusively through the medium of adventurers, little acquainted with either the country or people, who have been frequently more remarkable for boldness than principle.[119]

Compared to Crawfurd, most of these books and articles were tentative in their criticisms of British colonialism in South-East Asia. But like him, they hoped through their criticisms to move British public opinion and eventually the East India Company into taking a decisive position in South-East Asia. Each of these writings presented the reoccupation of Java and wider engagement in South-East Asia as a moral duty. For example, Raffles maintained that

> had Java remained permanently annexed to the British crown, the redress of the evils would have been, in a great measure, in the power of the English nation: the undertaking would have been worthy of their general character, and there was no other nation that could have possessed the means in an equal degree, even if it had indeed possessed the inclination.[120]

Raffles's criticism of British policy was that it had failed to live up to its civilising destiny. It needed to assert itself as colonial power more—not less—to defend the rights of native peoples. Raffles advocated what could be described as an indirect rule leading to guided independence, in which the subjected peoples became children needing education.

Raffles proposed that British indirect rule could be modelled on the ancient empire of Majpaht, in which 'Malay chiefs, though possessing the titles of Sultan, or Rajah, and in full possession of authority within their own domains' would be subordinate to British rule although it would be given an ancient title: 'yet all held of a superior, or Suzerain, who was King of the ancient and powerful state of Majopahit . . . who had the title of Bitara'.[121] Raffles argued that the British could reintroduce the legal structures of the Majpht Empire, giving the Governor-General of India the title Bitara, which 'would give a general right of superintendence over, and interference with, all the Malay states'.[122] Appealing to orientalist assumptions about Asian traditions, Raffles's idea of direct colonial intervention placed the development of Asian nations as the central purpose of government.

Articles published in the English Indian journals were generally supportive of Raffles's criticisms that British colonial policy lacked political spine in the face of a humanitarian need for empire. These arguments were aimed at the British Government, not the East India Company.[123] In contrast, when Crawfurd published his criticisms of the British East India Company, he met with a harsh response from Raffles and his followers. Raffles complained that Crawfurd's accounts of European involvement in Asia 'seem calculated for no other purpose than to heap abuse upon East India companies', and that in doing so, Crawfurd 'unfairly' compared the British with the Dutch.[124] With indignation, Raffles concluded that Crawfurd's 'remarks are intended to apply generally to the [British] company's administration in the east, we need only adduce the present state of our Indian possessions as a complete refutation of them'.[125] Another anonymous reviewer in the *Asiatic Journal* also looked disparagingly at Crawfurd's criticism of East India Company policy, arguing that Crawfurd wrote in a spirit of 'unfairness' in both his 'mode of reasoning' and 'misstatements'.[126]

Clearly irritated, both Raffles and the reviewer from the *Asiatic Journal* suggested that Crawfurd was disloyal to the Company, and even questioned his patriotism. Both of them argued that the East India Company exercised wise guidance in Asia, and it was the British government that was culpable. Raffles and his supporters were following the eighteenth-century pattern of using criticism to promote colonial reform.

Crawfurd's critique was unique in comparison to all other key writers on South-East Asia at the time who advocated an increase in colonial engagement. In 1824, the East India Company official, John Anderson, proposed that the British Empire should declare all of the Malayan States under British protection.[127] His reasons for this dramatic increase in British strategic responsibilities was to stop Siamese aggression into the Malay Peninsula because, as he stated, 'the inhabitants of the East . . . universally regard might as right' and, therefore, Britain cannot engage in 'pacific negotiation' or have a diplomatic relationship with them.[128] Similar to Raffles's idea of a Malayan confederation under the East India Company, Anderson's ideas would have seen a rapid expansion of British commitments in Asia. This is precisely what Crawfurd warned against: political alliance commitments in South-East Asia drawing more extensive colonial interventions.

The historian-administrators were coalescing around two divergent positions on the projection of colonial power. Raffles and his followers advocated maximum engagement and occupation of territory in Asia, whilst Crawfurd proposed a minimal engagement in Asia through carefully controlled trading ports. Although Raffles eventually followed Crawfurd's ideas with the creation of Singapore, this was Raffles's least favourite option. After the failure of his more grandiose ideas for retaining Java, Raffles advocated a confederation of Malay states under the East India Company's guidance. Crawfurd's ideas derived from a belief that the Europeans had already created major problems in South-East Asia, but the egg could not be unscrambled. The answer, therefore, was not more expansionist colonialism, but rather controlled minimalist colonialism.

Despite strident support for expansion of the empire by reviewers of Raffles's writings, it was Crawfurd's lone advocacy of limited colonialism that influenced policy makers in the first half of the nineteenth century. From 1814 onwards, Crawfurd published his ideas in the leading metropolitan journal the *Edinburgh Review*, and he probably also published anonymously in the London daily the *Morning Chronicle*, the paper that his father-in-law, James Perry, edited. In the 1830s, Crawfurd published review articles in the *Westminster Review* and some articles in *The Spectator*; later, he was a regular columnist in *The Examiner*.[129] Therefore, he developed strong connections with the metropolitan liberal and Radical press. He was the second expert called before the House of Lords inquiry into trade in South-East Asia. Neither Raffles nor his supporters were called before this committee, which largely accepted Crawfurd's call for free trade and lack of colonial entanglements.[130] After publishing his *History* and being presented before the House of Lords, Crawfurd successfully petitioned the Governor-General of India in 1820 for a diplomatic mission to the Kingdom of Siam, and following this was appointed as Resident of Singapore and later conducted a mission to Burma.[131] His influence regarding South-East Asia was paramount, leading Roderick Murchison to conclude, 'it may be affirmed, indeed, that during his Indian services all leading and public men sought for his counsel and advice'.[132] By the late 1820s, it was Crawfurd's idea of a colony and limited colonialism that resided at the centre of South-East Asian colonial policy.

As the following chapters demonstrate, Crawfurd became a leading liberal thinker. His ideas are important when understanding nineteenth-century liberalism. Rather than develop a regime of control and limit the expansion of democratic rights and the principle of equality to Asia (as some metropolitan liberal thinkers did), when faced with realities of Asia and the brutality of colonisation, Crawfurd responded with a program of colonial reform that aimed to democratise the colonies and recognise all people as equal.

Notes

1 Jane Rendall, 'Scottish Orientalism: From Robertson to James Mill', *The Historical Journal*, 25 1 (1982).
2 Koditschek, *Liberalism, Imperialism and the Historical Imagination.*
3 Michael Duffy, 'Kynynmound, Gilbert Elliot Murray, First Earl of Minto (1751–1814)', *Oxford Dictionary of National Biography*, (Oxford: Oxford University Press, 2004); online edn, January 2008 <http://www.oxforddnb.com.virtual.anu. edu.au/view/article/8661> date accessed 26 July, 2015.
4 Gilbert Elliot Minto and Emma Eleanor Elizabeth Elliot-Murray-Kynynmound Minto, *Lord Minto in India*, (London: Longmans, Green, and Co., 1880), p. 307.
5 Charles Assey, *Review of the Administration, Value and State of the Colony of Java, with its Dependencies, etc*, (London: Black, Parbury & Allen, 1816), p. 37. The publication was published anonymously but has been attributed to Assey.
6 Basil Hall, 'Article IV. Memoir of th eLife and Public Services of Sir Satmford Raffles . . . by his Widow', *The Edinburgh Review*, 51 (1830), p. 402.
7 Isaiah Berlin, *Liberty*, (Oxford: Oxford University Press, 2002 [1969]).
8 Mehta, *Liberalism and Empire.*
9 Koditschek, *Liberalism, Imperialism and the Historical Imagination*, pp. 74–76.
10 John Crawfurd, 'Crawfurd to Norton Shaw, 3 May', *Royal Geographical Society*, Royal Geographical Society, CB4/Crawfurd (1860).
11 Crawfurd, *HIA.*, vol. 3, p. 211.
12 Ibid., vol. 3, p. 211.
13 J.G.A Pocock, *Barbarism and Religion II: Narratives of Civil Government*, (Cambridge: Cambridge University Press, 1999), p. 3.
14 J.W. Burrow, *A History of Histories: Epics, Chronicles, Romances and Inquiries from Herodotus and Thucydides to the Twentieth Century*, (London: Penguin, 2009), p. 340.
15 Adam Smith, *The Wealth of Nations*, (London: Everyman's Library, 1981 [1776]); Samuel Fleischacker, *On Adam Smith's Wealth of Nations: A Philosophical Companion*, (Princeton: Princeton University Press, 2005). For an attempt to connect to South-East Asia see Sanjay Krishnan, *Reading the Global: Troubling Perspectives on Britain's Empire in Asia*, (New York; Chichester: Columbia University Press, 2007).
16 Smith quoted in Jack Harrington, *Sir John Malcolm and the Creation of British India*, (New York, NY: Palgrave Macmillan, 2010), p. 48.
17 Cited in Ibid. p. 47.
18 The Whigs were one of the two political parties in Britain in the eighteenth century; the other was the Tories. The Whigs were characterised by political philosophy that supported individual rights of property and the paramountcy of parliament.
19 Harrington, *Sir John Malcolm and the Creation of British India*, p. 46; Muthu, *Enlightenment against Empire*; Pitts, *A Turn to Empire.*
20 Charles Grant, *Mr. Grant's Observations on the State of Society among the Asiatic Subjects of Great Britain, Particularly with Respect to Morals; and on the Means of Improving it*, (London: The House of Commons, 1813).
21 Ibid. p. 8.
22 Anonymous, *The Present System of Our East India Government and Commerce Considered: In which are Exposed the Fallacy, the Incompatibility, and the Injustice of a Political and Despotic Power Possessing a Commercial*

Situation Also, Within the Countries Subject to its Dominion, (London: J. Gillet, and sold by Sherwood, Neely, and Jones, 1813). The authorship of this manuscript is debated Alexander Nowell is the author listed in Google Books, but John Bastin attributed the manuscript to John Crawfurd see: John Bastin, 'Sir Stamford Raffles's and John Crawfurd's Idea of Colonizing the Malay Archipelago', *Journal of the Malayan Branch of the Royal Asiatic Society*, 26 1 (1953).

23 Mary Quilty, 'British Economic Thought and Colonization in Southeat Asia, 1776–1850', (Australia: University of Sydney, 2001).

24 Crawfurd, *HIA.*, vol. 3, p. 213.

25 John Turnbull Thomson, *Glimpses Into Life in Malayan Lands*, (Singapore: Oxford University Press, 1984 [1864]), p. xiii.

26 Michael H. Fisher, *Indirect Rule in India: Residents and the Residency System, 1764–1858*, (Delhi; New York: Oxford University Press, 1991), pp. 95–101; Sudipta Sen, *Distant Sovereignty: National Imperialism and the Origins of British India*, (New York; London: Routledge, 2002), pp. 27–56.

27 Koditschek, *Liberalism, Imperialism and the Historical Imagination: Nineteenth Century Visions of Great Britain*; Alexander Bain, *James Mill: A Biography*, (New York: Henry Holt and Company, 1882).

28 Harrington, *Sir John Malcolm and the Creation of British India*.

29 George K. McGilvary, *East India Patronage and the British State: The Scottish Elite and Politics in the Eighteenth Century*, (London: Tauris Academic Studies, 2008).

30 Roy Porter, *Enlightenment: Britain and the Creation of the Modern World*, (London: Penguin, 2001), pp. 243–245.

31 James Buchan, *Capital of the Mind: How Edinburgh Changed the World*, (London: John Murray, 2004).

32 Arthur Keith, 'How Can the Institute Best Serve the Needs of Anthropology?', *The Journal of the Royal Anthropolgical Institute of Great Britain and Ireland*, 47 (January-June 1917), p. 17.

33 Anonymous, 'Death of Mr. John Crawfurd', *The Times*, (13 May, 1868).

34 Editorial, ibid.

35 Charles John Shore Teignmouth, Baron, *Sketches of the Coasts and Islands of Scotland and of the Isle of Man, Descriptive of the Scenery and Illustrative of the Progressive Revolution in the Economical, Moral, and Social Condition of the Inhabitants of Those Regions*, (London: J.W. Parker, 1836), vol. ii, p. 311.

36 Clifford N. Jupp, *The History of Islay, from Earliest Times to 1848*, (Port Charlotte: The Museum of Islay Life, 1994), p. 146.

37 A. Campbell, *The Grampians Desolate: A Poem*, (Edinburgh: J. Moir, 1804), p. 291.

38 Jupp, *The History of Islay, from Earliest Times to 1848*, p. 136.

39 Ibid.

40 (Margret Campbell) was Crawfurd's mothers name Editorial, 'Death of Mr. John Crawfurd', (13 May, 1868).

41 Teignmouth, *Sketches of the Coasts and Islands of Scotland and of the Isle of Man, Descriptive of the Scenery and Illustrative of the Progressive Revolution in the Economical, Moral, and Social Condition of the Inhabitants of those Regions*, vol. ii, pp. 308–309.

42 James MacDonald, *General View of the Agriculture of the Hebrides, or Western Isles of Scotland: With Observations on the Means of their Improvement, Together with a Separate Account of the Principal Islands; Comprehending their Resources, Fisheries, Manufactures, Manners, and Agriculture*, (Edinburgh: Sir R. Phillips, 1811), p. 67.

43 Jupp, *The History of Islay, from Earliest Times to 1848*, p. 174.

44 Ibid. p. 136.
45 John Crawfurd, 'Papers relating to Java and other areas of East Asia, ca. 1811–1823', East India Company, British Library, MS 30353.
46 Rendall, 'Scottish Orientalism: From Robertson to James Mill', p. 45.
47 The Asiatic Annual Register: Or, A View of the History of Hindustan, and of the Politics, Commerce and Literature of Asia, Volume 8, Editors lawrence Dundas Campbell, E. Samuel, Publisher J. Debrett, 1809, p. 63; The East India Military Calendar: Containing the Services of General and Field Officers of the Indian Army, Volume 3, The East India Military Calendar: Containing the Services of General and Field Officers of the Indian Army, The East India Military Calendar: Containing the Services of General and Field Officers of the Indian Army, Author John Philippart,1826, p. 179.
48 J.W. Kaye, *The Life and Correspondence of Major-General Sir John Malcolm, G.C.B.: Late Envoy to Persia, and Governor of Bombay; from Unpublished Letters and Journals*, (London: Smith, Elder, 1856), p. 106.
49 M.H. Fisher, *Indirect Rule in India: Residents and the Residency System, 1764–1858*, (New Delhi: Oxford University Press, 1991), p. 98.
50 Charles Edward Wurtzburg and Clifford Witting, *Raffles of the Eastern Isles*, (London: Hodder and Stoughton, 1954), p. 191.
51 Panular and others, *The British in Java, 1811–1816: A Javanese Account: A Text Edition, English Synopsis, and Commentary on British Library Additional Manuscript 12330 (Babad bdhah ing Ngayogyakarta)*, (Oxford; New York: Published for the British Academy by Oxford University Press, 1992), p. 19.
52 See: John Crawfurd, 'Of the Eastern Penisular of India', *Edinburgh Review*, 22 44 (1814); John Crawfurd, 'History and Languages of the Indian Islands', *Edinburgh Review*, 23 (1814); John Crawfurd, 'Publications Respecting the Eastern Peninsula of India', *Edinburgh Review*, 22 44 (1814).
53 Crawfurd, *HIA.*, vol. 3, p. 218.
54 James Mill, 'Bruce's Report on the East-India Negotiation', *The Monthly Review*, LXX (January 1813), p. 23.
55 Edward Gibbon, *The History of the Decline and Fall of the Roman Empire*, (London: The Folio Society, 1997 [1788]), vol. 1, pp. 76–77
56 J.G.A Pocock, *Barbarism and Religion IV: Barbarians, Savages and Empires*, (Cambridge: Cambridge Universtiy Press, 2005), p. 13.
57 Gibbon, *The History of the Decline and Fall of the Roman Empire*, vol. 1, pp. 40, 411; vol. 3, pp. 193, 340, 361.
58 Crawfurd, *HIA.*, vol. 3, p. 218.
59 Thomas Stamford Raffles, William Marsden, and John Barrow, 'Crawfurd's History of the Indian Archipelago', *Quarterly Review*, 28 55 (1822).
60 Crawfurd, *HIA.*, vol. 3, p. 217. Raffles, Marsden, and Barrow, 'Crawfurd's History of the Indian Archipelago'.
61 Crawfurd, *HIA*, p. 217.
62 Ibid., vol. 3, p. 217.
63 Ibid., vol. 3, p. 218.
64 Ibid. p. 217.
65 Ibid., vol. 3, p. 217.
66 Ibid., vol. 3, p. 219.
67 Ibid., vol. 3, p. 220.
68 Ibid., vol. 3, p. 220.
69 Ibid., vol. 3, p. 220.
70 Ibid., vol. 3, p. 220.
71 Ibid., vol. 3, p. 220.
72 Ibid., vol. 3, p. 221.
73 Ibid., vol. 3, p. 232.

74 Ibid., vol. 3, p. 229.
75 Ibid., vol. 3, pp. 229–232.
76 Ibid., vol. 3, p. 221.
77 Ibid., vol. 3, p. 221.
78 Johnson defines this as 'consisting of farms'. Samuel Johnson, *A Dictionary of the English Language: In which the Words are Deduced from their Originals, and Illustrated in their Different Significations by Examples from the Best Writers: To which are Prefixed, a History of the Language, and an English Grammar*, (London: W. Strahan, 1755), p. 1552.
79 Crawfurd, *HIA.*, vol. 3, p. 221.
80 Ibid., vol. 3, p. 228.
81 I am using the term liberal radical to describe Crawfurd's politics rather than connecting him to an actual political group. There were three broad political groupings in early to mid-nineteenth century British politics: the Whigs/liberals, the Tories and the radicals. The radicals consisted of breakaways from the Whigs/liberal grouping. The radicals had a variety of names and forms, being known at times as 'philosophical radicals', 'Utilitarians', 'Free traders', 'Cobdenites' and others. These radical groupings were shifting alliances that differed on key issues such as free trade, suffrage, taxation, religion, imperial and defence policy. Broadly, however, the radicals can be identified as liberal radicals.
82 Crawfurd, *HIA.*, vol. 3, p. 269.
83 Anonymous, 'Mr Crawfurd's History of the Indian Archipelago', *Asiatic Journal*, 10 56 (1820), p. 146.
84 J. MacQueen and Z. Macaulay, *The Colonial Controversy: Containing a Refutation of the Calumnies of the Anticolonists, the State of Hayti, Sierra Leone, India, China, Cochin China, Java, &c., &c., the Production of Sugar, &c., and the State of the Free and Slave Labourers in those Countries, Fully Considered in a Series of Letters Addressed to the Earl of Liverpool, with a Supplementary Letter to Mr. Macaulay*, (London: Khull, Blackie, 1825).
85 James Mill, 'Colony', in *Supplement to the Encyclopedia Britannica* (London: J. Iinnes, 1825).
86 Henry Thomas Petty th marquess of Lansdowne Fitzmaurice, *Report—Relative to the Trade with the East Indies and China- from the Select Committee of the House of Lords, Together with the Minutes of Evidence Taken in Sessions 1820 and 1821, before the said Committee: 11 April 1821*.
87 Ibid. p. 17.
88 Ibid. p. 19.
89 Ibid.
90 Ibid.
91 Crawfurd, *HIA.*, vol. 3, pp. 217, 330.
92 Ibid., vol. 3, p. 263.
93 Ibid., vol. 3, p. 263.
94 Ibid., vol. 3, p. 263.
95 The word colonialism was infrequently used in 1820. Although the word was used in the late eighteenth century, it went out of favour during the early nineteenth century and had not gained popularity after 1870. <https://books.google.com/ngrams/graph?content=colonialism&year_start=1700&year_end=1900&corpus=15&smoothing=3&share=&direct_url=t1%3B%2Ccolonialism%3B%2Cc0 > I am using the word colonialim in the modern sense of the word, meaning the ideology of colonial expansion. Crawfurd's depiction of the East India Company's administrative control of large swathes of land and people backed by force accords with the modern definition of the word colonialism.
96 Crawfurd, *HIA.*, vol. 3, p. 270.
97 Ibid., vol. 3, p. 221.

98   Ibid., vol. 3, pp. 263–264.
99   The settler colonial experience in North America and Australia was predicated on the idea that large tracts of land were uninhabited, although there were clearly large populations of people already living there at the time of colonial settlement. As nomads, these people did not constitute a nation or kingdom in British colonial thought, and therefore did not possess the land.
100 Anonymous, 'Letter from Captain Forrest to Bengal, 8th June 1784', Striats Settlemetns Factory Records, British Library, Vol 1. Prince of Wales Island, Consultations.
101 Crawfurd, *HIA.*, vol. 3, p. 271.
102 John Crawfurd, 'Raffles's History of Java', *Edinburgh Review*, 31 (March 1819), p. 412.
103 Crawfurd, *HIA.*, vol. 3, pp. 63, 67.
104 Ibid., vol. 3, p. 216
105 Ibid., vol. 1, p. 154.
106 Cited in Sen, *Distant Sovereignty*, p. pxxvi.
107 Crawfurd, *HIA*, vol. iii, p. 269.
108 John Crawfurd, *Notes on the Settlement or Colonization of British Subjects in India*, (London: J. Ridgway, 1833), p. 18.
109 Ibid.
110 John Crawfurd, 'To the inhabitants of the Borough of Marylebone, transcribed by Terr Ellingson', (1834).
111 Anonymous, 'Radical Club', *Phoenix; or, The Christian Advocate of Equal Knowledge*, (26 February, 1837).
112 Mehta, *Liberalism and Empire*; Pitts, *A Turn to Empire*.
113 British term for East India Company official who resided in an Asian royal court. A Resident was similar to an ambassador; however, over time, the Residents gained control of the native state's foreign policy. See Fisher, *Indirect Rule in India*.
114 William Marsden, *The History of Sumatra: Containing an Account of the Government, Laws, Customs and Manners of the Native Inhabitants, with a Description of the Natural Productions, and a Relation of the Ancient Political State of that Island*, (London: Printed for the author by J. McCreery and sold by Longman, Hurst, Rees, Orme and Brown, 1811), p. 214.
115 Anonymous, 'Letter from Captain Forrest to Bengal, 8th June 1784'.
116 Frances Light, 'Report on Junk Ceylon [Phuket]', Warren Hastings Papers, *East India Office Records*, British Library, Add 29210 (c.1784), p. 220. Circa 1784.
117 John Joseph Stockdale, *Sketches, Civil and Military, of the Island of Java . . . Second Edition, with Additions*, (London: J.J. Stockdale, 1812); Crawfurd, 'Of the Eastern Penisular of India'; Crawfurd, 'History and Languages of the Indian Islands'; Assey, *Review of the Colony of Java*; Thomas Stamford Raffles, *The History of Java*, (Kuala Lumpur: Oxford University Press, 1965 [1817]); Anonymous, 'Raffles History of Java', *The British Review*, 11 21 (1818); Crawfurd, 'Raffles's History of Java'; Crawfurd, *HIA*; Anonymous, 'History of the Indian Archipelago; Containing an Account of the Manners, Arts, Languages, Religions, Institutions and Comerce of its Inhabitants: By John Crawfurd, FRS.', *The British Review*, 32 (1820); Anonymous, 'Mr Crawfurd's History of the Indian Archipelago'; Raffles, Marsden, and Barrow, 'Crawfurd's History of the Indian Archipelago'.
118 Assey, *Review of the Colony of Java*.
119 Raffles, *The History of Java*, p. 231.
120 Ibid. p. 232.
121 Sophia Raffles, *Memoir of the Life and Public Services of Sir Thomas Stamford Raffles*, (London: James Duncan, 1835), vol. 1, p. 71.
122 Ibid., vol. 1, p. 80.

123 Anonymous, 'Raffles History of Java'; Anonymous, 'History of Java by Sir Thomas Stamford Raffles', *The Asiatic Journal and Monthly Miscellany*, (4 August, 1817); Anonymous, 'History of Java by Sir Thomas Stamford Raffles', *The Asiatic Journal and Monthly Miscellany*, (4 September, 1817); Anonymous, 'History of Java by Sir Thomas Stamford Raffles'; Anonymous, 'History of Java by Sir Thomas Stamford Raffles'; Anonymous, 'History of Java by Sir Thomas Stamford Raffles'.

124 Raffles, Marsden, and Barrow, 'Crawfurd's History of the Indian Archipelago', p. 130.

125 Ibid.

126 Anonymous, 'Mr Crawfurd's History of the Indian Archipelago', p. 146.

127 John Anderson, *Political and Commercial Considerations Relative to the Malayan Peninsula and the British Settlements in the Straits of Malacca*, (Prince of Wales Island: William Cox, 1824), p. ii.

128 Ibid. p. vi.

129 For references to Crawfurd writing in the Spectator see Thomas Carlyle, 'Thomas Carlyle to Margaret Carlyle', *Carlyle Letters*, 9 1 (1837). John Crawfurd, 'Thomas Carlisle's Lectures', *The Spectator*, (6 May, 1837), p. 421. For a discussion of his writing in *The Examiner* see appendix.

130 Fitzmaurice, *Trade with the East Indies and China—Select Committee of the House of Lords*.

131 Anonymous, 'Mr Crawfurd's Mision to Siam and Cochin China', *The Asiatic Journal and Monthly Miscellany*, 13 (1822), p. 406.

132 Murchison, 'Address to the Royal Geographical Society', p. cxlix.

2 Land, History and the Source of Civilisation

When Thomas Stamford Raffles (former Lieutenant Governor of Java) and John Crawfurd (former Resident of Yogyakarta) sat down to write their respective histories of Java and South-East Asia, land tenure was foremost in their mind. Whilst working in the British colonial government in Java between 1811 and 1816, both men argued over reforming land taxes. Raffles favoured the Roytwari system of taxing, which taxed the individual peasant cultivators who worked the land, whilst Crawfurd preferred the village-based system (based on the Zamindari system of Bengal) of taxing the village chiefs (*bekels*) who organised the peasant cultivators. By establishing a legal obligation to pay taxes on land, Raffles and Crawfurd not only introduced European ideas of private property in land into Java, but also European ideas of history. Their respective ideas of history were linked to their different positions on land, legitimacy and the role of a colonial power.

Both men were aware that pre-existing ideas of land title existed in Java. Raffles ordered an ethnographic survey to establish ownership and other relationships between the people and the land in Java. Crawfurd became one of the leading officials conducting the survey. The decision to survey land occupation was a practical administrative decision; however, the survey was also central to the British Enlightenment understanding of South-East Asian history.

The survey affected the way they understood history in two ways. On a personal level, it provided another mechanism to justify Raffles's and Crawfurd's different ideas when writing their histories. Yet, their argument over land tenure had a deeper importance for the European historiography of South-East Asia. On a second level, the survey into land tenure enabled Raffles and Crawfurd to integrate Javanese history with European history.

The settlement of land is the foundation on which the eighteenth-century Enlightenment historical narrative is constructed. Enlightenment historiography saw the settlement of land as constituting a beginning of national history. The settlement of land acted as the dividing line between the mythology of the wandering barbarian nomads and historical time of farming communities who organised themselves around the exchange of property and created the beginnings of government. For Enlightenment thinkers, the creation of government was the beginnings of civil history. The act of settling the land for farming by dividing it amongst tribe members formed the beginnings of a nation.

Thus, Enlightenment historiography saw the creation of private land ownership as the foundation of government. Customs and traditions emerged to govern the transfer of land and shape the national character. In keeping with this Enlightenment mindset, the historian-administrators believed that determining the original source of land ownership was essential. Flowing from the belief in the importance of determining origins of land ownership, the British maintained that if rights to land were pre-existing and indigenous then any decisions by the colonial government needed to respect those rights. Furthermore, such understandings were essential for understanding the legal origins of land rights but, also, all rights in Java.

Raffles and Crawfurd developed very different interpretations of the origins of Javanese custom and tradition. Raffles interpreted Javanese history as a series of invasions from external sources. He concluded that Java's civilisation was an extension of Indian history, with Indian colonists invading and settling Java. Raffles evoked this interpretation of history to argue for overhauling the system of land tenure in Java and recognise the peasant cultivator as the landholder, in much the same way as had occurred in India.

Crawfurd, however, interpreted Javanese history as a Javanese development of an 'indigenous civilisation'.[1] Crawfurd rejected the idea that the presence of Hindu relics in Java was evidence of an invasion and conquest of settlers from India. Instead, he presented a vision of history in which the Javanese borrowed from other cultures but maintained a unique identity. Crawfurd argued that the village was the basis of Javanese society, and therefore, that taxing the village chief was more consistent with Javanese tradition than taxing the individual cultivator.

History and Personality

Raffles was the first to publish, with his *History of Java* appearing in 1817, and in March 1819, Crawfurd anonymously critiqued it in the *Edinburgh Review*. He praised Raffles's work for providing the 'only authentic and detailed account . . . of an interesting race of people . . . whose history, it is now discovered, chiefly by the industry of our countrymen'.[2] Although Crawfurd cited the art of history as Raffles's achievement, he was also disappointed with the limits to Raffles's sketches, noting that 'the too ample details into [history] which Sir Stamford Raffles has entered on this subject, are indeed, in our opinion, among the greatest blemishes of his work'.[3]

It is clear that Raffles took exception to Crawfurd's observations and, in 1823, with the help of John Barrow and William Marsden, responded in kind to Crawfurd's 1820 *History of the Indian Archipelago*, writing a scathing 27-page dismissal of Crawfurd's three volumes.[4] The essence of Raffles's attack was Crawfurd's incessant theorising:

> The author advances a number of ingenious theories and speculations, while the reader is seldom furnished with such a full and impartial statement as to enable him to form his own judgement. In works of an historical nature such speculations can rarely be indulged without derogating from that character of impartiality and authenticity by which they should always be distinguished[5]

Most accounts of Raffles's and Crawfurd's relationship and approach to historical writing have concentrated on their personal animosity.[6] The historian John Bastin has surmised that their relationship went sour in 1813, when Raffles disregarded Crawfurd's advice on land tenure.[7] Raffles was the Lieutenant Governor of Java, and therefore, the senior administrator. Crawfurd reluctantly supported Raffles's policy.

Personality was probably the larger part of their dispute. It seems both men had healthy egos. Contemporary descriptions of Crawfurd paint him as opinionated and argumentative, whilst Raffles's career was also marked by disputes with his contemporaries, such as William Farquhar (Resident of Malacca and Resident of Singapore) and Robert Gillespie (military commander of British forces in Java). Crawfurd did not engage in any published personal slandering of Raffles, and he based his criticisms on scholarly differences of opinion. He even refers to Raffles as his friend in his writings.[8]

In comparison, Raffles's supporters made it clear that Crawfurd was not part of their group. One of Crawfurd's reviewers maintained that Crawfurd was not very original and accused him of only 'reservedly' acknowledging his substantial debt to Raffles.[9] Raffles also made a point of downplaying Crawfurd's role in contributing to his *History of Java*, not mentioning him as a major contributing figure in the introduction.[10] On the other hand, beyond his minor criticism in the *Edinburgh Review*, Crawfurd did not publish any negative commentary on Raffles until the 1850s, when he wanted to correct supporters of James Brooke, who lionised Raffles as a visionary, and presented Brooke as his disciple.[11]

Historiography has also favoured Raffles, often at Crawfurd's expense. Lady Sophia Raffles selectively published some of Raffles's letters which suggested that Crawfurd was campaigning against him.[12] The nineteenth-century historian and apologist for Raffles, Hugh Egerton, argued that Crawfurd 'hampered' Raffles, contradicting his orders and generally 'bore Raffles no great good will'.[13] Later in the 1940s, Charles Wurtzburg labelled Crawfurd 'a difficult person, dour, narrow-minded and close-fisted' who easily took 'offence' and although 'very resentful of criticism' was 'quite ready to criticize his superiors which in this case was Raffles'.[14] The basis for Wurtzburg's conclusions is unclear. Both Egerton and, later, Wurtzburg usually followed and extended Raffles's notes and blamed Crawfurd for Raffles's disasters. Often using very little original evidence, recent historians have been equally critical of Crawfurd, labelling him as 'crotchety' at best and a 'racist' at worst, or generally downright 'miserly'.[15]

Professional rivalry for the same patron probably contributed to their posturing. Both men looked to Lord Minto, Governor-General of British India, as their patron. Minto was also ultimately responsible for colonial actions in Java. Between April 1811 and September 1811, Minto commanded the British invasion of Java. He recruited for the expedition many of the leading officers from Penang and Malacca, such as Raffles, Leyden and Crawfurd, all picked for their knowledge of local conditions in archipelagic South-East Asia. After the success of the invasion, Minto returned to India and left Raffles in command of Java. Minto, however, continued to correspond with some of the junior officers (whom he had handpicked) who were now under Raffles's command.

Minto's decision to correspond with junior offices was not unremarkable. In the early nineteenth century, it was a normal part of administrative observational practice for senior officers to correspond with junior officers, with the purpose of encouraging juniors to report on the activities of their immediate superiors.[16] Raffles probably assumed that Crawfurd maintained a private correspondence with Minto and was undermining his position of authority.[17] Raffles's 1814 dispatches back to Bengal suggest he felt threatened by Crawfurd. In his *Substance of a Minute*, which outlined Raffles's policy on land tenure, Raffles substantially quoted Crawfurd's reports for factual evidence. Raffles edited the quotations, however, removing the strength of Crawfurd's argument, whilst also feeling the need to argue against Crawfurd.

Although personality and structures of patronage are important reasons for professional disagreement, Raffles's and Crawfurd's own words point to the argument being more than personal. Both men were critical of each other for their respective interpretations of history and of what constituted history. Crawfurd believed that Raffles's historical accounts were 'too ample' in 'details', whilst Raffles saw Crawfurd as too theoretical and, in the case of Crawfurd's claim for an archipelagic wide aboriginal Negro race (discussed in the following chapter), Raffles suggested that Crawfurd massaged the evidence.[18]

Despite their differences with each other, today we would consider few of their works as historical, with both men more concerned with current affairs in Java and South-East Asia. John Bastin characterised Crawfurd's approach in the following manner:

> a reader has to proceed through the whole of the first volume . . . and through half of the second before he will be treated to anything that can reasonably be defined as history proper; and having proceeded so far, he will doubtless be dismayed to read that, in the opinion of the author,

Indonesian history is too "defective in interest and dignity to demand the solemn and continuous narrative of regular history".[19]

History, for modern historians such as Bastin, is a narrative of past events describing change over time, constructed from different sources. Bastin's criticism is not new. Even Crawfurd's contemporaries thought he stretched the definition of history, with one reviewer complaining that Crawfurd applied 'the term history' to 'all that can be written which relates to the Indian islands'.[20] Crawfurd, however, was not alone—Raffles's *History of Java* is equally devoid of historical narrative until half way through volume two.

On one level, Bastin's comments support Raffles's criticism of Crawfurd that he engaged in excessive theorising. Crawfurd's other critics pointed to him as an 'individual of an active mind' (which was not a compliment) who used the 'jargon of analysis' and practised unconventional historical enquiry through 'questionable theories'.[21] All of Crawfurd's contemporary critics rejected his methodology of social theorising as history. Yet it would be ahistorical to use Bastin's comments to support Raffles's supporters' criticisms. For their criticisms were responding to a very different issue.

Bastin's summation of Crawfurd's use of history points to a modern problem of interpreting and understanding Enlightenment historiography—there is something about how Raffles and Crawfurd used the word 'history' in the early nineteenth century that is alien to us today. If we take their books as works of history—which is how Raffles and Crawfurd chose to describe their work—history as a reconstructed narrative of the past becomes in the hands of Raffles and Crawfurd a series of antiquarian and theoretical antecedents to a discussion about current affairs.

The form of history that Raffles and Crawfurd practised, with its preoccupation with philosophical history or nascent social theory, was about explaining the evolution of the present social condition. A paucity of sources meant that a historical narrative was not easy to construct. A narrative needed a beginning point and, in the case of Java, the beginning point could only be implied through the ruins and legacies of Hindu culture, which suggested layers of development. The phrases 'stage of society', 'civil government' and 'liberty' were central to this thinking.

These analytical tools for understanding Java were the tools of the antiquarian, a point the editor of the *Java Gazette* observed soon after the founding of the newspaper in 1812, when he asked for readers to report from the field about 'information [that] will naturally be expected, interesting to the politician, the merchant, the antiquarian, the naturalist'.[22] Antiquarians in Britain examined ancient folklore, rudimentary philology and provided speculation around ruins and practised nascent archaeological investigations.[23] Antiquarians blurred the lines between scientific methodology and romantic imagination, with their work often inspiring romantic historical novels in the eighteenth and nineteenth centuries.[24]

In using the approaches of the antiquarian, late eighteenth- and early nineteenth-century writers in the colonies were not arguing that a journey to the colonies was a step back in evolutionary time, as was claimed in the late nineteenth century. Instead, what we see in the colonies at this time is an ambiguity surrounding the nature of historical questions.

The reach of Enlightenment historiography was very broad. The phrases 'stages of society', 'civil government' and 'liberty' also peppered colonial dispatches and were used to justify or explain colonial action. When presenting his policy decision to the higher government in Bengal, Raffles felt the need to include a chapter on the history of 'Tenures of Land and State of Society among the Javanese'.[25] In the colonies, the tools of history could apply to understanding the contemporary condition of the 'natives' or colonised peoples. Modern historical methodology emerged out of the antiquarian mindset when, as the historian John Burrow argues, the antiquarians looked for the 'barbarian and medieval antecedents of modern legal institutions and customs'.[26] A similar process existed with historiography in the colonies, whereby colonial officials used the tools of the antiquarian to understand the legal and social structures of the society they had to govern.

In 1811, the central political question of colonial policy facing Raffles and his officers in Java was land tenure. In Asia, understanding land tenure appeared important in understanding the customs of land management and ownership necessary for colonial administration. Raffles and Crawfurd wrote their histories to support their respective arguments on land reform, but in doing so, they were also writing histories about nations in South-East Asia. Their personal differences reflected a deeper division between them on the role of history and development of a national cultural identity in Java.

History, Custom and Land in Enlightenment Historiography

Raffles and Crawfurd's differences on the origins of Javanese land tenure rested on their two different ideas on the origins of customs. Enlightenment historiography saw the settlement of land as central to explaining how those differences in customs developed. Land and its settlement explained the creation of civil government for Enlightenment historians.

The seventeenth and eighteenth centuries saw Europeans encounter vastly different people who lived in vastly different 'states of society'—which resembled aspects of what they knew of their own barbarian past. Historians made analogies between the hunter-gatherer peoples that Europeans encountered and the barbarian peoples of the European past. Such historical reasoning was a regular occurance within colonial reports and despatches. In his report on establishing a colony in Penang, Thomas Forrest recalled Julius Caesar and the ancient British tribes as an analogy to the social change he was living through:

> Things have been continually changing, and will continue so to do; how fast the Change in Hindostan [sic], how vast the change in America, and

all within the space of a few years! Had any one told Julius Caesar, when he landed in Britain, "This Island in process of time will make Italy tremble", and mode of fighting will be entirely altered; he could not have conceived how such a Change could happen.[27]

Forrest made the above pronouncement in the context of colonial policy in Asia. His argument was part of this historicising tradition, in which Forrest used an imagined understanding of the British and European past to interpret Asian societies. Similarly, the seminal Enlightenment historian Edward Gibbon (who wrote the *Decline and Fall of the Roman Empire*) compared the natives of North America with the German barbarian tribes to make analogies about how the German barbarians lived, based on reports of hunter-gatherers in America.

The identification of 'stages of society' was part of a broad philosophical approach to history known as either conjectural or stadial history. This philosophical belief held that societies existed on a trajectory towards civilisation, but the trajectory was marked by different stages, with each stage being like a step in the onwards advancement of civilisation. Every society was at a different point in the trajectory towards civilisation. Eighteenth-century and early nineteenth-century historians, antiquarians and orientalists all realised that every society progressed through this pathway differently. Therefore, conjectural or stadial history held the potential to explain the differences in customs and characters of different nations or societies.[28]

There is some debate amongst historians that stadial history, with its sociological approach, was the opposite of narrative history, and that the philosophers David Hume and Adam Smith followed the stadial approach, whilst the historians Edward Gibbon and William Robertson followed the conjectural or narrative approach. As Robert Nisbet has written:

> Throughout the eighteenth century there had been, side by side with the kind of history a Gibbon or Robertson wrote, that other kind of "history" well described in the French by the phrase *histoire raisonnee*: "conjectural," "hypothetical," "natural" history, the purpose of which was not to record and analyze actual events in time but, rather, to seek, through reason, the natural laws or the development, the progress, of mankind as a whole.[29]

Although modern writers can distinguish differences in style between the stadial and conjectural styles, in reality, many historians at the time did not differentiate between the two.[30] In South-East Asia, the historian-administrators mixed the two styles. For Crawfurd, Hume's and Robinson's styles were not distinguishable, and Crawfurd's reviews of his fellow historians also suggests a blending of styles was commonplace in the writing of late-Enlightenment South-East Asian history.[31] Whilst writing a eulogy for Mountstuart Elphinstone, a British historian-administrator of India, Crawfurd reflected on the style of history he and his fellow historian-administrators used, seeing no distinction between conjectural and stadial history:

> Mr Elphinstone did not write history like Tacitus any more than does Sir Archibald Alison! He wrote like a gentleman emulating the style of his countrymen and mine Hume and Robertson who never professed to write like Tacitus.[32]

Although Crawfurd saw little difference between the different styles of Hume and Robertson, Raffles and his followers argued Crawfurd's style of writing history more closely corresponded to the style of philosophic or conjectural history.[33] For Raffles's followers, Crawfurd's style drew heavily on the theoretical speculation of conjectural history.

The edifice of Enlightenment conjectural or stadial historiography rested on barbarian tenure of the land. The barbarian occupation of Western Europe during the decline of the Roman Empire marked the beginning of feudalism and a new 'stage of society' in history. The feudal 'stage of society' began and ended with the establishment and transformation of land tenure. The type of land tenure shaped the type of civil government that existed. Occupation of the land was therefore at the core of history.

Enlightenment thinkers also saw that the barbarian was key to understanding the development of private property in European history. The barbarian invasions destroyed the Roman system of property in Dark Ages Europe. The new rulers in Europe were the nomadic barbarians who underwent a transition to feudal lords ruling peasant labourers. Historians of feudal tenure in Europe noted that these tenures were not originally land grants to veterans for patriotic service to the republic (as in the ancient Roman tradition), but rather payment to a free barbarian warrior, whose obligations were limited to personal ties of honour.[34] Feudal tenure evolved from a grant existing at the precarious whim of a monarch to the full heritability of tenure by a fief for a tax, only forfeitable by the monarch under strict codified rules.[35] Historians in the Enlightenment period therefore looked to the feudal institutions of barbarian land tenure to explain the evolution of limitations on the power of European sovereigns by the existence of private property.

This form of historiography was limited as an explanation for the existence of private property. Although land tenure provided an explanation for the type of civil government that existed, questions beset the antiquarian/historian. How did government and land tenure develop in the first place? What roles and responsibilities transferred from that initial inception? These questions search for a beginning to civil history, which was transition from a tribal nomadic savage or barbarian horde to a settled farming society on the pathway towards civilisation.

Most Enlightenment historians approached the idea of a beginning to history by assuming the validity of Genesis and biblical origins. The stories of the Bible were universal and linked all people back to a common origin of Adam and Eve, created by God. Consequently, the antiquarians of the Middle Ages and even the sixteenth and seventeenth centuries traced the lineage of European dynasties back to Jesus and the biblical patriarchs. Enlightenment and nineteenth-century figures overwhelmingly accepted Mosaic history as fact, even though they saw problems with its application.

With the predominance of Mosaic history in mind, Raffles opened his history with a discussion of Genesis and whether Java was named in the books of ancient Israel.[36] Through his text, Raffles made the frequent assumption that future research would eventually demonstrate the connection back to ancient Israel.[37] Similarly to Raffles, Crawfurd also played with the idea of Genesis in Javanese history. In the period of 1812–16, when Crawfurd penned his initial thoughts on the origins of Javanese historical writing, he began with the Mosaic narrative.

Unlike Raffles, however, Crawfurd looked to Javanese sources and found that Javanese chronologies began with the Abrahamic figures of Adam and Seth, followed by indigenous figures such as Noorchoyo, Noor Aso, Jung Yivang Wannang, Jung Yivang Toongool and, finally, Jung Yivang Gooroo.[38] Although the Javanese chronicle tradition began with the biblical stories, Crawfurd was critical of interpreting them as indicative of the Mosaic narrative, labelling it as mythology with no relationship to history:

> The commencement of Javanese History or rather Mythology opens with a strange tissue of those incongruities and absurdities, which were totally unworthy of narration; did it not afford a striking illustration of the Character of the people and new proof of the miserable weakness of the human reason in the Infancy of society.[39]

Crawfurd rejected the Mosaic narrative. The stories of the Abrahamic patriarchs were mere mythology to him and not the source of real history. His rejection is not just of Javanese history, but the entire Mosaic narrative. For Crawfurd, the reliance on mythology as a beginning to history demonstrated a lack of reason.

Crawfurd made a clear distinction between history and mythology. He concluded that the Asian historical tradition was 'not very solicitous in separating truth from falsehood'.[40] Nevertheless, he also understood that mythology made historical claims and was suggestive of history, calling it a' distant approximation to a knowledge of events', but Crawfurd was adamant that this was not history.[41] Instead, Crawfurd was arguing for a reasoned analysis of Java's past, in which history was divided from mythology.

Mythology was important, he argued, but only to the extent that it gave reference to the state of society in Java and South-East Asia. Mythology therefore became raw data needing interpretation to connect it to the broader idea of history. For South-East Asian history, he proposed that 'time and patience, with some critical skill, are required to ascertain the value of each report, to confront, to compare, to reconcile, to retain the genuine account and reject that which is not satisfactorily proved'.[42] Crawfurd wanted a historical narrative deduced from reasoning. Unlike Raffles, he rejected the Mosaic narrative when looking for the beginnings of Javanese history.

Crawfurd's reasoned approach to the beginning of history did not necessarily need to rely on a narrative of origins; instead, it could use conjectural or stadial theory to deduce a beginning from the surviving evidence. This theoretical approach allowed historians to move away from and discard aspects of the Mosaic narrative that they found politically awkward, such as the Mosaic narratives' support for patriarchy and the rights of kings over their subjects. The theoretical approach allowed philosophers to deduce a historical narrative, such as the development of a political society, and philosophers could use arguments from the material relationship between people, the land and commerce as evidence for that historical narrative.

The importance of land in the British Enlightenment tradition of historiography goes back to John Locke's *Two Treaties on Civil Government* (1690). In this text, Locke demonstrated how historians could break away from the Mosaic narrative by introducing a new mechanism for deducing the development of society by placing the creation of property at the beginning of history. Locke introduced a way of understanding history before recorded time that continued to influence historians throughout the eighteenth and nineteenth centuries.

Locke developed his theoretical approach to history in response to a political problem of his time, whereby royalists used biblical scripture to support the rights of kings over commoners as a continuation of the patriarchal rights of the biblical patriarchs.[43] In the first of his *Two Treaties*, Locke contended that far from government being a construction of the patriarchs, if Adam and his descendants had a government, it 'was rather a commonwealth than an absolute monarchy'.[44] He defined a commonwealth as a political society being formed out of the 'consent of the people' for their 'comfortable, safe, and peaceable living one amongst another, in a secure enjoyment of their properties, and a greater security against any that are not of it'.[45]

In the second of Locke's *Two Treaties*, he established that the creation of commonwealths had the creation of private property at its core. Locke argued that governments evolved in response to the creation of private property.[46] His argument was that before history, humans did not own private property. Humans were God's creation, along with the rest of the earth, and the earth was a collective resource.

Locke adopted the ahistorical position of Thomas Hobbes, that before the creation of history, people lived in a 'state of nature'. A state of nature was ahistorical, because it was untraceable and had no basis in any recorded scripture. The state of nature was theoretical and deduced only through reason. The state of nature became a dividing line between nature (pre-history) and history. Locke reasoned that out of this state of nature, humans first cleared land for farming.

This act, Locke argued alienated the land from common ownership and created private property.[47] With the creation of private property, Locke surmised that people needed to coordinate their rights to that land and trade in the produce derived from farming the land. This desire to coordinate the rules regarding property rights created the need for government. He proposed that communities of individuals developed to settle 'the bounds of their distinct territories and by laws within themselves regulated the properties of the private men of their society, and so, by compact and agreement, settled the property which labour and industry began'.[48]

Paradoxically, although Locke made an ahistorical argument, he created a theoretical framework based on anthropological observation that was inherently historical.[49] Locke rejected traditional British approaches to history in favour of the French approach of 'returning facts to their context'.[50] Locke's approach was to recreate the social structure of earlier societies through an anthropological reasoning.[51] The application of such an ahistorical argument was universal in that it could explain the creation of government in all societies.[52] Despite being ahistorical, Locke's argument was an explanation of historical evolution of political systems based on property. His text became one of the leading ideological keystones of the Whig/liberal political tradition in Britain which emphasised the rights of property owners, be they lords or wealthy commoners, against the powers of the king.[53]

Eighteenth-century historians focused on the settlement of land to frame the stages of society. The creation of property generated the need for government and, therefore, civil history. The writing of global history during the Enlightenment becomes the story of the development of civil government, and a source of explanations for deviations from the standard notion of development that Locke laid out. Locke's arguments extended the sixteenth- and seventeenth-century examination of European Feudalism to explain 'states of society', the role of 'liberty' and 'despotism' of government and the 'national character' in any society across the globe.

The use of Locke's arguments also meant that Enlightenment historiography was comparative. Societies in Asia could easily be compared to the barbarian hordes that occupied the land in Western Europe at the end of the Roman Empire. The settlement of land by farmers represented the beginning of civil history. The implication for Raffles's and Crawfurd's histories was that they focused on the settlement of land, connecting it to the construction of laws and society.

The System of Land Tenure in Java

When the British occupied Java in August 1811, they wanted to determine the original laws of land ownership across the island. They soon discovered a system of land tenure which diverged from district to district with local customs varying considerably. In addition to land tenure differing according to local customs, there was a mix of Javanese kingdoms and Dutch colonies claiming sovereignty over different territories throughout the island. The old the Vereenigde Oostindische Compagnie, or Dutch East India Company (VOC) collapsed in 1800, with the colonial territories reverting to the Netherlands Government. After 1811, these territories fell directly under British rule.

The Dutch occupation of Northeast Java was piecemeal. In the 1740s, the VOC gained political control over the Kingdom of Mataram by supporting the sovereign against rebels and other enemies. The Dutch had previously gained control of Cirebon, which historically was subordinate to Mataram, but under the Dutch was autonomous.[54] The agreement between the VOC and the *Susuhanan* or Emperor of Mataram required the *Susuhanan* to deliver stipulated quantities of products to the VOC from his land at fixed prices. In 1749, Susuhanan Pakubuwono II, on his deathbed, asked the Dutch Governor-General to look after his state, signing a contract on December 11 'freely and unconditionally ceding the entire estate of Mataram to the Company'.[55] Three days later, his son signed an agreement acknowledging that 'control of the kingdom of Mataram came to him solely as a favour granted by the Company'.[56] Although these events appear profound, at the time, the Dutch did not enforce their supposed rights of sovereignty over all of Matram and the Javanese aristocracy did not recognise them. Sixty years later, the British found the treaty in the Dutch archive and interpreted the contract to legally cement their power.

The Susuhunan of Matram was the pinnacle of a hierarchical state, structured around patron-client relationships. The land surrounding his court was termed *Negaragung* and was reserved for the private use of his family. Beyond that were the *Mancanegara* lands, granted to leading retainers and officials who resided at court. The Dutch called these retainer-officials 'regents'. In the Javanese language, they were called *bupati*. The regent or *bupati* received an *apanage*, that is, a grant of land from the Susuhanan. The principles governing these grants were similar across Java. The size of an *apanage* or land holding increased depending on the seniority of the official. The holder of the *apanage* had the right to exploit the land but was expected to make regular payments to the overall ruler of the kingdom. The *apanage* was payment for service to an official, with officials liable to lose their *apanage* and means of family support when dismissed from office. Unlike European concepts of private tenure, the *apanage* was not hereditary and could be removed at any time.[57]

The *apanage* holders were meant to oversee their lands, but in practise, often they rarely had any physical connection to the land, preferring instead to reside at court rather than on their *apanage*. A *bekel*, who handled the administration of *apanage* for the *bupati* or regent, conducted the actual administration of the land. In some instances, another layer of officials called a *demang* existed between the *bupati* and the *bekel*. The *bekel* organised the cultivators working the land. The cultivator received the produce of the land and paid a rent (in produce) to the *bekel*, who after taking his share, passed the rent up the line until it reached the sovereign.[58]

The *bekel* was a leading figure of the village community, and in some regions was elected by the village. Nevertheless, similar to the *bupati* holder of the *apanage*, the *bekel* possessed an insecure position that could be removed at any time. If the sovereign dismissed the *bupati* holder of the *apanage*, it was routine for the new *bupati* to dismiss the previous *bekel*. In some instances, numerous people in the village would still support the old *bekel*, and reportedly, open violence often erupted between forces of the old *bekel* and the new *bekel*.[59] Under the Dutch, regents had greater security than they had under the pre-colonial system, in which the *bupati* could be replaced at any time. The Dutch granted the *bupati* a quasi-hereditary position in the colonial government.[60] This was not the case in regions still under Javanese rule, such as Yogyakarta, where, according to Crawfurd, it was often the case that the grandchildren of former high-ranking officials were often mere peasants.[61]

In addition to paying a rent in produce, the cultivators also paid tribute through corvée labour (unpaid labour by the cultivators in lieu of taxes or rent to the holders of the *apanage*). The *bupati* traditionally had rights to direct the labour of the people on their *apanage*. In his study of the Sultanate at Yogyakarta, Peter Cary argues that the corvée system points to the militaristic origins of the Javanese state, whereby a corvée labour meant military service.[62] By the late eighteenth century, corvée labour extended to many other areas including public works, labour in the *bupati* household and other tasks. The Dutch required their regents in the northeast part of Java to organise labour for Dutch projects. According to the historian Robert Van Niel's recent work, most labour used by the Dutch was wage labour in Java, but they also made extensive use of the regent's capacity to call on corvée labour for regular work on cash crops.

Prior to the British occupation, the Dutch had already instigated major reforms. In 1795, the French revolution reached the Netherlands, with consequences for Java. Franco-Dutch revolutionaries invaded the Netherlands. The French General Charles Pichegru led the revolutionary invasion of the Netherlands, with the Dutch contingent under the direction of General Herman Willem Daendels. These revolutionaries quickly defeated the old Dutch order in the Netherlands. The Dutch empire now fell under the influence of French revolutionaries. As a reward for his services in the invasion of the Netherlands, Daendels was appointed Governor-General of Java (1808–11) and attempted reforms to gain greater control over the system of land tenure.[63]

In 1808, Daendels started the process of transforming the economy from being based on produce to a monetary system. Daendels ordered that European government servants receive fixed salaries from the government, replacing the previous system in which European Residents received payment from the regents in a variety of forms. Daendels also stipulated that the regents pay recognition money as tax to the central government. This recognition money was a type of land rent, which the regents had to raise from their *apanage*.[64]

Contingents of crops and corvée labour continued, but with the colonial government exercising greater authority. Although Daendels underwent a process of monetising the economy of Java, the colonial state still relied on forced labour. In fact, the extent of forced labour dramatically increased under Daendels with the major construction of new roads in 1808–9. Sea trade had previously connected the Dutch settlements in Java, but British privateers rendered communications between the Dutch colonies on the northeast coast of Java extremely precarious, necessitating the need for roads connecting the settlements through the interior of Java. The excessive use of forced labour left a lingering memory. When the British eventually invaded Java, they probably encountered local grievances that gave undue attention towards the impact of corvée labour.

The British had no practical experience of governing Java, and therefore, any dramatic change in the Javanese economy needed careful planning and research. Raffles and Crawfurd wanted to determine what system had existed before what they saw as Dutch contamination. In the central south of Java around Yogyakarta, land tenure existed under a system of local rule that, according to Crawfurd and Raffles, was unaffected by Dutch intervention. Both men saw the central south region of Yogyakarta as a model from which they could determine the original system of landownership. For the British, Yogyakarta land systems suggested that regional differences were variations on a common theme, of the Sovereign being the only owner of land who could give land and remove it at a whim.

British Objectives in Reforming Land

The initial imperative to reform Javanese land tenure was outlined by the Governor-General of India, Lord Minto, who led the British invasion. After the initial invasion of Java, Minto quickly returned to India and instructed Lieutenant Governor Raffles to introduce a 'fundamental change in the whole system of landed property and tenure', as well as ending the use of 'forced contingencies' (supplying of crops) and corvée labour (supplying of labour). Although the British overstated the extent of corvée labour under the Dutch, Minto wanted to further monetise the economic system in Java, as had occurred in British India.[65]

By the early nineteenth century, land systems in British India had been radically changed and monetised in order to prop up the British East India Company. In the late eighteenth century, the Company had gone from economic crisis to economic crisis as it struggled to deal with its growing territorial administrative responsibilities.[66] After the Battle of Plassey (1757), the Company took on the right to tax Bengal in the name of the Moghul emperor. The new responsibility initiated a debate about what type of tax system to introduce. Two schools of thought developed: the Zamindari and the Ryotwari systems.[67]

The Zamindari system was common throughout Bengal and northern British India. This system taxed the Zamindars, who, under the Moguls, were tax collectors appointed by the Mogul. However, by the time the British arrived, these officials appeared and acted as hereditary local ruler controlling and profiting from land. Therefore, the Zamindari system advocated recognising the Zamindars as hereditary landlords who paid taxes to the colonial government in return for recognition of the hereditary rights of occupation. The Ryots, who cultivated the land, would in turn pay taxes to the Zamindars, and as property lords, the Zamindars could reinvest capital into agricultural improvements.

The Ryotwari system, on the other hand, taxed the actual cultivators of the soil, the Ryots. This system emphasised the fact that the Zamindars were not rightful landowners, but mere officials of the Mogul state, and therefore it was wrong to grant them titles to land that they did not possess. Advocates of this system proposed taxing the Ryots directly and circumventing the Zamindars and thereby empowering the peasant cultivators. This was particularly the case in Southern India, where it was less common to find Zamindars as intermediaries between the princely rulers and the cultivators. If the Zamindari system was introduced into regions where it had not previously existed, some British officials concluded they would be giving people land who actually had no right to that land.[68]

In addition to increasing taxing powers of the new colonial territory, Minto was also interested in reforming Javanese ideas of private property. He believed that the recognition of private property would uphold the 'principle of encouraging industry in the cultivation and improvement of lands by creating an interest in the effort and fruits of that industry'.[69] In Minto's view, the protection of property rights would increase the quantity of labour and in turn allow for more land to be cultivated, and consequently, more taxes to be paid.[70]

Minto's ideas on property and labour relied on Enlightenment ideas of self-interest. As a born and bred Scotsman, he was infused, in particular, by Scottish Enlightenment ideas. Self-interest and dedication to vocation were at the heart of the Scottish Enlightenment idea of social improvement. Minto, a friend of David Hume, had attended Dugald Stewart's lectures on Adam Smith's political economy in 1801–2 before venturing out to India.[71] Therefore, Minto took his Scottish Enlightenment thinking on the relationship between labour and property with him to India and Java. Self-interest would mean that if individual Javanese peasants could keep some of the profits from their farming of their land, they would be driven by the desire to increase their profits. The desire to increase their profits would move the Javanese peasants from subsistence agriculture to overproduction for the benefit of global trade.

Minto and his British officers viewed the situation in Java as being in dire need of reform. From their perspective, the Dutch ruled through a system forcing native regents to supply produce to them at fixed prices. The regents in turn forced the peasant cultivators to farm commercial crops for no economic incentive. Such a system of forced labour resembled slavery. In February 1814, Raffles expressed these concerns when he reported to Minto:

> The system of contingents and of forced services reduced the people to the lowest state of vassalage and subjection; and as no person could be certain of the produce of his labour, it must be supposed that his labours would not be exerted beyond his actual wants. Where no security existed, priority and distress naturally followed.[72]

The system of forced contingents (produce) and labour did not encourage labour to move to where it was most productive. To make money with a system of contingents using forced labour, the colonial government was driven to be despotic, which, in the interpretation of British colonial thought, mimicked the despotic traditions of Asian governments.

Despotism is a continual trope of British descriptions of government in India and South-East Asia. They continually labelled Asian systems of government as despotic. Despotism meant that an individual had no rights, or none that were certain, and lived at the whim of their sovereign ruler. The concept of despotism had a long pedigree in European thought: the French philosopher Montesquieu defined it as 'extreme obedience' to the 'prince's will'. European critiques of Eastern despotism can be traced all the way back to Classical Greek criticisms of the Persian Empire.[73]

Land was central to the Enlightenment idea of despotism. The British tradition vested rights in the ownership of property. If a landholder had no certain title to their land, they were subject to despotism. Despotism was believed to usually accompany ill-defined rights to land. Crawfurd noted that 'earliest European observances of eastern manners and customs . . . generally pronounced the whole property of the soil to be vested in the sovereign throughout Asia'.[74]

James Mill published his history of British Indian whilst the British were in Java. Much of Mill's work was concerned with the economy of land ownership and creation of despotism as consequence of the sovereign's control over private property. Mill used the Lockean idea of land to condemn the system of Indian government as despotic. He argued that land in Asia was originally held 'in common', as Lockean theorists suggested occurred in Europe. Rather than commonwealths emerging based on private property, Mill maintained that 'the sovereign' gained all private property rights to the soil in Asia. He did this as 'the representative of the society' and held as that representative all 'property in the land which belongs to the society'. As the representative of society, the sovereign, 'parcels it [the land] out' to bureaucrats. According to Mill's understanding of Asian government, private ownership therefore existed only in the 'crop', not the 'land' from which the crop was drawn.[75] Mill argued that Asian government was despotic because it did not allow private property and therefore diverged from the natural path of property ownership and history set out by Locke.

Minto and the British had broad objectives of trying to reform the Javanese economy. They wanted to create freedom of labour following the ideals outlined by Adam Smith, John Locke and the broader economic ideas of the Scottish Enlightenment. To do this, they also believed that freedom of property needed to be introduced, as it had been in India. Although Minto, Raffles, Crawfurd and many of the British officers had knowledge of the systems of government in India, their knowledge of Java was limited.[76] Minto suspected that no property in the soil existed for individuals, but he was not sure, cautioning Raffles that he should undertake an 'investigation' into native customs of land ownership before introducing new 'regulations'.[77] In answering Minto's questions, Raffles would place Java within European historiography. He would trace how land ownership was created from the original lands held 'in common' and how that type of government developed in Java.

Finding the Proprietors of the Soil and the Birth of Javanese History

As an administrator with a scholastic bent, Raffles was quick to support Minto's order for detailed research into land tenure in Java. In January 1812 (three months after taking control of the government in Java), Raffles ordered a comprehensive review of the traditions of land tenure in the colonies directly ruled by Europeans and the independent states in Java.[78]

Raffles interpreted Minto's order as a search for the history of Java, and he responded with an investigation into the ancient origins of native customs in Java. A common phrase that Raffles used in his dispatches was that reforms needed to be in accordance with 'ancient usages' and 'institutions' of Java.[79] His focus on the ancient was the search for the original Java.

If customs were 'ancient', they were more than the mere creation of government. They bestowed rights that were almost mystical. If they were ancient, it meant that Raffles's officers had to adopt antiquarian research techniques to determine the nature of these customs and traditions and the rights they bestowed.[80] Raffles ordered his officers in outlying provinces to discover who constituted the actual 'proprietors of the soil' and determine if the people who were holders of land had any hereditary rights to the land. This investigation into 'proprietors of the soil' went to the heart of British understanding of the creation of custom and law.

Using the ideas of Locke and other Enlightenment thinkers on land tenure, Raffles saw 'proprietors of the soil' as potentially holding custodianship of that land since its original alienation from when it, along with all land, was originally held 'in common'. In exploring who constitutes a proprietor of the soil, Raffles was according to the Lockean interpretation of the creation of property, looking into the origins of government in Java. The original alienation of land created the ancient tradition and customs of government.

By determining the proprietors, Raffles could then determine the political relationship between the sovereign (meaning the sultan and supreme ruler of the territory) and the people and the rights the people had under the sovereign. Raffles needed to know if the people already possessed alienated rights to private property in land or if the British had to create it afresh with new land tenure laws.

Raffles appointed Colonel Colin Mackenzie, the leading survey engineer in British India, to head his commission into land tenure. Mackenzie had previously conducted surveys into land tenure in the conquered territories of Mysore in India. In 1811, Mackenzie accompanied Minto's invasion of Java as an engineer. After the invasion, he nominated to stay and tour the island before heading back to India. When not working on Raffles's land commission, Mackenzie spent time inspecting the Hindu and Buddhist ruins in the island and formed the opinion/belief that Java's civilisation was a product of Indian colonists.[81]

Mackenzie appeared to have the skills Raffles was looking for, and was one of the few officers on the island with no administrative responsibilities. Yet, Raffles soon became aware of the serious limitations of merely relying on Mackenzie's and the commission's advice. Mackenzie's commission into land tenure in Java was limited to a review of Dutch and Javanese records. This review of records was also challenged by linguistic hurdles, with all native records needing translation from Javanese to Malay to Dutch before Mackenzie could look at them.[82] By following the written records in the Dutch archive, Mackenzie was also relying on the accuracy of these written records in conveying the actual traditions of land tenure and cultivation in Java.

To what extent Raffles relied on the advice of Mackenzie is debated. John Bastin maintained that Mackenzie was influential, but more recently, the historian Robert Van Niel has argued that it is 'doubtful that the commission's reports ever had much effect on Raffles' plans for reform'.[83] Yet, these reports were instrumental in building Raffles's knowledge about Java.[84] Although he did not acknowledge Mackenzie as a major influence when writing a *History of Java*, Raffles drafted many of his ideas about Javanese history in his 11 February 1814 'Substance of Minute on Land tenure'. In this Minute, Raffles relied substantially on Mackenzie's research and followed Mackenzie's interpretation of Javanese tradition as emanating from Indian colonists. In the Minute, Raffles outlined how Javanese history reflected the importance of Hindu legal traditions and culture as the source of early Javanese greatness. The consequence of this was that Raffles would later reject any interpretation of Javanese culture and tradition which did not support his view that Javanese laws originated in India.

In 1812, Raffles conceived of a second approach to understanding the origins of Javanese custom and tradition. He ordered each of his officers in the various districts held under British jurisdiction and Residents in the areas outside of British control to conduct interviews with the Javanese to ascertain the local land laws and customs. Basil Hall travelled extensively through Java as a tourist during the British occupation and described Raffles's rationale:

> In order to execute such a task with any chance of permanent support from the mass of the people, it was obviously necessary, in the first instance, to ascertain correctly how the facts stood, and what it really was that the natives wished. For this purpose Mr Raffles instituted statistical enquires in every district in Java—ordered the whole island to be surveyed—took the utmost pains to discover who were the best informed natives, and communicated personally with them all—listened with unwavered patience to all they had to say—and let it be understood in every quarter, his sincere desire was, not to establish any particular views or theories, but to obtain correct information upon all points.[85]

Hall, perhaps too eagerly, adds to the 'great man' interpretation of Raffles in suggesting that the research was almost singlehandedly conducted by Raffles. But despite the drawbacks in his description, Hall seems even-handed in his emphasis on Raffles's need to get his officers to record oral sources to understand the traditions of Java as people lived them. Raffles seems to have appreciated that many of the laws and customs would not be written down or might be interpreted differently to those written down.

Raffles concluded that the areas not under British control would have been changed least—as they would not have been infected by Dutch colonial rule and maintained their original integrity. He looked to Crawfurd, who was conversant in Javanese and the Resident of Yogyakarta. Yogyakarta was still under Javanese sovereignty and administration and therefore an example of traditional law unaffected by Dutch rule.

Crawfurd's initial advice to Raffles supported the view that Raffles had from India, that:

> the sovereign is the undisputed proprietor. He gives one day and takes back the following, and these vicissitudes are so common and the principle so thoroughly acknowledged, that there is not an acre of land in the country to which their shadow of hereditary right or title could be made.[86]

Mackenzie supported Crawfurd's view, writing to Raffles: 'From every source of enquiry I could personally refer to, it has been constantly reported by natives as well as Europeans, that the right of Property has been invariably considered solely in the Sovereign or State'.[87]

As a consequence of this advice, Raffles came to the opinion that the course of Javanese history meant that limited rights existed for hereditary land ownership. Crawfurd's advice suggested that India and Java differed more in 'degree than in kind' and that a continuation existed between Indian political systems and the Javanese. He reported to Raffles that the 'ancient authority of the Crown' was 'less broken or diminished in Java' than Bengal with the 'sovereigns having contracted few obligations from their subjects'.[88] Although Crawfurd saw a connection to India in Javanese institutions and history, he interpreted that condition very differently to Raffles.

Indic and Islamic Colonisation and Mosaic Interpretations of Javanese Land Tenure

For Raffles, Javanese history was an extension of India's history. His historical narrative in his *History of Java* begins with a mythical account that interconnects with Mosaic history. The Javanese were 'exiles from Egypt' who travelled across the Red Sea and lived along the Indian Coastline and slowly made their way to Java. He conjectured that government in Java emanated from an Indian colony, either created by a Brahmin figure called Tritresta or by Aji Saka, who was the lawgiver and created the first state.[89] Raffles focused on Indian cultural connections and informed his readers that 'in the Sanscrit language, Saka means an era, and is applied to the founder of an era; and in the chronology of the Hindu princes of India, Saka is a name or title'.[90] His narrative claimed multiple waves of Indian migration occurred in the remote past.

His focus on the Indian colonial conquest of Java meant that Raffles dismissed Javanese accounts of their own past that suggest a peaceful adoption of Hindu culture. Raffles concluded that such accounts were 'a fiction invented by national vanity, for the purpose of concealing from posterity the successful invasion of foreign adventurers'.[91] His vision of Indian colonisation was not that of mass settlement, but rather resembled his own government, being a 'successful invasion of foreign adventurers'. Raffles interpretation meant that for him, colonialism was at the core of Javanese identity.

In his *History*, Raffles praised the Hindu culture of Majapahit. He devoted a chapter to Majapahit's antiquarian remains. This period fascinated Raffles and he believed it was at the core of understanding Java's traditions. He argued that the Javanese

> are still devotedly attached to their ancient [Indian] institutions, and though they have long ceased to respect the temples and idols of a former worship, they still retain a high respect for the laws, usages, and national observations which prevailed before the introduction of Mahomedanism.[92]

Raffles's emphasis on Indian Hindu culture sullied his view of the contemporary Islamic period. Raffles did not have a favourable view of Islam and believed the introduction of Islam was a backward step for Java. He concluded his section on ancient Javanese history with a lament to their current degeneration compared to their glorious Indian colonial induced past:

> Nothing, therefore, of the ancient history of the people, of their institutions prior to the introduction of Mahometanism, of their magnificence and power before the distraction of internal war and the division of the country into petty contending sovereignties, or of their relations either to adjacent or distant tribes, in their origin, language, and religion, could be accurately known or fully relied on. The grandeur of their ancestors sounds like a fable in the mouth of the degenerate Javan; and it is only when it can be traced in monuments, which cannot be falsified, that we are led to give credit to their traditions concerning it.[93]

For Raffles, Islam forced a degenerate corruption onto Javanese culture. Even Javanese accounts of their own past could not be trusted because of the corruption of Islam. Javanese sources needed antiquarian interpretation through the ruined monuments left behind and knowledge of Hindu law. This antiquarian research became, for Raffles, the only reliable way to discern the real laws that existed behind society.

Raffles's interpretation of Javanese history suggested Hindu legal traditions were directly shared when India colonised Java. He saw the peasants in Java as the equivalent of the Ryots of India. That is, they were the original cultivators and had a superior ancient claim to the land that preceded the arrival of Islam. In Raffles's eyes, this elevated the Javanese peasants to the rank of landholder:

> Anterior to the establishment of the Mahomedan religion in Java, the cultivators of the soil were considered to rank as the first class in the state; for according to the institutions of Majapait, it was ordained, "that next to the sovereign shall be considered and respected the cultivators of the soil: they shall be the first class in the state below the Sovereign".[94]

The consequence for his land tenure reforms meant that Raffles rejected contemporary evidence of land use if it did not fit within his framework of Indian colonisation. In his *Minute on Land Tenure*, Raffles painted Crawfurd's ideas on the history of land tenure as being overly influenced by contemporary 'Mohamodean Government', and therefore, Crawfurd misunderstood the 'ancient usage' of land.[95] If there was little contemporary evidence, Raffles maintained that was because the Islamic government had washed away the traces of ancient laws from India.

In comparison to Raffles's use of Mosaic history and his crude vision of waves of invasions and migrations colonising Java, Crawfurd uses much more nuanced terms. According to Crawfurd, the similarities between India and Java were not a result of colonisation but first, because both India and Java shared similar states of society, and, secondly, that the Javanese peacefully adopted Indian culture for practical mercantile reasons. Also using a Lockean theory of history, Crawfurd proposed that India had advanced beyond Java in the progress towards civilisation.[96] Java, for Crawfurd, still demonstrated the early progress towards civilisation, when the village was the centre of the community, like the early egalitarian commonwealths that Locke theorised.

Crawfurd argued that in the early stage of a society, 'a village and a nation were synonymous'[97] and that villages were still the central expression of community and identity:

> The Village community constitutes the most important part of the Javanese institutions. The Javanese village, like the Hindu, is an incorporation, in which the powers of self-government to a large extent are inherent. Its officers consist of the head man, his assistant or deputy, and the village priest, who are elected by the occupants of the land, and in a few cases, by its proprietors. With these village officers rests the collection of the public taxes, and the whole care of the police.[98]

Crawfurd's theoretical approach meant that as the population increased, migrants spread out from the village into new districts, building new settlements by clearing the land and tilling the soil. Crawfurd believed that this village pattern of development spread a similar political culture of independence to the new villages.[99]

Crawfurd believed that in these early village societies, the central political figures were elected and enjoyed a collective popularity in the community, and he concluded that this electoral tradition of the primitive commonwealth survived in Java.[100] He further proposed that the *bekel*, whose role was to organise the cultivators of the land, acted as a chief to the village.

Crawfurd termed the *bekel* a 'landholder' and although acknowledging he was an official of the state and therefore technically liable to dismissal at any time, he proposed that in practice, the *bekel* maintained practical control over the land:

> From the advantages acquired by actual possession and the Capital thus accumulated the *bekel*, generally speaking, becomes the fittest and ablest person to pay the superior the full rent of the land; it is therefore, not the advantage of the latter to remove him.[101]

Crawfurd saw the *bekel* as the equivalent of the Zamindar (or landholders) in Bengal, and he advised Raffles to recognise the *bekel* as the landholders and not the peasants. Although Crawfurd believed in a similarity between Bengal and Java, the connection he made was much more complex than the connection Raffles made.

Crawfurd approached the apparent Indian influence over Java in two ways. His first approach outlined a theoretical Lockean concept of a comparative evolution of a common social archetype, in which all societies go through common evolution of social conditions based on various systems of agriculture. Therefore, India and Java looked similar because of similar social evolutionary conditions, but they were unrelated.

Within this second approach, Crawfurd admitted that a direct Indic relationship existed. The legacies of Hindu culture were clearly present in Java. He explained the Hindu connection as a diffusion of Indian culture into an indigenous Javanese society that already practiced spirit worship.[102] He dismissed suggestions of a conquest concluding there was 'no evidence' and proposed that missionaries and regular contact with Indian merchants over the preceding 1,500 years were the more likely source.[103]

Similar to the adoption of Hindu culture, Crawfurd saw the adoption of Islam in Java as a peaceful transition in which new legal formations emerged overlaying earlier Hindu laws and customs. Unlike Raffles, who saw Islam as a degenerate religion, Crawfurd demonstrated no apparent dislike or disrespect towards Islam.[104] He did not see the practice of Islam as causing any consternation in Java and happily discussed the layers of Hindu cultural practices that remained in Javanese Islamic practice.[105] He painted a picture of an indigenous Javanese society that evolved based on local conditions but was also influenced by outside faiths.

The consequence for land reforms was that Crawfurd did not see a continuation of Hindu law as central, but instead, he was looking for practical solutions to the current systems of authority in Java. He proposed that making the *bekel* responsible for paying the land tax would best fit the local conditions in Java. Crawfurd advised Raffles that by recognising the *bekel* as having a hereditary right to alienate the land, the underlining power relations in Java would be minimally affected, while at the same time, the British policy of reform would be best served.

In comparison to Crawfurd's pragmatic recognition of the *bekel* as a landholder, Raffles stood firm in his belief that Java was colonised by Indian rulers. He rejected Crawfurd's preference for the Zamindari system and instead instructed his officers that:

> It has been a question with Government, how far either the bekels or demdangs ought to be considered in the light of land-holders, as suggested by Mr. Crawfurd in his Report on the Cadoe; and on a due consideration of the rights and pretensions of all classes, it has been considered, that there does not exist any proprietary right in the soil between the actual cultivator and the Sovereign, to establish the *bekel* as the hereditary landholder. To allow him to sub-let the land of a village at

pleasure, would be to grant him an authority and independence which never could have been expected, and to arm him with power prejudicial to the happiness of the people, and repugnant to the objects which Government have in view, in effecting the amelioration and improvement of the mass of the population.[106]

Although Raffles won the battle, a conflict in ideas had begun between himself and Crawfurd that would last until after Raffles's death. Crawfurd's ideas of colonial rule dominated the 1820s in South-East Asia. Crawfurd would go on to fight a similar battle over culture with James Brooke and his supporters in Sarawak during the 1840s, 50s and 60s. Both men would fight over how colonial policy responded to indigenous cultural interests. Although Crawfurd rejected traditional chronologies in South-East Asia as works of fiction, he ultimately was more sympathetic to the integrity of Javanese culture than Raffles was.

From Crawfurd's direct experience in interviewing Javanese people about their customs, Crawfurd began considering a new vision of history that was highly critical of colonial practices and aimed to reduce colonial involvement in Asian countries. Crawfurd's vision of history minimised the role of migrations and invasions that were a mainstay of the British historical imagination. He argued instead that history was a product of 'indigenous civilisation'. He looked to the origins of customs as coming from a decision within a civilisation and not as a product of external imposition. Crawfurd would develop a view of indigenous civilisation that would ultimately lead him to a polygenesis view of race and reject universal ideas of history.

Notes

1 Crawfurd, *HIA.*, vol. 2, p. 114
2 Crawfurd, 'Raffles's History of Java', p. 395.
3 Ibid. p. 409.
4 Victoria Glendinng argued that Raffles 'did not review Crawfurd's History of the Indian Archipelago' and that the article was completed by John Barrow V. Glendinning, *Raffles: And the Golden Opportunity*, (London: Profile Books, 2012). The John Murray III Register lists the article as being written by 'Sir Stamford Raffles & J. Barrow'; Jonathan Cutmore, the editor of the *Quarterly Review Archive*, lists the article as 'John Barrow, probably with Sir Thomas Stamford Raffles' but also provides the supporting quotation from a letter William Gifford (the founding editor of the *Quarterly Review*) to John Murrary (the publisher): '[Barrow] is very anxious for the article on Crawford which he & Marden say is sound & good; I suppose therefore it must be inserted, especially as Sir T Raffles is coming home & he expects much assistance from him. The paper is not very brisk, but tis sensible'. Using this quotation, it is clear that there are three authors: Barrow, Raffles and William Marsden. Barrow might have undertaken the main task of writing, but Raffles and Marsden certainly would have supported the arguments made. See Jonathan Cutmore, 'Quarterly Review Archive'.
5 Raffles, Marsden, and Barrow, 'Crawfurd's History of the Indian Archipelago', p. 112.

6   Hugh Edward Egerton, *Sir Stamford Raffles: England in the Far East*, ([S.l.]: T. Fisher Unwin, 1900); Raffles, *Memoir of the Life and Public Services of Sir Thomas Stamford Raffles*; Wurtzburg and Witting, *Raffles of the Eastern Isles*; Tim Hannigan, *Raffles and the British Invasion of Java*, (Singapore: Monsoon, 2012).

7   John Bastin, 'Malayan Portraits: John Crawfurd', *Malaya*, 3 (December 1954).

8   Crawfurd, *HIA.*, vol. 2, p. 216.

9   Anonymous, 'Mr Crawfurd's History of the Indian Archipelago', p. 145.

10 Ibid.

11 John Crawfurd, *A Descriptive Dictionary of the Indian Islands & Adjacent Countries*, (Kuala Lumpur; New York: Oxford University Press, 1971 [1856]), p. 363; Crawfurd*, 'A Visit to the Indian Archipelago in H.M.S. Maeander, with Portions of the Private Journal of Sir James Brooke, K.C.B. By Captain the Hon. Henry Keppel, R.N. Two Vols. Bentley', (19 February, 1853).

12 See Raffles, *Memoir of the Life and Public Services of Sir Thomas Stamford Raffles*.

13 Egerton, *Sir Stamford Raffles: England in the Far East*, pp. 68, 93.

14 Wurtzburg and Witting, *Raffles of the Eastern Isles*, p. 191.

15 Bastin, 'Malayan Portraits: John Crawfurd'; C.M. Turnbull, *The Straits Settlements, 1826–1867: Indian Presidency to Crown Colony*, (London: Athlone Press, 1972), p. 322; Ter Ellingson, *The Myth of the Noble Savage*, (Berkeley: University of California, 2001); Mary Quilty, *Textual Empires: A Reading of Early British Histories of Southeast Asia*, (Melbourne: Monash Asia Institute, 1998); Hannigan, *Raffles and the British Invasion of Java*.

16 Zoë Laidlaw, *Colonial Connections, 1815–45: Patronage, the Information Revolution and Colonial Government*, (Manchester: Manchester University Press, 2005).

17 A dispatch from 1 May 1812 explaining Raffles's decision to destroy Yogya is written by Raffles suggesting Minto has already received information from Crawfurd. I have to thank Tze Shung from the Australian National University for bringing this dispatch to my notice.

18 Crawfurd, 'Raffles's History of Java'; Raffles, Marsden, and Barrow, 'Crawfurd's History of the Indian Archipelago'.

19 John Bastin, 'English Sources for the Modern Period of Indonesian History', in *An Introduction to Indonesian Historiography*, ed. by Soedjatmoko and Cornell University, Modern Indonesia Project (Ithaca, NY: Cornell University Press, 1965), pp. 252–272.

20 Anonymous, 'Mr Crawfurd's History of the Indian Archipelago', p. 145.

21 Ibid. p. 146; Anonymous, 'History of the Indian Archipelago; Containing an Account of the Manners, Arts, Languages, Religions, Institutions and Comerce of its Inhabitants: By John Crawfurd, FRS.', pp. 327–328.

22 Anonymous, *Java Gazette* (29 February, 1812), p. 5.

23 George W. Stocking, *Victorian Anthropology*, (New York: Free Press, 1987), pp. 53–56.

24 Katie Trumpener, *Bardic Nationalism: The Romantic Novel and the British Empire*, (Princeton: Princeton University Press, 1997), pp. 6–7.

25 Thomas Stamford Raffles, *Substance of a Minute Recorded by the Honourable Thomas Stamford Raffles . . . on the 11th February 1814; on the Introduction of an Imprived System of Internal Management and the Establishment of a Land Rental on the Island of Java: To which are Added Several of the Most Interesting Documents therein Referred to*, (London: Printed (but not published) for Black, Parry, and Co., 1814), pp. 79–152.

26 Burrow, *A History of Histories*, p. 305; P. Rowley-Conwy, *From Genesis to Prehistory: The Archaeological Three Age System and its Contested Reception in*

Denmark, Britain, and Ireland, (Oxford: Oxford University Press, 2007); Alain Schnapp, *The Discovery of the Past,* (London: British Museum Press, 1993).

27 Thomas Forrest, '2 July 1784 letter from Capt Forrest, Extract of Bengal General Consultations', Factory Records: Straits Settlements, *East India Company,* British Library.

28 see R.L. Meek, *Social Science and the Ignoble Savage,* (Cambridge: Cambridge University Press, 1976). For historic analysis of stadial history and for a contemporary discription, see Crawfurd, 'History and Languages of the Indian Islands'; A. Smith and others, *The Glasgow Edition of the Works and Correspondence of Adam Smith: III: Essays on Philosophical Subjects: With Dugald Stewart's 'Account of Adam Smith': With Dugald Stewart's 'Account of Adam Smith',* (Oxford: Oxford University Press, 1980).

29 Robert Nisbet, 'Vico and the Idea of Progress', *Social Research,* 43 3 (1976), p. 629.

30 J. G. A. Pocock has demonstrated how Edward Gibbon used the methods of stadial history within his narrative. See Pocock, *Barbarism and Religion II: Narratives of Civil Government.*

31 Crawfurd, 'Of the Eastern Penisular of India'; Crawfurd, 'History and Languages of the Indian Islands'; John Crawfurd, 'Raffles's History of Java', ibid. 31 (March 1819).

32 Crawfurd, 'Crawfurd to Norton Shaw, 3 May'.

33 Anonymous, 'Mr Crawfurd's History of the Indian Archipelago'; Anonymous, 'History of the Indian Archipelago; Containing an Account of the Manners, Arts, Languages, Religions, Institutions and Comerce of its Inhabitants: By John Crawfurd, FRS.'; Raffles, Marsden, and Barrow, 'Crawfurd's History of the Indian Archipelago'.

34 J. G. A. Pocock, *The Ancient Constituion and the Feudal Law: A Study of English Historical Though in the Seventeenth Century,* (Cambridge: Cambridge University Press, 1987), p. 79.

35 Ibid. p. 81.

36 Raffles, *The History of Java,* vol. 1, p. 2.

37 Raffles constructs these references as a discussion of a common source; ibid., vol. 1, pp. 2, 57, vol. 2, chapter 1.

38 Crawfurd, 'Papers Relating to Java and Other Areas of East Asia, ca. 1811–1823', p. 27.

39 Ibid.

40 Crawfurd, 'Of the Eastern Penisular of India', p. 359.

41 Ibid.

42 Ibid. p. 332.

43 Locke was a political Whig who believed in the primacy of parliament over the sovereign in Britain. Seventeenth-century royalist historians such as Sir Robert Filmer wanted to argue that antiquity was on the side of the sovereign and not parliaments. Whig historians argued that the House of Commons was steeped in the immortal ancient constitution of Britain. Filmer argued that the Commons only existed at the King's will. Filmer's argument, forcefully outlined in *Patriarcha,* was a classic statement of Mosaic history Robert Filmer and Peter Laslett, *Patriarcha and Other Political Works,* (New Brunswick, NJ: Transaction Publishers, 2009). He proposed that the patriarchal family was the basis of nations, with Kings claiming genealogical authority back to Adam. John Locke, *Two Treatieses of Goverement,* (Cambridge: Cambridge University Press, 2004 [1698]), pp. 1.142–1.44. In writing *Two Treaties,* Locke wanted to demonstrate that these ideas were ahistorical and against scripture; yet in doing so, Locke posed a theoretical analysis conjecturing a basis for history that did not need a Mosaic narrative.

44 Locke, *Two Treatieses of Goverenment*, p. 1.146.
45 Ibid. p. 2.96.
46 Peter Laslett, 'Introduction', in *Locke: Two Treaties of Government*, ed. by Peter Laslett (Cambridge: Cambridge University Press, 2004).
47 'The labour that was mine, removing them out of that common state they were in, hath fixed my property in them'. Locke, *Two Treatieses of Goverenment*, p. 2.28.
48 Ibid. p. 2.45.
49 Pocock, *Ancient Consitution and the Feudal Law*, p. 235.
50 Mark Glat, 'John Locke's Historical Sense', *The Review of Politics*, 43 01 (1981), p. 623.
51 Ibid. pp. 625–627.
52 David Armitage, *The Ideological Origins of the British Empire*, (Cambridge: Cambridge University Press, 2000), p. 98.
53 Ibid.
54 Robert Van Niel, *Java's Northeast Coast, 1740–1840: A Study in Colonial Encroachment and Dominance*, (Leiden: Research School CNWS, Leiden University, 2005), p. 5.
55 Cited in ibid. p. 15.
56 Cited in ibid.
57 Peter Carey, *The Power of Prophecy: Prince Dipanagara and the End of an Old Order in Java, 1785–1855*, (Leiden: KITLV Press, 2007), p. 10.
58 Ibid. pp. 14–15.
59 Ibid. p. 15; Crawfurd, 'Papers Relating to Java and Other Areas of East Asia, ca. 1811–1823'.
60 Carey, *The Power of Prophecy: Prince Dipanagara and the End of an Old Order in Java, 1785–1855*.
61 Ibid. Crawfurd, 'Papers Relating to Java and Other Areas of East Asia, ca. 1811–1823'.
62 Carey, *The Power of Prophecy: Prince Dipanagara and the End of an Old Order in Java, 1785–1855*.
63 P. van 't Veer, *Daendels: maarschalk van Holland*, (Bussum: Fibula-Van Dishoeck, 1983).
64 Van Niel, *Java's Northeast Coast*, pp. 199–201.
65 Minto and Minto, *Lord Minto in India*, p. 312; John Bastin, *Raffles' Ideas on the Land Rent System in Java and the Mackenzie Land Tenure Commission*, ('s-Gravenhage: Nijhoff, 1954), p. 17.
66 C.A. Bayly, *Indian Society and the Making of the British Empire*, (Cambridge: Cambridge University Press, 1988); Jon E. Wilson, *The Domination of Strangers: Modern Governance in Eastern India, 1780–1835*, (Basingstoke: Palgrave Macmillan, 2010).
67 Ranajit Guha, *A Rule of Property for Bengal: An Essay on the Idea of Permanent Settlement*, (New Delhi: Orient Longman, 1982).
68 Ibid.
69 Thomas Stamford Sir Raffles, 'Minute on Land Tenure', Factory Records: Java, *British Library*, India Office Records and Private Papers, IOR/G/21/60 vol. 69.), p. 5.
70 Quilty, 'British Economic Thought and Colonization in Southeat Asia, 1776–1850', p. 248.
71 Rendall, 'Scottish Orientalism: From Robertson to James Mill', p. 45; Margot Finn, 'Slaves Out of Context: Domestic Slavery and the Anglo-Inidan Family, c. 1780–1830', *Transactions of the Royal Historical Society*, 19 (2009), p. 194.
72 Raffles, 'Minute on Land Tenure', p. 8
73 Anne M. Bailey and Joseph R. Llobera, 'The Asiatic Moe of Production: Science and Politics', (London, Boston and Henley: Routledge & Kegan Paul, 1981).

74 John Crawfurd, 'Description of India', India Office Library, *British Library*, British Library, Mss eur d 457/a (1832–3), p. 452.

75 James Mill, *The History of British India*, (London: Baldwin, Cradock, and Joy, 1820 [1817]), vol. 2, ch. 5.

76 John Bastin downplays the role of India in Raffles's thinking. He argues that Raffles was responding to an internal revenue crisis in Java. Raffles continued with the forced deliveries in early 1812 and expected high returns on the sale of coffee and rice. The continuing global war with France and the British war with America in 1812 meant the export trade collapsed and prices of commodities in Java fell to a one-fifth of their pre-war prices. John Bastin, *The Native Policies of Sir Stamford Raffles in Java and Sumatra: An Economic Interpretation*, (Oxford: Oxford University Press, 1957), pp. 17–18. The lack of exports meant the government in Java faced a financial crisis with a depreciating currency. Therefore, Raffles faced an urgent need to transform the government finances from trade to taxation. Ibid.

77 Minto and Minto, *Lord Minto in India*, p. 312; Bastin, *Raffles' Ideas on the Land Rent System in Java and the Mackenzie Land Tenure Commission*, p. 17.

78 Cited in William Cook Mackenzie and Colin Surveyor-General of India Mackenzie, *Colonel Colin Mackenzie: First Surveyor-General of India, etc. [With a portrait.]*, pp. ix. 230. (Edinburgh & London: W. & R. Chambers, 1952), p. 140.

79 The idea that customs in Java were 'ancient' was a thought that Raffles had which pre-dated his arrival in Java. Prior to the British invasion, Raffles issued declarations to the Javanese outlining British objectives in Java as concerned 'solely with the desire of securing to the Eastern nations the enjoyment of their ancient laws and institutions and of protecting everyone from violence, oppression and injustice'. Wurtzburg and Witting, *Raffles of the Eastern Isles*, p. 162.

80 For a recent publication on the influence of antiquarianism on Malay studies, see Martin Müller, 'Manufacturing Malayness', *Indonesia and the Malay World*, 42 123 (2014).

81 Bastin, *Raffles' Ideas on the Land Rent System in Java and the Mackenzie Land Tenure Commission*.

82 Ibid. see Nicholas B. Dirks, 'Colin Mackenzie: Autobiography of an Archive', in *The Madrass School of Orientalism: Producing Knowledge in Colonial South India*, ed. by Thomas R. Trautmann (New Delhi: Oxford University Press, 2009), pp. 29–47.

83 Van Niel, *Java's Northeast Coast*, p. 245.

84 With Raffle's track record of falling out with key people, it is a reasonable possibility that a falling out with Raffles was part of the reason Mackenzie never completed the work. Raffles initially praised Mackenzie's work in 1813–14 and used his research, but failed to substantially acknowledge him (along with Crawfurd and Farquhar) as a key intellectual whose research Raffles drew on when writing his *History of Java*.

85 Hall, 'Article IV: Memoir of th eLife and Public Services of Sir Satmford Raffles . . . by his Widow', p. 406. W.E. Houghton, J.H. Slingerland, and Wellesley College, *The Wellesley Index to Victorian Periodicals, 1824–1900*, (Toronto: University of Toronto Press, 1989). Attributes this article to the naval officer Basil Hall. Internal evidence in the article points to the writer having spent time travelling through the island of Java. B. Hall, *Fragments of Voyages and Travels by Captain Basil Hall, 3: Second Series*, (Edinburgh: Robert Cadell, 1832), p. 180. States he travelled 1000 miles through the island in 1815.

86 Crawfurd cited in Bastin, *Raffles' Ideas on the Land Rent System in Java and the Mackenzie Land Tenure Commission*, p. 36.

87 MacKenzie cited in Ibid. p. 68.

88 Crawfurd cited in Ibid. p. 36.

89 Raffles, *The History of Java*, vol. 2, pp. 75–77.

90 Ibid., vol. 2, pp. 72.

91 Ibid., vol. 2, p. 93.

92 Ibid., vol. 2, p. 2.

93 Ibid., vol. 2, p. 6.

94 Raffles, *Substance of a Minute Recorded by the Honourable Thomas Stamford Raffles . . . on the 11th February 1814; on the Introduction of an Imprived System of Internal Management and the Establishment of a Land Rental on the Island of Java: To which are Added Several of the Most Interesting Documents therein Referred to*, p. 134.

95 Raffles, 'Minute on Land Tenure', p. 102.

96 Crawfurd, 'Papers Relating to Java and Other Areas of East Asia, ca. 1811–1823', p. 43.

97 Crawfurd, *HIA.*, vol. 3, p. 6.

98 Crawfurd, *Descriptive Dictionary*, p. 183.

99 Crawfurd, *HIA.*, vol. 3, p. 8.

100 Crawfurd, 'Of the Eastern Penisular of India'.

101 Crawfurd, 'Papers Relating to Java and Other Areas of East Asia, ca. 1811–1823', p. 36.

102 Crawfurd, *HIA.*, vol. 2, p. 211.

103 Ibid., vol. 2, p. 228.

104 For a discussion of Raffles's attitudes to Islam, see Syed Muhd Khairudin Aljunied, *Rethinking Raffles: A Study of Stamford Raffles' Discourse on Religions Amongst Malays*, (Singapore: Marshall Cavendish Academic, 2005). Crawfurd and Raffles's debate on the coming of Islam has not ended. There is much contemporary debate on whether or not Islam was a peaceful transition in Southeast Asia or if it was a revolutionary change. Anthony Reid takes the Raffles line and argues that the coming of Islam was violent and revolutionary. Anthony Reid, 'Islamization and Christianization in Southeast Asia: The Critical Phase, 1550–1650', in *Southeast Asian in the Early Modern Era*, ed. by Anthony Reid (Ithaca: Cornell University Press, 1993), pp. 151–179. Figures such as Anthony Milner and Michael Laffan maintain that the transition to Islam in Southeast was not particularly violent. Anthony Crothers Milner, 'Islam and the Muslim State', in *Islam in South-East Asia*, ed. by M.B. Hooker (Leiden: E.J. Bril, 1983); Michael Francis Laffan, *Islamic Nationhood and Colonial Indonesia: The umma Below the Winds*, (London: RoutledgeCurzon, 2003); H.M. Federspiel, *Sultans, Shamans, and Saints: Islam and Muslims in Southeast Asia*, (Honolulu: University of Hawai'i Press, 2007).

105 Crawfurd, *HIA.*, vol. 2, pp. 265–268.

106 Sir Thomas Stamford Raffles, *Substance of a Minute Recorded by the Honourable Thomas Stamford Raffles, Lieutenant-Governor of Java and its Dependencies, on the 11th February 1814, on the Introduction of an Improved System of Internal Management and the Establishment of a Land Rental on the Island of Java: To which are Added Several of the Most Interesting Documents therein Referred to*, (London: Printed (but not published) for Black, Parry), p. 45.

3   Searching for the Aboriginal Pre-History of the Savage

Raffles and Crawfurd's debates on the origins of Javanese civilisation were part of a broader philosophic argument amongst the historian-administrators over the existence of and meaning of aboriginal[1] people in South-East Asia. Many recent historians have maintained that aboriginality was a creation of colonial thought—their logic being that it was the colonists who labelled people aborigines: the colonised people did not give themselves the label.[2] However, the idea of aboriginality was a major problem for early nineteenth-century thinking. The existence and meaning of aboriginal people in South-East Asia had the potential undermine the integrity of a universal Mosaic narrative to history. The implication for colonial policy was whether or not the people of South-East Asia were passive actors who only responded to colonialism or if they were active agents that shaped their own destiny.

In South-East Asia, historian-administrators developed different ideas on aboriginality. They argued over whether aborigines were relics of the first human migrations or separate and innate creations distinct from other humans. William Marsden, John Leyden, Stamford Raffles and John Crawfurd went about historicising aboriginal peoples as part of a process of describing the transformation of savage tribes into barbarian nations. These arguments challenged perceived ideas of history and were at the cutting edge of then contemporary reasoning that discovered a deep past.

The early nineteenth century saw the words 'aboriginal' and 'indigenous' being increasingly used to replace the earlier eighteenth century terms of 'savage' and 'barbarian'. The word 'savage' spiked in 1780 and then again in 1785 along with the word barbarian. The spikes coincided with the vast publishing of philosophic history describing the peoples of America, Africa, Asia and Australia as well as the historical texts on Europe's ancient past. The words 'aboriginal' and 'indigenous' have a much slower but consistent rise from 1790 throughout the nineteenth century.[3]

The transition from using the terms 'savage' and 'barbarian' to 'aboriginal' or 'indigenous' was not a mere replacement of words. Instead, it introduced the idea of 'aboriginal' peoples as a distinct ethnic identity associated with social form. The aboriginal condition became a focus of study. The approaches to studying pre-history through identifying the original or aboriginal people had potentially major implications for a universal narrative of history.[4] The search for human origins meant a challenge to the biblical narrative within Mosaic history and directly fed into racial ideas of identity.

The Enlightenment saw historians, antiquarians and naturalists attempting to push known history back before the first barbarian farming settlements into the savage world of 'pre-history'[5]. As we saw in the previous chapter, the settling of land was believed to have created the beginnings of government and established the foundations of civil history. Enlightenment historians, however, now wanted to understand what existed before the settlement of land and the beginnings of civil history. There was clearly a chain of events that preceded the construction of a barbarian nation and possibly a savage tribe as well.

Savages Before History and Analogies Between America and South-East Asia

Ideas about aboriginality began with Enlightenment figures conceiving of a common savage original state for all humanity. Part of this intellectual endeavour was to establish a link or analogy between savages in America and savages in other parts of the world. In South-East Asian scholarship, William Marsden's 1783 *History of Sumatra* broke away from the traditions of travellers' narratives, founding an approach to studying the savage with historical rigour. Marsden's *History* followed the then new Enlightenment project of extending European historiography to the new worlds of America and Asia. Early ideas of aboriginality were strongly influenced by European interpretations of Native Americans, who were branded savages.[6] John Locke had argued that 'all the world was once America', making America analogous to the biblical Eden.[7] The analogy meant that before the beginning of civil history, all peoples lived in a condition similar to that of the Native Americans, in wildernesses like virginal landscape of North America—untouched by improvement.

The idea of a comparison between North America and Asia was on the minds of historian-administrators in South-East Asia. In 1784, Thomas George Forrest used the North American wilderness as a metaphor for untamed parts of South-East Asia whilst writing reports on sites for potential British settlements in South-East Asia. Forrest reported to the government in Bengal that mainland South-East Asia was 'like the Wilds of America, passable only by the Natives'.[8] The islands, he noted, were 'poorly inhabited' and in the case of the Andaman Islands populated by 'savages' who like 'the North Americans eat their prisoners' or 'adopted them'.[9] Also Forrest suggested that Borneo was the source of raw materials for developed societies, arguing that the trade relationship between 'Borneo' and 'China' resembled the 'trade from Europe to America'.[10] Although Forrest was far from saying that Asia was America, he was suggesting that parts of Asia were analogous to North America in society and wildness.

Marsden believed that the American savage represented one of the most original types of humans. He saw them as being as wild and uncultured as the savages that dwelt in the interior of Sumatra. In comparison to the savages of North America and the wild interior of Sumatra, the majority of Sumatrans used technology and engaged in international trade and, therefore, had some of the trappings of civilisation. For Marsden, technology and trade set the Malays apart from the savages living in the forest.

In a letter to Marsden, Alexander Dalrymple described the savages from the interior of the Philippine island of Luzon as resembling 'the savages of North America' in their war-like attitude and savagery. Dalrymple believed these savages were originally 'natural lords of the country' who now accepted 'tribute' from the 'people who settled in the low lands' for use of the 'woods and rivers'.[11] Areas of wilderness devoid of cities and civilisation in both America and Asia became Eden-like environments, symbolising the condition of original people who had a natural nobility. These people were 'savages' because they existed without government and therefore, for Enlightenment thinkers, had no civil history.[12] By comparing South-East Asia to America, Forrest, Marsden and Dalrymple suggested that wild tribes of South-East Asia constituted another model for understanding original peoples.

While investigating the original peoples of Sumatra, Marsden made 'inquiries amongst the natives concerning the aborigines' of Sumatra.[13] 'I have been informed', Marsden recalled, of 'two different species of people dispersed in the woods and avoiding all communication with the other inhabitants'.[14] These people were called Orang Cooboo[15] and Orang Googoo, both of which he described as 'primitive'. These people lived off 'whatever the woods afford[ed]'. The Googoo he describes as almost sub-human, 'differing in little but the use of speech from the Orang Utan of Borneo; their bodies being covered with long hair'.[16] Marsden questioned the sub-human aspect of the story and was clearly not convinced, but he concluded that it probably had 'some foundation in truth'.[17]

Marsden's suspicions reflect a deeper problem he had in asking people about aboriginality. We do not know exactly what he asked the inhabitants, but his questions must have been hard to communicate. The ideas of 'origins', 'indigenous' and 'aboriginal' had a particular culturally evolved meaning in eighteenth-century British thought, which could not have been translated easily across cultures. When he spoke to the Pangeran of Soongey Lamo, chief of the Rejangs, in Malay, the man responded 'No Malay, Sir; I am a genuine, original countryman'.[18] The word original was 'ooloo' or 'ulu/hulu', meaning the source of a river, head of an object or interior.[19] The Pangeran could have meant he originated from the interior of Sumatra and not the coast. Did Marsden ask any further questions to clarify what the Pangeran meant? Did he attempt to convey his interpretation of the idea of original to the Pangeran and include some other description? I suspect he did, and Marsden's recorded account is a vastly truncated version of a much longer exchange.

From the answers Marsden received, we have some idea of the way he must have described aboriginal people to the Sumatrans. Marsden used a stadial (or staged) approach to understanding human history (described in Chapter 2). Within that approach, Marsden used levels of agricultural and social development to determine the stages of civilisation a people went through in developing. Therefore, he probably asked a question something along the lines of 'are there any people who live in Sumatra with no manufactures or technology and no farming?' The response from the coastal Sumatrans was yes, they live up river. Whatever the case, Marsden's ideas on aboriginality contained underlying assumptions of savagery and primitiveness.

Marsden's assumption of an analogy between the savages of South-East Asia and America followed standard eighteenth-century thinking, as did his search for the Sumatran 'stages of society'.[20] Marsden proposed the stage of society as a problem, arguing that the Sumatrans 'though far distant from that point to which the polished states of Europe, have aspired, they yet look down, with an interval almost as great, on the savage tribes of Africa and America'.[21] For Marsden, it was a philosophical problem that needed to be answered because highly civilised people lived next to savages.

Marsden's arguments drew heavily on William Robertson's *History of America* in identifying American Indians as being one of the simplest societies.[22] Following Robertson, Marsden used comparative methodology to determine social development through an analysis of the different levels societies had reached in technology, mathematics, philosophy and language.[23] Marsden maintained that the different peoples living in Sumatra—who were often in close proximity to each other—displayed very different stages of social development. In Sumatra, he saw examples of both degeneration and progress. He concluded that tribes and nations could progress or degenerate and through the study of this progression or degeneration, the early history of a people could be determined.

Aborigines in the Interior: Migration and Colonialism

When considering the levels of social development of different tribes and nations, eighteenth- and nineteenth-century thinkers brought to the discussion their own experience of European history and the brutal history of European colonisation in the New World (America). The European encroachment into the New World was a seaborne migratory invasion that saw the displacement and killing of the Native American peoples from their original lands.

A similar pattern of European migration and displacement of nomadic or subsistence communities also occurred in South-East Asia. When Captain Light founded Penang, he met the 'original' inhabitants of the Island: the

Orang lut or sea gypsies, a semi-nomadic people who lived off fishing and forest products. These people initially supported the new colony, but many of them soon moved into the interior, away from the settlement.[24] Those that stayed in the settlement lost their identity, becoming indistinguishable from the Malay migrants from peninsular Malaya to the colonial community. British writers did not see a problem with migrant communities supplanting original communities. It was part of a natural order of civilisation and state formation. In the few instances where colonial officials did raise concerns, it was for utilitarian reasons.

In 1805, Colonel Robert Farquhar proposed that the approach of attracting migrants to fill the colony of Penang was not working. He argued that the Chinese and Indian migrants were 'itinerant' settlers who only came to the colony with the 'view of returning to their [original] country'.[25] These 'itinerants', Farquhar argued, drained the economy of the island-colony by continually stripping it of capital as settlers exported their wealth back to their home country. Farquhar proposed that the Malays should be encouraged to settle because it was their natural country; they had an ancestral connection to the soil and would therefore supposedly leave their economic capital in the colony.[26] Despite Farquhar's belief that the Malays were native, in fact, even the Malays were migrants. The Malays that Farquhar referred to were not the original people of the Island that Light had encountered 19 years previously.[27]

Farquhar's concerns reflected British ideas of history. Settlement was about moving into a foreign land, taking root and, finally, supplanting or blending with the original population. Colonial settlement as migration, conquest, blending or banishment of original peoples reflected Enlightenment interpretations of European history. Enlightenment historiography saw European history as the story of waves of invading hordes who displaced and annihilated previous occupants of the land, creating distinct ethnic and national identities inside of Europe.[28]

Stories of invasions and supplanting of people were at the core of the European tradition of national history. Enlightenment historiography charted these internal European invasions and supplanting of previous communities to explain the origins of the nations and states of eighteenth-century Europe. David Hume's six-volume *The History of England* published between 1754 and 1761 is an example of how Enlightenment thinkers saw migration and conquests in history. His first volume outlined the barbarian origins of English liberty and the construction of the different British nations of England, Scotland and Wales through a series of different barbarian colonising invasions. In the first thirty pages of his book, Hume describes the aboriginal population of Britain which was supplanted by successive migratory invasions by seaborne outsiders.

The Roman invasion pushed some aboriginal Britons into the land that became Scotland, whilst the remaining Britons blended with the Romans. These Romano-Britons were then supplanted by the Saxons, and the surviving remnants of Britons fled to the land of Wales. For Hume, the supplanting of one people by another was not about numbers of people migrating, it was about ideas and values. Civilisation and barbarian freedom dictated if a people were displaced.

Hume painted the aboriginal Britons as a barbarous people who were semi-nomadic and tribal. Their 'sole property', Hume maintained 'was their arms and their cattle'.[29] Conquest destroyed the nomadic way of life and spirit of the aboriginal Britons. According to Hume, 'the natives, disarmed, dispirited, and submissive, had left all desire and even idea of their former liberty and independence'.[30] The Britons under the Romans became subservient but civilised. Nevertheless, some Britons chose to move further into 'Caledonia' (Scotland) out of Rome's grasp. Hume described them as 'fiercer and more intractable spirits who deemed war and death itself less intolerable than servitude under the victors'.[31] In his narrative, the freedom-loving Britons became the Picts/Scots and maintained their tribal ways.

In comparison to the freedom-loving Picts/Scots, Hume argued that the Britons who submitted to Rome quickly became used to luxury, rather than liberty. He concluded that these Britons became domesticated subjects of the Romans: 'Unaccustomed both to the perils of war, and to the cares of civil government, they found themselves incapable of forming or executing any measures for resisting the incursions of the [Saxon] barbarians'.[32] Into this mix came the German barbarians, in the form of the Saxons. They defeated the Britons, whom he said were 'shut up in the barren counties of Cornwall and Wales'.[33] Hume's narrative of the creation of the three nations of Britain, England, Scotland and Wales, was the narrative of an aboriginal people conquered and banished by successive invaders from the sea.[34]

With a changing of the names, Hume's narrative of displacement could apply to the Americas, Australia and Southern Africa. His message was that invaders brought advanced civilisation or sanguine barbarian freedom which could displace aboriginal populations without much effort. Hume's narrative was not unique: it drew from historical reasoning that went back to Roman interpretations of their invasions of Western Europe.[35] The narrative of migration and displacement was at the heart of British thinking when considering the plight of tribal peoples. British writers could point to a repeated pattern of semi-civilised or civilised peoples invading and conquering aboriginal or original peoples, in which either the invaders subsumed the aboriginal people or the aborigines fled from the invaders and found refuge in the interior or wilderness.

When Marsden wrote *The History of Sumatra*, he had this narrative of migration, conquest and supplantation of aboriginal British peoples in mind. This narrative he related to the previously discussed aboriginal tribes, the Orang Cooboo and Orang Googoo. Marsden described these tribes as living deep in the interior of Sumatra and being subject to harassment by coastal communities.[36] Their origins were indeterminate, but they were forest dwellers and avoided dealings with coastal Malays. In the first 1783 edition, Marsden assumed the accepted view of Malay history that these tribes derived from Malaya. In his second 1811 edition, however, he changed his opinion, arguing that the Malays derived from Sumatra instead. In his 1811 account, he creates a narrative of migration, invasion and conquest by the Malays who supplanted a Negro indigenous population in Sumatra:

> The first instance adventurers from Sumatra, who, in the twelfth century, formed an establishment there, and that the indigenous inhabitants, gradually driven by them to the woods and mountains, so far from being the stock from whence the Malays were propagated, are an entirely different race of men, nearly approaching in their physical character to the negroes of Africa.[37]

The Malays in Marsden's 1811 narrative are an adventurous, commercial and imperial people who left Sumatra to supplant the indigenous tribal population of Malaya. Pushed into the interior, the aboriginal peoples were an isolated distinct people. His 1784 edition suggested a racial difference between Malays and the aboriginal people of Sumatra. In his 1811 edition, he was more explicit suggesting the aborigines were like the Negros of Africa. The dichotomy between the aboriginal people living in the wild interior and invaders living along the coastal regions was analogous with the European historical experience. The analogy implied to readers in the late eighteenth century a naturalness of conquest by advanced maritime peoples over primitive savages.

John Leyden, in an essay also published in 1811, went further than Marsden and argued that the Papuans or 'oriental Negros' were the original people found throughout the archipelago, but, by the time he wrote, they were 'for the most part confined to the interior of these islands'.[38] Leyden wrote this in an essay on languages in the region. In it, he did not pay the Papuans much attention, apart from describing them as constituting an earlier migration into the region. He suggested that most of them had disappeared over time, with only isolated communities left scattered throughout the archipelago:

> Some of their divisions have formed small savage states, and made some advances towards civilization; but the greater part of them, even with the example of more civilized races before their eyes, have betrayed no symptoms, either of a taste or capacity for improvement, and continue in their primitive state of nakedness, sleeping in trees, devoid of houses or clothing, and subsisting on the spontaneous products of the forest.[39]

By 1811, it had become an accepted fact that dark-skinned people lived in the hinterland of the islands throughout the archipelago and that these people represented the descendants of the first inhabitants. In 1817, Raffles equally accepted that a race of Papuans had populated the islands of

South-East Asia only to be supplanted by the Malays and Javanese and targeted for slavery by their conquerors. Crawfurd took the idea further, proposing that 'whenever they [Negro races] are encountered by the fairer races, they are hunted down like the wild animals of the forest, and driven to the mountains or fastnesses[40] incapable of resistance'.[41]

Each of these writers constructed a narrative of displacement surrounding indigenous peoples. Their histories focused on Malay colonialism, narrating a history of South-East Asia in which aboriginal peoples are continually displaced by invading peoples. This reasoning, common to British thinkers at the time, legitimised displacement and destruction of indigenous peoples as a natural reality. Therefore, throughout the world, aboriginal peoples became the displaced losers in the face of migrating invaders.

Origins of Humans and Mosaic History

As the previous chapter has argued, the idea of determining an original source of property was at the core of Enlightenment historiography. The creation of private property initiated the creation of history. But before the dawn of history, there existed a savage stage of society that preceded the creation of property. Although this savage state existed before history, Enlightenment thinking still attempted to historicise the savage: to speculate on what the savage's original state would have been.

Marsden littered his *History of Sumatra* with statements about determining the customs of 'original inhabitants' as opposed to the 'Mohometan' developments of later ages. His *History* aimed to uncover the central character of the Sumatrans. The book was, in his words, 'aiming at a more particular detail, in what respects the customs, opinion, arts and industry of the original inhabitants, in their most genuine state' were like.[42] These fragments of 'original inhabitants' are indicative of his commitment to an Enlightenment quest to discover an original source for the historical narrative—a quest that his followers, Raffles and Crawfurd, would continue. Although he was searching for origins, Marsden, like all Enlightenment thinkers, did not have a clear idea of what he meant by origins of a people.

Ideas about origins in the Enlightenment could be both religious and historical. Judeo-Christian tradition provided a story of origins, but by the 1780s, naturalists researching in geology and biology rarely accepted the biblical idea of Genesis in its entirety. Biological theory, which was the study of life and living organisms, including their structure, function, growth, evolution, distribution and taxonomy, was in its infancy in the late eighteenth century. Biological theory meant that naturalists understood that their knowledge had deficiencies and they could not provide a scientific explanation of ultimate human origins. Marsden did make vague speculations on the origins of some Sumatran peoples, connecting them back to the orangutan, but he made these speculations very briefly and in passing.[43]

Nevertheless, there were other ways of understanding origins within an accepted idea of migration.

Samuel Johnson's 1755 dictionary defined an 'original' or 'aboriginal' people as the 'earliest inhabitants of a country' or 'those of whom no original is to be traced'.[44] Johnson's definition was indicative of the multiple ways of understanding origins. For example, his first definition of the 'earliest inhabitants' suggested a story of migration, in which aboriginal people are the first to inhabit a particular land after they arrived from somewhere else. Origins in this instance referred to a distinct people beginning the moment they broke away from another tribal or national grouping. The accepted truth of Mosaic history in which history began with the biblical patriarchs meant that the origins of humans was the Garden of Eden and that the expansion of people out of the holy land amounted to the early stages of history. At the breakaway moment when a new group distinguished itself as a new branch of the human tree, that can be traced back to Adam and Eve. Most historians in the eighteenth century did not bother questioning this orthodoxy.

Johnson's second definition, the idea that there are people from which 'no original is to be traced', suggested a people who existed before traceable history and whose migration cannot be attributed to another tribe or nation. Such a people also could exist outside of the framework of Mosaic history or the universal history narrative. The thought that there might be people who could not trace their ancestors to the Garden of Eden led some thinkers such as Lord Kames (Henry Home) to suggest the possibility of multiple separate creations, a position known as polygenesis that could stem from autochthony (meaning originating where found).[45]

Decades later, the German philosopher, Alexander von Humboldt defined the German variant of the word 'autocthoni'[46] in a way that encapsulates the problem of locating indigenous people within Mosaic history:

> I make use of the word indigenous ("autocthoni"), not to indicate a fact of *creation*, which does not belong to history, but simply to denote that we are ignorant of the "autocthoni" having been preceded by any other people.[47]

Humboldt's footnote published in 1853 summarises the positions on indigeneity that by then were well defined. Samuel Johnson wrote 100 years earlier, when such ideas were less defined. But in Johnson's definition, we can still see the basis of von Humboldt's position that to define a people as aboriginal was to label their origins unknowable or in the realms of speculation.

Marsden avoided any substantial discussion of what constituted aboriginality. In their recent studies of Marsden, both Diana Carroll and Sandra Manickam point to the search for aboriginal origins of the Sumatrans as a central theme in Marsden's research.[48] However, their claim needs to be tempered by the fact that Marsden only twice used the words 'aboriginal' and 'aborigine' in the first edition of his 1783 *History of Sumatra*.[49] He also infrequently used the word 'indigenous' as well. In 1783, Marsden used the word 'indigenous' six times, although by 1811, Marsden had doubled his usage of the word. Carroll argues that the audiences were different for the two versions, with the 1783 *History* intended as a scholarly work explaining and providing evidence for Marsden's linguistic theories, whilst the revisions to the 1811 *History* aimed to improve its practical usefulness and reflect the changed intellectual context of the early nineteenth century. Carroll proposes that Marsden's idea of race was transformed between the two editions, with 'the history of humankind becoming the history of races and definitively distinguished from the history of language'.[50]

Carroll's reading of the two editions supports the notion that the idea of racial origins was not predominant in eighteenth-century thought, but a shift that occurred in the early nineteenth century. Differences between the 1783 and 1811 editions show that the search for origins in the eighteenth century was framed around determining a linguistic source, whilst in the nineteenth century, the aim was to determine a racial source, with race increasingly connected to biology.

Migration, Mosaic History and the Austronesian Thesis in Marsden, Leyden and Raffles

At the heart of identifying an indigenous or aboriginal people was the problem of migration in Mosaic history. As Chapter 2 discussed, the European historic tradition, with its basis in biblical history, approached identity through an understanding of people emanating out first from Eden then Babel and then the world of biblical patriarchs. At its core, European historiography saw human existence as emanating from an original Adam and Eve, with languages and physical characteristics gradually emerging as people became more distant from one another.

Philology, which is the study of changes in languages over time, became a means of tracing these origins. William Jones' pioneering work in the late eighteenth century into the connections between Sanskrit and Latin pointed to 'some common source, which perhaps, no longer exists'.[51] In the pantheon of Hindu gods, Jones saw similarities to the polytheistic gods of Ancient Greece and Rome. Jones's papers for the Asiatic Society of Bengal placed Indian history into a framework of Mosaic history. He attempted to find a monotheistic core to each of the Asian religions so he could trace Indian history back to Noah and the repopulating of the earth after the Biblical flood.[52] Although the discipline of philology had emerged in the seventeenth century, it was Jones's eighteenth-century discovery of a linguistic connection between Sanskrit and Latin that caused a revolution in writing the history of nations.

Jones's discovery meant it was possible to trace the divergence of language groups and demonstrate their link to a common original language. In 1811,

John Leyden expressed the importance of this methodology in understanding human history and the origins of ethnic, national or racial differences:

> In the paucity of existing monuments, relative to the Indo-Chinese [South-East Asian] nations, no better method presented itself, either for classing their tribes, or laying a foundation for historical researches, than by examining the mutual relation of the several languages which are current among them. This method, when applied on an extensive scale, is always the surest clue for developing the origin of a nation, and indicating the revolutions to which it may have been subjected, either by foreign conquest or colonization.[53]

The spread of humans was baffling to eighteenth-century thinkers. They lived at a time when extremely well-equipped European expeditions, such as Captain Cook's Endeavour Expedition to the Pacific, were continually discovering people living on remote islands. In the case of Easter Island, the inhabitants possessed no oceangoing sailing vessels. 'How did people arrive at these destinations?' was the question on their minds.

Marsden tried to answer this question a few years after his 1779 return to Britain from his long residence in Sumatra. Through his friendship with Thomas Forrest, Marsden came to regularly attend Joseph Banks's breakfast gatherings of men of science. On one of these occasions, Marsden addressed the gathering with a comparative wordlist of Sumatran and Polynesian languages that demonstrated a linguistic connection between the Malay and Polynesian languages. Marsden's paper was no more than four pages long, but Banks realised the importance of Marsden's observations. He published it soon after and encouraged Marsden to follow up with a detailed account of Sumatra.[54]

Marsden's *History of Sumatra* was largely written to substantiate his belief that there was a general language spoken which was 'indigenous to all the islands of the eastern sea' and extended from 'Madagascar to the remotest of Captain Cook's discoveries' in the Pacific Ocean.[55] When he first published his *History of Sumatra* in 1784, Marsden proposed that this indigenous language symbolised an ancient social and political community that he associated with the Malays. He proposed that this ancient Malay people 'comprehended a wider extent than the Roman or any other tongue has yet boasted', but over time, 'it has been more or less mixed and corrupted' and began to display local differences.[56]

Marsden saw himself as following the Mosaic tradition, claiming, 'I am engaged in an attempt to render this comparison of languages more extensive, and as far as possible, to bring specimens of all those spoken in the known world, into one point of view'.[57] Marsden also saw himself as a rival to William Jones at the time.[58] He did not, however, believe in a polygenic position or that the aboriginal peoples of South-East Asia were autochthonous. He was still of the opinion that although one large linguistic group linked the peoples from Madagascar to Easter Island, this ancient linguistic group descended from an earlier linguistic tradition that came from continental Europe or Asia.

In 1811, John Leyden published his account of the Indo-Chinese languages. In this account, Leyden somewhat disingenuously rewrote Marsden's thesis to paint him almost as a supporter of polygenesis. Like Crawfurd, Leyden was a gifted linguist who emanated from a Scottish Highland community. Prior to travelling to India, he distinguished himself amongst Scottish intellectuals by recording Scottish folklore. Whilst at the University of Edinburgh, Leyden joined the circle of Lord Minto, who was soon to become Governor-General of British India and Leyden's patron.[59] In India, Leyden immersed himself in Sanskrit and modern Indian languages. During a spell in Penang—where he also became close friends with Stamford Raffles and John Crawfurd—Leyden was exposed to Malay and numerous other South-East Asian languages.

Leyden agreed with Marsden that traces of the Malay language existed across South-East Asia and the Pacific. Nevertheless, he disagreed with Marsden on the originality of the Malay language. Discerning the originality of a language was an important part of Enlightenment philology. Originality signified that the language could not be traced to an early common root language. Consequently, an original language could signify an aboriginal people.

Leyden quoted Marsden in such a way as to suggest that Marsden proposed that Malay was the original language of South-East Asia and was unconnected to the mainland languages of Asia: 'is sufficient to give it claim to the highest degree of antiquity, and to originality, as far as that term can be applied'.[60] Although these were Marsden's words, Leyden used them to set Marsden against William Jones, stating that Jones 'admitted' but had not 'confirmed' Marsden's findings.[61] Leyden downplayed the true import of Marsden's work for his own ends.

Marsden had clearly stated that he believed all languages were traceable to one original language and therefore supported the original unity of all mankind. Despite Marsden's belief in the unity of mankind, Leyden contended that Marsden was trying to disconnect Malay from other Indo-European languages. He stated that Marsden 'seems inclined to think that the Malay language was indigenous in the Malay Peninsula, from which it extended itself among the eastern isles, till it became the lingua franca of that part of the globe'.[62] After massaging Marsden's argument, Leyden concluded that Marsden 'by attempting to prove too much, however . . . has failed essentially'.[63] The intellectual hatchet-job that Leyden conducted on Marsden cleared the ground for his own theory, which was that Malay shared a common origin with Sanskrit.[64]

Leyden's main argument was to challenge the antiquity of the Malay language. He proposed that Javanese was the ancient language, citing that the 'Javanese language is admitted by the Malays to be that of a more ancient nation than themselves'.[65] Leyden asserted the primacy of the Javanese language in 1808, three years before the British occupied Java, when knowledge of the Javanese language was minimal. For Leyden, the antiquity of Javanese discounted Marsden's claim that Malay was the ancestral language of South-East Asia. Leyden was careful in wording his argument. He wanted to argue that Malay was a derivative of Javanese, but he did not quite have the evidence to support his argument. So he used the carefully qualified phrase that Malay 'appears to be a corrupt derivative' of coastal Javanese.[66] Using the framework common to Enlightenment and early nineteenth-century ideas of aboriginality or originality, Leyden proclaimed that the interior of Java provided the purist examples of the Javanese language.[67]

Although Leyden saw Javanese as an older language than Malay, his ultimate argument was that both Malay and Javanese, along with all other South-East Asian languages, were derivatives of Sanskrit. The language of the Javanese interior (which Leyden believed was older than the coastal language) demonstrated a 'close and intimate connection with Sanscrit'.[68] The Sanskrit origins, he argued, presented a 'more natural inference' than Marsden's indigenous Malay origin.[69] In addition to the linguistic connections, Leyden also cited the Hindu cultural heritage in Java and Bali to emphasise India as the source of South-East Asian culture.

Leyden transformed Marsden's words and the nature of British scholarship on South-East Asia. Although Marsden believed that South-East Asian peoples ultimately connected into the pattern of Mosaic history, he did not pursue the connection further, claiming instead that 'the circumstances and progress of their separation are wrapped in the darkest veil of obscurity'.[70] Leyden, although rejecting the originality of the Malay language group, was trying to understand the linguistic connections linking people of insular South-East Asia back to continental Asia and therefore furthering Mosaic history.

Leyden's ideas on languages influenced Raffles and Crawfurd's divergent views on South-East Asian history and identity. For Raffles, Leyden provided the linguistic evidence that linked Java and the Malay world to India. As the previous chapter demonstrated, Raffles was not an original thinker, but rather, a compiler of views. In the preface to his *History of Java*, Raffles declared that Leyden, if he had lived, was more qualified to write the tome than he was.[71] Raffles's homage to Leyden, which is highly emotional, with references to Leyden dying in Raffles's arms, points out that Leyden had already established a narrative of 'national migration'. In his 1813 address to the Batavian Society, Raffles outlined Leyden's narrative of migration: 'I am convinced . . . that he [Leyden] would have found it no difficult task to have traced the connection which formerly subsisted between the Eastern Islands and Western India'.[72]

Raffles's idea of history was that Javanese civilisation derived from India and that this 'fact' legitimised his policies of land tenure. Raffles's dogged assertion that Javanese customs emanated from India had their origins in

Leyden's speculations. In his *History of Java*, Raffles combined Marsden's and Leyden's thinking. He began by repeating the original thesis of Marsden that 'one original language seems, in a very remote period, to have pervaded the whole Archipelago, and to have spread (perhaps with the population) towards Madagascar on one side, and to the islands in the South Sea on the other'.[73] Raffles then propagated Leyden's ideas to produce a civilisational thesis that negated the arguments that religion, culture, law and civilisation were indigenous to South-East Asia: 'Sanscrit terms', he argued, direct us 'at once, to the source whence civilization flowed towards these regions'.[74]

Raffles leaned towards Leyden's view that South-East Asian people migrated there from India, although his writing suggests he thought this migration probably occurred in multiple waves. In a letter to William Wilberforce in September 1819, Raffles summarised his opinion: that although a 'woolly-headed race [is] scattered over these Islands from the Andamans to New Guinea', he was sceptical that these people represented an aboriginal population, reasoning that 'there have been wanting persons who consider them as the aborigines of the country'.[75] Raffles used the word 'aboriginal' to mean autochthony (meaning an independent creation) rather than first migration (as we would today), and seemingly he believed all aboriginal peoples needed to resemble African Negros. Raffles went on to reject the 'aboriginal' thesis, concluding that 'I am far from concurring in the opinion regarding aborigines of these Islands, and rather consider the Caffres we now find in the region to have been brought by traders in remote periods as slaves'.[76]

Raffles was committed to the idea of waves of migration into South-East Asia. This opinion conformed to the tenets of Mosaic history. It also meant colonial migrations were a normal part of South-East Asian history. Marsden had tacitly raised the possibility of an original people existing in South-East Asia, but Leyden and Raffles both argued for an intrinsic connection with India and rejected the hypothesis. Nevertheless, the idea of aboriginal races in South-East Asia would not die, and John Crawfurd would reinvigorate the belief and develop a non-Mosaic and non-universal narrative of South-East Asian history.

Crawfurd and Autochthony Polygenesis

Crawfurd's and Raffles's differing views of history are interconnected with their opposing views of the antiquity and originality of Javanese laws and customs. As the previous chapter proposes, when considering the traditions of land tenure in Java, Crawfurd believed the Javanese were an ancient culture that, although influenced by external forces, was indigenous to the islands and region of South-East Asia. In comparison, Raffles believed Javanese civilisation was a colonial import from India, and therefore contemporary land tenure was a Mohammedan corruption of older Indian land tenure. The aboriginal pre-history of Java, therefore, was part of broader debates on colonial administration.

On 13 February 1820, Raffles confided to Marsden his apprehension about Crawfurd's forthcoming book: 'I expect from him a somewhat new view of the literature, history, and antiquities of Java, as he appears in his review of my work in the *Edinburgh [Review]* to have thrown a cloud over that part of my story'.[77] Raffles was expecting Crawfurd to produce a major leap in historical reasoning, acquiescing that 'I shall be happy to stand corrected where I am wrong . . . but I hope he will give something more than assertion as to the dates which he disputed'.[78] Although Raffles was expecting something big, he was not expecting the re-interpretation of Java's past that Crawfurd published.

Crawfurd made a fundamental break with Mosaic history. He rejected all previous attempts to narrate the ancient history of the populating of South-East Asia. Previous attempts had been conducted by 'superficial observers', he argued, who believed the Negro peoples of South-East Asia originally arrived as a 'colony from Africa' and everybody else came through an 'emigration from Tartary'.[79] These hypotheses he dismissed as 'violent suppositions' that go against the 'physical state of the globe, the nature of man' and therefore are 'too absurd to bear the slightest touch of examination'.[80]

Crawfurd rejected Leyden and Raffles's proposition that the people of South-East Asia came from India, declaring that the limited nature of Sanskrit connections merely suggested the adoption of some Sanskrit terms after the introduction of Hinduism.[81] His argument focused on the type of words in local languages with a Sanskrit base, leading to a conclusion 'that the language [Sanskrit] was not introduced by conquest, but propagated by the slow and gradual means of religious conversion, effected, just as in later times, the Arabic, by the Mahomedans [sic], through the activity and intrigues of a few dexterous priests'.[82] Therefore, Crawfurd saw the introduction of Hindu practices in South-East Asia as being little different from the more recent introduction of Islam and that both religions represented waves of influence over an indigenous South-East Asian community and culture.

In ruling out migrations and invasions from Tartary or India, Crawfurd still had to account for the early populating of South-East Asia. His answer was to break with the accepted traditions of Mosaic history. Crawfurd proposed that each original tribe had an 'aboriginal language'. Crawfurd's evidence for this hypothesis was his observation that amongst savage peoples, there was a proliferation of languages, but amongst civilised societies, there were few languages.[83]

He looked to geographical and other barriers (Crawfurd indicates these barriers were more like sexual racial selection such as 'colour, complexion, and physical configuration') to explain why each savage societies had numerous language. In 1820, he concluded that these divisions prevented wide-scale ancient migration, proposing that 'languages are of course original and unmixed, in proportion as circumstances have kept the tribes distinct'.[84] The consequence for historical thinking from Crawfurd's mode of thought was that South-East Asia did not need to be populated from continental Asia. Instead, it was populated by a series of autocrondi aboriginal peoples.

In presenting an argument for polygenesis across the three volumes, Crawfurd's narrative is confused, meandering and easily misunderstood by readers today. His contemporaries did not miss the implications of Crawfurd's conclusions, and their response gives a sense of why Crawfurd wrote in an opaque style:

> What does he mean by aboriginal and indigenous, words so perpetually used by him? That the population of the islands took place at a remote period, we are willing to admit; but an indigenous or aboriginal population implies something more, and is an hypothesis wholly repugnant to the only rational explanation of the problem, that which is contained in the Hebrew account of the creation.[85]

Crawfurd was not just raising an intellectual conjecture, he was challenging the historical traditions of the Bible—questioning the story of human creation told in the Bible as real history. The anonymous review above implied that Crawfurd was presenting a heretical argument that was repugnant to the 'Hebrew account of creation'.

Not only were Crawfurd's opinions heretical, for an early nineteenth-century reader, they bordered on the fantastic. Raffles easily mocked Crawfurd's racial opinions, musing 'for our own parts, we had (however "weakly") supposed that men originally sprang from a common stock'.[86] Such responses suggest that Crawfurd's opaque style was a deliberate ploy to mitigate such responses. The consequences for researchers proposing a challenge to the historical validity of Mosaic history could be extreme. Robert Chambers chose to write his *Vestiges of the Natural History of Creation* anonymously, and 30 years later, Charles Darwin agonised over the printing of his *Origins of the Species*.[87] Both texts radically changed ideas of history, extending the limits of what was understood as history. Challenges to biblical worldviews were almost inevitably at the cutting edge of scientific and historical thinking in the early nineteenth century. Yet, an open challenge was extremely risky.

I am not arguing that Crawfurd was developing a proto-evolutionary position. Crawfurd was quick to declare that he was not attempting to propose a theory on the creation of humans—he explicitly avoided conjecture around the origins of humans, writing it 'appears to me to be one far beyond the compass of human reason'.[88] Rather, I am arguing that the early nineteenth century saw many ideas that challenged received ideas of history and that Crawfurd was at the forefront of contemporary reasoning in trying to understand the deep past.

The early nineteenth century was a cauldron of bubbling ideas that challenged the established Christian worldview of history, which limited geological time to a few thousand years and treated the historical traditions of the Bible as unassailable fact. Throughout the late eighteenth century, geologists and antiquarians concluded that the earth was much older than previous understandings of Mosaic history. Evidence such as the slow degradation of historically known lava flows on Mount Vesuvius outside of Naples, the existence of fossilised animals with no living equivalents and the existence of human remains in layers of sediment contemporaneous to fossils of extinct animals all suggested that the earth existed in deep time. This idea of deep time contradicted narrow definitions of biblical time in Mosaic history.

Although there were many challenges to Mosaic time in the early nineteenth century, relatively few thinkers challenged the idea of monogenesis. Lord Kames (Henry Home), in his 1734 *History of Man*, reasoned that the physical characteristics of human diversity were so extensive that the races originated from separate sources.[89] Charles White, in his 1799 *Account of the Regular Gradation in Man*, proposed that all humans existed in a gradated chain. This was not an evolutionary argument, but rather, a classificatory chain of being, ordering animals and humans according to a gradated hierarchy. White concluded the various races of man were different species and should equally be gradated.[90] How the different races were created White did not speculate. White's concern was that science should realise that humanity was separated into different species. In 1817, the great French comparative anatomist George Cuvier also proposed a racial classification that bordered on polygenesism.[91] In the nineteenth century, two of Cuvier's protégées, Louis Agassiz and Robert Knox, went on to advocate that the different races constituted different species of humans.

Proponents of polygenism often advocated hierarchical differences between the species of humans. White, Cuvier, Agassiz and Knox all, to varying degrees, proposed the superiority of white races over darker skin races. Many studies have demonstrated the interconnections between polygenism, imperialism and slavery.[92] Nevertheless, the interconnections between polygenesis, slavery and imperialism were complex. Most advocates of monogenesis also believed that Europeans were superior, but all advocates of polygenesis were not necessarily discriminatory.

Lord Kames, for example, believed in polygenism, but he did not believe in a racial hierarchy and, in 1778, he freed a black Jamaican slave, Joseph Knight, from James Wedderburn, his master. Equally, Cuvier's pre-1817 writings tended towards racial equality. Whilst Knox, although he espoused a belief in the biological and mental inferiority of Africans and dark-skinned people, as well as race being the source of political conflicts, he also believed that colonialism and imperialism ultimately destroyed dominant races. As previous chapters have demonstrated, Crawfurd believed in racial equality, with all races having equal rights to vote in legislatures. Although some advocates of polygenesis stipulated racial superiority, that position was not universal.

Crawfurd used polygenesis to advance conceptions of cultural unique-ness among the peoples in South-East Asia. By arguing that different peo-ples were aboriginal, Crawfurd was maintaining that many of the social developments that occurred in South-East Asia were indigenous to the local environment. South-East Asia was not a blank page on which invasions introduced culture, but rather, South-East Asians actively exerted agency to develop their own path.

Crawfurd's deployment of polygenesis was part of his endeavour to go beyond recorded history. His contemporaries, however, were not convinced of Crawfurd's ingenuity. Raffles believed that Crawfurd used polygenesism purely to support his other speculations into the remote past regarding the existence of an ancient civilisation that left no trace except remnants in the languages of South-East Asia:

> This strange paradox appears to be brought forward solely for the pur-pose of supporting another equally strange; namely, the discovery of a *dead language* of unparalleled extent, propagated by a great and power-ful nation, of whose history and name every trace had been obliterated, and which our author is pleased to denominate the *Great* Polyesian.[93]

Crawfurd had a distinctive interpretation of Marsden's observation, that previously there was a 'general language spoken' throughout South-East Asia and the Pacific. Marsden had not specifically stated that this was an original language unconnected to mainland Asia. He had in fact proposed that all languages throughout the world could ultimately be traced back to an original source language. Nevertheless, Leyden had presented Marsden as suggesting that an original language existed in South-East Asia uncon-nected to continental Asia. Marsden was probably not comfortable with Leyden's misrepresentation, but he was certainly against Crawfurd's conclu-sions and worked with Raffles in writing the scathing critique of Crawfurd's *History of the Indian Archipelago* in the *Quarterly Review*.[94]

Crawfurd appears to have latched onto Leyden's distorted interpretation of Marsden, proclaiming that 'in imitation of Mr Marsden, I have called [this language] the Great Polynesian'.[95] This Great Polynesian language, Crawfurd admitted, left no trace of its civilisation, but he reasoned that did not mean it did not exist. The linguistic similarities between the languages of South-East Asia and the Pacific were the means of discovery. Crawfurd used the principles of philology, by exploring the meanings of words shared by peoples across South-East Asia and the Pacific, to try and develop a picture of this society:

> On the evidence of language, we may pronounce as to the state of civil-isation of such a nation, that they had made some progress in agri-culture,—that they understood the use of iron,—had artificers in this metal, and in gold; perhaps made trinkets of the latter;—were clothed

with a fabric made of the fibrous bark of plants, which they wove in the loom,—were ignorant of the manufacture of cotton cloth, which was acquired in after times from the continent of India,—had tamed the cow and buffalo, and applied them to draught and carriage,—and the hog, the domestic fowl, and the duck, and used them for food . . . The wide spread of their language across many seas proves that they had made considerable progress in maritime skill.[96]

This description of Crawfurd's Great Polynesian people is very similar to modern deductions regarding the culture and society of the Austronesian peoples (the name by which modern scholars have named the language grouping that Marsden identified) that populated South-East Asia between 4000 BCE and 300 BCE, as the following 2009 textbook definition demonstrates:

These Austronesians brought with them domesticated pigs and dogs, grew rice and millet, used bows and arrows, had looms for weaving, and possessed a knowledge of tattooing, which became a common practice in Austronesian societies. Some early Austronesians built sophisticated ocean-going sailing vessels with multilayered hulls and manoeuvrable square sails known as balance-lugs.[97]

Crawfurd's ideas were speculative and, for all his contemporary reviewers, little more than flights of fancy; nevertheless Crawfurd was attempting to develop a deep sense of South-East Asian history and culture. He was pushing back the limits of known history to develop a pre-history in South East Asia out of new techniques. In pushing back the limits of history, Crawfurd challenged the validity of Mosaic history and the idea of a universal history narrative. He also rejected the idea that South-East Asian societies were passive actors subject to invaders that introduced new cultural and racial paradigms. Instead, Crawfurd proposed a vision of South-East Asia in which civilisation was an indigenous creation.

Savage Tribes and the Creation of Nations

By musing on the existence of a Great Polynesian nation, Crawfurd was attempting to conjecture a history of South-East Asia before written records. Like Raffles, Leyden and Marsden before him, Crawfurd gave credit and homage to the findings of William Jones in the search for origins before recorded human history. Unlike his predecessors writing about Sumatra and Java, however, Crawfurd decided that there was no correlation to a Sanskrit origin in South-East Asia, and consequently, he reinterpreted Jones's philological methods to produce a pre-history of South-East Asian savage and barbarian society that presented South-East Asia as an indigenous culture unconnected to the Asian mainland.[98]

In developing his pre-history narrative, Crawfurd also drew on the Scottish Enlightenment historical tradition developed by figures such as Adam Smith, Adam Ferguson, James Burnett (Lord Monboddo) and David Hume. The Scottish tradition focused on conjectural or theoretical reconstructions of history in the absence of written records.[99] Crawfurd used the approaches of philology and conjectural history to propose a narrative of pre-history for South-East Asia that explained the racial diversity of South-East Asia but also the existence of the Great Polynesian nation. This pre-history did not merely conjecture how society operated in the savage state, it also traced the development of identity from the savage tribe to the barbarian nation.

Crawfurd's theory of pre-history was that in the beginning, there were many tribes in the archipelago and all were equal; however, he did not rule out the idea of providence for the creation of future nations, proposing that circumstances could be either be 'natural or fortuitous'.[100] Marsden, Leyden and Raffles had all argued that conquests by one tribe over another formed nations in South-East Asia.[101] Although Crawfurd saw religious conversion in South-East Asia as a pacific process, in 1820, he shared the eighteenth-century belief in the central role of conquest in transforming the savage tribe into a barbarian nation, believing that:

> It is by conquest only that we can suppose the languages of rude nations to produce a material influence upon each other and the notion of partial and occasional subjugation is not excluded by such circumstances, as ultimately prove obstacles to the union of two or more tribes, to the formation of one nation and one language.[102]

Nevertheless, in believing that war created tribal and national groupings, Crawfurd saw this transition as a cultural transformation, in which conquest resulted in one language becoming dominant. Campaigns of conquest by one tribe over others unified the diverse savage tribes into a united nation. His belief in one language for every aboriginal tribe meant that each of these tribes had an identity, but assimilated with the new conquering tribe.[103] Although he placed emphasis on war and assimilation through violence, Crawfurd believed that nations were cultural constructions. He defined a nation as the expansion (in imperial terms) of one tribal language over other tribal languages.

Crawfurd believed ethnicity did not exist in the savage state and one of these tribes would 'conquer one or more of these [tribes],—adopting, as in savage society, the conquered as captives'.[104] Crawfurd's logic was also steeped in pre-national terms. Before the nineteenth century, states and empires did not focus on the ethnicity of their members—the important thing was gaining subjects and then controlling them.[105] The historians Anthony Milner and James Scott have both argued that the capturing of people was central to the operation of political systems in South-East Asia. Scott pointed to people moving and changing their ethnic identity across one generation within South-East Asia. Most polities within South-East Asia saw major movements of people as the ruler gained subjects through incentives or, as Scott argued, through coercion.[106] Milner, however, argued that people wanted to move towards these centres of power in Asia, and maintained that 'representatives of developing European nation states would certainly have seen the region as politically fragmented, but as characterized as well by competition and fluidity' for people.[107] As we saw in the previous chapter, the need for people and labour mattered more to rulers than land in South-East Asian political thinking.

Crawfurd saw the movement of people as a common theme of South-East Asian history. The blending of people, for Crawfurd, became an impetus for the construction of a core national culture:

> The languages of the conquered and conquerors would amalgamate, the latter chiefly giving it its form and character. Progressive conquests of this nature would, in the course of ages, though after many reverses and fluctuations, reduce a country under the sway of one people, and reduce to one its many dialects.[108]

The expansion of one savage tribe over the others created a unity among tribes, with subservient tribes' adoption of the traits of the master tribe producing a nation. Crawfurd was not making a racial argument or advancing the idea of racial domination. His focus was racial blending, not biological purity. Later in life, he termed this blending of races 'commixture'.[109] For his conception of history and interpretations of history in the early nineteenth century, Crawfurd's narrative of the creation of nations followed a standard Enlightenment line that was little different from the writings of any of his contemporaries. Most Enlightenment theorists, be they French or British, saw the nation beginning with a tribe which conquered other tribes and then blended with those tribes. Such theorising went back to Roman times, with Roman accounts of their own foundation being a union of neighbouring tribes (such as the Sabine) through a mix of conquest and negotiation. At first glance, there was very little new in what Crawfurd was posing. The newness of his argument was in the autochthony implications of this theory.

That Crawfurd believed in polygenesis, that there were multiple aboriginal peoples created in South-East Asia, did not mean that he saw every nation having an aboriginal origin. For Crawfurd, the aboriginality of each tribe meant they had an original identity that existed at creation, with each tribe having an original language, and that the blending of these unique original identities created distinct nations with distinct national characters. How they received this original language Crawfurd did not say, arguing that it was 'beyond the compass of human reason'.[110] By maintaining the aboriginality of each tribe, Crawfurd presented a very different idea of history. History ceased to be something that all humans shared in common, as in the Mosaic approach, in which the tribes and nations branched out from an original Adam and Eve. Instead, history, for Crawfurd, became highly localised and unique to each culture.

The separate creations of races did not mean an absence of human unity. Crawfurd continually made comparisons with other cultures, despite believing each culture was a unique creation. He made these comparisons to understand the general path of human development. This theoretical approach constituted an archetype with deviations rather than a shared story, in which each culture was influence by similar forces of biology and environment. For example, he argued that all nations followed the same path from the savage 'primordial horde' to a 'semi-barbarous nation':

> The necessity of supporting an increasing population would be the incentive to industry, invention, and improvement, and, in this manner, we can trace the progress of the savage state to semi-barbarism, until some natural obstacle, as the barrier of seas and mountains, interrupted the geographical progress of improvement. This, in short, is the progress of society in every part of the world.[111]

Although the archetype shaped the general early progress of human groups, Crawfurd believed that once they achieved the 'semi-barbarous' stage, divergence emerged at that point. He proposed that geography, environmental conditions and the national character formed from the moment of aboriginal creation shaped the future progress of the semi-barbarous nation.

The historian-administrators in South-East Asia were at the forefront of debates on extending the limits of known history, and one in particular challenged the tenets of Mosaic history, with its accepted biblical origins of human society. The idea of the aborigine was central to these debates. Although the aborigine was a construction of colonial thought, in the colonial South-East Asia debates, the aborigine was a search for either evidence of an original language (unrelated to other languages) or the first human migration.

The consequence of Crawfurd's ideas was that he rejected the notion that people in South-East Asia were passive actors subject to civilisation introduced by colonial invaders. He argued for an organic view of South-East Asian society, in which civilisation developed independently of colonial interventions. Despite Crawfurd's rejection of the central role of colonialism in promoting civilisation, Crawfurd's ideas also promoted racial concepts of South-East Asia. By arguing that aborigines were separate creations, Crawfurd was rejecting the unity of human species. His vision of aboriginality necessitated a much more complex vision of race and identity.

Notes

1   I am deliberately not capitalising the word 'aborigine' or the word 'indigenous'. In Australia, 'Aborigine' is a proper noun, but in the context in which I am using the word through this chapter and book, the word 'aborigine' refers to a type of

people, not an actual ethnicity. I also do not want to be in the business of identity creation in this book. Therefore, I am choosing to use the lowercase 'aborigine'.

2 A.R. Pagden, *The Fall of Natural Man: The American Indian and the Origins of Comparative Ethnology*, (Cambridge: Cambridge University Press, 1982); Bain Attwood, *The Making of the Aborigines*, (Boston: Allen & Unwin, 1989); Patrick Wolfe, *Settler Colonialism and the Transformation of Anthropology: The Politics and Poetics of an Ethnographic Event*, (London: Cassell, 1999), pp. 178–179; Lynette Russell, *Savage Imaginings: Historical and Contemporary Constructions of Australian Aboriginalities*, (Melbourne: Australian Scholarly Publishing, 2001); Ian J. McNiven and Lynette Russell, *Appropriated Pasts: Indigenous Peoples and the Colonial Culture of Archaeology*, (Lanham, MD: AltaMira Press, 2005).

3 See Google, 'Ngram Viewer for the words 'savage', 'barbarian', 'aboriginal', 'indigneous' date range 1700–1850'.

4 See Ibid.

5 I am using the term pre-history not as the modern discipline pre-history, but instead as a descriptive term for the problem of understanding the past before history. Therefore, I have chosen to use pre-history and not pre-history so the reader will not be confused.

6 Pagden, *The Fall of Natural Man: The American Indian and the Origins of Comparative Ethnology*; Roger Bartra, *Wild Men in the Looking Glass: The Mythic Origins of European Otherness*, (Ann Arbor: University of Michigan Press, 1994).

7 Locke, *Two Treatieses of Goverenment*, ch. 5, section 49, p. 301.

8 Thomas Forrest, 'Report on Pulo Penang', Warren Hastings Papers, *East India Office Records*, British Library, Add 29210 (c.1784)., p. 216; Forrest, '2 July 1784 letter from Capt Forrest, Extract of Bengal General Consultations'.

9 Forrest, 'Report on Pulo Penang', p. 216; Forrest, '2 July 1784 letter from Capt Forrest, Extract of Bengal General Consultations'.

10 Thomas Forrest and David K. Bassett, *A Voyage to New Guinea and the Moluccas, 1774–1776 . . . With an Introduction by D. K. Bassett*, (Kuala Lumpur, etc.: Oxford University Press, 1969), p. 405.

11 William Marsden, *The History of Sumatra, Containing an Account of the Government, Laws, Customs, and Manners of the Native Inhabitants, with a Description of the Natural Productions, and a Relation of the Ancient Political State of that Island* (London: The Author, 1784), p. 258.

12 Pocock, *Barbarism and Religion IV: Barbarians, Savages and Empires.*

13 William Marsden, *The History of Sumatra, Containing an Account of the Government, Laws, Customs, and Manners of the Native Inhabitants, with a Description of the Natural Productions and a Relation of the Ancient Political State*, (London: printed for The Author, and sold by Thomas Payne and Son; Benjamin White; James Robson; P. Elmsly; Leigh and Sotheby; and J. Sewell, 1783).

14 Ibid.

15 The 1811 version was spelt as Orang Kubu and Orang Googoo was spelt as Orang Gubu Marsden, *History of Sumatra 1811.*

16 Marsden, *History of Sumatra 1784*, p. 35. The Orang Kubu is the Malay name for a hunter-gather communities that live in the jungles of Sumatra; Kubu means fort or protection. The forest is their fort.

17 Ibid.

18 Ibid. p. 36.

19 John M. Echols and others, *An Indonesian-English Dictionary*, (Ithaca: Cornell University Press, 1989), p. 214.

20 Pagden, *The Fall of Natural Man: The American Indian and the Origins of Comparative Ethnology*; Meek, *Social Science and the Ignoble Savage*; Pocock, *Barbarism and Religion IV: Barbarians, Savages and Empires*. For examples from the time, see Guillaume Thomas Franc ois Raynal, *A Philosophical and Political History of the British Settlements and Trade in North America*, (Edinburgh: printed by C. MacFarquhar. Sold by the booksellers, 1776); William Robertson, *The History of America*, (London: Printed for W. Strahan; T. Cadell . . . ; and J. Balfour, at Edinburgh, 1777).

21 Marsden, *History of Sumatra 1784*, p. 267.

22 Ibid., p. 168; Diana Carroll, 'Savages and Barbarians: The British Enlightenment and William Marsden's Contribution to a Malayo-Polynesian Discourse', *Signatures*, 5 (2002).

23 Marsden, *History of Sumatra 1784*, p. 168.

24 Alexander Kyd, 'Report into Island of Penang', Straits Settlements, *East India Compay*, National Library of Australia, vol. 9 (1787); Francis Light, 'A List of the Inhabitants of Prince of Wales's Island', Ibid. National Library, vol. 9 (1788).

25 William Farquar, 'Report upon the Company's affairs at Prince of Wales Island, and on the General Interests of the British Government in the Eastern Seas', Ibid. *East India Compay Library*, National Library of Australia, vol. 9 (1806).

26 Ibid.

27 I make this conclusion based on the census records. The population increased dramatically from immigrants from peninsular Malaya.

28 Burrow, *A History of Histories*; Pocock, *Ancient Consitution and the Feudal Law*; Pocock, *Barbarism and Religion II: Narratives of Civil Government*.

29 David Hume, *History of England*, (Indianapolis: Liberty Fund, 1983 [1778]), vol. 1, p. 5.

30 Ibid., vol. 1, p. 10.

31 Ibid., vol. 1, p. 10.

32 Ibid., vol. 1, p. 13.

33 Ibid., vol. 1, p. 24.

34 Recent archeological and historical research has raised questions and doubts about the validity of the Saxon invasion of Britain. See Francis Pryor, *Britain AD: A Quest for Arthur, England and the Anglo-Saxons*, (London: Harper Perennial, 2005).

35 Simon Schama, *Landscape and Memory*, (London: Fontana, 1996), pp. 75–100.

36 Marsden, *History of Sumatra 1784*, p. 35.

37 Marsden, *History of Sumatra 1811*, p. 326.

38 John Leyden, 'On the Languages and Literature of the Indo-Chinese Nations', *Asiatick Researches; Or, Transactions of the Asiatic Society of Bengal*', 10 v. 10 (1811), pp. 160, 218.

39 Ibid. p. 218.

40 Samuel Johnson defined Fastnesses as 'a strong place, a place not easily forced' Johnson, *A Dictionary of the English Language: In which the Words are Deduced from their Originals, and Illustrated in their Different Significations by Examples from the Best Writers: To which are Prefixed, a History of the Language, and an English Grammar*, p. 777.

41 Crawfurd, *HIA.*, vol. 1, pp. 24–26.

42 Marsden, *History of Sumatra 1784*, p. vi.

43 R.B. Cribb, H. Gilbert, and H. Tiffin, *Wild Man from Borneo: A Cultural History of the Orangutan*, (Honolulu: University of Hawaii Press, 2014); G. Forth, *Images of the Wildman in Southeast Asia: An Anthropological Perspective*, (London: Routledge, 2008), pp. 118–119.

44 Johnson, *A Dictionary of the English Language: In which the Words are Deduced from their Originals, and Illustrated in their Different Significations*

by *Examples from the Best Writers: To which are Prefixed, a History of the Language, and an English Grammar*, p. 59.

45 Lord Kames, *Six Sketches on the History of Man*, (Philadelphia: R. Bell, 1774); Roy Porter, *Flesh in the Age of Reason*, (London: Penguin, 2004), p. 249 One such text was Samuel Smith, *An Essay on the Causes of the Variety of Complexion and Figure in the Human Species, to which are Added Strictures on Lord Kames's Discourses on the Original Diversity of Mankind*, (Edinburgh: C. Elliot, 1778), which used the climatic theory to explain diversity and was scathing of Kames.

46 Modern spelling for autocthoni is autochthony.

47 A. von Humboldt, A. Bonpland and T. Ross, *Personal Narrative of Travels to the Equinoctial Regions of America: During the Years 1799–1804*, (London: Henry G. Bohn, 1853), vol. 3, pp. 81–82.

48 Carroll, 'Savages and Barbarians: The British Enlightenment and William Marsden's Contribution to a Malayo-Polynesian Discourse'; Diana Carroll, 'William Marsden and his Malayo-Polynesian Legacy', (Ph.D. Thesis, Australian National University, 2005). Sandra Khor Manickam, 'Taming Race: The Construction of Aborigines in ColonialMalaya, 1783–1937', (Ph.D. Thesis, Australian National University, 2010). Manickam's thesis will be published by NUS Press as *Taming the Wild: Aborigines and Racial Knowledge in Colonial Malaya*.

49 Marsden, *The History of Sumatra 1783*, in a footnote on page 35 and another footnote on page 268 where he was quoting a French writer.

50 Carroll, 'William Marsden and his Malayo-Polynesian Legacy'.

51 Cited in Stocking, *Victorian Anthropology*, p. 23.

52 Ibid. p. 23.

53 Leyden, 'On the Languages and Literature of the Indo-Chinese Nations', p. 162.

54 William Marsden, 'Remarks on the Sumatran Languages, by Mr Marsden: In a Letter to Sir Joseph Banks, Bart: President of the Royal Society', *Archaeologia or Miscellaneous Tracts Relating to Antiquity*, 6 (1782).

55 'Indigenous to All the Islands of the Eastern Sea; from Madagascar to the Remotest of Captain Cook's Discoveries; Comprehending a Wider Extent Than the Roman or Any Other Tongue has Yet Boasted.' Marsden, *History of Sumatra 1784*, p. 200.

56 Ibid.

57 Ibid. p. 163.

58 Carroll, 'William Marsden and his Malayo-Polynesian Legacy'.

59 Wurtzburg and Witting, *Raffles of the Eastern Isles*.

60 Leyden, 'On the Languages and Literature of the Indo-Chinese Nations', p. 166.

61 Ibid.

62 Ibid. p. 167.

63 Ibid.

64 Ibid.

65 Ibid. p. 189.

66 Ibid. p. 190.

67 Ibid.

68 Ibid.

69 Ibid. p. 167.

70 Marsden, *The History of Sumatra 1783*, p. 35.

71 Raffles, *The History of Java*, vol. 1, p. x.

72 Quoted in Raffles, *Memoir of the Life and Public Services of Sir Thomas Stamford Raffles*, vol. 2, p. 390.

73 Raffles, *The History of Java*, vol. 2, p. 369.

74 Ibid.

75 Raffles, *Memoir of the Life and Public Services of Sir Thomas Stamford Raffles*, vol. 1, p. 405.

76 Ibid., vol. 1, p. 405.
77 Ibid., vol. 2, p. 83.
78 Ibid.
79 Crawfurd, *HIA.*, vol. 1, p. 27.
80 Ibid., vol. 1, p. 27.
81 Ibid., vol. 2, p. 78.
82 Ibid., vol. 2, p. 108.
83 Crawfurd first described this argument in Ibid., vol. 2, pp. 94–98; however, at this stage his argument was observation. By 1856, he argued it as a universal linguistic theory. Crawfurd, *Descriptive Dictionary*, pp. 259–264. By the 1860s, Crawfurd was using this argument to reject Max Muller's Aryan thesis and also evolution John Crawfurd, 'On Sir Charles Lyell's "Antiquity of Man", and on Professor Huxley's "Evidence as to Man's Place in Nature" ', *Transactions of the Ethnological Society of London*, 3 (1865); John Crawfurd, 'On the Physical and Mental Characteristics of the European and Asiatic Races of Man', *Transactions of the Ethnological Society of London*, 5 (1867); John Crawfurd, 'On the Theory of the Origin of Species by Natural Selection in the Struggle for Life', *Transactions of the Ethnological Society of London*, 7 (1869).
84 Crawfurd, *HIA.*, vol. 2, p. 80.
85 Anonymous,'History of the Indian Archipelago; Containing an Account of the Manners, Arts, Languages, Religions, Institutions and Comerce of its Inhabitants: By John Crawfurd, FRS.', pp. 328–329.
86 Raffles, Marsden, and Barrow, 'Crawfurd's History of the Indian Archipelago', p. 118.
87 Robert Chambers, *Vestiges of the Natural History of Creation*, (London: W. & R. Chambers, 1884); Charles Darwin, 'On The Origin of Species by Means of Natural Selection', in *Charles Darwin, On The Origin of Species*, ed. by Joseph Carroll (Peterborough: Broadview Texts, 2003 [1859]).
88 Crawfurd, *HIA.*, vol. 1, p. 27.
89 Kames, *Six Sketches on the History of Man*.
90 Charles White, *An Account of the Regular Gradation in Man*, (London: Printed for C. Dilly, 1799).
91 Stocking, *Victorian Anthropology*, p. 26.
92 For example: Kay Anderson, *Race and the Crisis of Humanism*, (Milton Park, Abingdon, Oxon; New York: UCL Press, 2007); Edward Beasley, *The Victorian Reinvention of Race: New Racisms and the Problem of Grouping in the Human Sciences*, (London: Routledge, 2010); B. Douglas and C. Ballard, *Foreign Bodies: Oceania and the Science of Race 1750–1940*, (Canberra, A.C.T.: ANU E Press, 2008); Stocking, *Victorian Anthropology*; Adrian Desmond and James Moore, *Darwin's Sacred Cause: How a Hatred of Slavery Shaped Darwin's Views on Human Evolution*, (New York: Houghton Mifflin Harcourt Publishing Comapany, 2009); Stephen Jay Gould, *The Mismeasure of Man*, (New York: W W Norton & Company, 1981).
93 Raffles, Marsden, and Barrow, 'Crawfurd's History of the Indian Archipelago', p. 117.
94 Ibid.
95 Crawfurd, *HIA.*, vol. 2, p. 99.
96 Ibid., vol. 2, p. 85.
97 Craig A. Lockard, *Southeast Asia in World History*, (New York; Oxford: Oxford University Press, 2009), p. 15.
98 Crawfurd, *HIA.*, vol. 2.
99 Burrow, *A History of Histories*; Meek, *Social Science and the Ignoble Savage*; Rendall, 'Scottish Orientalism: From Robertson to James Mill'; Buchan, *Capital of the Mind*.

100 Crawfurd, *HIA.*, vol. 2, p. 95.
101 Marsden, *History of Sumatra 1784*, p. 173; Leyden, 'On the Languages and Literature of the Indo-Chinese Nations'; Raffles, *The History of Java*.
102 Crawfurd, *HIA.*, vol. 2, p. 97.
103 Ibid., vol. 2, p. 30 every 'original language with every primitive horde'.
104 Ibid., vol. 2, p. 95.
105 Perry Anderson, *Lineages of the Absolutist State*, (New York: New Left Books, 1974).
106 James C. Scott, *Weapons of the Weak: Everyday Forms of Peasant Resistance*, (New Haven; London: Yale University Press, 1985); James C. Scott, 'Hill and Valley in Southeast Asia . . . or Why the State is the Enemy of People who Move Around . . . or . . . Why Civilizations Can't Climb Hills', in *The Concept of Indigenous Peoples in Asia: A Resource Book*, ed. by Christian Erni (Copenhagen: International Work Group for Indegenous Affairs, 2008).
107 Anthony Milner, *The Malays*, (Oxford: Wiley-Blackwell, 2008), p. 53.
108 Crawfurd, *HIA.*, vol. 2, p. 96.
109 John Crawfurd, 'On the Commixture of the Races of Man as Affecting the Progress of Civilization (Europe)', *Transactions of the Ethnological Society of London*, 2 (1863).
110 Ibid., vol. 1, p. 27.
111 Crawfurd, *HIA.*, vol. 2, p. 96.

4   Race and the Natural
History of the Savage

The language of racial thinking permeates nineteenth-century writing. Many historians consider that the racial language of nineteenth-century figures was a result of colonial superiority.[1] Racial thought undoubtedly fed into a Late Victorian colonial culture of superiority. This chapter argues, however, that the move to racial thinking was not a product of a belief in their own superiority but, rather, an attempt by historian-administrators to deal with gaps in their knowledge as they attempted to explain the unexplainable. The nineteenth-century idea of race is part of a process that described God's work and the influence nature had on the civil history of humans. Race was a name for symptoms of what could not be explained by the historical record.

In the nineteenth century, the Enlightenment ideas of civilisation represented in the debates between Raffles and Crawfurd were transformed into ideas about race. Over the course of his life, Crawfurd's research reflected this transition as he moved from debates with Raffles, relating to the originality of languages, to his final work as President of the Ethnological Society of London, when he battled over ideas of race and evolution. In his research into South-East Asia, Crawfurd developed his ideas of race as he and others grappled with human qualities which appeared to exist outside of the processes of civil history.

Recent scholarship often maligns Crawfurd's role in the Ethnological Society. According to Jane Rendall, much of his writings in the 1860s were characterised by an attempt to justify 'European superiority on racial grounds'.[2] In his generally laudable book *Machines as the Measure of Men*, Michael Adas summarised Crawfurd's ideas on Asia: 'For Crawfurd, a tendency towards despotism, like indifference or hostility to innovation, was inherent in the racial composition of the Asiatic peoples'.[3] Whilst Ter Ellingson's *Myth of the Noble Savage* is the most comprehensive attempt to understand Crawfurd's work to date, it reduces his ideas to little more than a racial conspiracy theory to misrepresent Jean-Jacques Rousseau as the source of the 'the noble savage' concept.[4]

In an even more bizarre example of misquotation, Edward Beasley totally misquotes Catherine Hall's account of the 1865 Birmingham conference for the British Association for the Advancement of Science.[5] Beasley maintained

Crawfurd presented a paper arguing that the African Negro was a 'uniform-looking black race of smelly, prognathous, pointy-toothed people unable to write books', provoking 'widespread laughter'.[6] In fact, the opposite occurred—Crawfurd presented a paper lambasting the cruelty of European civilisation by inflicting slavery and perpetuating racial inequality, even after the emancipation of African slaves in British colonies.[7] It was the moral message of racial equality despite racial difference that Crawfurd promoted, which the crowd rejected responding with widespread laughter.

Crawfurd's writings from the 1860s are fertile grounds for slapdash attempts to find a personified caricature of nineteenth-century racial thinking. In each instance, his writings have been selected out of context and were used to simplify nineteenth-century thought to the point of misrepresentation.

In the twenty-first century, race is a concept of biological or pseudo-scientific thinking.[8] Race, as a theory of human identity and action, pre-scribes that the physical and genetically transferable characteristics of a person are at the core of identity and in some way determine a person's capacity. Race, therefore, is an immutable mark of division between peoples based on physical and hereditary characteristics. The problem is that people at the beginning of the nineteenth century did not make such a clear distinction between culture and biology. Nor did they conceive of race in such terms. Thinkers at the beginning of the nineteenth century always used cultural evidence to understand racial divisions, with language being one of the paramount sources of evidence.

Early nineteenth-century thinking on humans' relationship to nature and each other was still dominated by the religious concept of the chain of being, which was a hierarchical system of ordering connecting the lowly ant to the human and ultimately to God. This chain of being also linked the separate biological (or physical) and cultural (or socially created) spheres of human identity. Religious approaches to the past denoted what fell into the sphere of history, this religious basis to thinking about the past also applied to developing ideas about racial differences. Biology or nature was the creation of God and, therefore, physical form fulfilled the will of God. The next logical step in thinking was that the physical differences between peoples expressed God's will in some way.

Each of the historian-administrators of South-East Asia divided their works into civil history and natural history. The anthropologist James Boon characterised this nineteenth-century approach to history in South-East Asia as the theme of 'man' and 'nature', in which racial ethnology emerges at the intersection between human history and natural history.[9] In this chapter, I follow Boon's pathway through the accounts of race in South-East Asia by examining the development of race as a concept in the writings of Marsden, Raffles, Crawfurd and later, Alfred Russell Wallace.

Wallace was a naturalist and co-discoverer of evolution. He spent many years in South-East Asia and observed the geographical distribution of flora and fauna as well as humans. Wallace used his understanding of flora and fauna distribution to conceive of a theory of evolution by natural selection with Charles Darwin.[10] Wallace's approach to race was to synthesise polygenesis and monogenesis ideas with the approach of natural selection. After the deaths of Raffles and Marsden, Wallace was the only 'expert' on South-East Asia to openly debate Crawfurd on South-East Asia.[11]

Describing the Physical Characteristics of People Before the British Occupation of Java

The Enlightenment practice of describing the physicality and character of different peoples preceded nineteenth-century racial theory.[12] Unlike racial theory (which connected peoples' physical characteristics to social traits within a hereditary framework), eighteenth-century descriptions were primarily practical illustrations of physical differences. Describing the physical features of exotic people was an essential part of the Enlightenment travel narrative.

Eighteenth-century ideas of character were also essential to travel writing at the time. Most Enlightenment travel texts included a chapter on manners and morals or national character. These chapters began as outlines of social customs and accepted practices. Like the illustrations, the descriptions were practical in nature and informed readers of different habits of exotic people. Yet, as Chapter 2 demonstrated, Enlightenment philosophers increasingly focused on questions of character formation as a nascent form of sociology. Philosophers saw that this raw social data had broader uses and could be used comparatively to understand social development.

Most of the metropolitan philosophers rarely ventured out of their home cities. For example, although the philosopher Adam Smith travelled around Western Europe as a tutor, he spent most of his life in Edinburgh, whilst the Prussian philosopher Immanuel Kant never left Königsberg.[13] Despite their seclusion, these Enlightenment philosophers used travel literature to open their minds and develop a universal idea of history. They had very little understanding of the alien peoples they were reading about. Illustrations, therefore, gave a degree of familiarity.

The origins of racial theory, however, were in the connecting of the physical descriptions to the social and cultural descriptions. The linkage between the two forms of description allowed for a new form of civilisational theory which explained social change (or lack of) through physical characteristics. The historian-administrators in South-East Asia were at the forefront of debates on linkages between physical and social theorising.

In 1814, John Crawfurd was an emerging scholar looking to make his mark as a philosophic historian. He saw the theoretical potential of unifying the physical and social descriptions to make a new form of history that explained social development in different parts of the globe. The *Edinburgh Review* commissioned the young Crawfurd to write a synopsis of recent writing on South-East Asia.

By 1814, the format of travel writing was generally accepted. Travellers wrote descriptions of the people they encountered and metropolitan philosophers then compiled the different accounts into theories of human society.[14] Yet Crawfurd was appalled at what he found when it came to reporting from South-East Asia. He believed the travel writers were confusing themselves with theorising philosophers and the consequence was the poverty of both disciplines:

> we find no small difficulty in extracting a plain, intelligible, and consistent account from the narrations of travellers into those regions. The greater part, unfortunately, have been ambitious of the character of philosophers and historians, rather than of the merit of recording plainly what fell under their own observation.[15]

Crawfurd believed that travel writers should observe, not theorise. William Marsden was one of Crawfurd's targets, and Marsden took the opportunity to make similar criticisms about Crawfurd six years later.[16] The reason why Crawfurd believed that travellers made poor philosophers was his belief that their sample size was too small. Accounts of the people of individual kingdoms or even islands such as Sumatra were too narrow, he argued, for comparative conclusions, making the account 'unconsciously distorted'.[17] He believed that what was needed was a wider regional study that cross-referenced multiple societies and different stages of society.

Crawfurd's criticisms outline the divisions of labour between metropolitan philosophers and colonial observers but also show a desire for a new form of theorising. Crawfurd's 1814 criticisms of his contemporaries' writings focused purely on reports concerning the natives' manners and customs. Manners and customs represented the highpoint of Enlightenment discourse on civilisation, yet Crawfurd was clearly looking towards a deeper understanding of peoples, one which went to their very core, beyond the idea of civilisation. He wrote of the Malays, 'from what country they originally sprung or to what causes their dispersion is to be ascribed, remains among the secrets of Oriental history'.[18] The search for a deeper primordial root to culture would eventually lead Crawfurd to aboriginality and polygenesis, yet in 1814, he only hinted at such blasphemous ideas.

When he did publish his polygenesis ideas in 1820, Crawfurd also demonstrated that he was abreast of the latest form of theorising. He talked about 'race', not as a throwaway descriptive term that could mean nation or civilisation, but as a biologically framed concept, in which a person's physiology was as much under examination as a person's character.

The focus on 'race' was a major development in nineteenth-century thought. The defining of 'races' was certainly a focus in biological thought by 1800. In France and Germany, savants and philosophers such as Immanuel Kant, Johann Blumenbach and Georges Cuvier were coalescing around the idea that race was 'organic and hereditary'.[19] In the British world, the acceptance of the 'organic and hereditary' nature of race saw a much slower take-up and the adoption of race had a slightly different trajectory. In using the concept of race, Crawfurd saw himself as perfecting an already established descriptive tradition of discussing manners and characters of people in South-East Asia.

In Britain by 1800, there was an established tradition of writing down observations on peoples' appearances. For example, James Cook wrote the following description of the Tahitians on his first voyage to the Pacific Ocean:

> with regard to the people, they are in general rather of a larger make than Europeans. The males are tall, robust, and finely shaped. The females, of the superior class, are likewise generally above our common size; but those of the lower rank are rather below it, and some of them are remarkably little. Their natural complexion is a fine clear olive, or what we call brunette; their skin delicately smooth, and agreeably soft. The shape of their faces is in general handsome, and their eyes are full of sensibility and expression: their teeth are likewise remarkably white and regular, and their breath entirely free from any disagreeable smell; their hair is, for the most part, black. Their motions are easy and graceful, but not vigorous; their deportment is generous and open, and their behaviour affable and courteous.[20]

Cook's account was more illustrative than scientific. He was traversing into the unknown and describing people unfamiliar to Europeans. Such descriptive activity was practical. Most readers of eighteenth- and early nineteenth-century travel accounts of Asia had very little comprehension of the world they were reading about.

Any illustration, whether it be written or a woodcut, gave the reader a sense of the place. The illustrators however were also prone to misunderstanding. Cook complained that his editor, Dr Hawkesworth, botched Cook's original manuscript whilst supposedly improving the language. Equally, woodcuts were open to falsehoods. Cook's journal depicts and demonstrates phenomenal detail in the images of botanical and material culture specimens brought back to Europe, but the illustration of a Maori in a family at Dusk Bay looks more like a stylised patriarchal Celt than a Maori (Figure 4.3).[21]

Although the Celtic comparison was partly a product of an illustrator drawing on an image he was already familiar with, it also had a deeper meaning that connected to stadial history. The image contained assumptions connecting the Maori with European history, presenting the Maori as being at the same stage of development as an ancient Celt. Classical European imagery was common in eighteenth-century depictions of Asia. Thomas Forrest's *Voyage to New Guinea* was also full of images that bore more of a resemblance to Europe than to Asia. His image of a wedding party in Mindanao looked more like ancient Athens than the sultanate of Mindanao. Forrest's image also made a claim about civilisation—he was claiming that the people of Mindanao were equal in civilisation to the ancient Greeks (Figure 4.4).

Illustrators could also misinterpret even the specimens brought back from voyages to Asia. Surviving Dutch natural history texts from South-East Asia provide interesting examples of why written descriptions are important. It was common for patrons to organise illustrators to colour the woodcuts after publication. In some instances, the illustrators clearly could not read: one such example is from Albertus Seba's *Accurate description of the very rich thesaurus of the principal and rarest natural objects,* where the illustrator painted animals in vivid exotic colours that are clearly impossible, such as opossums with aqua claws.[22]

Both words and illustrations could easily be misinterpreted. Writers therefore used detailed descriptions of the people to reduce misinformation. Yet as we can see from Cook's account, he went beyond mere description. His account connected the physical appearance of people to their status in life, with high-status people being large and low-status people being small. He also made comparisons between peoples, for example declaring that the Tahitians were 'in general rather of a larger make than Europeans'. Although such descriptions were not deliberately 'racial' descriptions, Cook's description connected cultural attitudes to physical form.

Thomas Forrest, writing 12 years after Cook in 1780, also at times noted the physical appearances of the people he encountered as comparisons, proposing that the Papuan people 'had their frizzled black locks sticking out a great way from their heads, and were as black as African Coffres'.[23] Although Forrest used Africans as an analogy, later writers developed such phrases to argue that a Negro race occupied the hinterlands of island and peninsula South-East Asia.

Following on from Forrest, Marsden also described the people of Sumatra in 1783. He provided the first portrait of Malay from Sumatra (Figure 4.5) and gave general physical descriptions of the Malays as a people, for example, noting that 'their eyes are uniformly dark and clear' and their hair is 'strong and of a shining black'. Nevertheless, most of Marsden's description of the people related not to biological characteristics, but instead about how they groomed or deformed their bodies. For example he noted 'pubic boys' rubbing their face with '*chunam* (quick lime)' to prevent hair growth, or women flattening their noses, which he called a 'preposterous custom', or the fact that 'persons of superior rank encourage the growth of the hand-nails'.[24]

In these descriptions, Marsden may have been judgemental, but he was not racial in his views. His accounts describe the people but also connect the Malays to a stadial level of civilisation. His descriptions detail the physical characteristics of manners and customs, for example, the custom of women deliberately flattening their noses. Racial thinking assumes a person's innate exterior appearance is indicative of their inner intellectual and emotional capacities. In comparison, Marsden's descriptions of physicality did not focus on the innate mentality of the people, and were therefore not racial in nature.

Raffles's concept of physical descriptions was little changed from that of Marsden. His observations were, like Marsden's, intermingled with details of clothing, customs and food. The only exception was Raffles's new focus on illustrations. His *History of Java* was lavishly illustrated with portraits of Javanese and Papuan peoples. In comparison, Marsden's illustrations were predominantly focusing on natural history specimens (flora and fauna), his ethnographical illustrations followed the examples set out by the illustrators from the Captain Cooke's *Endeavour voyage*, portraying material culture and a couple of scenes of mountains and villages.

Raffles placed the people at centre stage of his illustrations. Whereas Marsden merely gave one detailed image of a Malay boy (Figure 4.5), Raffles provided eleven images of individuals. Each illustration represented a Javanese person of a particular social rank. He also included an image of 'Dick', a Papuan slave boy whom Raffles took back to Britain (included within Figure 4.8).

Raffles's images were not anthropological: the images did not fixate on the physical form, but rather, as Anthony Forge has argued, the images 'reduce facile exoticism and present the Javanese as "civilised" in a European sense'.[25] In his study of the images, Forge compared the final versions published in the *History of Java* with the draft versions held in the British Museum (see Figures 4.6 and 4.7). Forge maintained that the images were altered under Raffles's direction, removing exotic elements from the images. Raffles's images were not designed to be comparative, but rather, to demonstrate the nobility and civilisation of the Javanese. Although Raffles concentrated on illustrating the physical form, his images were a continuation of Enlightenment discourses on civilisation and not a move towards discussion of the innate physical form of different peoples.

Crawfurd made the first move in South-East Asian historiography to racial theorising. In 1814, he argued for a new form of comparative theorising that looked at a region and not just an island and attempted to understand deeper currents and divisions within history.[26] When he published his *History of the Indian Archipelago* in 1820, he wanted it to be an intellectual break from the cultural descriptions and illustrations of the past. Although he also blended cultural descriptions and illustrations with physical descriptions and illustrations, Crawfurd presented a new focus on the physical form.

In his *History*, at the beginning of his second chapter on the 'physical form of the inhabitants of the archipelago', Crawfurd provided two illustrations of the 'brown' and 'Negro' race. 'Katut, a native of Bali' exampled the brown race, while also reprising Raffles's image of the Papuan boy 'Dick', which was recast as representative of the 'Negro'. The combined image invited readers to make comparisons between the 'brown' and 'Negro' races of the archipelago (Figure 4.8). Crawfurd presented the pictures of the two boys in stark contrast to each other. The images mirrored Crawfurd's argument that the two races were completely different from each other.

Crawfurd presented the images as types of people; therefore, he represented a break from eighteenth-century practices of mere illustration. Raffles complained about Crawfurd's use of his original image and argued Crawfurd was comparing a Papuan child with a full-grown Balinese man (although there is no evidence that Katut was a man and to me, both of them appear as children, although at different ages). Nevertheless, Raffles did not complain about Crawfurd's use of comparisons to demonstrate physical form, but rather, the particular individuals chosen. Crawfurd's use of images invited readers to make theoretical comparisons between different forms of people and looked toward comparisons that appeared more scientific.

In the eighteenth-century accounts of South-East Asia, race was largely irrelevant. Writers focused on using physical form to make a case for civilisational stages, but these were as much cultural as racial/biological. In Crawfurd's writing, we see the beginnings of a change and the move to new forms of theorising that did propose race as a fundamental social division. Images in his *History of the Indian Archipelago* illustrate Crawfurd's desire to identify deeper historical processes underpinning civilisation.

Nature and Human History in Raffles's and Crawfurd's Writings

The mid-nineteenth century saw the explosion of racial theory as an explanation for the differences between humans. Race became an elucidation for human relations of dominance and subordination and for many advocates, a means of explaining world events. Reflecting the transition towards racial explanations, the South-East Asian histories of Raffles and Crawfurd both included racial concepts in their explanations of history. The pathway to this point for both men was a debate about the role of nature in history. Similar to debates on land and aboriginality, race (in the context of South-East Asian colonial debates) was connected to the role of God in creation.

A vision of God's creation underpinned the limits of what was historical. The world fell into two spheres: the work of God and the work of humans. As discussed in Chapter 2, the work of humans was Mosaic history—or the spreading out of the biblical lands—followed by civil history, which charted social progression through a rise and fall dialectic. In comparison, the natural world was a product of God, and therefore, the purpose of natural history was to understand the plan of the almighty Creator.[27]

These two forms of history (natural and human) were not mutually exclusive. Natural history was central to both Marsden's *History of Sumatra* and Raffles's *History of Java*, and the historians were certainly aware that natural history affected the course of human history. Although they were both tracking Mosaic and civil history and the development of civilisation in Sumatra and Java, both Marsden and Raffles saw natural history as an essential part of the historical narrative. Natural history explained the place of humans in the world and God's overall plan for the world.

Both forms of history represented extrapolations in the chain of being, connecting the world of God and nature to the world of man. The chain of being had its origins in the Ancient Greek philosophy of Plato, and since that time, the chain of being has been a continual theme in Western thought. The historian of ideas, Arthur Lovejoy, summarised the chain of being as the connection between the 'otherworldliness' and the 'this-worldliness'.[28] In the eighteenth century, nature represented a sphere of the otherworldliness. Although nature was clearly physical and existed as an influence in human history, the reason for that influence could only be explained through God. For example, the natural world was provided by God to benefit humans and, as such, natural history was the flipside of human history. Nevertheless, what encompassed the parameters of natural history was often far from what we today would understand as historical thinking.

The difference in parameters between natural history and civil history is apparent in Raffles's 1817 announcement of Thomas Horsfield's proposed *Zoological Researches in Java* (which was not published until 1824) as being the natural history companion to Raffles's own civil *History of Java*. Far from being historical, Horsfield's *Zoological Researches* is a catalogue of Fauna, and his discussion of history is limited to iterations of scholarly debates across time surrounding the correct identification of an animal's genus. However, Horsfield maintained that he was describing a deeper history rather than mere scholarly debate. For example, at the beginning of his account of the *Semopithecus Maurus*, which is a type of gibbon, he wrote, ' My principal object at present is to give an accurate figure, both of the adult and the young subject, illustrated by its history, as I observed it in Java'.[29] His history of the *Semopithecus Maurus* is little more than a physical description of the animal, with no sense of the animal in its natural environment. At this time, natural history only meant the description and classification of animals.

Description had an important purpose in the chain of being. The mere act of classification contributed to understanding where species existed within the chain of being connecting God to humans. Natural history was not therefore about cause and effect (which are the normal domains of civil history), but rather, natural history was about order and place. The role of natural history was to describe the relationship between the human and the natural world. This relationship was one that did not appear to change much. Natural history therefore had only a limited focus on change. The Mosaic narrative held that God had created the world and that causation had no place in explaining the gradiated differences between species.

In comparison to natural history, which was overwhelmingly a process outside of normal processes of civil history (which explained causation and change), civil history was the history of man after God's act of creation. As previous chapters have demonstrated, civil history tracked the trans-formations in personal and national character through political and social changes. Humans therefore had two parts to their characters: first, God's original plan shaped by their biology and innate psychology, and second, their character shaped over time as a result of historical change. These assumptions were early iterations of nature versus nurture.

William Marsden had devoted his *History of Sumatra* primarily to civil history and, therefore, he addressed the 'nurtured' aspects of human iden-tity. However, he did explore one aspect of human identity that possibly fell outside of civil history: the diversity of human skin colour, a key aspect of what would become racial thought.

When Marsden first wrote in 1783, the climatic theory of skin colour was still the predominant explanation for the varying degrees of darkness in differ-ent populations of people. Climatic theory held that in hotter climates people were of a darker skin and sunburn was the process by which people became darker.[30] Marsden used his experience in Asia to disprove the argument, main-taining that European children were as 'fair as those born in the country of their parents' and even after the second generation, he observed the same phenomenon.[31] Although he observed skin difference as hereditary, Mars-den attributed this to some form of 'secretion' which theoretically could be changed. Therefore, although Marsden rejected climate, he was still proposing that skin colour was connected to some environmental element that produced these secretions rather than a process that was primordial and unchanging.

Marsden was identifying a problem of the ways in which forces outside history affected the identity of humans. Raffles also speculated that soil type might influence identity but did not develop the point further. Both men were identifying nature as an influence on human identity and physical form. However, neither of them devoted much attention to try and under-stand identity outside of the processes of history.

Mosaic history, with its emphasis on a single act of creation, meant that racial identity was non-existent, for the human was essentially the blank page that God created. Raffles supported the blank-page hypothesis, believ-ing that:

> As we approach the limits of savage life, and recur to that inartificial unimproved state of society, in which the primitive divergence may be supposed to have taken place, we shall find the points of resemblance increased, and the proofs of a common descent multiplied.[32]

In Raffles's logic, the primitive states shared not only language and customs, but also physical characteristics. The savages were truly blank pages, ready to be imbued with civilisation and therefore identity.

Civilisation was not an onwards and upwards trajectory. Raffles saw decline and degeneration as much as progress in creating racial and national differences. For example, he argued, 'Mahometan institutions had considerably obliterated their ancient character, and had not only obstructed their improvement, but had accelerated their decline'.[33] Although his portrayal of Islamic-induced decline was indicative of Raffles's dislike of Islam, it demonstrated that he saw racial identity (the physical and mental expression of humans) as generally a process inside of history. This meant that racial identity became a trait that could be changed through education.

When Raffles used the term 'race', he was describing a very mutable structure, which was in line with eighteenth-century thinking on race and identity. Raffles was not attempting to present any new opinions on the creation of racial identity, but rather, providing a synthesis of eighteenth-century thought.

The forming of a race was an unresolved paradox in the minds of Marsden and Raffles—as it was for all naturalists in the early nineteenth century. As we have seen, Marsden rejected climatic theories, whilst Raffles looked to the soil as a solution. Both of these ideas acknowledged the possible existence of processes outside of human agency or civil history to understand the creation of racial differences, but they did not explore them further. Both Raffles and Marsden assumed that nature or the environment provided a mechanism to influence humans, but did not give much attention to attempts to understand the process.

Unlike Marsden and Raffles, Crawfurd certainly believed events outside of civil history were very important for understanding human identity and the progress of civil history. Crawfurd was in two minds about how nature shaped identity and would reflect on both approaches throughout his career. Unlike Raffles, Crawfurd believed humans were influenced by events that history could not explain. His racial theory was underpinned by his belief in polygenesis. For Crawfurd, multiple creations explained human differences. Polygenesis meant that the basic identity of the different human races was determined by different acts of creation.

Nevertheless, Crawfurd believed that race was not the only explanation for human actions which history could not explain. Crawfurd looked to geography and a rehashed version of the Enlightenment tradition of environmental conditions, to provide another possible source of explanation for human differences. As early as 1820, he played with the importance of food and geographical zones as solutions:

> No country has produced a great or civilized race, but a country which by its fertility is capable of yielding a supply of *farinaceous* grain of the first quality . . . [And that] Man seems never to have made progress in improvement, when feeding on inferior grains, *farinaceous* roots, on fruits, or on the pith of trees . . . Civilisation originated in the west, where are situated the countries capable of producing corn. [and therefore] Man is there most improved, and his improvement decreases, in a geographical ratio, as we go eastward, until, at New Guinea, the

termination of the Archipelago, we find the whole inhabitants an undistinguished race of savages.[34]

In the above passage, Crawfurd provided a clear idea of the geographical spread of civilisation from West to East. His argument was that the knowledge of agriculture spread in an Easterly direction and supported the development of large-scale states. Although he described that the feeding on certain crops appeared to sustain particular types of societies, he was not presenting a racial argument. Instead, Crawfurd was pondering the environmental effects on civil history. Crawfurd's argument was that environments stimulate and enable different types of social adaptations.

In 1856, Crawfurd published his second edition of *History of the Indian Archipelago* as a descriptive dictionary, and in his essay on 'Man', he again reflected on why civilisational differences exist between the brown and Negro races of South-East Asia. He postulated that geography was an alternative to racial explanations, even declaring that 'the question of race may be soon dismissed'.[35] Locality he considered the most important factor, with rich soils and rivers capable of providing irrigation always being a source of 'indigenous and independent civilisation'. In places where these conditions did not exist, he maintained, 'we are sure to encounter rudeness and barbarism'.[36] Therefore, in the intervening 36 years, Crawfurd had refined his geographical arguments to develop a thesis on how the environment affects the course of human history.

In his *Descriptive Dictionary of the Indian Archipelago*, he described in turn each of the dominant islands in the archipelago and considered their history in relation to soil fertility. He maintained that islands needed to possess fertile soils with mountains high enough to generate continuous water to allow for irrigation. Advancing his point, he pointed out that

> islands on the western side of Sumatra afford striking illustrations of the position which I am endeavouring to establish. Thus, the island of Nias has a fertile and well-watered soil, and the result is a peaceable agricultural population of 200,000, while the other islands in its neighbourhood are for the most part still covered with forest and have a rude or savage population, not estimated at about one-twentieth part of that number.[37]

After five pages of evidence outlining his argument for geographical determinism, Crawfurd concluded

> that from the facts now stated, it will appear that the causes which have contributed to the advancement or retardment of civilisation in the Indian islands, have been mainly the same as in other parts of the world. Wherever the conditions have been propitious, indigenous civilisations have spontaneously sprung up, in a degree proportioned to their favourableness.[38]

Despite this conclusion, Crawfurd then outlined a counterpoint:

> What then, it may be asked, hindered civilisation in Java from attaining the same maturity as in these localities [Valleys of the Nile, the Assyrian rivers, the Ganges, and the great rivers of China]—for that it never did so is unquestionable?[39]

His conclusion marked the limits of his geographical argument: 'The solution will probably be found in the inferior intellectual capacity of the races occupying the Malayan Archipelago, for it is difficult to find any other'.[40] This conclusion saw Crawfurd revert to race when he could no longer explain the limits of historical reasoning.

Crawfurd's reversion to race as an explanation was an acknowledgement of his failure to find a historical explanation for social change between the different types of peoples. He concluded that the reason for difference must have existed in forces beyond civil historical explanation. He wanted to explain the forces that appear to exist outside of civil historical explanation, namely the environment and the natural or biological factors to human identity. He understood that these forces affected the course of civil history. Race, therefore, was an explanation of last resort, after his attempts at using geography as an explanation had failed. In this respect, Crawfurd was really using race as a description of symptoms, not as an explanation for the symptoms. Race became a means of labelling the unexplainable.

Developing an Idea of Race in South-East Asia

Crawfurd saw himself at the forefront of understanding the transition of the savage to the civilised through the concept of 'race'. Marsden and Raffles, as well as lesser writers, all followed the eighteenth-century descriptive approach that included chapters on 'manners, customs and character'. In 1820, Crawfurd followed this descriptive style. Before proceeding to include a chapter on 'manner, customs and character', however, he opened his book with a chapter titled the 'Physical form of the Inhabitants of the Archipelago'. Crawfurd placed the physical form over and above social character. None of his contemporary reviewers noticed the importance of this change: for the first time in South-East Asian studies, somebody had placed the study of the physical form in a preeminent position of focus.

Crawfurd's opening sentence made the change clear: 'There are two aboriginal races of human being inhabiting the Indian islands, as different from each other as both are from all the rest of their species'.[41] His declaration was a powerful statement of racial thought, in which he declared race as a means of understanding global history. He went on to suggest basic comparative observations that would become indicative of nineteenth-century racial thought:

the brown and negro races of the Archipelago may be considered to present, in their physical and moral character, a complete parallel with the white and negro races of the western world. The first have always displayed as eminent a relative superiority over the second as the race of white men have done over the negroes of the west.[42]

Statements about the inherent inferiority of dark-skinned people to fairer-skinned people are at the heart of nineteenth-century racial thought, yet are often misunderstood. Crawfurd saw the possibilities of using race to explain the factors which he perceived existed outside of historical explanation. For Crawfurd, only the brown race developed indigenous civilisations, with the Negro race consistently living 'in the lowest and most abject state of social existence'.[43] He also suggested that the Negro race 'disappeared' wherever it was in close contact with the civilised brown race.

Crawfurd's use of language poses a problem for modern historians reflecting on nineteenth-century ethnology and racial thought. In a recent essay on representations of Papuans by nineteenth-century ethnologists, Chris Ballard cited Crawfurd's approach as representing 'negrophobic assumptions'.[44] In a slightly earlier interpretation, James Boon maintained that Crawfurd's account of a brown and Negro race represented the 'semiotics of prejudice'.[45] Crawfurd's statements, therefore, in the eyes of modern scholars represent an example of a European projecting a pejorative racial idea of inherent inferiority onto a dark-skinned 'other'.

The problem with Ballard's and Boon's interpretations of Crawfurd's writing is that Crawfurd was not actually saying the Negros were inferior or were lesser human beings. His argument was that fair-skinned people have superiority over Negro people. There is a subtle difference between the two statements (at this point, I ask you, the reader, to bear with me before making a judgement).

The underlying issue behind Crawfurd's claim of European superiority over African peoples was the atrocious fact of the Atlantic slave trade. This trade resulted in the exploitation and murder of millions of Africans by Europeans through the forced transportation of African people to America, who then worked as slaves in the production of plantation crops for the benefit of Europeans.

Although Britain banned the Atlantic slave trade in 1807, slavery continued in the British Empire until 1838 and in the United States of America until 1865. Even in England, Scotland and Wales, where former slaves were free, they existed at the lowest socio-economic level of society. In 1820, Crawfurd was describing the status quo in which Europeans exploited Africans, making analogies between South-East Asia and the Atlantic world. His arguments are not 'negrophobic assumptions' or the 'semiotics of prejudice', but rather, a statement of a brutal reality which he wanted his readers to acknowledge.

The interpretations of Crawfurd's arguments as racist are even more problematic when we consider that modern scholars of South-East Asian pre-history[46] still accept the basic tenet of Crawfurd's argument: that an Austronesian population supplanted a darker-skinned Papuan population.[47] The linguistic evidence for South-East Asian pre-history points to an Austronesian migration into South-East Asia from Taiwan or Southern China. South-East Asia was not a series of empty islands before this Austronesian migration. Archaeological and linguistic evidence points to earlier migrations into South-East Asia, including earlier waves of hominids such as *Homo erectus* and possibly others such as *Homo floresiensis*.

The general agreement now amongst prehistorians is that a hunter-gatherer population existed in South-East Asia before the Austronesian migration, and that these people spoke Papuan languages.[48] Over time, the Austronesian peoples supplanted the Papuan peoples. That is, Crawfurd's conclusions still hold, although modern scholars discuss the existence of an Austronesian migration without using the racial language of the nineteenth century. If Crawfurd's racial writings appear as 'negrophobic assumptions' or as the 'semiotics of prejudice' to us today, it is not because of what he writes, but the way he writes.

For Crawfurd, race was a means to justify his polygenesis assumptions. As we saw in previous chapters, he saw culture as having an indigenous hereditary source. How this was expressed, as he admitted, was beyond his 'reason'.[49] In addition to racial explanations for differences between people, he explored geographical arguments as a source of cultural difference, but he found them wanting as a means of explaining human development or lack of development. Development, he argued, was ultimately a result of interactions between aboriginal races.

Crawfurd had promoted racial blending as a colonial policy in his 1820 *History of the Indian Archipelago*. In 1837, he responded to a lecture by Thomas Carlyle, wherein Carlyle had argued that it was the German race's purity that was the reason for its success. Crawfurd responded in his review of Carlyle's lecture by stating:

> We are not quite sure, indeed but that the breed has been in some cases even improved by crossing and transplanting, as in the instances of the English and Americans compared with the pure Germans, and the French compared with their part progenitors the Germans and the Scandinavians. Wherever the German influence has not extended, as among the Sclavonic nations, societies is still in a languid and semi-barbarous state.[50]

It was the blending of races through a process that Crawfurd would later call commixture that, he argued, created distinct nations as opposed to races. In 1863, Crawfurd read a paper on commixture to the Ethnological Society, where he declared that colonisation and settlement rarely destroys the aboriginal peoples but rather adds to them, and cited the English example, claiming: 'It follows that, although as to race a bastard people, we are, to say the least, not the worse for being so. We are not exclusively Britons or exclusively Saxons, but most probably a good deal more of the first than of the last'.[51]

Crawfurd was concerned with the aboriginal qualities of race. He argued that aboriginal purity continued regardless of the migrations and occupations. Colonisation did have an effect, with new migrant populations being infused into the aboriginal population, but this colonial influence was minor. Reflecting on the role of colonial migrations affecting the 'aboriginal' population of the French nation, he maintained:

> The immigrants must at all times have been few in comparison with the natives; and hence it may be concluded, that the infusion of foreign blood has not effected any material change, and that, in mind and person, the people of France are not essentially different from the Gauls of Caesar, nearly two thousand years ago.[52]

He believed that aboriginality existed outside of history, that it was determined at the moment of first creation. Unlike an aboriginal race, which was a product of the first creation, nations were a product of history—of migrations and settlement creating a new mixed population. In 1833, Crawfurd explained this distinction as follows: 'the character of nations is produced by circumstances and situations, and to distinguish the original qualities of the race from those superadeded [sic] by culture and civilisation'.[53] Crawfurd therefore overlaid the eighteenth-century idea of civilisational development onto his idea of aboriginal races. For example, in his unpublished 1833 chapter on 'race in Hindustan', Crawfurd argued that Indians were naturally gifted people who had suffered defective governments rendering them a lesser race than the European race. His conception of racial character is clearly not a static condition: 'Had the circumstances of the society, in which their vices have been generated, been favourable to the growth of the opposite virtues I believe they would have sprung up with the same certainty . . . as Europe'.[54] In 1863, he made the same argument in relation to the French, declaring, 'The change from semi-barbarism to the highest civilization, is no doubt immense; but this is a matter wholly apart from physical form and innate mental capacity'.[55] Race was the basic building material in Crawfurd's worldview, but they were building blocks which could be transformed by the influences of history.

Key to this transformation was the mixing of populations producing social advancement.[56] Although Crawfurd presented a polygenesis argument whereby all races were distinct creations, they were not fixed. All races progressed based on historical processes and were not limited by 'physical form and innate mental capacity'.[57]

From Polygenesis to Natural Selection

Crawfurd's polygenesis ideas found a fertile response with the naturalist Alfred Russell Wallace. Wallace synthesised the polygenesis position and

Crawfurd's idea of mixing of races with the Darwinian theory of natural selection. Wallace's importance to nineteenth-century thought is that he discovered or realised the theory of evolution as a process of natural selection concurrently with Charles Darwin. His conception of evolution, however, had its origins in racial thinking.

Unlike many of the naturalists in Britain, Wallace was poor, financing his passion for natural history and ethnology by collecting specimens to sell to museums and by the publishing of his travel memoirs. His first collecting expedition (to the Amazon in the 1840s) ended in disaster with him losing most of his specimens (and therefore a big percentage of his saleable assets) in a ship fire. Undaunted, with his insurance money and support from the Royal Geographical Society and Sir James Brooke (the Rajah of Sarawak), Wallace launched a new collecting expedition to South-East Asia.[58]

Wallace was an avid reader of ethnology and natural history. In 1844, when the proto-evolutionist Robert Chambers published his anonymous *Vestiges of Creation*, Wallace quickly interpreted its implications for human history, reflecting back on his young self in his 1905 autobiography that 'if the theory of the *Vestiges* is accepted the Negro, the Red Indian and the European are distinct species of the genus Homo'.[59] In this instance, Wallace recast the polygenesis versus monogenesis debate in his own mind. He envisioned how it was possible to accept the separateness of races as distinct species, but through evolution maintained that the genus Homo united these species. Chambers had not articulated how the process of evolution could work and, although *Vestiges of Creation* was overwhelmingly popular, it was widely criticised at the time.[60] In his musings, however, we can see that Wallace was beginning to conceive how the events, which did not exist within the then contemporary historical understandings, could be historicised through evolution.

Wallace was eventually going to encounter Crawfurd, who was the leading scholar on South-East Asian issues. Wallace would have almost certainly been aware of Crawfurd's reputation, and had more than likely read his books either before embarking for Singapore or whilst he was in Sarawak, living with James Brooke. Crawfurd was aware of Wallace from at least 1857 being an anonymous referee for some of Wallace's submissions to the Royal Geographical Society's journal.[61] The first recorded meeting between Wallace and Crawfurd was at the Royal Geographical Society in 1863, after Wallace had only recently returned from South-East Asia.[62] Crawfurd told Wallace he found the argument on geographical divisions 'enlightening' but, sensing a polygenesis grounding to Wallace's argument, Crawfurd went on to ask if Wallace 'had said something about the human inhabitants of these regions' and got Wallace to 'promise' to spell out his theories in relation to humans.[63]

In South East-Asia, Wallace followed Crawfurd's argument that there were two distinct species of humans: a brown Malay race and a Negro Papuan race. Whereas Crawfurd used race to describe processes outside of the historical narrative that he did not understand, Wallace historicised Craw-furd's racial arguments through the mechanism of 'survival of the fittest'.[64] Wallace developed the theory of 'survival of the fittest' in 1858, whilst staying on the island of Gilolo, where he wrote in his notebooks that he had found the 'exact boundary between the Malay and the Papuan races'. After this realisation, he caught a fever and during a hallucinated daze, he connected the dots, developing the idea of evolution whilst still on Gilolo Island.[65]

Wallace realised that the divisions between types of people also applied to flora and fauna. He posed, 'The western and eastern islands of the Archi-pelago, as here divided, belong to regions more distinct and contrasted than any other of the great zoological divisions of the globe'.[66] His comments resonated with Crawfurd's opening passage in his *History of the Indian Archipelago* (which Wallace would have read):

> There are two aboriginal races of human beings inhabiting the Indian islands, as different from each other as both are from all the rest of their species. This is the only portion of the globe which presents so unusual a phenomenon.[67]

Wallace proposed that a line divided the archipelago into biological regions: an Asian and an Australian/Papuan region. In the Australian zone, he observed the 'marsupial order constitutes the great mass of the mammalia', whilst in the Asian zone, 'not a solitary marsupial animal exists'.[68] The site of this division is now known as the Wallace Line. He came to this conclusion, however, through connecting the natural world and the human world in a way that suggested the polygenesis approach.

The zoologicial differences suggested to Wallace that the races had different pre-histories and origins. The Malayan race, he believed, 'resembles physically the East Asian populations, from Siam to Manchuria', and he reasoned that the archipelago was probably connected to the Asian main-land during 'the human period'.[69] In language that again harked back to Crawfurd's 'Great Polynesian nations', Wallace proposed that the Papuans along 'with the natives of Gilolo and Ceram, the Fijian, the inhabitants of the Sandwich Islands and of New Zealand (and perhaps even of Australia), are all varying forms of one great Oceanic or Polynesian race'.[70] Wallace was arguing that the Oceanic peoples and Australasian fauna were products of a long-lost continent and unrelated to mainland Asia.[71] This argument ran very close to polygenic racial thought and outlined the possibility of a separate centre of creation. The only point separating Wallace from the polygenic position held by Crawfurd was Wallace's qualifying statement that at a 'very remote period . . . the two continents of Asia and Australia were separated'.[72] This qualification places Wallace's ideas within the con-text of Darwinian evolution and the belief that all species stem from one source. The tone of Wallace's argument, however, fits closely with the poly-genesis camp, and indicates an influence from polygenic positions.

Many biographers of Wallace see his discovery of the geographical regions and evolution as a classic example of rigorous positivist observation, where Wallace zigzagged the islands of South-East Asia, carefully documenting the local environments.[73] This view of Wallace is misleading, as he developed his ideas based on pre-existing literature, of which Crawfurd was certainly one source. By 1859, numerous Dutch naturalists had observed the geographic division between Australian and Asian fauna. Wallace had more than likely already read summaries of Dutch research on the geographical division in the writings of George Windsor Earl, James Logan and John Crawfurd. Using Dutch sources, Earl, Logan and Crawfurd had all proposed some form of line dividing Australia from Asia that crossed somewhere between islands of Flores, Timor and New Guinea—Wallace would have used these arguments in developing his ideas.[74] One of the key figures that Wallace acknowledged inspired him in the lead-up to his discoveries was the barrister and amateur ornithologist Philip Sclater. Wallace's debt to Sclater underlines the importance of racial polygenesism at the time.

On 16 June 1857, Sclater announced to the audience at the Linnaean Society that the primary problem in natural history was determining 'what are the most natural primary ontological divisions of the earth's surface?'[75] He suggested that all naturalists should commit themselves to answering this problem through focusing on it in their own areas of expertise. Wallace received a copy of this paper whilst in South-East Asia, and quickly committed himself to Sclater's project.[76] Sclater was concerned with determining the original centres of distribution of flora and fauna types. He argued that 'it was well-known and universally acknowledged' that the different regions of flora and fauna in of the world 'have been the result of distinct creations'.[77] Therefore, the role for naturalists was to determine how many centres of creation originally existed.

Although Sclater's paper focused on the centres of creation for birds, his real focus was on humans. He reasoned that if there were distinct centres of creation for flora and fauna, there were probably distinct regions for humans as well. Sclater attributed his inspiration to the Swiss-American naturalist and polygenesis advocate Louis Agassiz. Agassiz was one of the leading naturalists of the nineteenth century and had argued that the natural world consisted of centres of original creation.[78] Although Agassiz was against African American slavery, he supported the pro-slavery American racial writers Josiah Nott and George Gliddon by writing a preface to their *Types of Mankind* advocating that the distribution of different types of humans also corresponded to these original centres of creation.

Historians have long pointed to the issue of slavery as a division within the politics of nascent anthropology.[79] Using the London Ethnology Society minutes, historians such as George Stocking and John Burrow identified that the divisions over slavery were interconnected to the division between advocates of monogenesis and polygenesis in British intellectual circles.[80]

The treatment of non-European peoples was a key concern of early nineteenth-century ethnology and anthropology. The intellectual foundation figure of the Ethnological Society of London was James Cowles Prichard. In his *Natural History of Man* (1848), Prichard railed against the immorality of the polygenesis position, connecting it with the Atlantic slave trade and the cruel treatment of colonised peoples:

> Those who hold that the Negro is of a distinct species from our own, and of a different and inferior grade in the scale of organised beings . . . observe that it cannot be much more criminal to destroy such creatures when they annoy us than to extirpate wolves or bears.[81]

For Prichard and his followers, proving the unity of the human race was a moral question that upheld the Bible and necessitated ethical treatment of non-European peoples. In making his moral case, Prichard simplified the intellectual debates of the time. He was effectively arguing that you are either for the unity of the human race or against it, and if you are against the unity of the human race, you were against those humans you saw as created separately from you. Or in short: those who supported or believed polygenesis were immoral.

Prichard's moral absolutes have influenced subsequent historians' conclusions about the politics of mid-nineteenth-century ethnology. Most recently, Adrian Desmond and James Moore have passionately represented the monogenesis versus polygenesis argument in *Darwin's Sacred Cause*. Their argument is that Darwin's hatred of slavery drove him to write *Origin of Species* and demonstrate the fallacy of Americans who used polygenesis as a crutch to morally support slavery.

Although polygenesis was popular in the slave-owning Southern states of the United States of America, advocates of polygenesis in Britain were not necessarily supporters of slavery. In his review of the pro-polygenesis racial writer Samual Morton's *Crania America*, Crawfurd criticised Prichard and his followers for being ideological zealots, rejecting evidence because it did not fit with their moral view:

> The differences of conformation between what are called Varieties of men seemed to him [Morton] great enough and constant enough to justify him in regarding them as Species. This therefore, is the distinct result to which all the reasonings [sic] and discoveries of himself and his commentators tend. It is not a question on which we desire to enter controversially, and it is matter of regret to us that such unquestionable and very valuable contribution as this book makes to the science of which it treats, may be expected to meet with bitter opposition from the mere use that will be made of its arguments against the moral and intellectual equality of the negro.[82]

Before the publication of Darwin's *Origin*, the majority of ethnologists tended to support the polygenesis view. Overwhelmingly, the advocates of physical anthropology (the researchers who examined differences in the skeletal form of humans) supported a belief in polygenesis.[83] It was not as common among followers of the philology approach; nevertheless, many people were moving towards polygenesis. This broad sweep of the scientific and the ethnological establishment means that we cannot interpret the divisions simply as an ethical and political dichotomy between monogenesis, who constituted the anti-slavery position, and polygenesis, who represented the pro-slavery position.

In his paper on birds, Sclater noted that 'the idea of the original unity of the human race' was 'still strongly supported by many Ethnologists' in Britain. He summarised the contemporary attitude amongst naturalists, feeling confident that most 'philosophical zoologists' assumed that there were multiple centres of creation.[84] As the editor of *Ibis* (the Journal of the British Ornithologists' Union) and secretary of the Zoological Society of London, Sclater was an establishment figure in the community of naturalists. Therefore, his arguing for the innate logic of multiple creations for animals and humans (polygenesis) carried intellectual force. He concluded the case for monogenesis was almost ridiculous, henceforth relying on an:

> awkward necessity of supposing the introduction of the red man into America by Behring's Straits, and of colonizing Polynesia by stray pairs of Malays floating over the water like cocoa-nuts.[85]

Wallace found Sclater's paper inspiring and wrote to Sclater of his hopes that his South-East Asian collection would elucidate the problem that Sclater identified. He agreed with Sclater that there were six 'grand zoological provinces'. Wallace's polygenesis-inspired zoological regions were interconnected with his path to discovering the theory of evolution. According to the historian of anthropology George Stocking, this realisation of Wallace's changed the 'context in which the debates between monogenists and polygenists was carried out, it established the basis for what seemed a new monogenism'. In fact, as Stocking makes clear, it was actually a synthesis of the polygenic and monogenic positions.[86]

By the 1850s, much of the ethnographic scholarly community accepted Crawfurd's polygenic position. Natural historians also favoured the principle of multiple centres of creation. The belief in multiple centres of creation represented a collective belief that natural history could not be reconciled to one act of creation, and that most acts of species creation were not acts of history, but rather, acts of God's successive processes of creation.

Crawfurd's ideas on race, however, developed after he had already tried to use geographical and historical explanations for the development of civilisational and physical and cultural differences. Crawfurd concluded that although the geographical environment was crucial to the historical process, it could not explain everything. Therefore, race became the catchall concept to describe factors that were unexplainable. Crawfurd used the word 'race' to label all that he could not explain.

Wallace started from the same premise as Crawfurd; however, whilst Crawfurd chose not to pursue the means of creation, Wallace thought about the mechanism of creation. Wallace saw that differences in geography corresponded to different types of flora, fauna and humans. Therefore, Wallace reasoned, they had transformed over time in relation to their geographical environment. Wallace therefore accepted the polygenesis position, but rather than understand them as separate creations of God, Wallace theorised that the different races were the result of different evolutionary histories, but they all shared a common origin.

Wallace introduced a real sense of historical change into ideas of human diversity. By developing a theory of evolution, Wallace historicised human differences and diversity into a process of social change that appeared to explain biological as well as cultural differences. In achieving this, Wallace transformed race from being a catchall phrase that labelled the unknowable to an explanation of human difference made explainable through natural selection. In doing so, Wallace placed the creation of humans inside the historical narrative.

Notes

1 For example, Michael Adas, *Machines as the Measure of Men: Science, Technology, and Ideologies of Western Dominance*, (Ithaca: Cornell University Press, 1989); Beasley, *The Victorian Reinvention of Race*; David Bindman, *Ape to Apollo: Aesthetics and the Idea of Race in the 18th Century*, (London: Reaktion Books, 2002); Christine Bolt, *Victorian Attitudes Towards Race*, (London: Routledge, 2013); Douglas and Ballard, *Foreign Bodies*; McCarthy, *Race, Empire, and the Idea of Human Development*; Rendall, 'Scottish Orientalism: From Robertson to James Mill'; Said, *Orientalism*.
2 Rendall, 'Scottish Orientalism: From Robertson to James Mill', p. 69.
3 Adas, *Machines as the Measure of Men*, p. 302.
4 Ellingson, *The Myth of the Noble Savage*, p. 294. In trying to understand nineteenth-century racial thought, Ellingson's crib is a journey to find the source of the statement 'the noble savage', which is often misattributed to Jean-Jacques Rousseau. Ellingson blames Crawfurd, with the only evidence for this Elingson's failure to find an even earlier source that uses the phrase 'noble savage' and Rousseau in the same passage. Ellingson looked for conspiracy, when in reality all he found was Crawfurd making a literacy analogy to John Dryden's play *The Conquest of Granada* (1672) and an ideal attribution to Rousseau as part of a general dismissing of eighteenth-century philosophical ideas of natural man. Did Crawfurd intentionally misrepresent Rousseau, or did he merely misunderstand Rousseau's argument, as many people have done since? Rather than providing a detailed analysis on complex ideas of race, progress and mid-nineteenth-century bio-geographical thinking, Ellingson's critique of Crawfurd's conflation of the noble savage metaphor with Rousseau verges on being a conspiracy theory.
5 Hall, *Civilising Subjects*, pp. 399–400.
6 Beasley, *The Victorian Reinvention of Race*, p. 18.

7 John Crawfurd, 'On the Physical and Mental Characteristics of the Negro', *Transactions of the Ethnological Society of London*, 4 (1866); Anonymous, *Thirty-Fifth Meeting; Held At Birmingham In September 1865: 34*, (London: Murray, 1866); Hall, *Civilising Subjects*, pp. 399–400.

8 Anderson, *Race and the Crisis of Humanism*; George M. Fredrickson, *Racism: A Short History*, (Princeton: Princeton University Press, 2003). For an alternate interpretation see Vincent Sarich and Frank Miele, *Race: The Reality of Human Differences*, (Boulder, CO: Westview Press, 2004). Who argues that in dismissing race as a concept, 21st century thought has rejected the role of physical anthropology in understating human diversity.

9 James A. Boon, *Affinities and Extremes*, (Chicago: Univeristy of Chicago Press, 1990).

10 Charles R Darwin and Alfred Russell Wallace, 'On the Tendency of Species to Form Varietiesl and on the Pepetuation of Varieties and Species by Natural Means of Selection [Read 1 July]', *Journal of the Proceedings of the Linnean Society of London: Zoology*, 2 20 (1858).

11 Most published discussions/debates with Crawfurd were conducted behind the veil of anonymity for both Crawfurd and his opponents.

12 Bindman, *Ape to Apollo*.

13 James Buchan, *Adam Smith and the Pursute of Perfect Liberty*, (London: Profile Books, 2006).

14 This model of centre-periphery scientific research dominated colonial research. Bruno Latour, *Science in Action: How to Follow Scientists and Engineers through Society*, (Cambridge, MA: Harvard University Press, 1987). The metropolitan centre claimed the right to discover, name and theorise, whilst the colonial periphery merely collected. Jim Endersby, *Imperial Nature: Joseph Hooker and the Practices of Victorian Science*, (Chicago: Universtiy of Chicago Press, 2008). Nevertheless, the periphery often attempted to challenge the centre and theorise for themselves and even at times supplant the centre. See Gareth Knapman, 'Museum Anthropology and Imperial Networks as Cultural Status: The Colonial Ethnology Museum in Nineteenth Century Melbourne', *History of Anthropology Newsletter*, 31 (2011); Gareth Knapman, 'Curiosities or Science in the Natinal Museum of Victoria: Procurement Networks and the Purpose of a Museum', in *Curating Empire: Museums and the British Imperial Experience*, ed. by Sarah editor Longair and John editor McAleer (Manchester: Manchester University Press, 2012), pp. 82–103.

15 Crawfurd, 'Publications Respecting the Eastern Peninsula of India', p. 332.

16 Raffles, Marsden and Barrow, 'Crawfurd's History of the Indian Archipelago'. For evidence of Marsden's involvement see John Barrow, '653 Article 5: Crawfurd, History of the Indian Archipelago: With Maps and Engravings; *Proceedings of the Agricultural Society*, established in Sumatra. Vol. I; *Malayan Miscellanies*, Vol. I, pp. 111–138: Author: John Barrow, probably with Sir Thomas Stamford Raffles', in *Quarterly Review Archive*, ed. by Jonathan Cutmore (1822). '[Barrow] is very anxious for the article on Crawford which he & Marden say is sound & good; I suppose therefore it must be inserted, especially as Sir T Raffles is coming home & he expects much assistance from him. The paper is not very brisk, but tis sensible'.

17 Crawfurd, 'Publications Respecting the Eastern Peninsula of India', p. 344.

18 Ibid. p. 361.

19 Douglas and Ballard, *Foreign Bodies*, p. 41.

20 James Cook, *Captain Cook's Voyages of Discovery*, (Switzerland: Heron Books, c.1975), pp. 37–38.

21 G.W. Anderson and James Cook, *A New, Authentic, and Complete Collection of Voyages Round the World, Undertaken and Performed by Royal Authority:*

Containing an Authentic, Entertaining, Full, and Complete History of Captain Cook's First, Second, Third and Last Voyages, Undertaken by Order of his Present Majesty, for Making Discoveries in Geography, Navigation, Astronomy, &c. in the Southern and Northern Hemispheres &c. &c. &c. . . . the Whole Comprehending a Full Account, from the Earliest Period to the Present Time, (London: Printed for the proprietors), p. 54. see also [Hodges, William] 1744–1797 A family in Dusk Bay, New Zealand. London; Alexr. Hogg [1784?], *National Library of New Zealand*, <http://tapuhi.natlib.govt.nz/cgi-bin/spydus/NAV/GLOBAL/OPHDR/1/135242>

22 Museum Victoria, 'Albertus Seba's depiction of the southern common opossum Didelphis marsupialis in the 18th century Thesaurus held by the Museum Victoria Library.', (2009).

23 Forrest and Bassett, *A Voyage to New Guinea and the Moluccas, 1774–1776 . . . With an Introduction by D. K. Bassett*, p. 64.

24 William Marsden, *The History of Sumatra*, (Kuala Lumpur: Oxford University Press, 1966 [1811]), pp. 44–45.

25 Anthony Forge, 'Raffles and Daniell: Making the Image Fit', in *Recovering the Orient: Artists, Scholars, Appropriations*, ed. by C. Andrew Gerstle and Anthony Crothers Milner (Chur, Switzerland: Harwood Academic Publishers, 1994), p. 147.

26 Crawfurd, 'Of the Eastern Penisular of India'.

27 William Paley, *Natural Theology*, (Oxford: Oxford University Press, 2008 [1802]).

28 Arthur O. Lovejoy, *The Great Chain of Being: A Study of the History of an Idea*, (Cambridge, MA: Harvard University Press, 1957), p. 24.

29 T. Horsfield, *Zoological Researches in Java, and the Neighbouring Islands*, (London: Kingsbury, Parbury, & Allen, 1824), p. 23.

30 Bindman, *Ape to Apollo*, pp. 58–59.

31 Marsden, *The History of Sumatra*, p. 46.

32 Raffles, *The History of Java*, vol. 1, p. 56.

33 Ibid., vol. 1, p. 57.

34 Crawfurd, *HIA.*, vol. 1, p. 15.

35 Crawfurd, *Descriptive Dictionary*, p. 259.

36 Ibid.

37 Ibid. p. 260.

38 Ibid. p. 264.

39 Ibid.

40 Ibid.

41 Crawfurd, *HIA.*, vol. 1, pp. 17–18.

42 Ibid., vol. 1, p. 80.

43 Ibid., vol. 1, p. 79.

44 Chris Ballard, "Oceanic Negroes': British anthropology of Papuans, 1820–1869', in *Foreign Bodies: Oceania and the Science of Race 1750–1940*, ed. by Bronwen Douglas and Chris Ballard (Canberra, A.C.T.: ANU E Press, 2008), pp. 157–201.

45 Boon, *Affinities and Extremes*, p. 37.

46 I am using 'pre-history' in the modern sense of the word.

47 Peter Bellwood, *Man's Conquest of the Pacific: The Prehistory of Southeast Asia and Oceania*, (Auckland; London: Collins, 1978), pp. 40–45.

48 Peter Bellwood, 'Southeast Asia before History', in *The Cambridge History of Southeast Asia*, ed. by Nicholas Tarling (Cambridge: Cambridge University Press, 1999), pp. 102–103); Lockard, *Southeast Asia in World History*, pp. 12–13.

49 Crawfurd, *HIA.*, vol. 1, p. 27.

50 Crawfurd, 'Thomas Carlisle's Lectures', (6 May, 1837) p. 421. This publication is identified as being by Crawfurd in Carlyle, 'Thomas Carlyle to Margaret Carlyle'. The publication also corresponds to Crawfurd general arguments regarding aboriginality, race and history.

51 Crawfurd, 'On the Commixture of the Races of Man as Affecting the Progress of Civilization (Europe)', p. 206.
52 Ibid.
53 Crawfurd, 'Description of India', p. 41.
54 Ibid. p. 66.
55 Crawfurd, 'On the Commixture of the Races of Man as Affecting the Progress of Civilization (Europe)', p. 206.
56 See Crawfurd's entry for 'Man' in Crawfurd, *Descriptive Dictionary*. Also Crawfurd, *HIA.*, Crawfurd, 'On the Commixture of the Races of Man as Affecting the Progress of Civilization (Europe)'.
57 Crawfurd, 'On the Commixture of the Races of Man as Affecting the Progress of Civilization (Europe)', p. 206.
58 John Crawfurd, 'John Crawfurd Letters', Royal Geographic Society, CB4/Crawfurd (1850–61)., RGS/CB4Wallace, A.R.
59 Cited in Stocking, *Victorian Anthropology*, p. 97.
60 J.A. Secord, *Victorian Sensation: The Extraordinary Publication, Reception, and Secret Authorship of Vestiges of the Natural History of Creation*, (Chicago: University of Chicago Press, 2000).
61 Crawfurd refereed at least three Wallace manuscripts and accepted all of them: 1857 'account of the Arru Islands' Crawfurd, 'John Crawfurd Letters',, RGS/JMS/8/22, 1859 'New Guinea' ibid., RGS.JMS/13/99; 1861 'On the trade of the Eastern Archipelago with New Guinea' ibid., RGS/JMS/13/126.
62 Alfred Russell Wallace, 'On the Physical Geography of the Malay Archipelago', *Proceedings of the Royal Geographical Society of London*, 75 (1863), pp. 210–211.
63 Ibid.
64 Alfred Russell Wallace, *The Malay Archipelago*, (New York: Dover Publications, 1962 [1869]), pp. 446–458. Also Stocking, *Victorian Anthropology*.
65 Wallace, *The Malay Archipelago*, pp. 446–458.
66 Ibid. p. 174.
67 Crawfurd, *HIA.*, vol. 1, pp. 17–18.
68 Wallace, *The Malay Archipelago*, p. 172.
69 Ibid. p. 211.
70 Ibid. p. 212. The Polynesian connection was also supported by James Brooke, Wallace's mentor and protector in South-East Asia.
71 Ibid. p. 214.
72 Ibid.
73 Michael Shermer, *In Darwin's Shadow: The Life and Science of Alfred Russel Wallace: A Biographical Study on the Psychology of History*, (Oxford: Oxford University Press, 2002), p. 122. For example, Michael Shermer attributes the Wallace line to a moment of brilliance: 'One day in 1858, upon ruminating on the closely allied species of the Malay Archipelago, Wallace noticed that some are more allied than others as a function of the geography in which they are found'. According to Shermer, Wallace was also reading 'a paper by the British ornithologist Philip Lutley Sclater, on the "Geographical Distribution of Birds", in which the author noted a break in bird distribution between the western and eastern islands of the Malay Archipelago. This caught Wallace's attention, because he too had noticed a similar division'. Peter Raby, *Alfred Russel Wallace*, (London: Chatto & Windus, 2001) and Ross A. Slotten, *The Heretic in Darwin's Court: The Life of Alfred Russel Wallace*, (New York: Columbia University Press, 2004) present similar arguments, essentially that Wallace spent more time in the field in South-East Asia than any other naturalist, and this experience led him to that discovery. None of these writers address the social context that contributed to the development of Wallace's thoughts. Desmond

and Moore in *Darwin's Sacred Cause* demonstrated that Darwin's thinking was not a result of positivism, but the social political issue of slavery.

74 In 1845, George Windsor Earl presented a paper 'On the Physical Structure and Arrangement of the Islands of the Indian Archipelago'; this was the nucleus to the Wallace Line. Earl had recorded depths sounding between the colony of Port Essington and the Malayan peninsular. He found that shallow seas linked Sumatra, Java and Borneo to continental Asia, whilst New Guinea and the Arru Islands were connected by shallow seas to Australia. In between, however, was a 'chain of islands which extends from Java to Timor'. These islands, he argued, are 'separated from each other by narrow channels of unfathomable depth' and in another paper went on to use species distribution to understand the ancient formation of the continents. George Windsor Earl, 'On the Physical Structure and Arrangement of the Islands in the Indian Archipelago', *Journal of the Geographical Society*, 15 (1845), p. 359; G.W. Earl, *A Correspondence Relating to the Discovery of Gold in Australia*, (London: Pelham Richardson, 1853), p. 5. In 1848, James Logan continued Earl's train of thought, arguing 'that there is a real and not merely a fanciful connection between the Archipelago and Asia'. However, he realised that previous arguments 'neglected the all-important evidence of the comparative distribution of the living flora and fauna, which seems to prove that the ancient southern continent'. James Richardson Logan, 'The Present Condition of the Indian Archipelago', *The Journal of The Indian Archipelago and Eastern Asia*, 1 (1847), p. 349. In 1856, John Crawfurd noted that the 'zoology of the Archipelago is still more restricted to localities than its botany'. He then gave an account that described the flora and fauna divisions in the archipelago. In the account, he describes the fauna of the western part of the archipelago as extending out of Asia. More importantly, he went on to argue that '[m]arsupial quadrupeds, unknown in the western islands of the Archipelago and in the Philippines, are first time seen in Celebes, and from thence exist in several islands as far as New Guinea, in which there is an opossum and tree-kangaroo'. Crawfurd had neatly articulated the fauna distribution underlining the Wallace Line. However, he went further, stating that '[b]irds, with the exception of those that are migratory, are nearly as limited in their geographical distribution as quadrupeds'. Although Crawfurd did not state there is a line dividing the archipelago, he did describe the existence of a line. Crawfurd, *Descriptive Dictionary*, p. 15.

75 Philip Lutley Sclater, 'On the General Geographical Distribution of the Members of the Class Aves', *Journal of the Proceedings of the Linnean Society of London*, 2 7 (1858), p. 130.

76 Alfred Russell Wallace, 'Letter from Mr. Wallace Concerning the Geographical Distribution of Birds (S52: 1859)', in *Alfred Russell Wallace Page*, (1859).

77 Sclater, 'On the General Geographical Distribution of the Members of the Class Aves', p. 130.

78 L. Agassiz, *An Essay on Classification*, (London: Longman, Brown, Green, Longmans & Roberts & Trübner, 1859), p. 57.

79 Adrian Desmond, *The Politics of Evolution: Morphology, Medicine, and Reform in Radical London*, (Chicago: University of Chicago Press, 1989).

80 Beasley, *The Victorian Reinvention of Race*; J.W. Burrow, *Evolution and Society: A Study in Victorian Social Theory*, (London: Cambridge University Press, 1966); Stocking, *Victorian Anthropology*; Ellingson, *The Myth of the Noble Savage*; Hall, *Civilising Subjects*; David Brion Davis, *The Problem of Slavery in Western Culture*, (Harmondsworth: Penguin, 1970).

81 James Cowles Prichard, *The Natural History of Man*, (London: H. Bailliere, 1855), pp. 6–7.

82 John Crawfurd*, 'Types of Mankind; or Ethnological Researches, Based upon the Ancient Monuments, Paintings, Sculptures, and Crania of Races, and upon

the Natural, Geographical, Philological, and Biblical History: Illustrated by Selections from the Indeited Papers of Samuel George Morton, M.D., and by Additional Contributions from Prof. L. Agassiz L.L.D.; W. Usher M.D.; Prof H.S. Patterson, MD. By J. C Nott, M.D. and Geo. R. Gliddon. Philadelphia: Lippincott, Grambo, and Co.', *The Examiner*, (Saturday 20 January, 1855).

83 Stocking, *Victorian Anthropology*, pp. 66–67.

84 Sclater, 'On the General Geographical Distribution of the Members of the Class Aves', p. 131.

85 Ibid.

86 Stocking, *Victorian Anthropology*, pp. 101–102.

5 Singapore and Competing Visions of Colonialism

Raffles and Crawfurd shared a unified concern for the advancement of civilisation in South-East Asia, but they approached the advancement of civilisation from different angles. Raffles favoured intervention in native states, arguing that South-East Asians shared a passive culture in which invaders introduced civilisation. Crawfurd, in comparison, argued that culture was inherently indigenous to South-East Asia, with local conditions shaping identity. European intervention more often ruined well-functioning societies.

The argument presented here is the opposite to the dominant interpretation that emphasised Raffles's messianic role in the establishment of Singapore and in the development of colonial policy in South-East Asia. In his pioneering work on Raffles and Crawfurd, John Bastin developed a misleading characterisation of the approaches of the two men to colonisation. He argued that the distinction between Raffles's and Crawfurd's individual approaches to colonisation was that Crawfurd advocated European migration and settlement to Asian colonies. In comparison, Bastin characterised Raffles's approach to colonisation as a synthesis of the colonial model of entrepot ports developed in the eighteenth century in South-East Asia. Raffles's creation of Singapore became the culmination of British colonising logic, whilst Crawfurd, in Bastin's narrative, is the purveyor of a failed colonial policy. In reality, the situation was reversed.

Two distinct ideas of colonial policy did exist. Crawfurd's approach favoured maintaining distance through the establishment of island colonies such as Singapore and thereby avoiding colonial entanglements and supporting the indigenous growth of civilisation through trade. It was Raffles who promoted the idea of colonial intervention, whilst Crawfurd advocated non-intervention and the maintenance of indigenous systems of government.

Raffles and the Founding of Singapore

Raffles's *History of Java* proposed the retention of Java as a British colony, and he also advocated an interventionist colonialism to promote civilisation. As part of the peace established after the Congress of Vienna in 1815,

Britain handed Java back to the Dutch. British decision-makers in London decided that a strong Netherlands was more important than retaining a large island colony in Asia.

Raffles's career floundered after the British left Java. The new Governor-General of India, Lord Francis Hastings, relieved Raffles of command of Java in 1815 before the colony reverted to Dutch control. Raffles faced charges of corruption for selling government lands in 1813 without prior authorisation from India. Whilst Raffles was Lieutenant Governor of Java, he bought the land as a silent partner.[1] Although (by twenty-first-century standards) the stench of corruption permeates the deal, in the early nineteenth century, it was reasonably common for governors to profit from their executive powers, and the consequent inquiry exonerated Raffles.[2] In 1818, Raffles gained a new posting at Bencoolen, which he described as the 'most wretched place I ever beheld', full of 'ruin and dilapidation'.[3] Bencoolen was an unimportant backwater to which the East India Company had banished him, a point that he recognised calling it his 'Elba'—likening himself and Bencoolen to the island where Napoleon Bonaparte was exiled in 1813.[4]

Raffles, however, decided not to see the posting as a punishment. Instead, he used the colony as a platform to challenge the return of Dutch power in South-East Asia by trying to unite the Malay sultans of Sumatra into a political confederation. He concluded treaties with the rulers of Minangkabau that stipulated that he was to be the British 'Representative in all the Malay States'.[5] For Raffles, the 'ruin and dilapidation' in Sumatra meant there was a need to reform and a chance for him to bring the colony and Sumatra back to its former glory which existed in his historical imagination. He attempted to conclude treaties with Acheen and Rhio, with the aim of securing Sumatra as a British sphere of influence.[6]

Raffles's ideas on Sumatra were broad and bold in nature, with designs to gain a new colonial empire. He was not advocating a policy of free trade, but, initially, a new land rent system in Sumatra and later, the broad acquisition of territory. His relations with native states demonstrate that he wanted to embroil the East India Company in Sumatran affairs. Such entanglements would invariably lead to more colonial acquisitions, until the island of Sumatra was fully under British control. Lord Hastings (the Governor-General of British India) rejected these initiatives.

After his grand schemes for Sumatra failed, Raffles formed a new colony at the tip of the Malay Peninsula called Singapore. Although the British authorities were not prepared to support Raffles's Sumatran adventures, they were concerned that after the return of Java and Malacca to the Dutch in 1816, the Dutch were closing off British access to South-East Asia and China. Farquhar had argued as early as 1816 for 'a new British settlement' situated 'near the S.E. entrance of these Straits, so as to lie as nearly as possible in the direct route of shipping passing to and from China and the Eastern Archipelago'.[7] Singapore is strategically located at the entrance of the Straits of Malacca with access to the South China Sea, and therefore, building a station at Singapore answered many of Farquhar's concerns. Raffles certainly used the Dutch exclusionist policies to justify his actions, and received from Governor-General Hastings orders 'to secure the free passage of the Straits of Malacca' by the 'establishment of a Station beyond Malacca, such as may command the southern entrance of the Straits'.[8]

Although late nineteenth- and early twentieth-century historians attribute the success of Singapore as a sort of monument to Raffles's vision, Crawfurd painted a picture of Raffles's lack of vision. In a moment of frustration in 1853, after reading writings that memorialised Raffles as a means of justifying British colonial expansion in Borneo, Crawfurd decided to set the record straight. Crawfurd maintained that Raffles's decision to found Singapore was the 'exception' to Raffles's colonial ideas and was 'a happy accident to which his enterprising sprit was driven by the barrenness of his proper locality', which was Bencoolen. As evidence for his rejection of Raffles's wisdom and vision, Crawfurd declared:

> That the foundation of Singapore was only a happy hit, and not the result of such sagacity and forecast as established an Alexandria, is sufficiently testified by the founder's next attempt. This consisted in the seizure and occupation of the island of Nias, on the naked, out of the way and barren western coast of Sumatra, without harbour, or any other qualification of an emporium.[9]

Crawfurd's comments painted a picture of Raffles as an opportunist who had little commercial logic and cast doubts on the view that Raffles was a systematic, strategic thinker.

Raffles only spent nine months in Singapore.[10] The success of Singapore, therefore, was only possible because of the other founding residents: William Farquhar and Crawfurd, who both worked to transform the fledgling settlement into a profitable trading port.[11] Farquhar was always annoyed at Raffles's attempts to negate his role in the foundation of the colony. Farquhar even claimed that Raffles stole the idea of Singapore as a colony from him, which would explain Crawfurd's argument that Raffles accidently created Singapore.[12] Viewed from the vantage point of 1818, the founding of Singapore was a desperate attempt by Raffles to salvage some lasting legacy from his time in South-East Asia.

Singapore as a New Settler Society

Raffles grudgingly accepted Crawfurd as the Resident of Singapore in 1823. Crawfurd inherited a colony that had grown exponentially under Raffles and William Farquhar. The society at that time was truly a multi-racial society. When first founded in 1819, the colony had a population of 200 to 300 inhabitants, who Crawfurd described as 'piratical Malayan fishermen'.[13]

By the time Crawfurd left in 1825, the population of Singapore had grown to over 10,000 inhabitants.

Many of the inhabitants of Singapore migrated in the first years of settlement from the older colony of Malacca. Formerly a Dutch colony, Malacca, which the British seized during the Napoleonic Wars, was handed back to the Dutch in 1815—only to be ceded back to the British in 1824. The political uncertainly in Malacca probably contributed to many of the inhabitants moving to Singapore. Whilst the British occupied Malacca, they estimated the population to be 25,000. When the Dutch regained possession in 1815, they estimated the population to be 22,000. By the 1827 census, the population of Malacca had dropped to 16,000.[14] In 1824, Crawfurd notes that most of the Malays in Singapore were emigrants from Malacca.[15] Along with Malay emigrants, many Baba Chinese—who were people of mixed Chinese and Malay descent—also moved to Singapore. William Farquhar, who Crawfurd replaced in Singapore, had previously been the longstanding Governor of Malacca and it was probably through his influence that many inhabitants followed him from Malacca to Singapore.[16] In addition to this older population of migrants from Malacca, a new population also developed in Singapore.

These new emigrants were Chinese. In 1825, 3,518 people migrated directly from China to Singapore. The following year, the number of new Chinese migrants grew to 5513. Most of these migrants did not stay in Singapore, but filtered to other parts of the archipelago. However, sufficient numbers stayed on in Singapore for Crawfurd to see a new British led Chinese-Malay society developing in the new colony. Crawfurd identified three groups of Chinese migrants. He preferred the Fokien (Fujian) Chinese, which he believed were 'considered superior, both in respectability and enterprise, to the rest to their countryman'.[17] Next came the people from the Canton (Guangzhou) region of China, followed by the Portuguese-influenced Chinese of Macao. In later works, he also identified the migrants from other regions of China: Chekiang (Zhejiang) and Kiangnan (Jiangnan).[18]

From his experience in Java, Crawfurd held mixed feelings towards the Chinese. In Java, the Chinese occupied an intermediary position within the colonial state. They often worked in trade, but also at minor levels of the colonial government. Crawfurd's frustration with the Chinese in Java is demonstrated by his descriptions of them. He called them 'at once enterprising, keen, laborious, luxurious, sensual, debauched, and pusillanimous'. He also said 'they very seldom condescend to work as day-labourers' and considered they were the 'least conscientious people alive', requiring 'constant prospect of gain or advantage' to 'induce them to fulfil their engagements'.[19]

His experiences in Singapore dramatically changed his attitudes towards the Chinese. Crawfurd became overwhelmingly impressed by the Chinese, who he argued were 'in many respects . . . the most active and valuable agents in developing the resources of the Archipelago'.[20] Physically, he believed 'the Chinese are an athletic, powerful race, even beyond our own countrymen'.[21]

After encountering large numbers of people directly from Fokien, he commented that these people demonstrated 'uncommon civility' and 'were remarkable for the earnestness of their hospitality'.[22] He still believed the Chinese to be 'an industrious, money-making, and money-spending people', but his descriptions after his time in Singapore are extremely positive and devoid of negative assumptions.[23] In 1830, when asked his opinion of the Chinese by a House of Lords Committee, he said, 'They are a very industrious people in every way; they are a business-like people; their manners more resemble Europeans in that part of their character'.[24] In a co-authored publication on commerce in China with Peter Gorden, Crawfurd described the Chinese as like any other population:

> The merchants and other men of business are acute, methodical, and enterprising. Among the lower classes of tradesmen, it is true, chicanery is not unfrequently practised; but among the higher order of dealers, extensive commercial intercourse produces its usual effect of a regard for character, and hence these are in general punctual as well as faithful to their engagements.[25]

Unlike in Java, the Chinese in Singapore readily took up many of the labouring, commercial positions as well as most of the artisan work in the colony.[26] After 10 years of settlement, Crawfurd believed the Malays had become 'incapable of maintaining competition in almost any line with the Chinese' and consequently, the Malay population 'had rather diminished than increased'.[27] He cited that Chinese labour was highly valued and consequently, the Chinese labourers earned higher wages than the Malays.[28] Crawfurd saw an economy developing whereby the British and Europeans provided the capital and administrative structures to the new settlement. The Chinese provided the majority of the labour, and the Malays took the roles of woodcutters, fishermen and petty farmers.

Crawfurd increasingly became convinced that the Chinese made ideal settlers. 'Of all the Asiatic settlers in our eastern settlements, the Chinese are the most obedient to the laws' and 'afford the least employment to the courts of justice'.[29] Crawfurd's reasoning for his belief that the Chinese made ideal settlers was the underlying belief he had in the narrative of social improvement within British settlements. 'Men go to Colonies', Crawfurd maintained, 'to better themselves'.[30] He believed that the Chinese who chose to emigrate were in general 'poorest of the lower orders, men who emigrate from poverty at home. No educated man and no man of property is ever to be found among them'.[31] He saw the alleviation of poverty as the driving mechanism behind free settlement in Singapore, declaring before a House of Lords Committee in 1830:

> That no sooner they land than their condition is prodigiously improved: they meet their countrymen, and probably their friends or relatives; they

find immediate employment in a congenial climate, and in countries where the wages of labour are perhaps three times as high as in China, and the necessaries of life perhaps by one half cheaper.[32]

Overwhelmingly, the migrants were male. Crawfurd argued that the migrants were exclusively male, stating, 'I have never seen or heard of a female amongst the emigrants, and never saw a Chinese woman except at Hue, the capital of Cochin China, where two or three were pointed out to me as objects of curiosity, who has been kidnapped and brought there when children'.[33] Initially, he believed that this was because the Chinese government refused to give females permission to leave, but later, he reasoned that the 'real cause seems to be the reluctance of the Chinese to quit their native country, and the hope which those who emigrate always cherish of returning to it'.[34] If migration was only going to be temporary, there was no need for women to migrate.

Despite the desire to return home, he concluded that 'the great majority of the Chinese remain permanently in their adopted countries, and all who prosper invariably do so'. Many adopted Malay wives who then became part of the Peranakan population of localised Chinese. By 1859, Crawfurd believed that the Chinese settlers had greater attachment to Singapore than China:

> Thus, in Singapore which has only existed forty years, they constitute the majority of the inhabitants, and among them are to be found holders of land and house property, and of great ships, many of them men of wealth, whose whole interests and attachments are local, and who are as deeply concerned in the tranquillity and prosperity of the settlement as the English settlers themselves.[35]

This story of attachment and feelings towards Singapore is bound in Crawfurd's narrative of wealth creation through individual freedom. In Crawfurd's narrative, Singapore is a wealth creator, in which poor Chinese migrants arrive and make their fortune, and that fortune creates a reason for settling and permanently committing to Singapore and the British Empire.

Ideas of Freedom and Equality

In each of his writings on the Chinese in Singapore, Crawfurd maintained that the Chinese made good settlers in British colonies because 'in the British possessions the Chinese are on a footing of equality with all other British subjects'.[36] In 1820, before he became the Resident of Singapore, Crawfurd wrote his *History of the Indian Archipelago*, where he presented a decisive argument for democracy and universal voting in the Asian colonies. He maintained that anybody who pays taxes should have a representative voice in government. His ideas on democracy were radical and did not exist anywhere in British Empire. In the 1820s, voting in both metropolitan and colonial parliaments was limited only to white, landowning males. Crawfurd's ideas would not be realised until the twentieth century.

As the Resident, Crawfurd's powers were limited. Although he wanted to introduce representative democracy, he did not have the authority to achieve such a radical reform. Despite Crawfurd's ideas being a visionary dream, he tried to create legal equality. Crawfurd's belief in representive government and legal equality for all subjects was a direct reference to the American War of Independence, mirroring the American claim of no tax without representation, but also his own childhood in Islay. He believed that colonies needed political freedom and that political representation should be spread as evenly as possible.

Freedom and equality were central to Crawfurd's and many of his contemporaries' ideas of Singapore as an example of the virtues of free trade. As Mary Quilty has argued, Crawfurd and his contemporaries deliberately blurred the distinction between freedom of trade with other ideas of freedom.[37] The eighteenth-century philosopher and economist Adam Smith used the term 'free trade' to mean trade unencumbered by government monopolies and taxation. Many of the British country traders that plied the South-East Asian trade route also called themselves 'free traders'.[38] In this sense, the term 'free traders' distinguished a body of merchant men who were independent and distinct from the East India Company.[39] They were free in the sense that they worked outside the constraints of monopoly. Free trade could also mean free trade in labour. Raffles, Crawfurd and other historian-administrators identified a continuation between free trade in goods and free trade in labour.[40] Slavery for them was an anathema. Both Raffles and Crawfurd wanted to identity the successes of Singapore with free labour and, in doing so, they connected free trade to ideas of individual freedom.

As a new colony, immigration was essential. The principal migrants were from China, India and the local Malay states. However, Crawfurd wanted to create the multi-racial society based on the colonisation principle that he outlined in 1820. The East India Company had always restricted British emigration to India, believing that widespread British migration would destabilise the colonial regime. Crawfurd objected to this argument. He wanted widespread European migration into the Asian colonies: 'no license was demanded, and they were permitted to own property in the land, upon terms as liberal and easy as can be supported in any new settled country'.[41]

Free trade in Singapore also meant freedom from taxation. Singapore was a free port, and this meant taxes were minimal. In Java, where the economy was based on agriculture, Raffles and Crawfurd had argued over how to raise taxes to support the cost of colonial government. They both argued that a land rent was the best mechanism. In comparison, in Singapore, there was no agriculture to tax and the economy was based on trading transactions. Believing it was an anathema to tax trade, Raffles and Crawfurd made Singapore an economic burden on India, with the colony not raising enough tax revenue to support its own administration. Crawfurd even cut taxes on trade further. Raffles had left Singapore with port charges as a government service and monopoly. Crawfurd wrote with pride that 'the wooding, watering, and ballasting of ships was thrown open to general competition, and no fee or charge of any sort whatsoever was levied either on account of the Government or its officers'.[42] As a consequence of the market-based reforms, Crawfurd saw competition reduce the prices far below the recommended maximum guidelines. Crawfurd also abolished the customs-house inspections of importations and exportations, replacing it with an honest system of reporting. He reasoned that with no taxes 'there were few motives for concealment'.[43]

The problem for Crawfurd was that in cutting government revenue on trade, he created an environment whereby the government had very little choice for raising public revenues. Therefore, Crawfurd created a colony where the revenues of the East India Company subsidised the tax-free growth of the Singapore economy. After Crawfurd retired as Resident of Singapore in 1826, the East India Company tried to make Singapore pay its own costs of administration, with the Company trying to levy a 2.5 percent duty on goods transiting between warehouses in Penang, Singapore and Malacca. The initiative was blocked by the House of Lords.[44] In 1828, Crawfurd resigned from the East India Company and took up the position as commercial agent for the Merchants of Calcutta (India) on a salary of £1,500 per annum, with the purpose of lobbying to oppose tax rises on Country Traders, who were merchants independent of the East India Company.[45] The Singapore merchants also continued to use Crawfurd's services as a lobbyist against tax rises throughout the 1830s.[46] Therefore, Crawfurd helped and continued to sponsor a belief that freedom of trade meant freedom from taxation.

Despite his reluctance to support taxation on trade, Crawfurd did consider how taxation could be used to support a belief of individual freedom within Singapore. Crawfurd turned to vices—opium and gambling—for the answer. Opium and gambling were government monopolies. Opium for sale and consumption in Singapore was limited to a government farm, and gambling was licensed and regulated by the police. Crawfurd chose opium and gambling as sources of revenue because they were morally questionable. In the 1820s, there were calls to make the sale of opium illegal and some colonies had tried to ban gambling. Crawfurd grew up in the town of Bowmore, a whisky-producing town known for its legal and illegal distilleries. In 1795, when he was 12 years old, Britain outlawed the production of whisky due to a shortage of grain. In Bowmore alone, 90 illegal stills were confiscated, but illegal production continued.[47] Whilst he was a doctor in Penang, he also witnessed attempts to outlaw gambling in the colony. But the attempts produced a 'universal corruption', with even European officers taking bribes to look the other way. Therefore, he argued prohibition would merely create corruption and smuggling.[48]

Crawfurd was firmly of the belief that opium was, and should continue to be, a legitimate, tradable commodity. He linked it to the consumption of brandy, wine, whisky and gin, and questioned the evidence that opium was widely abused by consumers.[49] From his experience in Singapore, 'the professed opium smokers, whom I have myself seen, were very few in number'.[50] In a later article, he cited the evidence of Dr Parker from a hospital in Canton, who stated that, out of 14,000 patients he encountered, only 15 'suffering from the excessive use of opium', which Crawfurd argued was 'little more than one in a thousand'. He also believed that moralism over the smoking of opium was racial hypocrisy when alcohol abuse was so common amongst the British, declaring 'could any medical man in England, Scotland, or Ireland, on the same exercise, say as much for the innocency [sic] of whiskey or gin?'[51] For Crawfurd, it was a matter of individual right to intoxicate the body:

> All the races of men, in whatever part of the globe, desire or require some one thing or another productive of intoxication; and whether this be beer, spirits, wine, or opium, seems a matter of taste or indifference. At all events, the affair is one with which the moralist or the legislator has no pretence for interference.[52]

His argument with moralists over opium was also about the principle of equality of individuals. He wanted Singapore to promote legal equality amongst the races. He continually maintained that the Chinese and other races had legal equality within the British Empire with each other and the Europeans. He was also quick to correct his peers on this point. In 1830, a House of Lords committee read Crawfurd a letter written by Raffles arguing that Indians were foreigners and not British. Crawfurd responded that the 'natives of India, are not foreigners, but British subjects'.[53] In his limited capacity, Crawfurd did try to enforce legal equality by introducing mixed juries as an initial attempt to force racial mixing:

> I was anxious to introduce the forms of a jury trial, both in civil and criminal cases; and an attempt was made with this view, which was defeated by the repugnance of the Europeans to sit as jurors with the natives, unless under legal sanction.[54]

Although Crawfurd failed in three years to introduce the racial integration that he wished, he believed the overall benefit of Singapore was that European merchants did deal directly with Chinese and Malays and therefore, a mixed society would hopefully develop.[55] Relating his experience of Singapore to an 1832 Select Committee on the Affairs of the East India Company, Crawfurd declared that all Asian people 'ought to be admitted to every privilege of British-born subjects; every situation ought to be as open to them as to British-born subjects or natives; all classes ought to be put on an equality. Their intelligence is equal to the education they receive'.[56]

Sovereignty and Freedom of Private Property

The main mechanism by which Crawfurd believed equality was enshrined in Singapore was through private property and the ownership of land. By granting property, Crawfurd believed individuals had an incentive to clear, cultivate and improve their land. In doing so, the individuals would add value to the land, and therefore, their attachment to the land would be as much economic as sentimental. This, he believed, would create long-term settlement and integrate the different races.

Crawfurd first published his ideas on the need for private property of land on his return from Java in his 1820 *History of the Indian Archipelago*. He reasoned that 'we have to legislate for Europeans, for Chinese, and for a mixed mass of native inhabitants'. He saw legal equality of the races as necessary, and concluded that 'the Law should make no distinction between them'. The 'first point' to achieve this reality of equality, he believed, was 'to establish a right of private property in the land'.[57] In establishing this right of private property, he believed prior occupation needed to be recognised—as he had experienced in Java—but for all unused lands, the government should auction lands for private ownership: 'The sovereign's right to the soil, with the reservation of a land-tax, should then be sold to the highest bidder'.

The problem Crawfurd faced in Singapore was that the 'sovereign's right to the soil' was not his to sell. As he readily admitted, the 'the island was desert when first occupied by us, and the right of property and sovereignty in it belonged to a native prince'.[58] Raffles and Farquhar had both side-stepped the issue of sovereignty of the island, with the settlement initially founded merely as a trading factory with 'no territorial cession' or 'legal right to legislation', with the only law being the 'Malay code'.[59] Farquhar expanded the colony within the confines of it being a mere trading factory and followed the spirit of the agreement with the Malay rulers.[60] Raffles, however, dismissed Farquhar and began acting as a sovereign ruler.[61] Crawfurd, however, saw the issue of resolving sovereignty as crucial for the development of his ideas of private property.

Singapore was originally part of the Johor-Riau Lingga sultanate, the successor state to the earlier Kingdom of Johor. Sultan Mahmud III of Johor, the last sultan of the Johor-Riau Lingga sultanate, died in 1811, leaving behind two illegitimate sons, Hussein and Abdul Rahman.[62] Mahmud's chief ministers divided the territory, with the Bindhara (or first minister) taking Abdul Rahman to Trengganu, whilst the Temenggong (or chief judge) took Hussein to the island of Riau. The Temenggong was residing on Singapore when Farquhar and Raffles arrived to establish a settlement for the annual payment of $3,000 Spanish dollars to the Temenggong and $5,000 Spanish dollars to Hussein, whom Raffles recognised as the 'His Highness the Sultan Hussein Mahomet Shah Sultan of Johor'.[63]

The treaty did not, however, give sovereignty to the British. It merely gave them the right to build a trading station, and the civil administration needed to be shared.[64] Farquhar abided by the spirit of the treaty and worked with the Malay rules, but Raffles was incensed. In his instructions to Crawfurd, he complained that 'the extraordinary principle assumed by Lieutenant Colonel Farquhar, and maintained by him in opposition to my authority, that the disposal of the land was vested in the native chiefs, that the government of the country was native and the port a native port'.[65] Under this arrangement, the British merely had jurisdiction over Europeans and Indians, whilst the Temenggong and the Sultan had held veto rights on most land sales and exerted authority over the Malays and technically the Chinese as well, although in practice, Chinese were self-governing.[66]

The historiography of the transfer of sovereignty from the Malays to the British has maintained that it was solely a British affair, in which the Malay rulers were victims of the scheming of Raffles and Crawfurd.[67] The dominant version of events holds that after he dismissed Farquhar, Raffles made his first moves to exert real sovereignty over the island, although it was *de facto*, not *dejur*. Raffles had made moves to creating a permanent system of private property in Singapore by making an agreement to buy out the Sultan and the Temenggong's judicial powers and rights to land under the 7 June 'Convention' of 1823 between Raffles Sultan Hussein and the Temenggong, with the mechanics of the 'Convention' being left to Crawfurd to organise.[68] Therefore, Crawfurd's role is minimised, and the transfer of sovereignty becomes an exclusively British-Malay transaction. In these accounts, other sizable interest groups, such as the Chinese and Baba community in Singapore, are totally ignored.

When Crawfurd took control of the island, tensions certainly were running high between Sultan Hussein and the British authorities. The Malay rulers (Sultan Hussein and the Temenggong) continued to exercise their rights as sovereigns in taxing Malays and also charging taxes for the clearing of land for cultivation despite Raffles's June 7 'Convention'. Sultan Hussein and the Temenggong also imprisoned Malays who failed to adhere to their directives. Sultan Hussein more than likely saw the settlement in traditional Malay terms, where he owned all the land and leased it out to different agents. The terms of the treaty supported this understanding. Crawfurd was certainly against this system of South-East Asian land tenure and had listed it as one of the underlining reasons for poverty in South-East Asia.[69]

In his account of the early settlement of Singapore, Abdullah bin Abdul Kadir maintains that Crawfurd tricked the Malay rulers into signing away sovereignty in 1824. Although there is no supporting evidence for Crawfurd's trickery, the account probably reflects the Malay rulers' realisation after signing the treaty, that they were in a much weaker position.[70] Animosity developed into hostility, with what Crawfurd called 'assassinations' within the Malay community, with the culprits claiming immunity because they were under the directive of the Sultan and the Temenggong.[71] The Sultan and Temenggong controlled a large number of armed personnel that would have outnumbered the token Sepoy force that Crawfurd had at his disposal. Crawfurd issued a directive for all Malays to disarm, as they were 'the only armed class of the inhabitants'. Both the Sultan and the Temenggong urged their followers to resist this campaign, with the Sultan telling his followers that if any person 'attempted to do it, he would order him to be krissed on the spot'.[72]

Crawfurd has left us four different account of the events. The first account was derived from his despatches to Bengal in which he presents his actions as being driven by orders from Bengal: 'In obedience to the instructions contained in your despatch . . . I lost no time in opening a negotiation with the Sultan and Tumungong [sic] for the cession of this island'.[73] The second account was published after the event in his journal of and embassy to Siam.[74] The final version of events were accounts he provided to later parliamentary inquires, first in 1831 and then again in 1847.[75]

These accounts differ considerably, In the first account, Crawfurd presented the conflict as a purely British-Malay affair; however, the later accounts provide increasing importance to the role of the Chinese community in demanding action and also supporting Crawfurd in taking a hard line against the Sultan and the Temenggong.

The situation nearly resulted in civil war. The Malay population totalled 4,580 in 1824, although not all of them were followers of the Sultan and the Temenggong, The Malay rulers could guarantee support from a large body of followers, whose previous experience in piracy meant that they were experienced fighters.[76] In comparison, Crawfurd had a mere 100 sepoys to call on. 'The chief Chinese merchants came to me, and told me, that if I had any apprehension at all that the military force was not quite strong enough, they were perfectly ready to come and protect the British settlement, and that they had 2,000 of the best young men at my service'.[77] Presumably, the Chinese had access to weapons for them to suggest this as an option, bringing a lie to Crawfurd's claim that the Malays were the 'only class of inhabitants' with weapons.

Faced with demands from the Chinese community within Singapore for an end to Malay 'assignations' and from Bengal for a full transfer of sovereignty, Crawfurd was confronted by the possibility of having to launch an Anglo-Chinese coup against the Malay rulers. Launching any form of military option would have resulted in wide-scale bloodshed and destruction of the settlement. Faced with this option, Crawfurd chose to use diplomacy in order to gain sovereignty of the island, by offering the Sultan and the Temenggong an annual salary of 24,000 Spanish dollars for the remainder of their lives, rather than destroying the settlement through war. In Crawfurd's words, the standoff ended when the 'Malays quietly and peaceably acquiesced' to the order to disarm.[78]

In his immediate despatches to Bengal, Crawfurd chose not mention how close he came to presiding over a civil war in the settlement. To the East India Company, any war would have appeared as a rebellion and Crawfurd would be held responsible. He only chose to reveal details of the Chinese support after his career in the East India Company had ended. In each instance, he mentioned the Chinese offer of military support so as to demonstrate that the Chinese were loyal settlers in British colonies.

Crawfurd had finally established real British sovereignty within the island and was able to enact his land reforms. The standard form of British land grant in newly settled colonies was a 'Quit-Rent', which was a feudal tenurial system of landholding in grants of land that made landholders tenants of the crown.[79] Land grants in both colonial New South Wales (Australia) and America were conducted through the system of Quit-Rents. These were grants at the discretion of the Governor or the Crown, usually to figures within the colonial establishment. In the case of New South Wales, it was stipulated that officers received them as a bequest on retirement, and other British who were supportive of the government also received lands at the Governor's discretion.[80]

Crawfurd was contemptuous of this system of colonisation. He saw it as being little different from feudal systems of landownership, whereby '[t]he British government had been heretofore in the habit of disposing of colonial lands, pretty much after the fashion in which the Vandals and other barbarians disposed of their conquered territories'.[81] For Crawfurd, the system of land grants resembled the South-East Asian system of landownership, which he detested. He would later write in the *Singapore Free Press*:

> I beg, however, to observe that I wholly object to the principle of letting the land on short leases, or indeed any leases at all, except such as are substantially equivalent to a permanent and perpetual grant to the soil. Except by a private and indefeasible right in the soil, no colony that I am aware of has ever flourished, nor do I think ever can flourish. I object even to a fixed quit-rent, except in town lots, where they are easily determined, and collected, and which has a substantial value, even from the earliest planting of a settlement.[82]

Crawfurd identified this system of free grants as being inherently unequal and unproductive, based on providing land to 'to influential aristocrats, to favourites and to the Church, who like dogs in the manger would neither make the right use of them themselves, nor let the labours do so'.[83] For Crawfurd and other free market economists in the early nineteenth century, the price of land was determined by the amount of labour added to the improvement of the land; as he argued in 1834, land 'acquires value only from the capital that is invested in its improvement'.[84] Crawfurd wanted land to be divided based on equality of opportunity and not as an autocratic grant.

Despite his objection to land grants based on Quit-Rents, Crawfurd proposed a dramatically modified version of this system. Raffles had initially granted tracts of land, similar to other colonial territories. Both Raffles and Crawfurd had tried to auction off territory; however, in Crawfurd's words, 'they turned out [to be] fictitious sales; nobody paid, and we were obliged to cancel them'. Instead, Raffles 'gave away the land' under the condition that recipients 'built a house', believing that was enough to give long-term certainty to investors.[85] The East India Company's Government in Bengal rejected these grants, arguing they 'created a reality in the land, accompanied by all the difficulties of a transfer', and wanted 99-year leases.[86] Hearing this news, Crawfurd organised public support within the colony and lobbied the Government in Bengal to support long-term ownership.[87] Crawfurd modified Raffles's grants making them 999-year leases instead, with a 'inconsiderable' yearly levy.[88] The process of creating private property began before the East India Company gained sovereignty over Singapore. Crawfurd saw 999-year Quit-Rents as a means 'to obviate the many legal difficulties which would arise in a commercial settlement'—the legal difficulty being that he did not have authority to grant private freehold.[89]

Crawfurd saw land as a means of gluing society together. Another reason he reluctantly introduced Quit-Rents over freehold was his desire to create land as Personal Property (which normally refers to Chattels) rather than as Real Property (which is always land) as a means of including as many different cultural groups into this system of landed property:

> This form of grant was adopted in order . . . to make the land a personal instead of a real property, with a view to the accommodation of a very heterogeneous population, the great majority of whom differed wholly from ourselves in the principles of the law of inheritance.[90]

From his concept of inheritance laws, personal property provided greater freedom to be disposed of at the individual's discretion, based on differing cultural norms.[91] He cited 'security of life and property' as his greatest achievement in Singapore. He proudly told an 1847 government enquiry that all people were able to purchase and settle land regardless of their race, and that 'everybody that wanted land bought [it], there was no prohibition'. When the government owned the land, it had no value—as realistically demonstrated by the fact that nobody would buy it. But since the land had 'fallen into the hands of individuals, the land had assumed a totally different character': the land had been developed and Singapore was built.[92] However, this society was based on the acquisition of sovereignty. Although Crawfurd was against widespread colonisation, he advocated absolute colonisation of island colonies as a means of preventing colonial expansion and enabling a society to exist on the negative freedoms of private property.

Crawfurd's Vision of Strategic Policy in South-East Asia

Already stretched across the globe and pursuing a peace dividend of military decommissioning, the British government and the East India Company had little interest in pursuing new colonial targets in Asia. By the mid-1830s, British colonial policy aimed to curtail imperial adventures and the expansion of empire. The island colonies of Penang and Singapore provided clear geographical limits to the expansion of empire in Asia. Consequently, British colonialism in South-East Asia largely followed the lines that Crawfurd had proposed in 1820, with settlement being limited to a few entrepot colonies.

Although Crawfurd's work was scathing of the previous practices of the East India Company, it appeared not to harm his career, which actually flourished. Following his time in Singapore, the Company dispatched him to Burma in 1826 to also conclude a commercial treaty with the Kingdom of Ava.[93] By 1830, Crawfurd had retired from the East India Company and reverted to his criticism of Company policy as part of a campaign to join the Radicals in the House of Commons. He mounted four attempts at winning a seat, all of which failed.[94] A Glasgow voter complained that Crawfurd, although a good writer, 'was unable to speak' and that he was a 'stranger' to the electorate—the 'stranger' theme appeared in each of the four electoral campaigns he attempted.[95] Clearly, Crawfurd's experience in Asia did not interest electors, who were more concerned with local issues, and his radicalism probably also scared many voters. Despite his lack of success, Crawfurd maintained a close friendship with Radicals in parliament and gained a newspaper column in *The Examiner*, in which he promoted commercial interests in South-East Asia, whilst also cautioning against colonial aggrandisement.[96]

Throughout the 1830s and 1840s, Crawfurd was regularly asked to give evidence before committees or advise government on Indian and Asian affairs. In 1830, he maintained that China's dislike of foreign ships and sailors entering their ports should be respected, and that this would not greatly impede access to Chinese markets. The reason he believed the British should respect Chinese policy was that Chinese junks would continue to conduct trade with British settlements regardless of Chinese government policy.[97] In 1832, he wrote a submission arguing for non-intervention in the native states and a reduction of Britain's imperial obligations. He critically cited his own experience in Java, arguing that before he became Resident of Yogyakarta, the 'sultan of Java, had a fertile territory, and about a million and a half of subjects'. Yet, he painted his time as Resident of Yogyakarta as a failure for exercising colonial rule and thereby destroying the country:

we exercised, during our possession of Java, the same kind of interference which we exercise in the administrations of Hydrabad, Oude and Mysore, or the Guicowar . . . After a quarrel with him [the Sultan of Java], which followed almost immediately on the conquest of the island, and which arose out of a desire to throw off the yoke of the European supremacy, which terminated in hostilities, tranquillity was afterwards tolerably maintained during our remaining occupation of the island . . . The same medley, indeed, with the other native princes of Java, had, on previous occasions, produced exactly similar effects.[98]

When it came to states exercising 'independent sovereignty' and in 'the immediate neighbourhood of British dominions', he suggested,

> the less we interfere in their internal affairs the better. Political residents are at present maintained by us, both at Ava and Nepaul [sic], in virtue of treaties with these courts. I confess I am unable to discover any utility in these agencies . . . The presence of a British diplomatic agent . . . seems to me more likely to be the source of irritation than of conciliation . . . The presence of a resident agent is notoriously viewed by the Indian princes as a mark of vassalage or thraldom

Crawfurd's views on the meddling influence of Europeans had changed little since he wrote the *History* in 1820. His experience in Singapore confirmed his earlier opinions. European Residents in Asian states along with treaties between European powers and local rulers all acted as forces pushing colonial expansion. This, he concluded, was not in anybody's best interest. In his submission, he pointed towards trade and revenue decreasing in India and Asia if the British continued to interfere. He argued for a reduced influence and pointed to island colonies like Singapore being the solution in South-East Asia.[99]

Raffles retired in 1824, but lost most of his fortune in a ship fire in Sumatra before departing for England. With little money, he petitioned the Company for a yearly pension of £500. On receiving the petition, the Company's response was to wave any outstanding accusations of mismanagement with the proviso that Raffles pay £22,000 for discrepancies in salary. Discrepancies in salary were common and often waived—but in this instance, the ignominy of a bill for £22,000 was more than likely a rebuke of Raffles's time in Asia.[100]

Raffles left no distinct or lasting vision of colonial policy in South-East Asia. His ideas were opportunistic and focused on grand, sweeping expansions and intervention, rather than limited colonial entrepots. Instead, it was Crawfurd's vision of free trade, limited colonial involvement and cultural integrity of the native nations in Asia that fitted colonial policy following 1815, which was decidedly against imperialism.[101] The disgraced Raffles died in 1826, whilst Crawfurd was in Burma negotiating a trade treaty with the Kingdom of Ava. At the time of Raffles's death, Crawfurd was widely regarded as the primary expert on South-East Asia.

Although Raffles's and Crawfurd's careers as colonial administrators were over by the late 1820s, they left two distinct ideas about colonialism in South-East Asia. It was Crawfurd and not Raffles who consistently argued for limited colonial engagement, in which Britain took control of small islands and promoted them as trading ports. Raffles's approach, on the other hand, was bold and romantic and advocated intervention into large swathes of the archipelago to civilise the people.

The battle of ideas between Raffles and Crawfurd did not end with Raffles's death. Raffles's romantic ideas of promoting civilisation by controlling large swathes of colonial territory appealed to future generations of historian-administrators. This next generation looked to justify colonialism as a British national duty to civilise the native.

Notes

1 Hannigan, *Raffles and the British Invasion of Java*, pp. 255–258; Wurtzburg and Witting, *Raffles of the Eastern Isles*, pp. 327–331.
2 John Crawfurd also purchased four lots of land in Singapore. John Crawfurd, 'Notes on Port Essington in Colonial Land and Emigration Commission'. In Anonymous, 'Colonial Land and Emigration Commission: General Report of the Colonial Land and Emigration Commissioners', *HOUSE OF COMMONS PAPERS; REPORTS OF COMMISSIONERS*, (1843), pp. 40–44. John Crawfurd, 'Land Regulations', *The Singapore Free Press and Mercantile Advertiser*, (11 October, 1838). Leong Foke Meng 'Earl Land Transactions in Singapore: The Real Estates of William Farquhar (1774–1839), John Crawfurd (1783–1868), and their Families' *Journal of the Malysian Brach of the Royal Asiatic Society*, 77 1 (2004).
3 Raffles, *Memoir of the Life and Public Services of Sir Thomas Stamford Raffles*, vol. 1, p. 293.
4 Hannigan, *Raffles and the British Invasion of Java*; John Bastin, *Raffles and Hastings: Private Exchanges behind the Founding of Singapore*, (Singapore: Marshall Cavendish Editions, 2014).
5 Bastin, *Raffles and Hastings*, p. 19.
6 Ibid. p. 24.
7 Cited in Ibid.
8 Cited in Ibid. p. 27.
9 Crawfurd*, 'A Vist to the Indian Archipelago in H.M.S. Maeander, with Portions of the Private Journal of Sir James Brooke, K.C.B. By Captain the Hon. Henry Keppel, R.N. Two Vols. Bentley', (19 February, 1853).
10 Hannigan, *Raffles and the British Invasion of Java*, p. 341.
11 Nadia Wright, 'Image is All: Lt-Colonel William Farquhar, Sir Stamford Raffles, and the Founding and Early Development of Colonial Singapore', (Australia: University of Melbourne, 2012).
12 William Farquhar, 'Memorial of Lt. Col. Farquar'; Java, *East India Company*, British Library, MS 542 (1824); Wright, 'Image is All: Lt-Colonel William Farquhar, Sir Stamford Raffles, and the Founding and Early Development of Colonial Singapore'.
13 John Crawfurd, *Journal of an Embassy to the Courts of Siam and Cochin China* and Thomas Lord Wallace,, 'First Report from the Select Committee on the Affairs of the East India Company (China trade.)', *HOUSE OF COMMONS PAPERS; REPORTS OF COMMITTEES*, (1830), p. 308.
14 John Crawfurd, *Journal of an Embassy to the Courts of Siam and Cochin China*, (New Gupta Colony: Isha Boks, 2013 [1830]), vol. 1, p. 56.
15 Ibid., vol. 2, p. 328.
16 Wright, 'Image is All: Lt-Colonel William Farquhar, Sir Stamford Raffles, and the Founding and Early Development of Colonial Singapore'.
17 Crawfurd, *Journal of an Embassy to the Courts of Siam and Cochin China*, vol. 2, p. 381.
18 Crawfurd, *Descriptive Dictionary*, p. 96.
19 Crawfurd, *HIA.*, vol. 1, pp. 135–136.
20 Crawfurd, *Descriptive Dictionary*, p. 96.
21 John Crawfurd*, 'The Opium Debate', *The Examiner*, (15 April, 1843).

22 Crawfurd, *Journal of an Embassy to the Courts of Siam and Cochin China*, vol. 1, p. 75.
23 For example, in his *Descriptive History*, which is the second edition of the HIA, Crawfurd did not reprint the description he wrote in 1820.
24 Wallace, 'First Report from the Select Committee on the Affairs of the East India Company (China Trade.)', p. 296.
25 H. Murray and others, *An Historical and Descriptive Account of China: Its Ancient and Modern History, Language, Literature, Religion, Government, Industry, Manners, and Social State; Intercourse with Europe from the Earliest Ages; Missions and Embassies to the Imperial Court; British and Foreign Commerce; Directions to Navigators; State of Mathematics and Astronomy; Survey of Its Geography, Geology, Botany, and Zoology*, (Edinburgh: Oliver & Boyd, 1836), vol. 3, p. 51. Crawfurd, however, distanced himself from this publication. At a meeting of the Royal Geographical Society, he 'protested against being held responsible for the opinions that have been attributed to him. He said the book that had been published in his name had been written by a clerk of his named Peter Gordon, who had used his name without any authority'. Anonymous, 'Royal Geographical Society', *The Examiner*, (15 December, 1860). Despite Crawfurd's reluctance to acknowledge inaccuracies with the text, the majority of the chapter on commerce in volume three that is attributed to him, and Peter Gordon is consistent with Crawfurd's use of language and ideas.
26 John Crawfurd*, 'Chinese Settlers', Ibid. (29 October, 1859).
27 Crawfurd, *Journal of an Embassy to the Courts of Siam and Cochin China*, vol. 2, p. 382.
28 Ibid., vol. 2, p. 384. See Quilty, 'British Economic Thought and Colonization in Southeast Asia, 1776–1850', p. 88. On the hierarchical racial economy of nineteenth-century Singapore.
29 Wallace, 'First Report from the Select Committee on the Affairs of the East India Company (China Trade.)', p. 297.
30 John Crawfurd*, 'New South Australian Colony', *The Westminster Review*, 21 42 (1834), p. 448.
31 Crawfurd*, 'Chinese Settlers', (29 October, 1859).
32 Wallace, 'First Report from the Select Committee on the Affairs of the East India Company (China Trade.)', p. 297.
33 Ibid. p. 298.
34 Crawfurd, *Descriptive Dictionary*, p. 96.
35 Crawfurd*, 'Chinese Settlers', (29 October, 1859).
36 Crawfurd, *Descriptive Dictionary*, pp. 97–98.
37 Quilty, 'British Economic Thought and Colonization in Southeat Asia, 1776–1850', p. 88.
38 Fitzmaurice, *Trade with the East Indies and China—Select Committee of the House of Lords*, p. 17.
39 Quilty, 'British Economic Thought and Colonization in Southeat Asia, 1776–1850', p. 88.
40 Ibid. pp. 97, 121–123.
41 Crawfurd, *Journal of an Embassy to the Courts of Siam and Cochin China*, vol. 2, p. 383.
42 Ibid., vol. 2, p. 376.
43 Ibid., vol. 2, p. 377.
44 Wong Lin Ken, 'The Trade of Singapore, 1819–69', *Journal of the Malaysian Branch of the Royal Asiatic Society*, 33 4 (1960), p. 172.
45 Wallace, 'First Report from the Select Committee on the Affairs of the East India Company (China trade.)', p. 533; Anonymous, 'The Stamp Tax', *The Asiatic Journal and Monthly Miscellany*, (27 May, 1829).

46 Anonymous, 'Singapore', *Singapore Chronicle and Commercial Register*, (9 January, 1836).

47 Jupp, *The History of Islay, from Earliest Times to 1848*, p. 166.

48 '[E]very man of the smallest financial experience must be satisfied, at once, that the suppression of the opium trade is impossible as long as the taste for it is general and intense over a population of 370 millions that can afford to pay for the drug,—as long as all India, all Persia, all Arabia, all Syria, all Asia Minor, to say nothing of a great part of America, can produce white poppies,—as long as there is an undefended coast of 2,000 miles by which to pour it in,—as long as numerous, active, and determined smugglers, native and foreign, exist for its dissemination; and as long as great profits and small risks tempt to the undertaking'. Crawfurd*, 'The Opium Debate', (15 April, 1843).

49 Crawfurd, *Journal of an Embassy to the Courts of Siam and Cochin China*; Crawfurd*, 'The Opium Debate', (15 April, 1843); Anonymous, 'Leeds Philosphical & Literary Society Lectures by Mr. J. Crawfurd, F.R.S.', *The Leeds Mercury*, (18 November, 1858).

50 Crawfurd, *Journal of an Embassy to the Courts of Siam and Cochin China*, vol. 2, p. 398.

51 Crawfurd*, 'The Opium Debate', (15 April, 1843).

52 Crawfurd, *Journal of an Embassy to the Courts of Siam and Cochin China*, vol. 2, p. 398.

53 Wallace, 'First Report from the Select Committee on the Affairs of the East India Company. (China Trade.)', p. 353.

54 Crawfurd, *Journal of an Embassy to the Courts of Siam and Cochin China*, vol. 2, p. 390.

55 Ibid., vol. 1, p. 361.

56 Hyde Villiers, 'Report from the Select Committee on the Affairs of the East India Company; with Minutes of Evidence in Six Parts, and an Appendix and Index to Each', *HOUSE OF COMMONS PAPERS; REPORTS OF COMMITTEES*, (1831), p. 316.

57 Crawfurd, *HIA.*, vol. 3, p. 63.

58 In the early nineteenth century, people used the word 'desert' to mean deserted.

59 John Crawfurd, *Journal of an Embassy from the Governor-General of India to the Court of Ava in the Year 1827*, (London: Henry Colburn, 1829), vol. 2, p. 402.

60 C.H. Wake, 'Raffles and the Rajas: The Founding of Singapore in Malayan and British Colonial History', *Journal of the Malaysian Branch of the Royal Asiatic Society*, 48 1 (1975).

61 C.M. Turnbull, *A History of Modern Singapore, 1819–2005*, (Singapore: NUS Press, 2009), pp. 39–40; Wake, 'Raffles and the Rajahs: The Founding of Singapore in Malayan and British Colonial History', p. 62.

62 Abdullah bin Abdul Kadir, *The Hikayat Abdullah: An Annotated Translation by A.H. Hill*, (Kuala Lumpur; Singapore: Oxford University Press, 1970), p. 141; B.W. Andaya and L.Y. Andaya, *A History of Malaysia*, (Basingstoke: Palgrave, 2001).

63 Turnbull, *A History of Modern Singapore, 1819–2005*, p. 29.

64 Wake, 'Raffles and the Rajas: The Founding of Singapore in Malayan and British Colonial History'.

65 Thomas Stamford Raffles, 'Arrangements with the Sultan and Toomoongong', 7 June, 1823, in *'Singapore Notices' Journal of the Indian Archipelago*, ed. by J.R. Logan, (Singapore: 1853), p. 344.

66 Kadir, *Hikayat Abdullah*, p. 158. 'The Chinese and Malays under the Control of the Sultan'. However, Turnbull, in *A History of Modern Singapore, 1819–2005*, wrote, 'Other Asians were put under the jurisdiction of their own *kapitan*, who

would keep the peace and settle disputes among their own community' and Far-quhar held court one a week in conjunction with the Sultan and Temenggong.

67 For example, see Kadir, *Hikayat Abdullah*; Anonymous, 'The Sultan of Johore', *Journal of the Indian Archipelago and Eastern Seas (New Series)*, 2 (1858); Charles Burton Buckley, *An Anecdotal History of Old Times in Singapore*, (Singapore: Malaya University Press, 1965 [1902]); Wurtzburg and Witting, *Raffles of the Eastern Isles*; Wake, 'Raffles and the Rajas: The Founding of Singapore in Malayan and British Colonial History'; Turnbull, *A History of Modern Singapore, 1819–2005*.

68 Turnbull, *A History of Modern Singapore, 1819–2005*, p. 39; Wake, 'Raffles and the Rajas: The Founding of Singapore in Malayan and British Colonial History'.

69 Crawfurd, *HIA.*, vol. 3, p. 63.

70 Kadir, *Hikayat Abdullah*, pp. 218–230.

71 The date of this hostilities varies in Crawfurd's accounts. In his account published in 1828, he stated that hostility developed in 1825. Crawfurd, *Embassy to Siam*, vol. 2, p. 392. Villiers, 'Report from the Select Committee on the Affairs of the East India Company, Appendix No. 8', p. 99. However, when giving evidence before a select committee in 1847, he recounted that the tension was a product of the treaty negotiations and was at the same time. Dudley and E. Harrowby Ryder, 'Report from the Select Committee on Commercial Relations with China; together with the minutes of evidence, appendix, and index', Ibid., (1847), p. 194.

72 Buckley, *An Anecdotal History of Old Times in Singapore*, p. 156.

73 John Crawfurd, 'Letter to G. Winton, Secretary to the Government, 3 August, 1824', in *'Singapore Notices' Journal of the Indian Archipelago*, ed. by J.R. Logan (Singapore: 1853), p. 350.

74 Villiers, 'Report from the Select Committee on the Affairs of the East India Company, Appendix No. 8', p. 99.

75 Dudley nd E. Harrowby Ryder, 'Report from the Select Committee on Commercial Relations with China; Together with the Minutes of Evidence, Appendix, and Index', Ibid., (1847), p. 194.

76 Wake, 'Raffles and the Rajas: The Founding of Singapore in Malayan and British Colonial History'.

77 Dudley and E. Harrowby Ryder, 'Report from the Select Committee on Commercial Relations with China; Together with the Minutes of Evidence, Appendix, and Index', Ibid., (1847), p. 194.

78 Crawfurd, *Embassy to Siam*, vol. 2, p. 392.

79 Enid Campbell, 'The Quit Rent System in Colonial New South Wales', *Monash University Law Review*, 35 4 (2009).

80 'Phillip's Instructions re Land Grants', (22 August, 1789), Frederick Watson, 'Historical Records of Australia', (Sydney: The Library Committee of the Commonwealth Parliament, 1914–1926), vol. 1, pp. 124–128.

81 Crawfurd*, 'New South Australian Colony', p. 450.

82 Crawfurd, 'Land Regulations', (11 October, 1838).

83 Crawfurd*, 'New South Australian Colony', p. 450.

84 Ibid.

85 Ryder, 'Report from the Select Committee on Commercial Relations with China', p. 193.

86 Ibid.

87 Crawfurd, 'Land Regulations', (11 October, 1838).

88 Crawfurd, *Embassy to Ava*, vol. 2, p. 395.

89 Ibid., vol. 2, pp. 395–396.

90 This was an important consideration in his mind, which he continue to reiterate to over the next 30 years. Crawfurd, 'Land Regulations', (11 October, 1838).

91 Crawfurd, *Embassy to Ava*, vol. 2, p. 396. Crawfurd, 'Land Regulations', (11 October, 1838); Crawfurd, *Descriptive Dictionary*, p. 429.

92 Ryder, 'Report from the Select Committee on Commercial Relations with China', p. 193.

93 Crawfurd, *Embassy to Ava*.

94 Glasgow in 1832, Paisley in 1834, Stirling Burghs in 1835, and Preston in 1837.

95 William Cobbett, 'Glasgow Election', *Cobbett's Weekly Political Register*, (27 October, 1832); Thomas Smith, 'To the Radical Reformers of Preston', *Preston Chronicle*, (24 December, 1836).

96 Murchison, 'Address to the Royal Geographical Society'; Anonymous, 'Mr John Crawfurd', *Examiner*, (16 May, 1868).

97 Wallace, 'First Report from the Select Committee on the Affairs of the East India Company (China Trade.)', p. 301.

98 Hyde Villiers, 'Report from the Select Committee on the Affairs of the East India Company; With Minutes of Evidence in Six Parts, and an Appendix and Index to Each', Ibid., (1831), 'Letter from John Crawfurd, Esq., to Thomas Hyde Villiers, Esq. 24 February, 1832' Appendix No. 8 page 93.

99 Ibid., 'Letter from John Crawfurd, Esq., to Thomas Hyde Villiers, Esq. 24 February, 1832' Appendix No. 8 page 93.

100 Hannigan, *Raffles and the British Invasion of Java*.

101 D.K. Fieldhouse, *The Colonial Empires: A Comparative Survey from the Eighteenth Century*, (London: Macmillan, 1982 [1966]), pp. 242–245.

Figure 1 John Crawfurd by unknown photographer, c. 1860 ©National Portrait Gallery, London

The large Temple at Brambanan

Figure 2 'The large temple at Brambánan', Thomas Stamford Raffles, *History of Java* (London : Black, Parbury, and Allen : and John Murray, 1817) Vol. 2, p. 18. Note that Raffles's image of the temple at Brambánan is indicative of his argument that Java originated as a Hindu colony. The architectural grandeur was a statement of Indian civilisation, and all achievements towards civilisation in Java were therefore a consequence of foreign colonisers. The decay of the temple in the modern era also represented the decay of civilisation in Java and was a subtle message to Raffles's readers that Java need a new colonising force from British India.

Figure 3 'A Family in Dusk Bay, New Zealand', drawn by William Hodges from George W. Anderson, *A New, Authentic and Complete Account of Voyages Round the World, Undertaken and Performed by Royal Authority. Containing an Authentic, Entertaining, Full and Complete History of Captain Cook's First, Second, Third & Last Voyages* (London: Printed for the proprietors, and published by Alex. Hogg, 1784). Note the detail in the material culture and the fauna. In comparison, the people have a very European complexion.

A MAGINDANO MARRIAGE.

Figure 4 'A Magindano Marriage', Thomas Forrest, *Voyage to New Guinea and the Moluccas* (London : G. Scott, 1779). Note the Grecian appearance of the subjects and the material culture in the background.

Figure 5 'A Javanese Ronggeng' ©The Trustees of the British Museum. Anthony Forge has identified this image as the original source illustration used in the production of 'A Ronggeng or Dancing Girl' in Raffles's *History of Java*. See Figure 7.

Figure 6 'A Ronggeng or Dancing Girl' in Thomas Stamford Raffles, *History of Java* (London : Black, Parbury, and Allen : and John Murray, 1817) Vol. 1, p. 342. Compare with Figure 6.

Figure 7 'A Malay, native of Bencoolen' from William Marsden, *History of Sumatra* (London : The Author, 1810–1811), p. 44. This is the only ethnographic image of a person in Marsden's history. It is one of the first racial images in South-East Asia published in English.

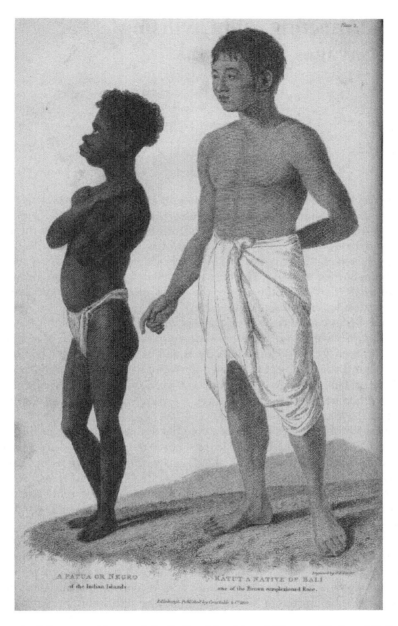

Figure 8 'A Papua or Negro of the Indian Islands' and 'Kutut a Native of Bali one of the Brown complexioned Race', John Crawfurd, *History of the Indian Archipelago*, 1820, p. 17. Crawfurd used these images to illustrate the 'two aboriginal races of human beings inhabiting the Indian islands'. The Image of the Papuan was a reproduction of Dick from Thomas Stamford Raffles's *History of Java*.

6 Protecting and Civilising Savages in Sarawak

Previous chapters of this book have sought to delineate a history of ideas in British understandings of South-East Asia. Colonial practices in Java, Penang and Singapore were largely by formed the substance of these historical debates of the late eighteenth and early nineteenth centuries. By the 1840s, however, the activities of James Brooke and his Royal Navy allies in northern Borneo caused a reprise to the debates between John Crawfurd, Stamford Raffles and others over the ethics of colonisation and imperial intervention in South-East Asia.

James Brooke went to South-East Asia with the intent to establish himself as a man of science, but by responding and taking advantage of a series of opportunities, he found himself as the Rajah of Sarawak, the only independent white British subject that ruled an Asian kingdom as an independent sovereign. His activities made him a Victorian-era celebrity and consequently, he became the subject of a vast volume of writing that Crawfurd labelled the 'Sarawak historians'.[1]

Despite Brooke's importance as a colonial figure and being a prolific journal and letter writer, he did not leave a consistent body of ideas. His journals were later published as embedded texts within the journals of Captains Henry Keppel (1846) and Rodney Mundy (1848) and in 1853, Brooke's letters were edited and published by John Templer. A careful reading of Brooke's journals and letters suggests that Brooke could radically change his opinions on the politics of Borneo from day to day.[2]

Although Brooke presented a personal inconsistency in his ideas, his apologist followers did present Brooke's achievements as a body of ideas that corresponded to a second wave of historical debates. Brooke's supporters argued that Brooke's rule was consistent with a desire to civilise the savages, end piracy and advance commerce in South-East Asia. The influential journalist James Augustus St. John argued that 'to extirpate piracy from the eastern seas is Mr. Brooke's principle object' and that pirates 'impeded the progress of trade', thereby preventing the commerce 'destined to carry the comforts and luxuries of civilization into the homes of the wild inhabitants of those vast but unconnected chains of islands'.[3] St. John simplistically saw Brooke's campaign as the advancement of civilisation through commerce and the suppression of piracy.

St. John's argument connected Brooke's project in Borneo to the civilising of the savage and historical debates over the ethics of colonialism that Raffles and Crawfurd debated. Much of Brooke's support in British government circles and among the public was based on the premise that he was suppressing piracy and advancing British colonial interests. Therefore, although Brooke did not engage debates directly, his empire in Sarawak was the subject of a new wave of debates.

Like the historian-administrators, Brooke did lambast colonial policies in South-East Asia for not being concerned enough with aborigines. Before he ventured to Sarawak in 1839, Brooke argued that British colonialism had been neglectful in failing to help or civilise the savages. This was different from the arguments Crawfurd made. Crawfurd had argued that British policies had destroyed indigenous society and therefore, the best policy was minimalist intervention to cause the least amount of harm to all concerned. In comparison, Brooke always proposed a more interventionist approach suggesting a colonialism that aligned with Raffles's ideas rather than Crawfurd's.

In comparison to Crawfurd, Brooke and his followers argued that Britain had a duty to protect and civilise people. Raffles had promoted the idea of protection, but Brooke developed it even further. Brooke and his apologist supporters capitalised on the romantic idea of empire that Raffles had propagated. In his writings, Brooke presented the colonisation of Sarawak in Borneo as a historical culmination of the protection of the natives that Raffles had advocated, whilst Brooke's supporters portrayed Brooke as a new Raffles.

Brooke's time as an empire builder coincided with the rise of the evangelical humanitarian movement in Britain that was meant to prevent imperial expansion. Brooke's ideas appeared tailored to fit this new era. He argued that colonialism needed to support the 'self-government' of aboriginal people.[4] In establishing a regime in Sarawak, Brooke used the humanitarian idealism of the 1830s and 1840s to legitimise his rule through civilisation. His colonising logic appealed to a universal idea of history, in which a British barbarian past legitimised the forceful introduction of civilisation amongst savages.

James Brooke and the Lure of Sarawak

Raffles's and Crawfurd's writings sponsored a desire for people to explore South-East Asia. In an attempt to redeem her husband's reputation and probably supplement her finances after his death, Sophia Raffles published Stamford Raffles's private letters and manuscripts as an edited memoir in 1830. The two-volume memoir romanticised Raffles's colonial endeavours to dominate South-East Asia. In the memoir, Raffles became the British hero who fought to exclude other European powers, civilise the barbarian Malays and reinvigorate the civilised yet degenerate Javanese.

The memoir brought attention to South-East Asia. In his *Edinburgh Review* of the memoir, Basil Hall lamented that for the general, untravelled public, the affairs of the Orient all appeared rather 'dull'.[5] He saw Raffles's romantic memoir, however, as an opportunity to direct public attention to South-East Asia. He saw it as acting as a conduit, allowing people to attach 'feeling' to the Javanese and Malays of South-East Asia and thereby 'engage our sympathies' and bring 'popularity to the topic' of colonial commitments in South-East Asia. The memoir had moderate success and was republished in 1835. The revised edition was an inspiration to the adventurous James Brooke who—as Rajah of Sarawak—advocated an interventionist colonialism to reform Asian societies.[6]

Raffles's memoir was probably Brooke's first foray into the intellectual literature of South-East Asia.[7] After reading the book, Brooke was enraged by what he saw as a failure of the British Government and the East India Company to support Raffles's colonising endeavours in Java and South-East Asia:

> It was in vain that Sir Stamford Raffles urged on them [the British East India Company] a line of conduct, which, had it been pursued, must eventually have ensured the ascendancy of the British over the space from Borneo to New Holland.[8]

Raffles's approach of introducing order, law, free trade and civil protections to South-East Asian peoples energised Brooke's imagination. The idea of civilising the people of South-East Asia kindled a desire in Brooke to travel to the region and pursue his own intellectual and possibly colonial endeavours.[9]

Before leaving Britain, Brooke wrote an essay on his goals and a critique of British imperial goals in South-East Asia for the *Geographical Society*. The unpublished draft essay was a call to arms for the British reoccupation of South-East Asia. Brooke condemned the 'vacillation and weakness' of the 1824 treaty, in which the British ceded Java, Sumatra and most of Borneo to the Dutch sphere of influence. Although clear connections existed between the *Geographical Society* and the expansion of the British Empire, Brooke's rampant political claims and even assertions that Britain should use 'hostility to regain what was foolishly thrown away' were too direct for the society and the journal.[10] As editor, Captain John Washington carefully removed all references to political objectives in the published version of Brooke's bellicose essay.[11]

In his biography of Brooke, Spencer St. John wrote favourably of Brooke's research before departing for Asia, but St. John's emphatic assertions actually highlight Brooke's ignorance more than his expertise.[12] Brooke asserted that Java still 'remembers the period of British possession' and blamed the Dutch for the 'internal dissensions' that destroyed Malay governments and gave rise to the petty states 'which thrive on piracy and fatten on the slave trade'.[13] He also pontificated on the trustworthiness and treachery of different nationalities throughout the archipelago. Although he had passion and opinions, his previous expertise did not extend much beyond a stopover in Penang and Singapore on his return to England via China from India. Brooke's embarkation essay was little more than a boldly written literature review consisting substantially of Sophia Raffles's 1835 reprinted memoir of Raffles's letters and George Windsor Earl's 1837 *The Eastern Seas*.[14] He did not refer to the wider publications from the region in his writings until 1841.[15]

Brooke's reliance on the written word was at the expense of practical experience. He did have some experience of Singapore and had previously failed in an attempt to become a trader in South-East Asia. There is little evidence that he sought out Crawfurd and other experts on South-East Asia before travelling there. A few years later, Crawfurd appeared before a select committee into Brooke's actions and expressed surprise that Brooke had never contacted him for advice.[16] Nor did Brooke use the expertise within the Geographical Society. Unlike many papers published by the society, none of Brooke's papers were read at society meetings. In addition, no record exists of the society subjecting Brooke's papers to referee—unlike other, less connected scholar adventurers.[17] Consequently, Brooke's contact with people knowledgeable about South-East Asia was probably minimal.

The actions of the Geographical Society's secretary, John Washington, suggest that he was actively trying to protect Brooke from criticism. To supplement Brooke's minimalist reading, Washington urged Brooke to read George Windsor Earl's writings and even suggested to Earl that he accompany Brooke as a surveyor, an offer Earl declined.[18] Washington published an outline of Brooke's plans in the *Athenaeum* and the Geographical Society's journal, calling him 'a well known member of the Yacht Club' and endorsed his expedition as a 'bold enterprise' to see 'how far individual exertion may be successful'.[19] The irony in Washington's tone suggested he expected to see Brooke return after only a short undertaking.

From his 1839 essay, Brooke was interested in extending the scientific and ethnographic knowledge of South-East Asia to the British public. Brooke planned to visit different islands. He aimed to engage in ethnology by talking to locals (or at least watching them) and recording his observations for science, whilst he would also pursue his interest in natural history by shooting and collecting any interesting creatures he might find and forwarding them back to the Geological Society. At that stage in time, this was not a man intent on empire building, but rather, taking a holiday.

Establishing a Regime in Sarawak

The establishment of Brooke's regime in Sarawak was initially surprising to British readers, but surprise turned to controversy, and the controversy continues with modern historians.[20] In his own account, Brooke maintained that he received the territory of Sarawak as a servant of the Sultan Omar Ali of Brunei, with the aim of pacifying and civilising the region. Joseph Hume, a contemporary critic of Brooke, proposed an alternative understanding a decade later. In Hume's narrative, Brooke was a manipulative opportunist seeking personal gain:

> Sir James Brooke seized the opportunity of the Sultan's distress, to wrest from him a new grant of the territory of Sarawak, absolving himself from the payment of a previously stipulated annual tribute of 2000 dollars.[21]

A later inquiry into Brooke was divided on the matter, with one commissioner maintaining that Brooke was a vessel of a foreign power (namely, the Sultanate of Brunei), whilst the other concluded that Brooke had led a popular revolution in Sarawak and established a new state.[22] Similar to Brooke's own time, many modern historians are either apologists for Brooke or critics who paint him as a manipulative, self-serving individual who aggressively built his private empire.[23]

The interpretation presented in this book is one in which Brooke was certainly eager to give his life purpose through empire building and used British military power to secure his kingdom, but he was one actor amongst many within Brunei and Sarawak. Brooke began his time like a 'babe in the woods', with local Brunei elites or *pangerans* looking to take advantage of him.[24] He was able, however, to transform his situation quickly, learning and adding to Malay structures of power. Behind Brooke's empire-building initiative was the threat, and fact, of superior British naval power.

When he first arrived in Sarawak, Brooke made connections with Pangeran Muda Hassim, Rajah of Sarawak. Brooke's Singapore and London connections had an intrinsic utility for Hassim, providing a new opportunity for Hassim to acquire increased wealth and prestige through trade. Hassim quickly went to work cultivating the naive Brooke, pandering to Brooke's ego, calling him a 'great man' and telling him that Sarawak was 'richer than any other locality along the whole line of coast'.[25] Brooke made clear his interest in natural history, and Hassim gave him the run of his country to visit the indigenous tribes and collect as many birds and animals as he wished.[26] He told Brooke of his dislike of the Dutch and his interest in a defensive alliance with Britain. Such musings stimulated an awareness of the commercial potential of Sarawak.

Up to this point in time, Brooke's life was nothing remarkable. In the 1820s, he served as junior army officer in India. During the second Anglo-Burma War, Brooke was severely wounded and sent back to Britain for recovery in 1825. He returned to India in 1830, but finding that his commission had lapsed, Brooke returned to Britain via Singapore and China. With his military career over, Brooke's future was bleak. Only his father's death saved him from genteel pauperism. In 1835, Brooke went from being an aimless and penniless discharged soldier to become the heir to £30,000 (equivalent to £94 million in 2011) inherited from his father's estate.[27] With this newfound wealth, Brooke decided to give his life greater purpose.

Brooke arrived at Sarawak River in July 1839 as part of his tour of South-East Asia. The Englishman added to the power and prestige of Hassim within Malay political discourse. Brooke's armed yacht provided extra military support to Hassim. The historian John Walker, however, maintains that Brooke also added to Hassim's *semangant*. *Semangat* is an abstract concept of power connected to social relations of dependence and the recognition of an individual as charismatic, or possessing *semangant*.[28] Walker's argument is that as a foreigner with his own warship, Brooke was a source of enhancing Hassim's *semangant*. Hassim must have sensed Brooke's desire for importance and actively ingratiated himself and pandered to Brooke. In a letter written with irony to his mother, Brooke reflected on Hassim's grooming: 'I am really becoming *a great man*, dearest mother; the world talks of me!'[29]

Brooke entered into a complex political environment which connected trade with political power. Prior to being sent to Sarawak, Hassim had acted as Sultan Omar Ali's Prime Minister and was a leading contender for the throne. One view was that the two men had grown distant and Ali had banished Hassim to the Sarawak backwater.[30] Another view of the situation, however, was that Sarawak, with its antimony ore trade, was instrumental for the economic development of Brunei. The second view would mean that Ali was sending his most senior official as a demonstration of how important the Sarawak region was to Brunei.[31] Hassim and Sultan Omar Ali were cousins, having the same paternal grandfather, but Hassim's sister was also Sultan Ali's mother and, therefore, Hassim was Ali's uncle as well as being his cousin.[32]

The Sultan of Brunei controlled Sarawak through the agency of Brunei installed *pengirans*, who in turn relied on the support of local Malay aristocrats. The relationship was one of suzerainty, in which the local Sarawak elites recognised the superiority of the Sultan of Brunei and consequently forwarded tribute to the sultan through his governors in Sarawak. In Sarawak at this time, however, the local elites were exerting their authority and resisting the tribute demands from Brunei. In an attempt to quell local unrest, Sultan Omar Ali dispatched Pengiran Indera Mahkota to Sarawak in 1826. With the support of the neighbouring Sultan of Sambas (who also claimed authority over Sarawak), the local Malay elites rebelled against Mahkota and Brunei's rule.[33]

Ali dispatched the more senior Hassim to Sarawak to resolve a protracted dispute between Mahkota and the Islamic coastal population over Brunei's authority in Sarawak. Brooke described the political environment of Sarawak as one of civil war and rebellion, he was witnessing the natural unstable political system of the region, as local elites extended their autonomy from Brunei.[34] Mahkota wanted to use external military resources to end the rebellion and favoured requesting support from the Dutch backed

Sultan of Sambas. Fearing the implications of Dutch involvement, Ali sent Hassim to end the conflict without using European intervention.[35]

Although derided by Brooke and his cohort of apologists as a weak ruler who pandered to pirates, Sultan Omar Ali showed a consistency in motive. He wanted to resist European involvement in his affairs. In sending Hassim to Sarawak in 1837, and his later resistance to Brooke and British power in Sarawak in the 1840s, Omar Ali was trying to avoid any form of European hegemony in his domain, be it Dutch or British. Despite Ali's desire to end the problem internally, with no extra resources, Hassim appeared to achieve little in Sarawak. He controlled access to the coast and limited the rebels trade with the outside world but failed to quell the rebellion.

Brooke's initial visit in 1839 was innocuous. He was a tourist, and, although he forwarded Hassim's overtures for British support on to the merchants of and government in Singapore, Brooke did not engage in any military action himself at this stage. He did, however, determine that antimony ore was the most valuable export from Sarawak and a potentially lucrative trade.[36] In July 1840, he returned to Sarawak, supposedly for a mere 10-day visit to see his 'friend' Hassim, but the lure of speculation in antimony was also probably strong.[37] According to Brooke, Hassim persuaded him to join forces and win the protracted conflict in Sarawak and ensure 'the independence of Borneo'.[38] Brooke also claimed that Hassim offered him the governorship of Sarawak as a reward. The only surviving original material on Brooke's actions was written (or at least edited and published) after Brooke gained power in Sarawak; therefore, he and his supporters presented Brooke's actions as those of a selfless hero helping a friend.[39] For example, Brooke described his actions in fighting Hassim's battles as being that of an 'Englishman's honour' to a friend—for which he asked nothing in return.[40]

More than likely, Brooke did ask for something in return, and probably proposed that Hassim grant him a licence to trade antimony ore and provide a guaranteed supply of the ore for Brooke to sell in Singapore—this was Hume's and Crawfurd's interpretation of the events.[41] Monopoly deals were a common part of South-East Asian trade. The Dutch had used these deals to gain control of Java in the seventeenth century, and Hassim would have been aware that any monopoly deal with Brooke would impede the independence of Brunei and therefore was probably against Sultan Ali's wishes.

After defeating the rebels in 1842, Brooke returned to Singapore and purchased trade goods that he could then sell to Hassim.[42] When he arrived at Sarawak, Brooke gave the goods to Hassim, but there was no stockpile of antimony waiting for Brooke in return. There are two possibilities for Hassim's actions: one, that Hassim could not gain the quantity of antimony that Brooke requested, or two, that Hassim was attempting to get out of the arrangement and not be beholden to this Englishman. Possibly both reasons were at play at the same time. For whatever reason, Hassim could not, or chose not, to deliver on his commitment to Brooke.

A standoff developed. Brooke resided in his warship whilst Hassim and Mahkota stayed in their compounds. Brooke made connections with Dayak tribes in the interior, and powerful local Malay elites increasingly allied themselves to Brooke. Ostensibly, Hassim and Mahkota allowed a Dayak raiding fleet upriver to attack the peoples Brooke had just visited and also attempted to poison Brooke's interpreter.

Believing that Hassim was probably going to dishonour their deal, Brooke threatened to use his private warship, the Royalist, to attack Hassim's compound and create a new civil war unless Hassim delivered on his end of the bargain economically and also politically by stopping the Dayak raids upriver.[43] With the support of over 200 Malays, Brooke marched on Hassim's compound. Faced with open revolt, Hassim's response was to offer Brooke the title to his kingdom and make Brooke the Rajah of Sarawak. In confidential letters, Crawfurd narrated the events by painting Brooke as a fool who was fleeced by locals:

> There he sold his cargo to the native chief, but he the native chief being like all the rest a laggard, Mr Brooke would never get payment. The payment, at last was a line on the territory, informed eventually, the sovereign the Sultan of Borneo, also a laggard and pirate.[44]

Brooke was now the ruler of Sarawak and a vassal of the Brunei court. He was in a precarious position. He had little local reliable military support and needed the support of local nobles. Therefore, Brooke looked to draw strength from the British Empire. In his early days of rule in Sarawak, Brooke used the arrival of the East India Steamship *Diana*, which was merely there in Borneo to report to the Singapore authorities, but Brooke presented the ship to the Malays as a symbol of British support for his activities. This action was a deliberate misrepresentation of the *Diana's* mission by Brooke to the Brunei elite, but it served his goal.[45] Brooke needed military support if he wanted to solidify his position and change the dynamics of politics in Sarawak and Brunei.

His greatest threat was the Sekrang and Saribas Ibans or Sea Dayaks, as they were known at the time. In 1843, Brooke had some success convincing the Governor of Singapore, Samuel George Bonham, to give support for anti-piracy measures, but it was Brooke's meeting with Captain Henry Keppel in Penang that gave him the military power he needed. Keppel agreed to venture to Sarawak in a campaign against the Sekrang and Saribas Dayaks, concluding it was an extension of his naval duty in suppressing piracy.[46] Keppel's ship, the *Dido*, was armed with eighteen 32-pounder cannons and was the largest warship that had visited the area.[47] The two men agreed to attack the villages and bases of the Saribas who lived on the Saribas River and were estimated to be the strongest source of resistance. Brooke had to delay his plans to attack on the Sekrang until 1844 because Keppel received orders to proceed to China. In 1844, Keppel returned to Sarawak and they jointly attacked Sekrang using the same methods as they did against the Saribas. The raid resulted in the burning of 5,000 Sekrang homes, five forts and hundreds of boats.[48] Crawfurd in his summary of these 1843–44 raids gave his approval, but suggested further measures should not be necessary, concluding in his *Examiner* newspaper column:

> But the snake is now more than scotched, though perhaps not thoroughly killed; and there is at any rate no reason to apprehend future serious disturbance from that quarter, to the schemes of commercial enterprise and national improvement for which these two gallant and enterprising Englishmen have so efficiently prepared the way.[49]

After 1845, Brooke became both the Governor of Labuan and the consul to Brunei. With these positions, he had real support from the British government. Brooke was also charged with the duty of furthering British policy in Borneo, but he maintained his private empire of Sarawak as a separate concern. With official sanction as Governor of Labuan, he could use British military power to support his own interests. The fact that Brooke had the power to call on British support meant that local elites were naturally cautious in resisting Brooke's designs.

Colonialism and the Humanitarianism of 1830s

A key aspect of James Brooke's appeal for British government support in Sarawak was his appeal for the protection of aborigines. In 1846, Captain Henry Keppel published parts of Brooke's diary, in which Brooke presented his actions as part of a great humanitarian cause:

> To assist is a duty; but in the performance of this duty, to be gentle and feeling is godlike; and probably, between individuals, there is no greater distinction than in this tender sympathy towards distress. Poor, poor Dayaks! Exposed to starvation, slavery, death! You may well raise the warmest feelings of compassion—enthusiasm awakes at witnessing your sufferings! To save men from death has its merit; but to alleviate suffering, to ameliorate all the ills of slavery, to protect these tribes from pillage and yearly scarcity, is far nobler.[50]

Brooke maintained a similar line in his private correspondence with the British government, declaring that his rule was to support the 'freedom of the aboriginal inhabitants form the oppressions . . . exercised on them by the Malay Race'.[51]

Brooke presented his regime as nobly protecting the suffering and helpless savages who were almost infantile. The focus on aborigines marked a fundamental shift in thinking about humanitarian protection in South-East Asia. Twenty years earlier, Raffles had made a humanitarian appeal for

British public support in Java and to a lesser extent Sumatra; however, that was for the support of semi-civilised or civilised peoples. Brooke's appeal to protecting aborigines focused on savages, who had not ventured down the path of civilisation. Brooke presented the aborigines as children needing disciplining or protecting.

Later critics, connected to the Aboriginal Protection Society and the Radicals in parliament, argued that Brooke's humanitarian statements were merely self-serving attempts to present his private empire building as constituting a noble cause.[52] Critics wanted to depict Brooke as an insincere opportunist who used the language of aboriginal protection to facilitate his personal ego and empire. This criticism, that Brooke was disingenuous, recognises an ominous development in Brooke's claims—he was using protection to legitimise exploitation.

The appeal for British protective humanitarianism began before Brooke even ventured to South-East Asia. In his 1839 essay on the objectives of colonisation in South-East Asia, Brooke argued that the purpose of colonisation should be the 'development of native resources' and should acknowledge the 'indefeasible rights of the Aborigines'.[53] He committed himself to 'conciliate the good opinion' of the 'aboriginal inhabitants' and to discover their racial origins.[54] These activities promised not only to promote British interests in South-East Asia but also to uphold the new humanitarian purpose of imperialism that had gained currency during the 1830s.

Brooke's focus on protecting aborigines was a development on the deep-rooted historical legitimisations of colonialism in South-East Asia. As this book has demonstrated, the idea of reforming natives by advancing them up the stage of civilisation, was a continual theme in late eighteenth- and early nineteenth-century British colonial thought in South-East Asia. Although Raffles popularised some of these beliefs, we could equally list George Forrest or Francis Light from the eighteenth century as proposing the use of colonises to reform the peoples of South-East Asia.[55] Higher authorities in British India and London usually dismissed these ideas of civilising reform—favouring instead limiting colonial expenditure, balancing payments and extracting as much revenue as possible.

These sentiments of colonial protection appealed to a British sense of nationalism, with British citizens believing their colonialism was better than that of other European countries because it protected rather than harmed the subjected peoples. The existence of protected aborigines legitimated British imperialism to conscientious British citizens. Brooke's own writing and those of his apologist followers unashamedly appealed to this historical mandate of Britain civilising and protecting the peoples of South-East Asia. Crawfurd was scornful of their attempts and commented to Richard Cobden that Brooke's empire building pandered to

> one of John Bull's temporary paroxysms of monomania, a kind of hallu-
> cination [to] which he is institutionally addicted, but it must be allowed

for the poor child beast, that in time he comes to his senses, and is as hard on himself.[56]

Brooke's departure for Borneo in 1839 coincided with an historically important ideological moment in the British Empire that saw the idea of a civilising mission being raised in importance. The 1830s saw the rising power of humanitarian critics of the British Empire, as the anti-slavery movement was transformed into a movement for aboriginal protection. The anti-slavery movement successfully organised for a House of Commons vote abolishing slavery in 1833. Subsequently, one of the movement's leading protagonists, the parliamentarian Thomas Foxwell Buxton, used parliament to promote the protection of aborigines as a purpose of the British Empire.

Buxton organised for a *Select Committee Report into Aborigines* in 1836. The committee transformed into a de facto inquiry into Governor Benjamin D'Urban's administration of the war against the Xhosa people in the Cape Colony (South Africa). Through the Select Committee and other parliamentary activities, Buxton succeeded in getting D'Urban recalled as governor to answer for his administration—in the language of the early nineteenth-century British civil service, being recalled was tantamount to being dismissed.[57] The Secretary for Colonies at the time was Lord Glenelg, who, with Buxton, were veterans of the anti-slavery campaigns and part of an influential evangelical group known as the 'Saints' or 'Clapham Sect' that steered imperial policy towards a civilising mission in the 1830s.[58]

The 'Saints' changed the language of imperialism and made the promotion of civilisation the centre of imperial policy. The effects were found across the empire. In Africa, the 'Saints' organised new model colonies for returned slaves and to spread the Christian gospel. In the Australian penal colony of Van Diemen's Land, Lieutenant Governor Arthur went to great lengths to present his war against the Aborigines as having a humanitarian side, and employed the religious fanatic George Augustus Robinson, who had a distant connection to the 'Saints', to 'pacifically' end the conflict between settlers and Aborigines.[59] Arthur went on to be praised for his dealing with the Tasmanian Aborigines. The lessons for colonial governors were clear: D'Urban failed to respond adequately to the 'Saints' concerns, whilst Arthur, who adopted and appealed to the 'Saints' agenda, continued his career.

These global considerations are important for understanding both the context of Brooke's appeals to the British government and the British public as well as the wider context of government responses to Brooke. These changes occurred immediately before Brooke was planning his expedition to South-East Asia. Brooke himself cited the New Zealand Association's goal of the 'protection of the natives by the acquisition of their territory' as a model to follow.[60] Similarly, William Gladstone in the colonial office looked at the context of colonisation in New Zealand and Australia when considering how to deal with Brooke's advances to integrate Sarawak into the British Empire.[61] Therefore, Brooke's claims to facilitate civilisation in Borneo need to be placed in the context of the humanitarian turn towards empire in the 1830s.

Brooke championed both the idea of aboriginal protection and supressing slavery in South-East Asia. He criticised the approaches of the 'Saints' in his 1839 essay for failing to concern themselves with South-East Asia:

> These unhappy countries have failed to rouse attention or excite commiseration, and as they sink lower and lower, they afford a striking proof of how civilization may be crushed, and how the fairest and richest lands under the sun may become degraded by a continuous course of oppression and misrule.[62]

Directly contradicting Crawfurd's and the official British government's position of non-intervention, Brooke argued that territorial possession was necessary to reform a society. He believed it was the only means of protecting the indigenous populations of South-East Asia and advancing their individual civilisations. Yet we do not have to read between the lines to see the many contradictions in Brooke's argument. For example, in his 1839 essay, he acknowledged these contradictions, advocating 'indefeasible rights of the aborigines' and supporting their 'self-government', yet at the same time, he also believed that territorial possession by Europeans of their aboriginal land was crucial to achieving the goal of 'self-government'. Brooke seems to have been aware of this contradiction, and hence his emphatic assertion that colonial rule should exist for the benefit of aboriginal people and not for Europeans.

By December 1841, Brooke believed he had developed a new vision of territorial possession that would resolve some of the contradictions inherent in his 1839 essay. He argued that territorial possession should not be by conquest or occupation, but rather, protection and rule through existing native institutions. He explained his ideas as an 'experiment of developing a country' through the residency of a minimal number of Europeans who govern with the 'assistance of native rulers'.[63] The principle virtue of this system, he believed, was that it maintained the independence of the indigenous elites:

> Above all it insures the independence of the native princes, and may advance the inhabitants further in the scale of civilization, by means of this very independence, than can be done when the government is a foreign one, and their natural freedom sacrificed.[64]

Brooke believed that leaving compliant native princes and traditional forms of government intact was a new system of territorial possession that corresponded to the humanitarian impulse of the time. In reality, his ideas were a development of British practices of indirect rule developed in India, whereby a British Resident advised and controlled the local native rulers in economic development. The only distinction was that he proposed taking up the mantle of traditional rule himself—becoming a Rajah.

In his narrative, empire became a noble duty of protection for Brooke and the British people more generally. Brooke challenged the humanitarian impulses of the time to present the territorial expansion of the British Empire as being a humanitarian necessity to protect the innocent savage.

Reforming a Degraded State and Cultural Identity of South-East Asia

Although Brooke had convinced Keppel that the Sekrang and Saribas Dayaks were pirates, these tribes were equally a political threat to Brooke. Consequently, labelling rebellious tribes as pirates enabled Brooke to call on British naval power to entrench his regime in Sarawak. The ambiguity between a pirate and a rebellious tribe was central to Brooke's use of military power to reform what he saw as degraded native societies.

In 1845, Brooke wanted to deal with a new political threat, that of the pirates in Marudu Bay. In his new capacity as consul, he wrote a memorandum on *Piracy in the Eastern Seas for the British Government* on 31 March 1845.[65] Keppel later published the memorandum in 1847 as part of his bestselling account of Brooke's journals and the suppression of piracy, giving his readers a sense of Brooke's ideas being part of a consistent plan and body of ideas.[66]

Similar to Raffles's and Crawfurd's official writings on behalf of the East India Company, Brooke's argument was also based on a clear idea of historical reasoning. In the document, he argued that civilisation is an historic stage of development and that exogenous forces had an important role in either civilisation or degradation in Borneo. In writing this document, Brooke was following the pathway of Raffles and Crawfurd in using historical reasoning and ethnology to justify his suggested colonial policies.

In his 1845 Memorandum, Brooke outlines his policy towards the people that he defines as pirates and why his policy should become British government policy. He advocated a policy of 'conciliation with punishments' that recognised Malay governments whilst destroying pirate communities that refused to renounce piracy. Brooke was advocating government policy change from one of policing the oceans by looking for pirate ships to seeking out the communal basis of piracy. His methods advocated the total destruction of communities:

> I would especially urge that, to eradicate the evil, the pirate-haunts must be burned and destroyed, and the communities dispersed; for merely to cruise against pirate-parhus, and to forbear attacking them until we see them commit a piracy, is a hopeless and an endless task, harassing to our men, and can be attended with but very partial and occasional success; whereas, on the contrary principle, what pirate would venture to

pursue his vocation if his home be endangered—if he be made to feel in his own person the very ills he inflicts upon others.[67]

The above statement was a clear body of ideas designed to persuade the government to pursue an aggressive policy of attacking villages and creating social change in South-East Asia through overwhelming force. The problem for Brooke was that piracy occurred in the open waters, but he was advocating attacks on land-based communities.

In advancing his aggressive policy, Brooke was stretching the boundaries of what the British government considered piracy. Brooke knew that his definition of piracy was problematic and consequently opened his argument by declaring that 'Piracy in the Eastern Archipelago is entirely distinct from Piracy in the Western World'.[68] Piracy, as defined by the eighteenth-century British jurist William Blackstone, was an act of 'robbery and depredation on the high seas' in which an individual had 'renounced all the benefits of society and government'.[69] Blackstone's vision was that pirates lived outside society and still lived in a 'state of nature' and their piratical actions were tantamount to declaring war on humanity *'hostis humani generis'*.[70] Blackstone's idea of pirates as outsiders did not equate to the practice of piracy that Brooke saw in South-East Asia.

Pirates, Brooke argued, represented entire 'communities' that raided other communities as well as raiding ships and small vessels that ventured in the shallow coastal waters and up the creeks of Borneo. He believed that there were three types of pirates. The first made 'long voyages in large heavy-armed prahus, such as the illanus, Balagnini (sea Gypsies) etc'. These pirates operated on the High Seas (what today we would call international waters). The second groups of pirates consisted of 'Dayak fleets, which make short but destructive excursions in swift prahus, and seek to surprise rather than openly to attack their prey'. These pirates operated in the shallows and mainly attacked other native prahus. The final group consisted of people living in large settlements who were led by pirate chiefs:

> half-bred Arab Seriffs, who, possessing themselves of the territory of some Malay state, form a nucleus for piracy, a rendezvous and market for all the roving fleets; and although occasionally sending out their own followers, they more frequently seek profit by making advances, in food, arms and gunpowder, to all who will agree to repay them at an exorbitant rate in slaves.[71]

All of these groups were part of large communities in which Brooke identified piracy as integral to the economic fabric of the community and the region. Nevertheless, these pirate communities created a state of crime and distress throughout the region to such an extent that the sovereign governments such as the 'old established Malay Governments (such as Borneo and Sooloo)' were either 'participators, in or victims to piracy, and in many cases both—purchasing from one set of pirates and enslaved and plundered by another'.[72]

Brooke was faced with problems in identifying piracy in South-East Asia. The first problem was where the acts of piracy occurred. By the late eighteenth century, the idea of the High Seas constituting international waters was broadly accepted. Blackstone, therefore, was clear that it was on the High Seas and that piracy occurred and that this was a common problem for all humanity and should be combatted by all nations. Although Royal Naval actions were clearly justified on the High Seas, it was not so clear that naval action was justified in waters that were not adjacent to British territory and controlled by somebody else. The acts of parliament were vague in stipulating the legal extent of British power.

The original act from the sixteenth century, written during the reign of Henry VIII, stipulated broadly that piracy was acts of 'treason, felonies, robberies, murders and confederacies' that were 'committed in or upon the Sea, or in any other haven, river, creek or place where the Admiral or Admirals have or pretend to have power over or jurisdiction'.[73] This act was renewed numerous times without changing the word 'Sea' to 'High Sea' until February 1844. The act stipulated that naval commanders could only operate in maritime territory that fell within their jurisdiction; however, the act's wording, 'Admirals have or pretend to have power over or jurisdiction', gave admirals the right to interpret the extent of their jurisdiction.

By the time Keppel arrived in Sarawak in May 1844, the law had already changed to stipulate that piracy occurred on the High Seas, potentially making Keppel's and Brooke's actions illegal. Nevertheless, it was not that simple. Keppel was also governed by the 1825 Act of Parliament that granted rewards for the capture and or destruction of pirates.[74] The 1825 Act maintained the older wording of 'sea' but also gave commanders the power to support subjects of the British Empire against pirates and also any state 'potentate in amity' with the British Empire against pirates. The word 'potentate' means supreme power and 'amity' means friendship. As a British subject and also as a Rajah, Brooke was entitled to claim support under the 1825 Act, as long as the suppression of piracy was near his territory. Brooke and Keppel's actions were legal, as long as Brooke maintained a close following of the 1825 Act.

The 1825 Act empowered naval officers to support allied sovereign states, or states with aspects of sovereignty in the suppression of piracy. Nevertheless, jurisdiction was still a problem for Brooke and a key reason why he wrote the 1845 *Memorandum on Piracy*.[75] Brooke's dominion might legitimise the exercise of military power along the coast of Sarawak, but it did not legitimise the use of power in other parts of Borneo. To overcome this limitation of his power, Brooke included with his 1845 Memorandum a letter from Sultan Omar Alli requesting British support in the suppression of piracy.[76] This enabled Brooke and Keppel to attack the pirates in North Borneo, which fell under the dominion of Brunei.

Brunei's letter, however, was only a temporary solution. Piracy in South-East Asia was not an act of isolated individuals, but rather, a systematic activity by local elites that resembled warfare more than piracy. Territory and jurisdiction were still clear problems for Brooke, and therefore, the 1845 Memorandum sought to distinguish the difference between legitimate acts of war and piracy in South-East Asia.

The similarity between piracy and warfare was a clear legal and political problem for Brooke, and he acknowledged it as such: 'in our efforts to suppress it, we may not be interfering with the right of native states to war one upon another'.[77] His answer was to define the nature of a state by arguing that 'we can only concede the right of war to recognised states', and he made continual reference to the old Malay governments of Brunei, Sulu and Sambas. He argued that these old Malay states had dependencies and it was these dependencies that had no rights to make war, concluding 'all chiefs who have seized on territory and arrogate independence (making this independence a plea for piracy) can never be allowed the right of declaring war, or entering on hostilities with their neighbours'.[78] Brooke wrote the memorandum to convince the British government to consider these communities piratical and therefore enabled them to be destroyed.

In presenting his ideas of reform, Brooke branded indigenous elites as foreign and labelled his enemies pirates.[79] In doing so, he followed Raffles in presenting political identity in South-East Asia as passive, in which South-East Asians responded and developed only to external forces. Brooke's ideas of reform were contradictory: his ideas relied on depicting South-East Asian cultural identities as incapable of indigenous development, yet at the same time, he believed the people needed to be protected from detrimental foreign forces.

Brooke's ideas for reform were all based on the idea that Borneo and the Malay world more broadly were in a state of decay. The idea of decay was an interpretation of historical events which, as we saw in Chapters 1 and 2, was central to British conceptions of history. History acted as an explanation for the rise or decline of a society. Ideas of reform that Brooke wanted to introduce in Sarawak were directly connected to his interpretation of decline and savagery within Sarawak's political society.

In his 1839 essay, Brooke reiterated Raffles's idea of Malay degeneration brought about by colonialism of non-British Europeans. He believed that Malay governments were in a process of 'internal dissension' that 'destroyed all rightful authority' and had 'given rise to petty states, which thrive on piracy and fatten on the slave trade'.[80] His views therefore presented piracy and slavery as aberrations of Borneo's society and the consequence of Europeans weakening the internal fabric of Malay polities.

Brooke described Sarawak as consisting of a mixture of indigenous Dayak tribes and Malay settlements. His ethnic divisions, however, were instrumental in depicting a society in decay and legitimising his civilising claims. For example, Brooke (drawing from Raffles's published letters) argued that the Malays were recent migrants to Sarawak who were in a process of exerting authority over the independent inland Dayak tribes.[81]

Depending on his audience, Brooke used the word Malay in different ways. Earlier generations of historian-administrators used the word Malay to cover all followers of the Islamic faith on the Malay Peninsula or in the islands surrounding the Malay Peninsula that appeared to be semi-civilised.[82] This use of the word Malay, however, is a British construction of Malay identity. There is little evidence that these people described themselves as Malay in those terms.[83] Brooke was aware of greater nuances around the use of the term Malay. In his journals, Brooke took care to identify distinct ethnicities in Borneo and the Moluccas that were Islamic and not Malay.[84] However, in his Memoranda to the British government, he simplified ethnicity into three distinct ethnic groups: Malays (which he understood as descendants of Malays from the Malay Peninsula), Arabs and Dayaks. In simplifying ethnicity, Brooke was maintaining an accepted British understanding of the divisions between these three different groups.

The distinction between Malays and the indigenous Dayaks is not as distinct as the British believed. As we have seen in Chapter 3, the idea of Malays colonising South-East Asia pervaded British thought. Marsden, Raffles and Crawfurd all took different positions on the expansion of the Malays as well as the expansion of Islam throughout the region. Malay was the language of power and regional trade, and hence an incentive for local elites to adopt the Malay language as a means of connecting to this regional trading system.

Similar to the adoption of language, there were other talismans epitomising a desire to connect to the regional power system. Dutch writers from the eighteenth century commented on the existence of local elites in Borneo that claimed Hindu-Javanese royal ancestry, and Malay elites of Brunei claimed descent from Malacca-Johor royal families—which was a common facet of all claimants for power in the Malay world.[85]

There was probably a continual process of Malay conversion by indigenous people seeking to develop stable, settled authority and recognition in the broader Malay world through the adoption of Islam and Malay customs.[86] The people Brooke called Malays were more than likely descended from Dayaks who had chosen to adopt Malay civilisation to connect into the broader systems of power and commerce in the South-East Asian region.

In both his letters to government and his memorandums, Brooke used the term 'Malay' in a fashion that appealed to British preconceptions of the Malays as foreigners and Dayaks as aboriginal. He presented the Malays as distinct from the aboriginal peoples on the island, commenting in his 1841 Memorandum that 'the Dayak tribes are the aborigines of Borneo, inhabiting the interior of the island, and are in subjugation to the Malays who line the coast' and maintained a similar argument when pleading for support for his own government in 1846, writing to the Colonial Secretary the Earl of Aberdeen that the 'prosperity of Sarawak is based on' the 'freedom of the aboriginal inhabitants from the oppression heretofore universally exercised on them by the Malay Race'.[87] Although the Malays had strong connections to the Dayak tribes, Brooke used the label 'Malay' as a way of delegitimising the local elites. By branding them as Malays, he was connecting in to a well-established narrative that saw the coastal Malays as colonisers, whilst the peoples of the interior became innocent indigenous people needing protection. He even branded his most determined local rivals as Arabs, further presenting local elites as foreigners to his British readers. Therefore, Brooke was narrating Borneo's history to British readers, describing all local elites as being foreigners who were trying to colonise Sarawak.

In his 1841 Memorandum and again in his 1846 Memorandum, Brooke presented the Malays as practicing a form of economic predation on the Dayak, thereby stimulating Dayak barbarism. The system Brooke described saw the interior 'Dayak' tribes supply the coastal 'Malay' tribes with rice, whilst the coastal tribes supplied the interior with manufactured goods gained from international trade. Malays dispatched goods to the interior with the expectation that Dayak chiefs would pay on delivery, through supplying rice and forest goods to the coast. Yet the prices demanded by Malay *pengirans* (regents) were often more than the Dayaks were able to pay.

Brooke noted that rice harvests were often totally consumed by the coastal Malays, leaving the Dayak cultivators in the interior to starve.[88] Failure to pay resulted in the Malays subcontracting the Serebas and Sakarran Dayaks (collectively known by Brooke as the Sea Dayaks) to launch punitive head-hunting raids which plundered the other Dayak tribes of the interior and seized women and children as slaves. Brooke claimed that 'of the twenty Dayak tribes under this [Sarawak] government more than half have been robbed of their wives and children in part; and one tribe is without women or children amongst them'.[89]

The biggest act of barbarism that the Malays had performed on the Dayaks, Brooke believed, was piracy. He saw the actions of the Malays as facilitating barbarism amongst the Dayaks and interpreted the taking of women and children as slaving raids. Yet unlike the slaving raids of the Sulu pirates, who took able-bodied men to work, the coastal Malays and Sea Dayaks wanted women.[90] The taking of women as hostages to extract further payment from the Dayaks and as wives for the Malays and the coastal Dayak communities was part of normal customs of tribal war in Sarawak. However, for British readers, such practices equated to slavery.[91]

In addition to branding the elites as Malays, in his 1845 Memorandum, Brooke also chose to label key enemies as Arabs. In his dispatches, he called the leaders of the piratical hordes 'Arab Sheriffs' who had no deep connection with the people and merely employed the Dayaks on 'piratical excursions'.[92] The subjects of these attacks were primarily other aboriginal Dayaks who were either killed or enslaved and on some occasions merchants as well. He also described the Arab Sheriffs as protected by the Malays. Therefore, in Brooke's narrative, the barbarous Arabs and the Malays were ganging up to enslave the helpless Dayak savages. Brooke was correct in this labelling, with many of the Arab Sheriffs claiming Arab descent, but to British readers of his memoranda, it presented the Arab pirates as exogenous foreigners leading the passive Dayaks astray.[93]

Brooke's approach in his 1841 and 1845 memoranda was to create a dichotomy between 'the half-bred Arab Sheriffs', whom he described as the 'worst class', and the Dayaks, which he abrogated from some responsibility by arguing the Sekrang and Saribas Dayaks were 'employed' by the Sheriffs and the Malays. The logic of his argument for British readers was that the Dayaks were innocent aborigines under the influence of degenerate foreigners. He appealed to the British public using organic notions of culture and ethnic identity to support characteristics he favoured. At the same time, also branded people and characteristics he did not like as either foreign and/or pirates.

Brooke told the British government and the public that his subjects were on the threshold of civilisation. They were good, honest people 'desirous to suppress piracy, to encourage trade and to cultivate the mostly friendly relations with the British'.[94] Brooke used the word civilisation to legitimise his punitive action against his local enemies in Borneo. Although acts of piracy could easily be portrayed as uncivilised, Brooke was faced with a contradiction in his own logic—he admitted these 'piratical excursions' could also be labelled 'inter-tribal war' and a normal state of affairs.[95]

In comparison to his portrayal of the troublesome local rulers that he branded as Malays or foreign Arabs, Brooke chose to present his rule in Sarawak as supporting native rights and indigenous rule. He argued that he was giving 'freedom' to 'the aboriginal inhabitants from the oppressions heretofore invariably exerted on them by the Malay Race' and even argued British rule was in the name of 'aboriginal self-government'.[96] Brooke adopted Malay titles and aspects of traditional rule so he could portray his regime as quasi-indigenous.[97]

Brooke's choice of words in his memoranda and letters to government which depicted the foreign origins of the Malays and their colonising intent was for British consumption. Brooke was tapping into a well-established belief that the history of South-East Asia was driven by colonial invaders. By telling his British readers that all change was introduced into Borneo by invaders, Brooke was tacitly rejecting any sense of local authority and presenting himself and British rule as legitimate.

Brooke's memoranda presented the Malays in Borneo as being no different than the Europeans. The Malays in his memoranda became interlopers instilling the passive indigenous people of Borneo with foreign ideas and subjecting them to slavery and the deprecations of Malay barbarism. Every example of Dayak savagery Brooke attributed to being a learnt behaviour from the Malays. For example, according to Brooke, even the act of Dayak headhunting reached endemic proportions in Borneo because of Malay-sponsored piracy.[98]

For Brooke's readers in Britain, the image of Borneo was one of passive indigenous savages subjected to the deprivations of foreigners—be they Malays, Arabs or Europeans. Brooke therefore followed Raffles in viewing South-East Asia as a passive actor, waiting for foreigners to give it civilisation. This vision enabled him to delegitimise indigenous elites in his correspondence with the British government and the British public. It also meant that as a passive entity, the savage was innocent and worthy of protection from the barbarous and degenerate Malays.

Although Brooke's idea of a civilising colonialism in Borneo fitted with the time, his ideas were the direct opposite of those advocated by John Crawfurd and reprised the debates between Raffles and Crawfurd over the role of colonialism in South-East Asian history. Although Crawfurd had retired from the East India Company and had failed in his attempts to be elected to the House of Common, he was not without power and influence. From the late 1840s onwards, Brooke would face Crawfurd's system of anonymous campaigning to limit colonial expansion in South-East Asia.

Notes

1 John Crawfurd*, 'Borneo and its Resources', *The Examiner*, (12 January, 1850).
2 J.H. Walker, *Power and Prowess: The Origins of Brooke Kingship in Sarawak*, (Crows Nest, N.S.W.; [Great Britain]: Asian Studies Association of Australia in Association with Allen & Unwin, 2002).
3 For example, in a co-written article, James August St. John and Horace St. John concluded, 'The suppression of piracy is a "to extirpate piracy from the eastern seas is Mr. Brooke's principle object" '. Dublin uni mag. May 1848, p. 657.
4 {Brooke, 1838 #1743}
5 Basil Hall, 'Memoir of the Life and Public Servies of Sir Stamford Raffles, F.R.S., Partiqulary in the Government of Java in 1811–6; and of Bencoolen and its Dependencies, 1817–24: With Details of the Commerce and Resources of the Eastern Archipelago; and Selections from the Correspondence: By his Widow', *Edinburgh Review*, 51 111 (1830), p. 369.
6 Nicholas Tarling, 'Brooke Rule in Sarawak and its Principles', *Journal of the Malaysian Branch of the Royal Asiatic Society*, 65 1 (1992); Robert Pringle, *Rajahs and Rebels: The Ibans of Sarawak under Brooke Rule, 1841–1941*, (London: Macmillan, 1970).
7 The second edition of Raffles's 'Memoir of the Life and Public Services of Sir Thomas Stamford Raffles' had only just been published when Brooke was looking towards South-East Asia. He probably purchased this and then George Windsor Earl, *The Eastern Seas, or, Voyages and adventures in the Indian Archipelago in 1832–33–34: Comprising a Tour of the Island of Java, Visits to Borneo, the Malay Peninsula, Siam, etc.; Also an Account of the Present State of Singapore*, (London: W.H. Allen, 1837), both of which were published in the 1830s, before getting a copy Raffles's *History of Java*. He did not get a copy of Crawfurd's *Indian Archipelago* until the 1840s: see James Brooke and John C. Templer, *The Private Letters of Sir James Brooke, K.C. B Rajah of Sarawak*, (London: Richard Bentley, 1853), vol. 1, p. 126.
8 Brooke and Templer, *The Private Letters of Sir James Brooke, K.C. B Rajah of Sarawak*, vol. 1, p. 6.

9   Although Brooke did not plan to create an empire in Sarawak before leaving Britain, Brooke did make it clear in his 1839 essay that he wanted to advance British colonialism in South-East Asia in some fashion.

10 Brooke and Templer, *The Private Letters of Sir James Brooke, K.C. B Rajah of Sarawak*, vol. 1, p. 10.

11 See original manuscript, James Brooke, 'On the Malayan Archipelago: A Proposed Exploration', *Journal Mss South East Asia, Royal Geographical Society*, Royal Geographical Society, JMS/8/2 1838 (1838).and also published in Private letters of James Brooke in 1853. An edited version appears in Anonymous, 'Exploring Expedition to the Asiatic Archipelago', *The Athenaeum*, 572 (1838), p. 744. And later in James Brooke, 'Proposed Exploring Expedition to the Asiatic Archipelago', *Journal of the Royal Geographical Society of London*, 8 (1838).

12 Spencer St. John, *The Life of Sir James Brooke, Rajah of Srarwak from his Persoanal Papers and Correspondance*, (Edinburgh: W. Blackwood, 1879), p. 12.

13 Brooke and Templer, *The Private Letters of Sir James Brooke, K.C. B Rajah of Sarawak*, vol. 1, p. 7.

14 Tarling, 'Brooke Rule in Sarawak and its Principles'.

15 See Brooke and Templer, *The Private Letters of Sir James Brooke, K.C. B Rajah of Sarawak*, vol. 1, p. 126.

16 See John Crawfurd, 'Notes for a British Settlement on the North-west Coast of Borneo', July 10 1844 in Anonymous, 'Borneo 1844 to 1846', *Colonial Office*, (National Archives United Kingdom, CO 144/1), p. 229.

17 See Royal Geographical Society Archive; for an example, see George Windsor Earl's correspondence.

18 C.M. Turnbull, 'Introduction', in *G.W. Earl, The Eastern Seas*, (Singapore: Oxford University Press, 1971), pp. v-xviii (p. xi).

19 Anonymous, 'Exploring Expedition to the Asiatic Archipelago'.

20 Nicholas Tarling, *The Burthen, the Risk, and the Glory: A Biography of Sir James Brooke*, (Kuala Lumpur; Oxford: Oxford University Press, 1982); Pringle, *Rajahs and Rebels: The Ibans of Sarawak under Brooke Rule, 1841–1941*; Walker, *Power and Prowess*.

21 Joseph Hume, 'Piracy and Murder', *The Times*, (1852).

22 Anonymous, 'Commission of Inquiry into James Brooke', *Foreign Office*, National Archives UK, FO 881/482 (1855).

23 Steven Runciman, *The White Rajahs: A History of Sarawak from 1841 to 1946*, (London: Cambridge University Press, 1960) and Graham Irwin, 'Nineteenth-Century Borneo: A Study in Diplomatic Rivalry', (Martinus Nijhoff: 's-Gravenhage, 1955), pp. xi. 251. pl. 4. Both provide accounts that are highly apologetic of the Brooke regime. Runciman's work was even commissioned by the successor colonial regime in Sarawak. A more critical account develops in the works of Tarling: see Nicholas Tarling, *Piracy and Politics in the Malay World: A Study of British Imperialism in Nineteenth-Century South-east Asia*, (Melbourne: F.W. Cheshire, 1963); Tarling, *The Burthen, the Risk, and the Glory*. However Pringle, *Rajahs and Rebels: The Ibans of Sarawak under Brooke Rule, 1841–1941*. And Walker, *Power and Prowess*. He takes a much more critical line towards the Brooke regime to reconstruct the relationship between Brooke and his subjects. See also Nicholas Tarling, 'The British Empire in South-East Asia', in *The Oxford History of the British Empire: Historiography*, ed. by Robin W. Winks (Oxford: Oxford University Press, 1999), pp. 409–412.

24 John Walker presents a different view of Brooke, whereby Brooke quickly learnt the principle of projecting authority within Malay political society cosmology and played a long game with the Malay elites to present himself as a new, charismatic leader. Walker, *Power and Prowess*, pp. 35–47.

25 Brooke and Templer, *The Private Letters of Sir James Brooke, K.C. B Rajah of Sarawak*, vol. 1, p. 66.

26 Ibid.

27 Lawrence H. Officer and Samuel H. Williamson, "Five Ways to Compute the Relative Value of a UK Pound Amount, 1270 to Present," MeasuringWorth, 2013. URL: <www.measuringworth.com/ukcompare/>

28 Walker, *Power and Prowess*, p. 37. For his extended discussion of Semangat pages, pp. 17–21.

29 Brooke and Templer, *The Private Letters of Sir James Brooke, K.C. B Rajah of Sarawak*, vol. 1, p. 85.

30 Brooke presented this view to the British government, likening the situations to a Shakespearian play, and used the Wars of the Roses analogy: 'Borneo is divided into White Roese and Red. The Sultan representing the House of York, and Muda Hassam the House of Lancaster'. James Brooke, 'Memorandum', Borneo 1844 to 1846, *Colonial Office*, National Archives United Kingdom, CO 144/1 (1845).

31 Walker, *Power and Prowess*, p. 28.

32 James Brooke, Memorandum in Anonymous, 'Borneo 1844 to 1846', p. 203.

33 The Sultan of Sambas also had a claim on Sarawak. See Ib Larsen, 'The First Sultan of Sarawak and His Links to Brunei and the Sambas Dynasty, 1599–1826: A Little-known Pre-Brooke History', *Journal of the Malaysian Branch of the Royal Asiatic Society*, 85 303 (2012); Walker, *Power and Prowess*, pp. 24–26.

34 Bianca Maria Gerlich, 'Marudu 1845: The Destruction and Reconstruction of a Coastal State in Borneo', (Thesis (doctoral), Abera Universität Hamburg, 2003); Walker, *Power and Prowess*, p. 26.

35 Brooke and Templer, *The Private Letters of Sir James Brooke, K.C. B Rajah of Sarawak*.

36 Ibid., vol. 1, p. 55. John Walker argues that the conflict/rebellion in Sarawak was all about controlling antimony. This scenario was that the Brunei and Sambas were both competing for influence over the region, with Brunei having an ancient claim, but over the previous 20 years since the foundation Singapore, local elites in Sarawak had exerted their independence from Brunei. Walker, *Power and Prowess*, p. 29.

37 Brooke and Templer, *The Private Letters of Sir James Brooke, K.C. B Rajah of Sarawak*, vol. 1, p. 165.

38 Ibid., vol. 1, p. 167.

39 St John history and other histories. For a recent critical account, see Bianca Maria Gerlich *Marudu 1845*.

40 Brooke and Templer, *The Private Letters of Sir James Brooke, K.C. B Rajah of Sarawak*, vol. 1, p. 167.

41 John Crawfurd, 'Crawfurd to Richard Cobden February 10', Cobden Papers, *West Sussex Record Office*, MS 89, 90, 91 (1848).

42 Ibid.

43 Brooke and Templer, *The Private Letters of Sir James Brooke, K.C. B Rajah of Sarawak*.

44 Crawfurd, 'Crawfurd to Richard Cobden, 10 February'.

45 Walker, *Power and Prowess*, p. 45.

46 Tarling, *The Burthen, the Risk, and the Glory*, p. 56.

47 Ibid.

48 Walker, *Power and Prowess*, p. 72.

49 John Crawfurd*, 'The Expedition to Borneo of H.M.S. Dido, for the Suppression of Piracy: with Extracts from the Journal of James Brooke, Esq., of Sarawak (now Agent for the British Government in Borneo). By Captain the Hon. Henry Keppel, R.N. Two vols. Capman and Hall', *The Examiner*, (21 February, 1846).

50 Henry Keppel, *The Expedition to Borneo of H.M.S. Dido for the Suppression of Piracy: With Extracts from the Journal of James Brooke*, (London: Chapman and Hall, 1846), vol. 1, p. 270.

51 James Brooke, 'Brooke to Earl of Aberdeen 10 March', *Colonial Office*, National Archives United Kingdom, CO 144/1 (1846), p. 219.

52 Joseph Hume, House of Commons Hansard, 3rd Series vol. 113, 22 July, 1815, Supply-Labuan, p. 109 see also Louis Alexia Chamerovzow, Borneo Facts Versus Borneo Fallacies, An inquiry into the alleged piracies of the Syaks of Serebas and Sakarran, Second Edition, Charles Gilpin, London, 1851, (sectary of the Aboriginal Protection Society) and W.N., Borneo Remarks on a recent 'Naval Execution", London, Effingham Wilson, 1850.

53 Brooke and Templer, *The Private Letters of Sir James Brooke, K.C. B Rajah of Sarawak*, vol. 1, p. 12.

54 Ibid., vol. 1, p. 23.

55 Forrest, '2 July 1784 letter from Capt Forrest, Extract of Bengal General Consultations'; Forrest, 'Report on Pulo Penang'; Frances Light, 'Report on Junk Ceylon [Phuket]', ibid.

56 Crawfurd, 'Crawfurd to Richard Cobden, 10 February'.

57 Laidlaw, *Colonial Connections*, p. 80.

58 Stephen Tomkins, *The Clapham Sect: How Wilberforce's Circle Transformed Britain*, (Oxford: Lion, 2010).

59 Gareth Knapman, 'The Pacificator: Discovering the Lost Bust of George Augustus Robinson', *La Trobe Journal*, 86 (2010); Henry Reynolds, *Fate of a Free People*, (Ringwood, VIC: Penguin, 1995).

60 Brooke and Templer, *The Private Letters of Sir James Brooke, K.C. B Rajah of Sarawak*, vol. 1, p. 20.

61 Anonymous, 'Borneo 1844 to 1846', p. 45.

62 Brooke and Templer, *The Private Letters of Sir James Brooke, K.C. B Rajah of Sarawak*, vol. 1, p. 20.

63 Ibid., vol. 1, p. 176.

64 Ibid., vol. 1, p. 177.

65 Anonymous, 'Borneo 1844 to 1846', pp. 181–199.

66 Keppel, *The Expedition to Borneo of H.M.S. Dido for the Suppression of Piracy: With Extracts from the Journal of James Brooke*, vol. 2, p. 144.

67 Brooke, 'Memorandum', p. 191, but also Keppel, *The Expedition to Borneo of H.M.S. Dido for the Suppression of Piracy: With Extracts from the Journal of James Brooke*, vol. 2, pp. 144, 152. It is worth noting that was such an action taken today, it would be a clear war crime and forced dispersal of people and the destruction of their homes an act of genocide.

68 Anonymous, 'Borneo 1844 to 1846', p. 181.

69 Crawfurd*, 'A Vist to the Indian Archipelago in H.M.S. Maeander, with Portions of the Private Journal of Sir James Brooke, K.C.B. By Captain the Hon. Henry Keppel, R.N. Two Vols. Bentley', (19 February, 1853). See also William Blackstone, *Commentaries on the Laws of England in Four Books: Notes Selected from the Editions of Archibold, Christian, Coleridge, Chitty, Stewart, Kerr, and others, Barron Field's Analysis, and Additional Notes, and a Life of the Author by George Sharswood: In Two Volumes*, (Philadelphia: J.B. Lippincott Co., 1893 [1753]), vol. 2, p. 71.

70 Blackstone, *Commentaries on the Laws of England*, vol. 2, p. 71.

71 Anonymous, 'Borneo 1844 to 1846', p. 181.

72 Ibid.

73 1844 (22) Offences at sea. A bill for the speedier trial of offences committed on the High Seas.

74 1825 (174) A bill to make further provision for the payment of the crews of His Majesty's ships and vessels and for encouraging the capture or destruction of piratical ships and vessels.

75 Anonymous, 'Borneo 1844 to 1846', pp. 181–199.

76 Ibid. p. 175.

77 Ibid. p. 191; Keppel, *The Expedition to Borneo of H.M.S. Dido for the Suppression of Piracy: With Extracts from the Journal of James Brooke*, vol. 1, p. 153.

78 Anonymous, 'Borneo 1844 to 1846', p. 190.

79 Ibid. pp. 181–199.

80 Brooke and Templer, *The Private Letters of Sir James Brooke, K.C. B Rajah of Sarawak*, vol. 1, p. 5.

81 Pringle, *Rajahs and Rebels: The Ibans of Sarawak under Brooke Rule, 1841–1941*.

82 Ibid; Anthony Crothers Milner, *The Malays*, (Chichester: Wiley-Blackwell, 2011).

83 Anthony Milner, *Kerajaan: Malay Political Culture on the Eve of Colonial Rule*, (Tucson: University of Arizona Press, 1982); Milner, *The Invention of Politics in Colonial Malaya*; Milner, *The Malays*.

84 Walker Sarawak Museum Journal paper on Malays.

85 Pringle, *Rajahs and Rebels: The Ibans of Sarawak under Brooke Rule, 1841–1941*. Also Walker, *Power and Prowess*, p. 84.

86 Pringle, *Rajahs and Rebels: The Ibans of Sarawak under Brooke Rule, 1841–1941*, p. 17. Also see Milner, *The Malays*; Reid, 'Islamization and Christianization in Southeast Asia: The Critical Phase, 1550–1650'.

87 James Brooke, *A Letter from Borneo with Notices of the Country and its Inhabitants Addressed to James Gardner esq*, (London: L & G Shelley, 1842). Copy held in FO 12/21, p. 409; Brooke, 'Brooke to Earl of Aberdeen 10 March', p. 219.

88 Brooke and Templer, *The Private Letters of Sir James Brooke, K.C. B Rajah of Sarawak*, vol. 1, p. 160. Brooke, *A Letter From Borneo with Notices of the Country and its Inhabitants Addressed to James Gardner esq*, p. 11.

89 Brooke and Templer, *The Private Letters of Sir James Brooke, K.C. B Rajah of Sarawak*, vol. 1, p. 161.

90 James F. Warren, *The Sulu Zone, 1768–1898: The Dynamics of External Trade, Slavery and Ethnicity in the Transformation of a Southeast Asian Maritime State*, (Singapore: Singapore University Press, 2007).

91 The women in their new role as wives of the costal tribes enabled the costal people to better extract resources from the interior by providing common family connections between the coast and the interior—binding interior tribes into exclusive exchange relationships. The practice of exterior communities taking women from the interior and thereby connecting the two communities into an exchange relationship that was advantageous to exterior communities continued well into the second half of the twentieth century. Bernard Sellato, *Nomads of the Borneo Rainforest: The Economics, Politics,and Ideology of Settling Down*, (Honolulu: University of Hawaii Press, 1994). Although unequal and violent, this system of exchange advantaged both communities. The interior tribes gained access to manufactured goods and global trade, whilst the coastal tribes gained needed supplies. Nevertheless, it was a system which was inherently unstable, with trading relationships breaking out into violence.

92 Anonymous, 'Borneo 1844 to 1846', p. 185.

93 A clear example of this is the writings of James Augustus St. John. Discussed further in the following chapter.

94 Anonymous, 'Borneo 1844 to 1846', p. 179.

95 Ibid. p. 191a.
96 Ibid. p. 219.
97 John Walker goes further arguing that Brooke's regime developed out of systems of power from within northern Borneo culture. Walker, *Power and Prowess*.
98 Pringle, *Rajahs and Rebels: The Ibans of Sarawak under Brooke Rule, 1841–1941*, p. 23. And Brooke, *A Letter From Borneo with Notices of the Country and its Inhabitants Addressed to James Gardner esq*, p. 19. See FO 12/21, p. 415.

7   Resisting Colonialism in Sarawak

This chapter reveals for the first time the role that John Crawfurd played in preventing the incorporation of Sarawak into the British Empire and impeding calls for large-scale colonial expansion in South-East Asia. Using his position as a journalist with *The Examiner* and as the leading government advisor on South-East Asian matters, Crawfurd worked anonymously to orchestrate liberal Radical opposition to James Brooke's imperial adventures. In opposing Brooke, Crawfurd developed a moral opposition to European expansion in South-East Asia. Colonial control of large tracts of land and people, he argued, would result in 'death and economic waste'.[1] He preferred a colonialism that, in today's jargon, would have a small footprint: the colonialism of entrepot outposts in which people, goods and capital were free to come and go.

Crawfurd understood that ethnology was central to Brooke's claims for extending colonial rule in Borneo and developed his ethnological arguments along with his opposition to colonial expansion in Borneo. Crawfurd's ethnology informed his politics to the extent that he believed in separate and distinct races that were indigenous creations and that a dominant political culture developed within each distinct race. He was morally against Brooke's attempt to brand people 'pirates' as an abuse of power and means of legitimising the killing of thousands of people.

After his first career in the East India Company, Crawfurd's second career was that of professional lobbyist and journalist. The British Merchants in Calcutta hired him in 1827 to lobby against the Stamp Act of 1827. For the next three decades, Crawfurd continued in the pay of either Calcutta or Straits Settlements merchants—employed to lobby against the monopolistic activities of the East India Company.[2] In his lobbying capacity, he published pamphlets publicly as well as anonymously. In Britain, he regularly published anonymous opinion articles on Asia in the leading London liberal paper, *The Examiner* and various other review journals. He also actively worked behind the scenes, talking with government officials about policy, and purportedly was a trusted authority on all sides of government.[3] As a member of many London clubs, associations and the Masonic Temple, he probably had access to political and other leading figures through non-official channels.[4] The merchant associations of India and Singapore paid him to shift the political and public opinions of the British elite.

Crawfurd's discreet lobbying was a clear threat to some interest groups. In 1834, he published a scathing anonymous critique of the plan to settle South Australia in accordance with Edward Gibbon Wakefield's colonisation methods.[5] Robert Torrens, one of the key financial backers to the scheme, identified Crawfurd as the anonymous critic, publishing an open letter rejecting Crawfurd's criticisms.[6] Most critiques were published anonymously in nineteenth-century Britain and there was a general intellectual acceptance of this cultural norm. Torrens therefore must have perceived major benefits from not letting Crawfurd make anonymous attacks.

Brooke's supporters initially saw Crawfurd as an ally, and many continued to do so, with Crawfurd never publicly declaring himself against Brooke, his opposition always voiced behind the vail of anonymity.[7] In 1843, Brooke's commercial agent and business partner, Henry Herman Wise, made contact with Crawfurd and other former colonial officials to make the case for incorporating Sarawak into the British Empire.[8] John Anderson, the former East India Company diplomat from Penang, was easily convinced.[9] In comparison, Crawfurd saw the plan as diverging both from British policy and the type of limited colonialism that he had been advocating for the previous 20 years, and consequently, he refused to support Wise and Brooke's plans. Instead, Crawfurd protested privately to Lord Stanley (head of the Colonial Office) and Lord Haddington (head of the Admiralty) that Sarawak was an uneconomic swamp and that any colony would be a disaster leading to numerous entanglements with local political disputes and would result in colonial expansion throughout Borneo.[10]

At this stage, Crawfurd sought to mould the direction of Brooke's colonial endeavours rather than oppose them and advised Wise and Brooke to advocate Labuan as a colony. Crawfurd had suggested years earlier the potential of Labuan as a colony to support the China trade.[11] The advantages, he argued, were that it provided a safe harbour for shipping, whilst not involving Britain in the larger political affairs of Brunei.

On hearing Crawfurd's suggestion, Brooke was disgruntled, but accepted Crawfurd's advice. Nevertheless, in a letter to his friend John Templer, he complained that Crawfurd's approach was a 'very short-sighted view which ties us up in small islands'. He went on to outline why a mainland approach was preferable:

> The mainland affords (with an equal expense) the power of opening new resources from the interior; of benefiting the aborigines; of affording to British capital the advantages of a fine soil as well as commerce; and of rapidly increasing the number of inhabitants, and bringing the country to a degree of civilisation never to be obtained by sticking ourselves on an island on the coast.[12]

Brooke's designs on the Borneo mainland were the precise reasons why Crawfurd wanted Labuan rather than Sarawak. By 'tying' Europeans up in the Islands, Crawfurd was placing geographical limits on further colonial expansion. He lobbied Haddington and Stanley, trying to convince the British government that Sarawak had 'no harbour, and was out of the highway of commerce, and involved us in territorial acquisitions that had no limit'.[13]

Publicly, Crawfurd gave qualified support for Brooke in the early 1840s, hoping that he could channel Brooke's energies towards Crawfurd's ideas of limited colonialism. When the colonial office asked Crawfurd if he recommended Brooke as the governor of Labuan, Crawfurd responded that Brooke appeared to possess 'all the qualities which have distinguished the successful founders of new colonies,—intrepidity, firmness, and enthusiasm, with the art of governing and leading the masses'.[14] Writing in *The Examiner* after the publication of Captain Henry Keppel's edition of Brooke's Journals, Crawfurd called Brooke an 'excellent man' involved in a campaign of 'romantic heroism'. Yet in his newspaper columns, Crawfurd also made it clear he had never met Brooke and that this 'romantic hero' almost appeared unreal, with Crawfurd admitting he 'hardly knew how do describe' James Brooke.[15]

Keppel's account of his and Brooke's diaries brought the 'romantic hero' to public attention. Crawfurd's support for Keppel's book gave Brooke much-needed support from the scholarly and diplomatic establishment concerning South-East Asia. Notwithstanding his views about Brooke's Sarawak adventure, Crawfurd gave Keppel permission to publish his advice to the Colonial Office on the suitability of Labuan, which Keppel published as Chapter 10 in his account of Brooke's journal.[16] Clearly, Crawfurd saw public interest in Brooke's activities as an opportunity to further publicise his own policy objectives.

Crawfurd agreed that pirates were a problem in the region, but did not see it as a reason for transforming Sarawak into a British colony. In his submission to the Colonial Office, he cited Labuan as being advantageous in the 'suppression of Malayan piracy' and noted that crippled ships had to deal with the threat of either being 'extorted' by 'semi-barbarous nations' or were in 'danger of falling into the power of robbers and savages'.[17] But although he recommended Labuan as a safe harbour for shipping, Crawfurd did not see piracy as an overwhelming problem because Keppel's policing action meant 'there is at any rate no reason to apprehend future serious disturbance from that quarter'.[18]

Despite discreetly supporting Brooke as a possible governor of Labuan in government circles and through his review articles in *The Examiner*, Crawfurd opposed Brooke's proposals for Borneo. In October 1846, Crawfurd published an anonymous commentary in *The Examiner* titled 'On the projected colonisation of Borneo', in which he rejected the idea of colonising Borneo.[19] Probably with a view to try to maintain connections with Brooke and his supporters, Crawfurd was careful not to criticise Brooke directly, and avoided mentioning him throughout the article. He opened this lengthy article with a blunt call for a 'little knowledge and common intelligence' to 'substitute for the dense cloud of vapour and rhetoric'.[20] He went on to explain the folly of colonising Borneo, arguing that it was an unproductive jungle, with poor soil and a geography that had prevented any 'native civilisation' (we will return to his focus on indigenous civilisation). The only form of colonisation that was possible, he maintained, was whereby Europeans could become a 'dominant caste' that 'exist by the toil of an inferior race,—that is, by holding that race in virtual slavery'.[21] Such a statement did not advocate colonisation—Crawfurd intended it as a rebuff to those who advocated colonialism on humanitarian grounds. He also perhaps intended it as a shock to the senses alongside the shocking images he evoked of dead Englishmen and money buried on the 'monster' island:

> The colonization, or the conquest, or the settlement of Borneo, or of any portion of Borneo, will in our humble opinion, be a very good scheme for burying Englishmen and their money in a tropical swamp; also, for swamping no inconsiderable portion of English reputation of common sense and forecast; but good for nothing else. In reference to these questions, therefore, let us hear no more of the monster island;— no, not even under its exotic sounding[22] name of Kalamantan.[23]

Crawfurd's argument against colonisation in Borneo drew on all the intellectual resources he could gather. He argued that it was pointless, commercially and morally. He was trying to negate Brooke's arguments, which focused on potential commercial rewards and also a duty to civilise. Rather than civilise the savage, Crawfurd maintained that colonisation would see the destruction of the colonisers themselves and degrade their morals through the introduction of slavery.[24]

By the late 1840s, despite Crawfurd's efforts, advocates of colonialism in Borneo appeared to be winning the debate.[25] Crawfurd's apprehension is apparent in his letters to the Radical parliamentarian Richard Cobden. Cobden had requested a background briefing from Crawfurd on Labuan and Sarawak. In letters marked 'Private' written two years after his first public but anonymous criticisms of colonisation in Borneo, Crawfurd indicated that he was extremely apprehensive about Brooke's character and conduct.[26] Crawfurd warned Cobden that Brooke was dangerous. Rather than being a humanitarian, Crawfurd believed that Brooke was actually promoting aggressive colonialism for personal gain. 'Nothing but *death* and *wast* [sic] was to be got of it', Crawfurd wrote. 'I tried', he said, 'to arrest it, to stop the blowing of the trumpets', but the 'aldermen of London and the accompanying fishmongers would have none of it and allowed the trumpet to blow on'.[27]

Throughout the 1840s, Crawfurd played a careful strategy of trying to direct colonial endeavours away from Sarawak whilst not declaring himself in opposition to James Brooke. Through private conversations, he had urged the Colonial Office and the Admiralty to be cautious. Publicly, he backed the settlement of Labuan as a compromise. His campaign for Labuan was successful, but despite these efforts, Brooke's influence increased. Critics of colonialism such as Crawfurd and Cobden looked on as Brooke captured the humanitarian agenda and used it to legitimise his colonising plans.

Colonialism and Naval Corruption

Crawfurd's opposition fell on relatively deaf ears until 1849, when the public mood changed. On 31 July 1849, in collaboration with British naval forces, Brooke launched an offensive campaign to destroy the capacity of the Saribas and Sekrang Dayaks to commit acts of piracy. The campaign was centred on the Battle of Beting Marau. Opponents labelled the battle a massacre of the Saribas and Sekrang Dayaks and used news of the event to challenge Brooke's civilising claims and the legitimacy of colonialism in Borneo.

Throughout the 1840s, individual naval commanders profited considerably from supporting Brooke's anti-piracy campaigns, despite senior commanders increasingly believing north Borneo was a distraction from real anti-piracy campaigns. The 1825 Act for 'encouraging the capture or destruction of piratical ships and vessels' allowed commanders to claim £20 prize money for every pirate captured or killed and £5 for every pirate who was alive before the battle, but whose fate was unknown.[28] The act was intended originally to respond to pirates in the Caribbean, where pirate crew numbers were small. The engagements in Borneo, however, often involved large numbers of Dayaks fighting with spears, numbers which were even inflated by naval captains.[29] In 1844, Captain Belcher claimed £11,900 in head money for killing 350 pirates, but the Dutch Resident on the island of Ternate (from where the pirates came) reported only 16 deaths and 40 wounded.[30] Naval officers could easily make their fortune by agreeing with Brooke's request and slaughtering large numbers of poorly armed Dayak warriors and then further inflating the claims.

In 1849, supported by Naval Commander Arthur Farquhar, Brooke continued his campaigns from 1844 and 1846 against the Saribas and Sekrang Dayaks.[31] Both communities had suffered the wrath of Brooke a few years earlier, but had returned to what Brooke described as 'piratical' ways. Brooke had information that a large Saribas and Sekrang war fleet was assembled. He assembled his own force, which included 2,500 Dayak warriors, 70 Dayak war-prahus, his private warship the Royalist and the British naval forces of *H.M.S. Albatross* and an armed paddle steamer named *H.M.S. Nemesis*. Brooke and Farquhar's original plan was to destroy the Saribas villages as he had earlier in 1844 and 1846, but hearing of a large raiding fleet making its way up the coast, they decided to lie in wait and ambush the pirate fleet.

The engagement on 31 July 1849 turned into a slaughter. Farquhar later claimed that 300 pirates were killed, 88 prahus destroyed and that 500 wounded pirates would have later died in the jungle. Most of these deaths were caused by the steamer *Nemesis's* ploughing through the disorientated Saribas and Sekrang war fleet with its paddle wheels—chopping the 'pirates' into pieces. After the 'battle', Farquhar and his men claimed £20,700 (equivalent to approximately £2 million in 2013)[32] in head money, and Brooke reported that the Saribas and Sekrang Dayaks had agreed to give up their piratical ways and instead to live off agriculture and trade only.

Such a large sum of money awarded to Farquhar caught the attention of Radicals such as Cobden and Hume (within the House of Commons), who were always on the lookout for profligate spending on colonial and military escapades. The Radicals used the large sums being allocated for 'head money' as a means of criticising Brooke and his campaign in Sarawak. The Radicals in parliament already held serious reservations regarding Brooke's anti-piracy methods from the mid-1840s; the debate about head money allowed the Radicals to bring the argument to public attention, which Crawfurd had failed to achieve in the mid-1840s.

There were two stages to this campaign of criticisms. The first stage was limited to questioning the veracity of naval officers for claims being made for extravagant head money. These questions were first raised by Cobden, Joseph Hume and other Radicals in the British parliament. Outside of parliament, the Radicals also gained support from the Aboriginal Protection Society and the Peace Society. The second stage was the public campaign against Brooke led by Joseph Hume. Hume used parliament to make broad calls to establish a Commission of Inquiry into abuses of power by James Brooke as honorary Consul to Brunei.

At first glance, the personal vitriolic nature of the debate in the press and the British parliament can easily blind observers to the real issues the Radicals raised in their criticisms of Brooke. Contemporary defenders of Brooke claimed Cobden and Hume were besmirching his good and noble character. Until the 1970s, many historians had followed in this fashion, with most being quasi-apologists for Brooke.[33] Such views reduce the ideological differences in the nineteenth century to mere personality. The clear moral and material objections to colonial expansion into South-East Asia are lost in most historical interpretations.[34]

In his comprehensive 1955 study of the diplomatic relations surrounding Brooke in the 1840s and 1850s, Graham Irwin downplayed the significance of humanitarian critics. For Irwin, the humanitarians practised a level of hyperbole that muted their criticism.[35] Irwin also argued that the anti-Brooke forces were a construction of the British merchant Henry Wise, who manufactured claims to seek revenge for Brooke's blocking of Wise's commercial interests.[36] In Irwin's narrative, Wise used his skills as a lobbyist to promote discontent in London and undermine Brooke. Irwin also correctly claimed that Wise was supported by merchants in Singapore, who shared his views and resented the fact that Brooke tried to curtail British traders accessing Sarawak.

Irwin's argument presents the Radical critics, such as Richard Cobden and Joseph Hume, as ignorant pawns being manipulated by self-serving merchants. Such a narrative merely perpetuates the romanticism around Brooke without exploring the concerns of the Radicals. Wise had lots of sensitive information in his possession that he could use against Brooke; therefore, Wise's disaffection with Brooke certainly changed the dynamic, opening up opportunities for the Radicals. On 26 November 1849, Wise wrote to Lord John Russell, First Lord of the Treasury. Wise described his personal horror on hearing of the operation against the Saribas and Sekrang Dayaks, saying he felt:

> a deep feeling of regret at the recent dreadful proceedings against some of the Dayaks in Borneo. And I beg respectfully state that, in common with others who from much experience in the East are capable of forming an opinion thereon, I believe such proceedings to be not more inconsistent with Sir James Brooke's previous professions as a Christian philanthropist, incompatible with his duties as Governor of Labuan.[37]

Irwin rightly dismissed Wise's statement of distress as hypocritical. Wise had not objected to the previous anti-piracy operations, which had also resulted in hundreds of Dayaks dying. Although Wise was probably disingenuous, a careful reading of his letter to Russell suggests he was changing sides in a debate that was already raging. In his letter, Wise stated that he had been persuaded by the opinions of 'others who' had 'much experience in the East'. Wise does not name Crawfurd, but (as we saw in the previous section) the leading opponent of Brooke in the 1840s was Crawfurd, and he operated behind the scenes, leaving few traces. Crawfurd was one of the most sought-after commentators on South-East Asia, regularly giving advice to government and maintaining an interest in public debates on South-East Asia as a lobbyist.[38] When Wise initially contacted Crawfurd in 1843 to support Brooke's campaign to make Sarawak a colony, Crawfurd persuaded Wise to change Brooke's plans and support a colony in Labuan instead of Sarawak.[39] Crawfurd did not have a high regard of Wise, describing him as a 'speculator' to Cobden, but he knew that Wise was a self-serving individual and could easily be manipulated to change sides and become an informant for the Radicals.[40]

News of the operation against the Saribas and Sekrang Dayaks first reached Britain in late October 1849. The *Daily News* was one of the first British papers to convey reports of the operation from the *Singapore Times*. The *Daily News* article followed the reporting practices of the 1840s, which rarely questioned the legitimacy of punitive anti-piracy expeditions. The paper was supportive of the need to suppress piracy, maintaining that 'the punishment inflicted on these fierce barbarians had been most complete'.[41] Nevertheless, a change was in the air: *The Examiner* (for which Crawfurd wrote) took a much more critical line towards British actions, calling the attack a 'dreadful slaughter of pirates'.[42]

Nothing further happened until the more comprehensive *Straits Times* report arrived in late November 1849. It was soon republished in all the London dailies. The account was glowing in its praise for Brooke, and also condemned the Dayak savages for depravities towards their captives. The article was much more graphic in its depiction of the one-sided nature of the conflict:

> Of 120 prahus which it is said started on the expedition, and all of which were in the bay the preceding evening, more than 87 were destroyed, and the loss of life on their side must have been immense—indeed, it has been placed as high as 1,200 men. On our part, saving a few slight casualties, all were unscathed.[43]

The above account was the first description of the slaughter of Dayaks published in British newspapers that depicting the involvement of paddle steamers chopping bodies to pieces. The account made clear the immense disparity of technology, with of rockets and cannons on one side against spears and swords on the other. Such descriptions left many humanitarians wondering if the 'battle' had been more like a massacre. On 6 December, Cobden wrote a long letter to his colleague John Bright reflecting the moral indignation of the humanitarians over Brooke's escapades in Borneo: 'It shocks me to think what fiendish atrocities may be committed by English arms without rousing any conscientious resistance at home, provided they be only far enough off, and the victims too feeble to trouble us with their remonstrances [sic] or groans'.[44] Cobden's focus was on the apathy of the public. He saw it as a moral argument with religious overtones: 'We as a nation have an awful retribution in store for us for wicked deeds'.[45]

The massacre of the Dayaks was clearly a moral issue for Cobden. In the *Manchester Times*, he accused Brooke of exacting 'unsparing vengeance and exterminating violence' on the Dayaks 'simply because they have not emerged from the lowest state of barbarism'.[46] Cobden went as far as accusing Brooke of 'horrid butchery' and attempting to 'exterminate the tribes' and the action being a disgrace to Britain's advocacy of 'peace and humanity' throughout the world.[47]

Crawfurd saw the matter in more practical terms. He knew that there was too little reliable information to prosecute any hard claims. He avoided providing any immediate moralising commentary, although with the dry wit that marked all of his journalism, he noted that 'the story has been told to the public by the alleged fox, and not by the alleged lamb'.[48]

Instead of moralising, Crawfurd developed the three central arguments that the Radicals would promote: first, that the massacre of the Saribas and Sekrang Dayaks was a consequence of corruption in the Royal Navy; secondly, that this corruption was a threat to the peoples of South-East Asia; and thirdly, that the tribes of Sarawak and north Borneo were not practicing piracy, but rather inter-tribal war, with which it was not the role of the British Empire to interfere. Any intervention, Crawfurd maintained, would lead to even greater atrocities by British forces who did not understand the people or the environment in which they were operating.

In 1848, Crawfurd had argued that naval corruption leads to colonial expansion, a year before the furore over Brooke broke out. He summarised the problem, with Brooke as one in which the British navy grants too much power in the hands of naval officers. Crawfurd changed the focus from Brooke's actions and instead to the naval officers that chose to support Brooke. In his review of Captain Belcher's account of Sarawak, Crawfurd had begun to develop the grounds for a future challenge to Brooke, by questioning the role and function of the Royal Navy. He concluded that British naval captains had an 'enormous range of powers and functions':

> They make war and peace as their own conscience[s] dictate; they contract alliances and promote the foundation of colonies . . . Nominally they are responsible to the British Government; but as that Government knows nothing of the localities, persons, or relations with they have to deal, they are virtually independent. They are a sort of modern Vikingar, with all the polish, protestations of religious and moral earnestness, and superficial accomplishments, of the nineteenth century. Truly a remarkable mission for a race of men, not always overstocked with education or intelligence.[49]

Crawfurd's damning description of the intelligence of naval captains underlined a structural problem within the Royal Navy and the British Empire generally. He maintained that naval officers and other military figures had a vested interest in promoting colonial expansion. Such arguments were very similar to his contention almost 30 years earlier in his *History of the Indian Archipelago* that mercantile companies in eighteenth century abused their powers for self-interested reasons: when he argued that Europeans appeared as 'armed traders' and,

> did not fail to use the power which they had in their hands to possess themselves on their own terms, of the produce or property of the native states with which they traded . . . Treaties were either violently or surreptitiously obtained . . . every attempt on the part of the natives to evade the flagrant injustice, as well as absurdity, which an adherence to them implied, was construed by the traders of Europe exercising sovereign authority as a perfidious violation of their rights, and, accordingly, punished to the utmost of their power.[50]

Following Crawfurd's reasoning, in 1850, the humanitarians soon moved their argument from moral indignation to particular concerns mirroring the stance Crawfurd took a year earlier, when he was the only activist working against Brooke.

Cobden and his Radical followers took Crawfurd's suggested lead. By his anonymity, Crawfurd concealed much of evidence of his involvement in the campaign against Brooke. He pleaded to Cobden to maintain 'confidentiality' because Crawfurd argued 'such things are most biting when anonymous'.[51] Crawfurd destroyed many of his papers before his death, and most of the evidence for his role in the campaign is found in his letters to Richard Cobden and Cobden's letters to others (but not Cobden's letters to Crawfurd, since they were destroyed).[52] Nor do we have any of Hume's correspondence with Crawfurd, since all of Hume's correspondence was destroyed in a house fire.[53] It is fair to presume, however, that Hume was in regular contact with Crawfurd, because Crawfurd regularly referred to him as a friend and Hume campaigned on behalf of Crawfurd during Crawfurd's failed election campaigns.

Crawfurd's role as the strategic and intellectual leader in the campaign is further exemplified by Cobden's letters to others, which indicate that the two men were regularly exchanging notes on strategy.[54] Cobden in his letters makes it clear he deferred to Crawfurd's judgement, writing to the Quaker peace activist Joseph Sturge:

> As respects the proposal to print Gliddon account of [the] Borneo doings, I should be afraid that some passages are libellous or at least so coarsely personal that they ought to be suppressed,—I sent a copy to Jno [sic] Crawfurd for his opinion, and he says he considers the account generally quite correct, and even written with moderation.[55]

In late January 1850, the Aboriginal Protection Society met to discuss the issue at Cobden's urging. Cobden had proposed a 'public and solemn protest' of both the Peace Society and Aboriginal Protection Society. Although the meeting began as a castigation of British butchery in South-East Asia, it soon turned to the practical question of how to change British policy and stop the butchery. The meeting called for a repeal of the system of head money, resolving that the practice was 'barbarous and unjust in principle' and presented 'a direct temptation to the shedding of innocent blood'.[56] In the newspaper reports of this meeting, we can read the humanitarians' strategic decision to direct attention away from Brooke and instead towards systems and corruption within the Royal Navy that supported colonial expansion and wars of conquest.

The Radicals presented a bill for the total repeal of the head money payments in early February 1850. Their argument centred on the rational and transparent expenditure of government money. In parliament, they questioned why the royal navy was paying £100,000 as head money to naval officers for the extrajudicial killing of 'pirates' in Sarawak. The move was classic Cobden: Cobden regularly used question time and parliamentary committees to focus on colonialism and empire as an extravagant waste of money.

It was clear that the payments were open to abuse, and the government made it clear that it was open to amending the bill to prevent abuse of the system.[57] Although the Radicals failed in enacting a repeal, they did succeed in pushing for a new act that gave discretion to the Admiralty Courts to determine the merits of each payment of head money. This change prevented naval officers from determining who constituted a pirate and henceforth, any action would not necessarily result in financial rewards to naval officers.[58] These changes removed much of the financial imperative behind naval support for Brooke.

The Radicals, therefore, were successful in changing government policy. Despite the limited objectives of reducing funding, the debate in parliament descended into vitriolic abuse. Crawfurd's old friend Joseph Hume initially stuck to what was probably a predetermined script focused purely on naval operations. Cobden, however, wanted the morality discussed and called 'attention of the House to the subject of the Borneo massacres'. He laid the blame squarely on Brooke, arguing that these 'two small tribes had the misfortune to live contiguous to a place taken possession of by a man called the Rajah of Sarawak'.[59] Cobden accused Brooke of killing people for his own self-interest. By the May sitting of parliament, the attacks were personal and much more detailed, as it became apparent to the Radicals that £100,000 would still be paid even though the Head Money Act was amended. The Radicals were accused of being unpatriotic and besmirching Brooke's good name.[60] Despite its moral substance, the debate focused on one big technical question: how do you determine or define what constituted a pirate?

Ethnology and the Definition of Piracy

Cobden first raised the question of what constituted a pirate in parliament in February 1850 and called for a committee of investigation. He made the cautious claim that 'there was no evidence that they [the Dayaks] interfered with British commerce'. He also proposed in the February sitting of parliament that the tribes in Borneo were merely 'carrying on predatory wars with each other' and, by implication, this was not piracy.[61] Cobden's argument was that these Dayaks were not a threat to British subjects and, therefore, suppression by a technologically advanced navy was an illegitimate use of force.

By May 1850, the debate in parliament had come to centre on what constituted a pirate and whether savage or barbarian tribes were, in fact, pirates. The evidence for this debate relied on ethnological interpretations of Dayak communities. The debate was the perfect environment for Crawfurd to write his anonymous articles and shape the Radicals' evidence.

Previous historians have focused on the roles of Hume, Cobden and the Aboriginal Protection Society in questioning Brooke's right to define who constituted a pirate.[62] It was John Crawfurd, however, who provided the evidence and intellectual arguments that rejected Brooke and his cohorts' interpretation of piracy.

In 1848, James Augustus St. John, a Brooke supporter in Britain, replaced Crawfurd as the writer on South-East Asian policy in the *Edinburgh Review*.[63] St. John was a journalist and possible relative of Brooke.[64] He involved his sons in support of the Brooke regime. Spencer St. John became one of Brooke's key ministers and advisers in Sarawak and later replaced Brooke as British Consul to Brunei. Spencer's younger brother, James Augustus Junior, also worked within Brooke's employ.[65] Both brothers continually supplied their father and their younger Brother Horace with material from Borneo and Horace went on to publish a new *History of the Indian Archipelago* in 1853.

James Augustus St. John (snr) maintained that piracy was the scourge of the South-East Asia, with every island in the archipelago supporting different pirate tribes.[66] The 'hand of Nature', he argued, meant that every 'creek and bay' was full of 'desperadoes' and 'piratical stations'.[67] St. John believed the problem was so epidemic in South-East Asia that British colonial rule was needed to encompass the entire archipelago. Reiterating the approaches of Raffles and Brooke, St. John maintained that it was:

> Not enough to destroy a bad government, we must replace it by a good one. Otherwise the seeds of mischief, like those of trees in a spot cleared of jungle and abandoned, will shoot up again with astonishing rapidity.[68]

St. John's article was light on ethnological detail to support the premise that colonialism would redress the bad governments and characters that sprouted so readily in South East Asia. In *The Sunday Times*, St. John presented Brooke's endeavours as part of Britain's historic duty:

> We never desire conquest for its own sake . . . Our business is of mining, and weaving, and ship-building, and navigation, and clothing the naked, and feeding the hungry, and civilising the savage, all over the world—teaching morality and religion by showing men their true interests and duties.[69]

Throughout St. John's publications, Brooke is presented as having the twin aims of 'suppressing piracy' and supporting the 'diffusion of civilisation', and Brooke's endeavours were presented as the epitome of nineteenth-century colonialism.

St. John also reprised Raffles's argument that the people in South-East Asia were passive actors, easily malleable to foreign ideas. As we saw in the previous chapter, Brooke painted all the local rulers who resisted him as foreigners to Borneo. St. John used Brooke's evidence to argue that piracy was merely a product of Islamic influences and that all the pirate leaders were Arabs, maintaining that:

> Ever since Mohammedanism was planted in the Archipelago, Arab adventurers have strayed thither, with no resources but their courage

and their swords, in the hope of erecting sovereignties for themselves among a less energetic and civilised people . . . In making their appearance among a half-savage race, and bringing along with them a knowledge of the Koran and of the first principles of civilised society, they naturally asserted their superiority over the Malays and Dayaks; who willingly succumbed to the authority of their new masters.[70]

In St. John's narrative, the people of South-East Asia were passive, uncivilised actors who did not determine their own history. Civilisation was brought to South-East Asia through Arab colonialism, but St. John argues the Arabs introduced a divergent civilisation amongst the peoples of South-East Asia and British colonialism would correct this divergence:

> Mr. Brooke, therefore, is perfectly right in denouncing the Sheriffs as the worst enemies of civilisation in the Archipelago: because, though they reclaim and refine up to a certain point, they stop short there; and, by tolerating, or rather perhaps inculcating the most immoral principles, prevent the healthful and spontaneous growth of society.[71]

On reading St. John's anonymous review and probably his columns in *The Sunday Times*, Crawfurd was incensed. He responded in *The Examiner*, bemoaning the decline in the *Edinburgh Review's* standards and declaring, 'Its article on Malayan piracy is a case in point, for instead of sound views it gives us dreams, and for knowledge, strange or incoherent words'.[72] Crawfurd declared, 'the pirates of the Archipelago are a nuisance, but they are not formidable' and that 'in all the populous and more civilised parts of the Archipelago, piracy has long ago been swept away by honest industry'.[73] The astronomical number of people supposedly involved in pirate fleets, Crawfurd argued, was ridiculous, citing the Chief of Kaili, whom St. John claimed had 1,000 ships engaged in piracy. Crawfurd noted that would have involved more people than lived on the island.[74]

Crawfurd was equally scornful of the claims that Arab Sheriffs led these piratical hordes:

> the reader, after all we have said, will not be much surprised to find that this cutting out of kingdoms with Arabian scimitars is a thing of the imagination only. The native princes of the Archipelago, from Sumatra to the Philippines inclusive, are genuine natives of their respective islands, and, as far as record and tradition extend, such has been the case for the last five centuries.[75]

In rebutting historical comparisons and the Arab influence, Crawfurd aimed to demonstrate that South-East Asians were not passive actors who could easily be transformed by colonialism. Since his time with Raffles in Java, Crawfurd had long argued that civilisation in South-East Asia derived from an indigenous source. This argument was at the heart of his racial theories, in which all races derived from aboriginal sources. In pressing the importance of local sources of identity and rejecting St. John and Brooke's argument that leaders in Borneo derived from Arabic sources, Crawfurd was technically wrong. Many Malay Royal families all claimed descent from Islamic Hadhrami migrants.[76] Despite Crawfurd's overstretched beliefs in the indigenous character of South-East Asian royalty, St. John's broader argument for the proposed transformation of pirate stations into colonies was a *fool's errand* to Crawfurd that would not achieve its goals in changing the indigenous character of South-East Asians. More importantly, however, Crawfurd wanted to demonstrate that the idea was premised on a fallacy that piracy was endemic in the archipelago.

Crawfurd led the campaign to reject the idea that Borneo was plagued by a pirate problem. On 12 January 1850, he returned to the theme of piracy in his *Examiner* columns. Parliament would not debate the issue of head money for another month, but Crawfurd realised he needed to refute the recent writings on Borneo by Brooke's supporters, whom he labelled the 'Sarawak historians'.[77] These 'Sarawak historians', he argued, produced very little new knowledge: 'in truth', he confessed, 'they leave our knowledge of the great island pretty much where it was before they were written'.[78]

Crawfurd proceeded to remedy this by writing an ethnological description of the peoples of Borneo, using the writings of Robert Burns (the grandson of the poet Robert Burns and a commercial rival of Brooke) and John Dalton (a merchant who traded in Borneo and died in 1831). These men, Crawfurd argued, produced original research superior to that published by Brooke's supporters. He believed Burns had 'written by far the best and most authentic account of it [Borneo] that has ever been given to the public'.[79] Spencer St. John had a different view and called Burns a 'ruffian' and 'disreputable adventurer' employed by Brooke's enemies to 'obtain a letter from the Sultan of Borneo complaining of Sir James Brooke's conduct'.[80] Burns was certainly supported by humanitarians and probably asked to find evidence against Brooke as well as research the ethnology of Borneo.

Crawfurd's ethnographic account did not address piracy directly, but rather, portrayed the people of Borneo as tribal, with very limited technologies. Although Brooke and his supporters had focused the British public on the ferocity of the Saribas and Sekrang Dayaks, Crawfurd argued that the Kayans were actually the paramount tribe in Borneo. The Kayans were superior because they mastered how to render steel from iron, whilst Saribas and Sekrang had not done so:

> The Kayans, like the rest of the natives, hoard skulls and pickled heads, although the passion appears to be on the wane. Notwithstanding these evidences of occasional ferocity, and that they are engaged in perpetual warfare with neighbouring tribes, they are hospitable, kind to strangers, and altogether a good-natured people.[81]

In juxtaposing the importance of the Saribas and Sekrang with the Kayans, Crawfurd wanted to demonstrate that Saribas and Sekrang were not the fierce warriors that Brooke and his supporters made them out to be. Instead, all the tribes became in his article poorly armed aborigines that made war on their neighbours, who were equally poorly armed.

Citing Dalton and Burns, Crawfurd argued that none of the tribes used firearms and had a 'superstitious dread' or fear of these powerful weapons. Their only weapons were the 'sword, spear and shield'.[82] In this, Crawfurd did not discount the argument that there were pirates in Borneo, but instead argued that the people Brooke charged with piracy were people who were not a threat and were only participating in their inter-tribal wars rather than piracy. Cobden and the Radicals would use Crawfurd's evidence in their debates in parliament.[83]

Although Crawfurd did not publicly moralise like Cobden, he did provide intellectual support to Cobden's claims. In late May 1850, Cobden raised the issue of £100,000 claim for head money again. Drawing on Crawfurd's ethnological arguments, which he put in the public domain, Cobden openly attacked Brooke's definition of a pirate:

> [Brooke] had certain disputes with his next neighbours, whom he was pleased to call "pirates". Now, these people were just as much pirates when Sir J. Brooke knew them as they had ever been before. They were tribes who had been in a state of predatory warfare with each other for many years.[84]

Brooke's supporters responded in parliament that everybody knew that pirates infested the archipelago and therefore Cobden and his associates were besmirching Brooke's good name.[85] On 12 July, Hume raised the issue in parliament again. He demanded publication of all official correspondence over the naval orders for the attack on the Saribas and Sekrang in 1849 and requested a formal commission of inquiry.

Crawfurd's influence permeates the parliamentary campaign against Brooke. Hume received a petition and a series of documents from the Singapore merchants, in which they called on Hume to call for an inquiry. Crawfurd represented these same merchants as their political agent in London. Previously, he had written to Cobden, assuring him of their support in a campaign against Brooke and that the Singapore merchants considered Cobden 'one of themselves' and that this 'expresses as much reliance and affection as possible'.[86] Consequently, Crawfurd would more than likely have been the conduit connecting Hume and the Singapore merchants. It may well have been through Crawfurd that Hume acquired Brooke's letters to Wise, which he read in parliament, and which Crawfurd then published in *The Examiner* with an extended commentary. Crawfurd, ultimately, was reasonably forgiving of Brooke at this stage, concluding: 'we can neither look upon him as an imposter and murderer, as Mr Hume does, nor as a demi-god, as others do'.[87]

On 22 July 1850, Cobden used Crawfurd as an authority in parliamentary debates, stating, 'Crawford had distinctly stated before the Committee, that there were no pirates near Sarawak'.[88] Crawfurd's intellectual position needed to be challenged by Brooke's supporters. James Augustus St. John wrote disparagingly of Crawfurd in *The Sunday Times*:

> With regard to Mr. Crawford whose name was mentioned in Monday night's debate, his authority is not worth one farthing, one way or the other. It is, I believe, nearly a quarter of a century since he quitted that part of the world, and apparently it is only since his return that he has thought much on the subject—if one so crotchety and self-willed can ever be said to think. Of course, where he says anything in favour of Sir James Brooke, one accepts it for what it is worth; but it may be the profound ignorance of parliament that it should refer to the testimony of such a writer at all.[89]

In Singapore, a Brooke supporter also challenged Crawfurd's command of evidence, asserting that the 'writer in *The Examiner*' used 'singularly loose statements and baseless statistics' to produce a 'vagrant' and 'unworthy' article.[90] The Singapore article did not, however, question Crawfurd's argument that Saribas and Sekrang were not pirates, but rather, rejected Crawfurd's assertion that the tribes were harmless. In London, Brooke's supporters published in the *Globe*, providing a list of witnesses who could swear that the Saribas and Sekrang were in fact pirates.[91] In response, Crawfurd anonymously attacked Brooke, calling him a man of 'much enterprise and of stirring ambition' but 'unscrupulous about means'.[92]

The debates were getting personal, and Crawfurd must have been worried that the debate would focus on him and his opinions, rather than the merits of Brooke's case. Crawfurd reminded Cobden about the importance of maintaining his anonymity.[93] He was certainly aware that St. John and other Brooke supporters would easily transfer focus away from the ideas Crawfurd was making and instead attack his credibility—in a similar fashion to the attacks that Cobden and Hume continually received.

By December 1850, St. John was trying to attack Crawfurd's intellectual legacy, calling 'Crawfurd and his book . . . obsolete' and that 'a man of the present day would as soon think of quoting the letters of the Jesuits as his farrago of a compilation'.[94] St. John's attack was part of a broader attempt to displace the importance of Crawfurd as the leading scholar on South-East Asia. Horace St. John (another of James Augustus St. John's sons) wrote the two-volume work *The Indian Archipelago: its History and Present State*.[95] His history presented Brooke as a central historical figure who was transforming South-East Asia—the second volume focuses predominantly on the backwater of Sarawak. The text was designed to supplant Crawfurd's previous history, with Horace writing, 'I knew of' no history 'which professed to describe the whole region, and narrate the adventures of Europeans on its shores and waters'.[96] Crawfurd never reviewed St. John's history, but instead released a second edition of his own history in 1856.[97] In a review of his book he most likely wrote himself, Crawfurd retorted 'the volume stands alone. There is no other on the subject that approaches it in fullness, accuracy, and variety of information'.[98]

Throughout 1851, Crawfurd continued to give his largely anonymous commentary on Brooke and the question of piracy. In May 1851, Brooke returned to Britain to challenge his accusers. In *The Examiner*, Crawfurd placed his support behind calls for a commission of inquiry into Brooke, writing that 'if without such commission Sir James Brooke attempts to put down piracy, after his own or any other fashion, he commits an illegal act, and becomes himself, in the eye of the law, the pirate he denounces'.[99] A few years later, in a confidential letter to the foreign office, Crawfurd branded Brooke a 'pirate' for his actions against the Sultan of Brunei.[100]

In June 1851, Crawfurd again took up his pen to outline reasons why the Dayaks were not pirates and support calls for an inquiry. 'The existence of piracy in the Indian Archipelago', he admitted, was 'undoubted', but he maintained piracy was a product of advanced civilisations: 'the pirates of the Indian Archipelago known to Europeans were never alleged to be any other than the most advanced nations of that part of the world—Malays and natives of the Philippine islands'. 'Throughout human history', he maintained there was:

> no case where the pirates mere untutored savages, without arts or effective arms. The pirates of the American Archipelago were not the Caribs, nor any other sort of red men [but rather Europeans]; and the pirates of the Indian Archipelago were not mere Dayaks of Borneo, or any other savages, sailing in cockle-shell and destitute of any weapons which could make them dangerous even to an English long-boat. In fact, Dayaks were never, until the last seven years, even alleged to be pirates.[101]

Crawfurd proceeded to dissect the parliamentary papers, concluding that:

> the two proscribed tribes are only poor savages, somewhat less truculent than savages in the same state of society usually are in other parts of the world,—incapable, from sheer impotency, however willing, of committing piracy on the high or narrow seas, and mischievous only to their savage neighbours, who, as usual, retaliate by mischief for mischief. The public is either asleep, or not quite sober on this subject.[102]

In these passages, Crawfurd was presenting nobody as noble and displacing the romantic myths that Brooke and his supporters were touting. The savages were not nice people, Crawfurd was clear about that. Savages killed each other, but it was advanced and civilised people that were capable of brutal acts of barbarism on a large scale. His argument was that human nature was barbaric and that there was no difference between the savage and the civilised. When placed in a barbaric environment, all people resort to barbarism.

From the perspective of those arguing in London, one thing stood out from the debate: there was a lack of reliable data to make any strong conclusions. Most of the evidence relied on information provided by Brooke, which the humanitarians looked on with suspicion. Crawfurd and Hume had tried to use Robert Burns as an alternate source of information, but his premature death ended that opportunity. All the writers agreed that claims were being made in the absence of any real information. All sides relied on interpreting Brooke's journals and the evidence supplied by the naval officers. Outside of Brooke's published journals, the ethnological knowledge of the peoples in Borneo was still rather miniscule. Even a basic idea of the population of Borneo was unknown. All sides were moving to the position of supporting some form of inquiry.

The Commission of Inquiry and the Alienation of James Brooke

In 1852, a new government formed in Britain that relied on the Radicals' support for legislation to pass through the House of Commons. Hume's and Cobden's lobbying finally resulted in a commission of inquiry. Hume requested that the inquiry focus exclusively on piracy and if Brooke had violated any acts of parliament or the treaty of friendship between Britain and Borneo. To determine this, Hume asked for the commission to undertake the detailed ethnology of Northern Borneo regarding piracy, calling for the commissioners to:

> Carefully distinguish between the inter-tribal head-hunting feuds of the Dyaks who have been attacked by Sir James Brooke . . . What was the "evidence and precautions taken . . . to ascertain that such persons really were pirates before they were attacked . . . To obtain correct descriptions of the boats belonging to the Dayaks who were attacked", information of their tonnage, dimensions, and number on each occasion, the number of men on board of them respectively, the descriptions and extent of the fire-arms and other-warlike instruments, which they were supplied, the nature and degree of resistance they offered . . . To procure the fullest information of the number and extent (if any) of the towns, villages, and houses belonging to the Dayaks which have been burned, destroyed, or injured by Sir James Brooke . . . To ascertain with accuracy the number, names and position in life of the Dayaks who were taken prisoner by Sir James Brooke.[103]

Hume's questions derived from many of the lines of argument that Crawfurd had raised. Although Hume had previously raised the problem of Brooke's legal status, in his suggested inquiry, he gave it very little thought. He did, however, request that the commission explore the 'manner in which, the late Sultan of Borneo was induced to enter into, and conclude any, and what negotiations whatever with Sir James Brooke respecting the territory of Sarawak'. Despite Hume's focus on piracy, the Secretary for Foreign Affairs, the Earl of Clarendon (George Villiers), did not focus primarily on piracy, but rather, the legal status of Brooke as both as Rajah of Sarawak and Governor of Labuan and consul to Brunei:

> The first question to which the Commissioners will have to direct their inquiries is, whether the position of Sir James Brooke in Sarawak, either as holding the possession of the Sultan of Borneo, or, as he now alleges, as an independent Rajah, holding it by the free choice of the people, be compatible with his duties as British Consul-General and Commissioner for Trade, and with his character of a British subject. With reference to this portion of the inquiry, it is to be observed that by no act of Her Majesty's Government has countenance ever been given to Sir James Brooke's assumption of independence, and that his possession of Sarawak has never been considered otherwise by them than as a private grant bestowed by a foreign Sovereign upon a British subject.[104]

When the British attacked Brunei in July 1846, after the death of Hassim Murdu, Brooke used the opportunity to gain a fresh title to Sarawak from Sultan Omar Alli. His new title did not stipulate any ongoing tribute and therefore it appeared that Brooke had *de facto* sovereignty of Sarawak—a development that the British government was not aware of until 1852.[105] Brooke's potentially sovereign legal status meant that he had a potential conflict of interest as a British Commissioner for Trade. Consequently, Clarendon requested that the Royal Commission address the issue of Brooke's conflict of interest, as both an individual trader and Commissioner for Trade. Finally, the commission was to look at piracy and if Brooke 'should be entrusted with a discretion to determine which of those tribes are piratical'.[106]

The Senior Commissioner was Charles Prinsep, the Advocate-General of Bengal, who behaved erratically during the course of the commission and on his return to Bengal was certified as insane.[107] The second Commissioner was Humphrey Devereux, a longstanding officer in the Bengal Civil Service. Brooke initially rejoiced at the idea of the Commission, believing it would focus on the issue of piracy and he could easily discount Hume's and the humanitarians' accusations. However, after reading the terms of reference, he decided it was a political witch hunt, calling it a commission based on 'false instructions' and a 'positive wrong from [the] government'.[108]

When the Commission concluded, it exonerated Brooke of accusations of misusing his Public Office of Consul to Brunei to support his private empire in Sarawak, yet decided that his position as ruler of Sarawak was incompatible with holding an official British position. What was worse for Brooke was that the Commission placed him into a legal *never-never land*.

The commissioners did not agree on the most important problem for the British government: whether or not Brooke was the sovereign ruler of Sarawak. The senior Commissioner, Prinsep, concluded that Brooke was still 'a vassal of the Sultan of Brunei', whilst the other Commissioner, Humphrey Devereux, maintained that Brooke carried the will of the people of Sarawak in a revolution against Brunei. Nevertheless, although Devereux saw Sarawak as an independent sovereignty, he doubted Brooke could 'attain to the position of being an independent ruler of a foreign country' whilst still maintaining he was a British subject.[109] As a subject of Queen Victoria, Brooke could not claim sovereignty in his own name. Any territory that Brooke claimed, the sovereignty for that territory automatically flowed to the Queen. The British government could consequently claim Sarawak at any time without needing to compensate Brooke for his pains.

Both commissioners supported Brooke's claim that the Saribas and Sekrang Dayaks were pirates and therefore legitimate targets. Nevertheless, although agreeing with Brooke, they seriously addressed the premise that the Dayaks were merely conducting inter-tribal war. Although the British government made that question of piracy an auxiliary focus of the commission, the topic dominated the interviews conducted by the Commissioners in Singapore.

Much of the questioning focused on distinguishing differences between piratical activities, peaceful trade and legitimate conflict. When addressing Europeans, the questions attempted to establish if the witnesses could tell the difference between the different tribes they encountered, or the difference between war prows and trading prows. When William Napier (the former Governor of Labuan, dismissed by Brooke in 1851) was questioned on 29 September 1854, he was asked if he had 'satisfied your mind as to the piratical or inter-tribal character of the predatory expeditions of the Saribas and Sekrang Dayaks?' Napier's answer was:

> I have no doubt that the Dayaks have inter-tribal wars, and long standing feuds, and that these feuds and inter-tribal wars are the origin of many of their expeditions against each other, that their expeditions may also combine piracy by attacking the smaller trading prows they fall in with, I also think highly probable.[110]

Napier's evidence highlighted the general problem the inquiry faced. Were the Dayaks acting out of tribal war or piracy, and how could you tell the difference? In Napier's evidence, the motive was inter-tribal wars, and any act of piracy was mere opportunity and not the direct motivation. When the commission turned to asking the non-European inhabitants of Borneo, they asked the question, 'Do you know anything of the Saribas and Sekrang Dayaks?' and usually got the response in the affirmative and a long statement of how they attacked villages.[111]

Although the native accounts were horrendous, such attacks on villages were not necessarily piracy, but rather, legitimate inter-tribal war that Britain had no business getting involved with, as Napier's evidence and the long commentary in parliament by Cobden, Hume and other radicals demonstrated. Consequently, the commissioners needed to assess how these acts constituted piracy or legitimate warfare. Napier argued that there was some feud or disagreement at the source of the Saribas and Sekrang expeditions. In legal terms, this would amount to a *casus belli* (cause of war); therefore, when questioning the natives of Borneo, the Commissioners asked for a cause. For example, on 16 October 1854, they asked Mohamot Sally, 'What is the general character of these attacks, were they provoked?' He responded, 'No cause or bad feeling, their object is only to get head and plunder'. Similarly, on the same day, the commissioners questioned Hajji Mahomet Sahat, asking, 'what was the cause of offence given?' He responded, 'There was no cause but a mere desire to obtain heads'.[112] In his analysis of the evidence, Decereux noted the 'attacks were all on one side' and that there is a 'unanimous declaration that no cause of offence has been given'.[113]

By focusing on cause or the lack of cause, the commissioners were trying to establish the legitimacy of the attack. The evidence they received from the people of Borneo was that there was no legitimate reason for the Saribas and Sekrang attacks, and the only reason for doing so was to plunder the people. Although still not the normal definition of piracy, the focus on plunder without cause meant the actions of the Saribas and Sekrang Dayaks had, according to Prinsep, 'nothing of the character of inter-tribal warfare' and therefore were closer to piracy than they were to inter-tribal war.[114] Nevertheless, Prinsep concluded that it is 'in my opinion neither necessary nor prudent that he [Brooke] should be entrusted by the British Crown with any discretion to determine which of these tribes are piratical'.[115]

On receiving the Commissioner's report in August 1857, Crawfurd was not impressed. In May 1854, he had predicted that 'Sir James too anxiously anticipates an adverse judgement'.[116] But receiving the report, Crawfurd complained that 'notwithstanding this huge volume, it cannot be said that there is in law the report of a commission at all'. In describing the proceedings, he called Prinsep the 'professional member' but labelled Devereux the 'lay brother', whose report, Crawfurd believed, was an 'abstract of the evidence, in which we find a mere naked skeleton without muscle, sinew, or ligament, and above all things, without brains'.[117]

Devereux claimed that the killing of 1,000 Saribas and Sekrang Dayaks in 1849 was 'just and expedient, and in conformity with the obligation of treaty, that punishment should be inflicted on them, with a view to the repression of their atrocious outrages' and that Devereux saw no 'reasonable ground for sympathy with a race of indiscriminate murderers'. Crawfurd responded that proportionally, it is about the same thing as if in a single night from 200,000 to 240,000 adult Englishmen had been put to the sword.[118] Crawfurd was totally unconvinced by the Commissioner's conclusions:

To call, then, the Seribas and Sakarran savages of Borneo "pirates", that is, men guilty of the crime of robbing on the high seas (for that is the only legal definition of piracy), is about as extravagant and absurd as if we were to call the highwaymen and footpads of Bagshot heath a hundred years ago, corsairs and bucaneers.[119]

The consequence of the commission was to end Brooke's ability to call on naval support and effectively end British expansion in Sarawak. The Commission thus delivered a qualified victory to the Radicals trying to prevent the expansion of the British Empire. Although the Commission exonerated Brooke, it did not give him any grounds to be included within the British Empire or even to call on naval support to defend his territory. The debate about piracy had ongoing implications for Crawfurd's and Cobden's criticisms of colonial expansion. Both Crawfurd and Cobden focused on trying to control the actions of military figures on the periphery who wanted to expand the empire. In 1854, Crawfurd had supported Cobden in a campaign to reveal the injustices of the war against Burma.[120] Both men were aware that Brooke was one example of a wider malaise.

The Chinese Insurrection and the Humanitarian Response to the Arrow War

Although Brooke was exonerated by the Commission, he was forced to exert the independence of his regime from the British Empire.[121] Spencer St. John believed the Commission destabilised the position of Brooke with different power blocks inside Sarawak. St. John recounted a conversation with a Chinese headman from a Chinese goldworking company that suggested the commission opened the way for plots against Brooke from within Sarawak:

He asked me what had been the result of the Commission, and whether it was true that the Rajah was no longer friendly with the British Government; whether the Queen had ordered the navy no longer to protect Sarawak; and finally, whether I, the Consul-General, was about to leave the country for good? I soon found that these subjects had been greatly canvassed among them, and they acknowledged that their friends in Singapore had written to them about these affairs. I tried to remove their unfavourable impressions, but my efforts were useless. The Rajah had announced that the British Government was no longer friendly to him, and the fact remained that I was about to quit the country. The evil results of the Commission met us at every step.[122]

In 1857, Brooke's regime faced a new crisis. On 11 February, the Chinese community launched a surprise rebellion. The Chinese plot was focused on killing Brooke and seizing Kuching, the capital of Sarawak. They succeeded in capturing Kuching, but Brooke escaped. Most accounts point to Brooke being in a state of depression at the time and that it was his loyal followers who provided the initiative to retake the capital.[123] Brooke's forces were supported by the timely arrival of the North Borneo Company Steamer, along with the loyal following of Malays and Bidayan (what contemporary accounts called Land Dayaks). These forces enabled Brooke to retake the capital. Charles Johnson was governor of the Sekrang and Saribas Dayaks (who were also now loyal followers of the Brooke state). Johnson arrived with his army of Dayaks after the capital was retaken. The Sekrang and Saribas Dayaks were then unleashed on the fleeing Chinese population. Brooke estimated that 2,000 Chinese men were killed, and probably large numbers of women as well.

News of the rebellion reached London by cable on 25 April 1857. On the 29 April, *The Times* published a long letter by Brooke narrating the cause of events. *The Times* called Brooke's actions towards the Chinese a 'terrible punishment' and listed the death toll as about 2,000. *The Times* concluded its editorial of the events by stating, 'amid the maundering of humanitarianism and the foppery of professional generalship it is reassuring to met with a man who recalls the old days of British enterprise and personal heroism in the East'.[124] Although *The Times* editorial attacked the humanitarians, the humanitarians launched no criticisms of Brooke's 'terrible punishment'.

In his column, Crawfurd raised the lack of outcry as a concern: 'How is it that there is no outcry against Sir James Brooke for his vigorous measures for the suppression of the murderous insurrection in Sarawak?'[125] Crawfurd explained it away as public acceptance of the necessities of quelling a rebellion. However, the humanitarian silence was part of a broader setback resulting from the British war in China. Humanitarians had been critical of Crawfurd's and Cobden's friend John Bowring, the Governor of Hong Kong, for his creation of hostilities in Canton that became the Arrow War or Second Opium War.

The *causa belli* for the Arrow War was the October 1856, seizure of a ship called the *Arrow* by Chinese authorities in Canton for piracy. The Chinese government objected to the British export and sale of opium within China. Much of this trade relied on British merchants working with Chinese merchants to undermine the Chinese government's ban on opium. In resisting British demands for the free trade in opium, the Chinese government harassed Chinese traders who peddled British drugs. As a counter move, the British allowed Chinese merchants to register ships under the British flag. The *Arrow* was one such ship that had previously been registered under the British flag, but its registration had lapsed at the time of its seizure. Bowring used the incident to demand trading concessions from the Chinese and ordered the bombardment of Canton without any approval from London.

Cobden saw the Arrow War as a means to change British foreign policy. Despite his friendship with Bowring, on 26 February 1857, Cobden launched a motion in parliament to have Bowring recalled. The motion was carried with a narrow victory. Lord Palmerston, the Prime Minister, however, called a snap election, and Cobden and many of his close allies lost their seats. Crawfurd wrote to Cobden, '[you have] left office at present without damage to your reputation, for the Church, the Army and the Navy are too strong for you'.[126] By the time news of Brooke's reprisals reached London, Cobden and many of his allies were out of parliament and feeling their defeat.

Despite the defeat of the Radicals in parliament, Brooke was himself facing serious problems because of the Chinese rebellion. The Chinese had provided a major part of revenue for the state. In quashing the rebellion, Brooke forced the Chinese population to flee Sarawak. In addition, substantial parts of the government infrastructure needed to be rebuilt. Brooke could no longer finance his independence.

In 1858, Brooke toured Britain trying to raise capital and promoting the idea of selling Sarawak to the British government. Crawfurd was initially tired of the campaign, writing to Cobden, 'I shall be obliged at last to write on the dirty topic although I should have been glad to have avoided it'. He speculated to Cobden a line of argument:

> I think the course you and I support will be the least—to admit at once that Brooke is a man of talents of enterprise and courage as he undoubtedly is, and that if on these grounds, the House of Commons should think his services worthy of a reward, it should vote him, at one a handsome sum and get rid of him and his Bornean tropical morass.[127]

Cobden, however, persuaded Crawfurd to continue the fight. On 9 October 1858, Crawfurd wrote in *The Examiner*, 'we can no longer remain silent respecting this new agitation of the Sarawak question'.[128] He called merchants and manufacturers supporting Brooke 'ignorant' and proceeded to reiterate all the problems he had previously raised with Sarawak and why it should not be a British colony. Brooke was requesting to be reimbursed for all the money he had spent on Sarawak over the previous 17 years. Crawfurd rejected this, but as he outlined in his letter to Cobden, he suggested parliament give Brooke some form of token grant for his services. Cobden forwarded copies of Crawfurd's articles to other activists, requesting they lobby the government as much as possible against the purchase of Sarawak, trying to stop Brooke's momentum.[129] The government, however, listened to the arguments made by Crawfurd and Cobden and rejected the Brooke proposal. In his *Examiner* column, Crawfurd congratulated the government:

> We feel it our duty to offer Lord Derby and his colleagues our hearty thanks for the courage and intelligence they have shown on this occasion, qualities which, had they been displayed by their predecessors, would have saved the nation from an imposition, which from first to last has cost much money, much foolscap, and expense for printing, to say nothing of the slaughter of some 5,000 savages or barbarians.

Notes

1 John Crawfurd, 'Crawfurd to Norton Shaw, 29 February', *Royal Geographical Society*, Royal Geographical Society, CB4/Crawfurd (1860); John Crawfurd*, 'On the Projected Colonization of Borneo', *The Examiner*, (24 October, 1846).

2 Turnbull, *The Straits Settlements*, p. 322; G. Burgess and M. Festenstein, *English Radicalism, 1550–1850*, (Cambridge: Cambridge University Press, 2007), pp. 298–299; Anonymous, 'News', *The Singapore Free Press and Mercantile Advertiser*, (21 October, 1847).

3 Anonymous, *The Singapore Free Press and Mercantile Advertiser*, (15 April, 1847). In a letter to Cobden, Crawfurd notes that Brooke's supporters were asking him for support. John Crawfurd, 'Crawfurd to Richard Cobden, 31 December', West Sussex Record Office, Cobden Mss 3/12 (1850).

4 For reference to Crawfurd being a Mason, see letter to John Crawfurd, 'Crawrud to Norton Shaw June 8', *Royal Geographical Society*, Royal Geographical Society, RGS/CB4/Crawfurd (1860). Also, his obituaries state he was in most of the intellectual clubs. Anonymous, 'Death of Mr. John Crawfurd', (13 May, 1868); Anonymous, 'Mr John Crawfurd', (16 May, 1868).

5 Crawfurd*, 'New South Australian Colony'. Crawfurd was revealed as the author of this anonymous at the time by R. Torrens, *Colonization of South Australia*, (Longman, Rees, Orme, Brown, Green, and Longman, 1835), p. 1.

6 Torrens, *Colonization of South Australia*.

7 Crawfurd commented to Richard Cobden that many of Brooke's allies asked him to write memorials supporting Brooke's attempt to get Sarawak transferred to British colonial authority in John Crawfurd, 'Crawfurd to Richard Cobden October 16', Cobden Papers, *West Sussex Record Office*, Cobden s/111 (1858).

8 John Crawfurd, 'Notes for a British Settlement on the North-West Coat of Borneo', *Foreign Office*, National Archives, CO 144/1 (1844), pp. 318–320.

9 John Anderson, 'Memorandum respecting a British Settlement on Borneo', *Foreign Office*, National Archives, CO 144/1 (1844).

10 Crawfurd, 'Crawfurd to Richard Cobden February 10'. Ingleson, in his account on the annexation of Labuan, states that Wise's response from the Foreign Office was unfavourable, and Ingleson writes, 'Brooke emphasized idealistic motives, such as the spread of Christianity and civilisation'. John Ingleson, 'Britain's Annexation of Labuan in 1846', *University Studies in History*, 5 4 (1970), p. 42. I would argued that it was because the Foreign Office was receiving unofficial advice from Crawfurd. See CO 144/ 1 pages 1–50 for references to documents being sent to Crawfurd for his comment. Ingleson goes on to state that Wise changed his approach and focused on the strategic importance of Sarawak. From Crawfurd's letter to Cobden, it appears that Wise was responding to the way Crawfurd was setting the debate.

11 {Crawfurd, c.1820 #2004}

12 Brooke and Templer, *The Private Letters of Sir James Brooke, K.C. B Rajah of Sarawak*, vol. 1, pp. 308–309.

13 Crawfurd, 'Crawfurd to Richard Cobden 10 February'.

14 Crawfurd, 'Notes for a British Settlement on the North-West Coat of Borneo', pp. 318–320.

15 Crawfurd*, 'The Expedition to Borneo of H.M.S. Dido, for the Suppression of Piracy: with Extracts from the Journal of James Brooke, Esq., of Sarawak (now Agent for the British Government in Borneo): By Captain the Hon. Henry Keppel, R.N. Two vols. Capman and Hall', (21 February, 1846).

16 Keppel, *The Expedition to Borneo of H.M.S. Dido for the Suppression of Piracy: With Extracts from the Journal of James Brooke*.

17 Crawfurd, 'Notes for a British Settlement on the North-West Coat of Borneo', p. 318.

18 Crawfurd*, 'The Expedition to Borneo of H.M.S. Dido, for the Suppression of Piracy: With Extracts from the Journal of James Brooke, Esq., of Sarawak (now Agent for the British Government in Borneo): By Captain the Hon. Henry Keppel, R.N: Two vols: Capman and Hall', (21 February, 1846).

19 Crawfurd*, 'On the Projected Colonization of Borneo', (24 October, 1846). The article was syndicated/reprinted in other papers as well including the *Hampshire Telegraph and Sussex Chronicle* on 31 October, 1846 and even the *Sydney Chronicle* on 3 April, 1847.

20 Ibid.

21 Ibid.

22 The original version had a compositing error and was written 'sounding and exotic', possibly suggesting that Crawfurd's handwritten copy had additional comments that were edited out in the published copy.

23 Crawfurd*, 'On the Projected Colonization of Borneo', (24 October, 1846).

24 Ibid.

25 See John Ingleson, *Expanding the Empire: James Brooke and the Sarawak Lobby, 1839–1868,* (Nedlands, WA: Centre for South and Southeast Asian Studies, University of Western Australia, 1979) for a discussion on how Brooke's British supporters manipulated public opinion.

26 Crawfurd, 'Crawfurd to Richard Cobden February 10', John Crawfurd, 'Crawfurd to Richard Cobden 24 December', Cobden Papers, *West Sussex Record Office,* MS 3/11 (1850); Crawfurd, 'Crawfurd to Richard Cobden, 31 December'; John Crawfurd, 'Crawfurd to Richard Cobden, 22 March', Cobden Papers, West Sussex Record Office, MS 3/17 (1851); John Crawfurd, 'Crawfurd to Richard Cobden 16 October', ibid. *West Sussex Record Office,* Cobden s/111 (1858); John Crawfurd, 'Crawfurd to Richard Cobden 20 September', Cobden Papers, West Sussex Record Office, Cobden s/114 (1858).

27 Crawfurd, 'Crawfurd to Richard Cobden 10 February'.

28 1825 (174) A bill to make further provision for the payment of the crews of His Majesty's ships and vessels, and for encouraging the capture or destruction of piratical ships and vessels.

29 Irwin, 'Nineteenth-Century Borneo', p. 146.

30 Ibid.

31 Ibid. p. 138.

32 <http://www.measuringworth.com/ukcompare/> real price of that commodity is £1,874,000.00, the labour value of that commodity is £14,820,000.00, and the income value of that commodity is £22,790,000.00

33 St. John, *Life of Sir James Brooke,* S. Runciman, *The White Rajah: A History of Sarawak from 1841 to 1946,* (Cambridge: Cambridge University Press, 2011); Tarling, *The Burthen, the Risk, and the Glory*; Irwin, *Nineteenth-Century Borneo.*

34 Nicholas Tarling focuses on government policy. Tarling, *Piracy and Politics in the Malay World*; Nicholas Tarling, *British Policy in the Malay Peninsula and Archipelago: 1824–1871,* (Kuala Lumpur: Oxford University Press, 1969); Nicholas Tarling, *Imperial Britian in South-East Asia,* (Kuala Lumpur: Oxford Univeristy Press, 1975). Irwin rejects the Radicals' position totally, arguing the Radicals were misguided and had little knowledge of the situation in Borneo or South-East Asia generally. Graham Irwin, however, did not realise that Crawfurd was one of the main architects of the radical position; Irwin, *Nineteenth-Century Borneo.* Robert Pringle generally accepts Irwin's narrative, but does realise that the Radicals were presenting a strong moral claim and included a radical statement as an appendix. Pringle, *Rajahs and Rebels: The Ibans of Sarawak under Brooke Rule, 1841–1941.*

35 Irwin, 'Nineteenth-Century Borneo', pp. 141–145.

36 The argument that Wise was behind the humanitarian argument was first proposed by Brooke's supporters in parliament. It was Henry Drummon who stated, 'it was Mr. Wise who was the real author and instigator of this Aborigines Protection Society, and who had got up this public company that Sir J. Brooke Blew up'. Commons Sitting of Friday, 12 July, 1850, Hansard, 3rd Series, vol. 112, p. 1311. In the same speech, Drummon charged the Radicals of trying to gain the colony themselves.

37 Henry Wise, 'Wise to Lord John Russell, 26 November', *Foreign Office*, National Archives (UK), FO 12/7 (1849), p. 193.

38 August St. John described Crawfurd as having the most access to information on South-East Asia. James Augustus St. John, 'To the editor of the 'Examiner', Piracy in the Indian Archipelago', *The Examiner*, (16 December, 1848).

39 Crawfurd, 'Crawfurd to Richard Cobden 10 February'.

40 Ibid.

41 Anonymous, 'Singapore', *Daily News*, (27 October, 1849).

42 Anonymous, 'Foreign Gleanings', *Examiner*, (3 November, 1849).

43 Anonymous, 'The Expedition against the Sakarran and Sarebas Pirates', *The Morning Chronicle*, (21 November, 1849); Anonymous, 'Sir James Brooke and the Pirates of the Indian Ocean', *The Times*, (23 November, 1849).

44 John Morley, *The Life of Richard Cobden*, (London: T. Fisher Unwin, 1903), p. 520.

45 Ibid.

46 Richard Cobden, 'Rajah Brooke and the Bornean Massacre', *Manchester Times*, (8 December, 1849). Cobden is identified as the author in Morley, *The Life of Richard Cobden*, p. 520.

47 Cobden, 'Rajahs Brooke and the Bornean Massacre', (8 December, 1849).

48 Crawfurd*, 'Borneo and its Resources', (12 January, 1850).

49 John Crawfurd*, 'Narrative of the Voyage of H.M.S Samarang, During the Years 1843–46; Employed Sureying the Islands of the Eastern Archipelago; Accompanied by a Brief Vocabulary of the Pincipal Languages: By Captain Sir Edward Belcher, R.N. Commander of the Expedition: With Notes on the Natural History of the Islands, by Arthur Adams, Assistant Surgon, R.N. Reeve and Co.', *The Examiner*, (18 March, 1848).

50 Crawfurd, *HIA.*, vol. iii, p. 220.

51 24 December, 1850 Cobden MS 3/11.

52 Wallace also made reference to Crawfurd losing his papers. Crawfurd had also lost a paper he was meant to referee; see RGB letter.

53 R.K. Huch and P.R. Ziegler, *Joseph Hume, the People's M.P*, (Phillidelphia: American Philosophical Society, 1985), p. vii.

54 For Cobden's surviving letters, see Anthony Howe, Simon Morgan, and Gordon Bannerman, 'The Letters of Richard Cobden Volume II 1848–1853', (Oxford: Oxford University Press, 2010).

55 Ibid. p. 332. Note W.A. Gliddon was brother of the racial thinker and craniologist George Gliddon.

56 Anonymous, 'Meeting of the Aboriginal Protection Society over Borneo', *The Examiner*, (2 February, 1850).

57 'Pirates (Head Money) Repeal Bill', House of Commons, Monday, 11 February, 1850, *Hansard*, 3rd series, vol. 108, p. 662.

58 Irwin, 'Nineteenth-Century Borneo', p. 146.

59 Ibid.

60 'Pirates (Head Money) Repeal Bill', House of Commons, Monday, 11 February, 1850, *Hansard*, 3rd series, vol. 108, p. 662.

61 Ibid.

62 Irwin, 'Nineteenth-Century Borneo'; Pringle, *Rajahs and Rebels: The Ibans of Sarawak under Brooke Rule, 1841–1941*; Tarling, *Piracy and Politics in the Malay World*.

63 James St. John, 'Piracy in the Oriental Archipelago', *The Edinburgh Review: Or Critical Journal*, 88 177 (1848). Attributed by Houghton, Slingerland, and College, *The Wellesley Index to Victorian Periodicals, 1824–1900*. The supplanting of Crawfurd and Crawfurd's subsequent attack of St. John (John Crawfurd*, 'Piracy in the Eastern Archipelago', *The Examiner*, (21 October, 1848); John Crawfurd*, 'The Edinburgh Review and the Examiner', *The Examiner*, (16 December, 1848).) was part of a broader division between the *Edinburgh Review*, the *Westminster Review* and *The Examiner* newspaper. Mary Quilty observed that 'Crawfurd in his later life seems to have switiched, as regular contributor from the Edinburgh Review to the Westminister Review because of these journals' changing stances on "systematic colonisation" over a division over colonisation between John Bowring and Perronet Thompson on the one hand and James and John Stuart Mill, George Grote, Molesworth and Buller on the other'. Quilty, 'British Economic Thought and Colonization in Southeat Asia, 1776–1850', p. 70.

64 The argument that James Augustus St. John was a relative of Brooke is speculative and introduced here for the first time. I am suggesting this idea based on two points of evidence. First, St. John used the alias Grenville Brooke for his articles in the *Sunday Times*. He began using the alias from the early 1830s, way before Brooke was important. Secondly, two of his sons were employed by James Brooke. Brooke often used distant relatives as officers in his state of Sarawak.

65 Frank Middleton, Middleton-St.John genealogy wiki, <http://middleton-stjohns.com/wiki/James_Augustus_St.John_II>, date accessed 27 November, 2014.

66 St. John, 'Piracy in the Oriental Archipelago', pp. 68–69.

67 Ibid. p. 68.

68 Ibid. p. 88.

69 Greville Brooke, 'New Markets for British Trade in the East', *The Sunday Times*, (11 October, 1846).

70 St. John, 'Piracy in the Oriental Archipelago', p. 76.

71 Ibid. p. 77.

72 Crawfurd*, 'Piracy in the Eastern Archipelago', (21 October, 1848).

73 Ibid.

74 Crawfurd may have misunderstood the evidence here. Many of the ships would have derived from the Balangingi, who were part of the Orang Lunt (Sea Gypsies); these people did not live on the island. I thank John Walker for this clarification of Crawfurd's evidence. For a discussion of the Balangingi diaspora, see Warren, *The Sulu Zone*, pp. 190–197.

75 Crawfurd*, 'The Edinburgh Review and the Examiner', (16 December, 1848).

76 For example, the Royal house of Johor traces their descent back to the 'Aidarus of Aceh in Sumatra, who was a Sayyid from the Hadramaut in Southern Arabia'. Most other Royal houses in the Malay world are interconnected with Johor. Christopher Buyers, 'Royal Ark—Johor', (2000–2012). For an extended discussion of the role of Hadrami migrants in South-East Asia and their involvement in Malay royal houses, see E. Ho, *The Graves of Tarim: Genealogy and Mobility across the Indian Ocean*, (Berklery, CA: University of California Press, 2006).

77 Crawfurd*, 'Borneo and its Resources', (12 January, 1850).

78 Ibid.

79 John Crawfurd*, 'Robert Burns' and 'Sir James Brooke', *The Examiner*, (4 October, 1851).

80 St. John, *Life of Sir James Brooke*, p. 239.

81 Crawfurd*, 'Borneo and its Resources', (12 January, 1850).

82 Ibid.
83 James Augustus St. John attacked Cobden's use of Crawfurd in parliament. See Greville Brooke, 'The Peace Agitators', *The Sunday Times*, (8 December, 1850); Greville Brooke, 'Trade and Piracy', *The Sunday Times*, (28 July, 1850).
84 Commons siting Thursday, 23 May, 1850, HOC *Hansard*, 3rd Series, vol. 111, p. 295.
85 Mr Plowden, 'I had been in the China sea in the year 1809 or 1810, and at that time a piratical fleet infested the whole southern coast, and spread dismay in every quarter . . . Now with regard to the Malay pirates, the House would remember that the Malay pirates infested the whole of the Archipelago, and were of a most atrocious character'. Commons siting Thursday, 23 May, 1850, HOC Hansard, 3rd Series, vol. 111, pp. 297–298.
86 Crawfurd, 'Crawfurd to Richard Cobden 10 February'. Crawfurd was also close friends with Charles Wood, the editor of the *Straits Times*. It was Wood who organised the memorial (letter of protest) that was sent to Hume complaining of Brooke's actions.
87 John Crawfurd*, 'The Rajah Brooke', *The Examiner*, (27 July, 1850).
88 SUPPLY—LABUAN. HC Feb 22 July, 1850 vol. 113 cc106–22.
89 Brooke, 'Trade and Piracy', (28 July, 1850).
90 A.Z., 'To the Editor of the Singapore Free Press', *The Singapore Free Press and Mercantile Advertiser*, (21 June, 1850).
91 I don't have access to this article, only Crawfurd's refutation of it in John Crawfurd*, 'Bornean Piracy', *The Examiner*, (28 June, 1851).
92 Ibid.
93 Crawfurd, 'Crawfurd to Richard Cobden 24 December'.
94 Grenville Brooke (James Augustus St. John) The Peace Agitators, *The Sunday Times*, (8 December, 1850), page 2 issue 1470.
95 Horace Stebbing Roscoe St. John, *The Indian Archipelago; Its History and Present State*, (London: Longman, Brown, Green and Longmans, 1853).
96 Ibid., vol. 1, p. v.
97 Crawfurd, *Descriptive Dictionary*.
98 John Crawfurd*, 'A Descriptive Dictionary of the Indian Islands and Adjacent Countries', *The Examiner*, (16 August, 1856).
99 John Crawfurd*, 'Modest Merit', *The Examiner*, (31 May, 1851).
100 John Crawfurd, 'Crawfurd to F Rogers, 12 November', *Foreign Office*, National Archives (UK), FO 12/28 (1860), pp. 173–180.
101 Crawfurd*, 'Bornean Piracy', (28 June, 1851).
102 Ibid.
103 Joseph Hume, 'Mr Hume, M.P., to the Right Honorable the Earl of Clarendon, Her Majesty's Secretary of State for Foreign Affairs, 30 April', *Foreign Office*, National Archives (UK), FO 12/21 (1853).
104 Earl of Clarendon, 'Earl of Clarendon to Sir Charles Wood, 21 June', *Foreign Office*, National Archives (UK), FO 12/21 (1853), p. 3.
105 Irwin, 'Nineteenth-Century Borneo', p. 148.
106 Clarendon, 'Earl of Clarendon to Sir Charles Wood, 21 June', p. 3.
107 St. John, *Life of Sir James Brooke*, p. 270. M. Allbrook, *Henry Prinsep's Empire: Framing a Distant Colony*, 2014), p. 56. also Runciman, *White Rajahs*. It is also worth noting that Prinsep was the senior commissioner and his verdict was not as favourable to Brooke as Devereux. The evidence for his insanity goes back to St. John's version of events. As a supporter of Brooke, St. John has every reason to slander Prinsep.
108 Quoted in Tarling, *The Burthen, the Risk, and the Glory*, pp. 180, 83.
109 Final reports into James Brooke. Anonymous, 'Commission of Inquiry into James Brooke'.

110 Anonymous, 'Evidence of William Napia (Former Governor of Labuan and at the time Law Agent in Singapore court House) 29 September', *Foreigin Office*, National Archives (UK), FO12/20 (1854), p. 67a.

111 FO 12/20 this is usually the second or third question asked, with the first questions being devoted to establishing the identity of the informant.

112 FO 12/20 pp. 287, 293.

113 Anonymous, 'Commission of Inquiry into James Brooke', p. 22.

114 Charles Prinsep, 'Mr Prinsep to the Governor-General of India in Council, Opinion', *Foreign Office*, National Archives UK, FO 881/482 (1855), p. 4.

115 Ibid. p. 6.

116 John Crawfurd*, 'The Borneo Inquiry', *The Examiner*, (20 May, 1854).

117 John Crawfurd*, 'Results of the Brooke Inquiry', *The Examiner*, (25 August, 1855).

118 FO 881/482 Memorandum on Piracy of the Serebas and Sakarran Dyaks; ibid.

119 John Crawfurd*, 'The Brooke and Borneo Inquiry', *The Examiner*, (1 September, 1855).

120 John Crawfurd*, 'How Wars are Got Up in India: The Origin of the Burmese War: By Richard Cobden, Esq., M.P.', *The Examiner*, (20 August, 1853). John Crawfurd, 'Crawfurd to Richard Cobden, 12 August with Memoranda on Burmah', Cobden Papers, West Sussex Record Office, Cobden M, 3/4 (MF 3) (1853).

121 Tarling, *The Burthen, the Risk, and the Glory*.

122 {St. John, 1879 #1744}

123 St. John, *Life of Sir James Brooke*; Tarling, *The Burthen, the Risk, and the Glory*; Walker, *Power and Prowess*.

124 Anonymous, 'The Graphic Letter of Sir James Brooke', *The Times* (29 April, 1857).

125 John Crawfurd*, 'Sarawak and Canton Affairs', *The Examiner*, (2 May, 1857).

126 Crawfurd, 'Crawfurd to Richard Cobden, 22 March'.

127 John Crawfurd, 'Crawfurd to Cobden, 30 September', Cobden Papers, West Sussex Record Office, Cobden MSS 5/109, 5/110 (1858).

128 John Crawfurd*, 'Rajah Brook and his Claims', *The Examiner*, (9 October, 1858).

129 Cobden to Joseph Sturge in R. Cobden and others, *The Letters of Richard Cobden: Volume III: 1854–1859*, (Oxford: Oxford University Press, 2012), p. 409.

8 Civilisation, the Savage and Equality

In his anonymous writings in *The Examiner*, John Crawfurd became a defender of the savage's rights to equality. He argued that the savage had the right to live without civilisation being enforced upon them, and that civilisation did not justify the mass killing of people. In a cutting article titled 'The Lion-Worshipers', published in 1851, when Crawfurd was 68 years old, he castigated imperial nationalists, such as the supporters of James Brooke, for following a cult to force European civilisation onto South-East Asian peoples, writing:

> Under the designation of pirate, some three thousand of the male adult population of the two feeble tribes alluded to have from first to last been put to the edge of the sword,—without resistance. Our contemporary is pleased to call all this "extirpating piracy", "reclaiming savages", and introducing "the arts of civilised life". Substituting opium for brandy, which is vended by authority in Sarawak for the benefit of the State, the means pursued seem to us to be the very same by which the savages of another part of the globe have been either exterminated or brutalised.[1]

Crawfurd's article passionately expressed his belief in the rights of the savage to live free of imposed civilisation. It was, he said, the civilised who inflicted 'homicide as the best means of taming the savage and the barbarian'.[2] Crawfurd concluded that a civilising empire that protected Asian peoples by removing their rights to decide their individual destinies was tantamount to treating grown adults as children. He wanted Britain to recognise the natural individual rights of all peoples. Rather than protect savages as children with a civilising colonialism, Crawfurd proposed that the civilised should leave the savage alone. In places where the savage was already colonised, the savage should be treated as an equal to the civilised European and given full rights within the colonial state.

Crawfurd's belief in the savage having natural rights affected how he responded to James Brooke and the colonisation of Sarawak. His belief also affected his approach to ethnology. With the revival of colonialism in the 1840s and 1850s—which Crawfurd had campaigned against—he was forced to reconsider his approach to civilisation and the savage. From the 1840s onwards, Crawfurd's ethnology increasingly focused on the violent tensions between the savage and the civilised. Underlying his concern was a belief in freedom and equality of all races, despite his conviction in their separate creations. Yet, even as Crawfurd lobbied against colonisation, his views on the importance of race in determining human history hardened. His polygenesis vision of race meant his ideas could easily be used to support morally dubious attitudes towards non-European peoples. After 1859, Crawfurd faced a new challenge to his polygenic thinking. Charles Darwin's idea of evolution and the American Civil War forced Crawfurd to reconsider equality between the races. Although supporting the morality behind the monogenesis position and evolution, the conclusion that Crawfurd drew was that evolutionary theory created a hierarchy between the races and further supported the move to inequality between the races.

The Breakdown of Conjectural History of the Savage and the Barbarian

In 1858, when Crawfurd wrote his last words on Sarawak, he ended his article by stating that British involvement in Sarawak had resulted in the 'slaughter of some 5,000 savages or barbarians'.[3] This was a loose use of language, in which Crawfurd conflated the savage with the barbarian. Such looseness of language in his descriptions of the differences between the savage and the barbarian is a common facet of Crawfurd's writings from the 1840s onwards. Crawfurd was not alone: his contemporaries in the debates on Sarawak blurred the distinction between the savage and the barbarian, with one of his contemporaries claiming that 'savages could be reclaimed from barbarism'.[4] Crawfurd's lack of clarity in descriptive use of the terms 'savage' and 'barbarian' reflected a move away from the conjectural history methods of his early career towards a new anthropological model of race that was not bound by universal history.[5]

As we have seen, Crawfurd's early writings of the 1820s followed the eighteenth-century traditions of conjectural or stadial history. This approach to history identified societies as passing through key stages in social development: from the savage, to the barbarian, to the civilised stage of social development. Many Enlightenment historians also included numerous transitional stages between the three main stages, such as semi-civilised or semi-barbarian. Conjectural history was an inherently universalist form of history and presumed that all humans followed the same path of development towards civilisation. Local conditions could cause disruptions that prevented development or led to degradation, but the general stages were the same.

By the late eighteenth century, the conjectural framework of staged development was also connected to the circular idea of history, with Edward Gibbon's *Decline and Fall of the Roman Empire* being the preeminent example. This form of circular decline-and-fall history gave the barbarian an important role in human history. Barbarians became the warlike peoples that raided civilised empires, bringing waves of liberty into degenerate civilisation.

In the 1820s, Crawfurd used both conjectural and decline-and-fall methodologies to explain social development in South-East Asia. However, Crawfurd's polygenic ideas were a problem for him in developing a truly conjectural history. Conjectural history held that there was a universal history for all societies to follow. Crawfurd's belief in multiple separate creations for the different races meant that he could never truly subscribe to this universal view of history. The progress of a race's development through history was, for Crawfurd, always dictated by the mix of local geographic conditions and the inherent qualities the race was gifted with at its first creation.

Although Crawfurd's 1820 *History of the Indian Archipelago* used the circular decline-and-fall narrative as an explanatory tool, he also saw its limitations. He acknowledged that barbarians in South-East East Asia faced practical problems of filling the historical role of a barbarian hoard, failing to be able to move vast amounts of people across the water and supplying them with food in the way the Northern barbarians had done:

> The Indian islanders can never effect conquests on more civilized neighbours as did the barbarians of the north, from the want of those provisions, the existence of which was implied in the very nature of a Tartar camp, and the impossibility, therefore, of moving in great and overwhelming bodies.[6]

Although Crawfurd saw South-East Asians as equally as barbarous as the barbarians of northern Europe that overran the Roman Empire, he was noting that the sea prevented South-East Asians from moving as a hoard, and prevented them from having an equally important historical effect. Consequently, when writing in 1820 and considering which barbarians brought liberty to South-East Asia, he looked to the European trading companies as harbingers of barbarian liberty.

By the 1840s and 1850s, Crawfurd could no longer see colonialism and barbarism as positive forces. He wrote very little that was positive towards colonialism in his columns in *The Examiner*. His writing therefore no longer reflected the circular decline-and-fall view of civilisation, but rather, a critique of the amoral rapacious and ill-conceived attitudes of the civilised towards the savage. Much of his writing focused on the barbarities that Europeans, and in particular the British, were unleashing towards the savage under the guise of 'civilising' them.

When he chose to release the second edition of his *History of the Indian Archipelago* as the *Descriptive Dictionary of the Indian Archipelago*, he only used the word 'barbarian' three times as opposed to the 45 times he used the word 'savage' and the 64 times he used the word 'civilisation'. Crawfurd had made a deliberate decision to move away from the conjectural history of his youth. Instead, he began using a methodology that assessed societies as either being 'savage' or 'civilised', with indeterminate gradients in between.

Crawfurd recognised that the savage society and the civilised society were both idealised types. In 1858, he noted that both the savage and the civilised states were relative concepts. All savages, he argued, have 'made some advances towards civilisation' and the 'word civilization is, of course, merely a relative term, and which, although it always implies social advancement, it is impossible to fix or define'.[7]

The title of his 1858 paper and lecture, 'On the conditions which promote or retard civilisation', suggested his new focus was on degrees of civilisation as means of replacing conjectural history. Throughout his newspaper columns and his *Descriptive Dictionary*, Crawfurd focused on degrees of civilisation and what prevented civilisation from developing and prospering. Initially he focused on geographical causes, but when they did not appear strong enough, he reverted to blaming racial cause for improvement or lack of it.

On a political and strategic level, Crawfurd's descriptions of savages as ignoble and living a less than romantic way of life was a deliberate attempt to make colonisation appear less attractive to harbingers of a civilising empire. He wanted to make it clear that the people of Borneo were not imperial assets, but rather, problems. For example, he stated: 'There are probably not fewer than twenty petty tribes speaking twenty different and distinct languages, unintelligible to each other; ever at war, and far more intent on cutting off each other's head, to pickle and store than on anything else'.[8] These depictions of savagery were deliberately designed to be negative and derogatory towards the people of Borneo. Crawfurd wanted to warn the civilised to leave the savage to their own devices, for fear of courting disaster. In trying to stop colonialism, Crawfurd was actually trying to protect the peoples of Borneo from the designs of British builders of empire.

In 1858, Crawfurd also wrote his last series of articles rejecting the 'occupation' of Sarawak as a 'protectorate'. He believed these articles represented a 'complete case not very easy to answer'.[9] The political argument of labelling people savages was a central part of his dismissal of Brooke's agenda. He stated it was 'most unwise to entangle ourselves in the politics of savages and barbarians innumerable,—of men incapable of keeping the peace towards each other for a single week together'.[10] This advice was in keeping with Crawfurd's long-term political strategy railing against the expense of empire. But implicit within this political strategy was a new approach by Crawfurd to indigenous peoples.

The Civilised World Against the Savage and the Barbarian World

Whilst writing his final articles on Sarawak in October 1858, Crawfurd was also penning his lecture 'On the conditions which favour, retard, or obstruct the early civilization of man'.[11] This lecture was to be his keynote address, which he would rewrite and deliver several times over the next three years. Crawfurd was in his early 70's by the time he was writing and delivering this lecture. In an age when the average life expectancy was 44, he may have seen it as the culmination of his life's work.[12] Whatever the case, there is no doubt Crawfurd saw it as important and intended it to impact on the major philosophical debates of the day. He planned for the paper to sum-marise his long-held ideas on the importance of geography and their inter-section with his ideas on race. He had already articulated many of his ideas about geographical determinism in his 1856 *Descriptive Dictionary of the Indian Archipelago*. Yet, he found writing this new paper 'On Conditions that determine civilisation' forced him to expand his old ideas. As he com-plained to his old comrade Cobden, 'although [I am] long use to thinking on it, I find [it] somewhat tough'.[13] A deeper problem was on Crawfurd's mind.

Much of the final 1861 published paper had little to do with the topic in the title. Instead, Crawfurd devoted most of the article to arguing that there was nothing noble about savages, and they certainly were not innocent peo-ple living in an Arcadian bliss who needed protection.[14] The original paper delivered in 1858 had a very similar direction.[15] It began with Crawfurd's reassertion of his belief in multiple creations of humans for distinct regions of the earth. However, despite the separate origins of races, he argued that humans in their initial creation were all equal as savages and that they were 'miserable beings'.[16] In the paper, Crawfurd connected the indigenous tribes of Borneo with those in South America, Australia and South-East Asia more broadly as all living in a savage condition that was harsh and brutal.

Crawfurd promoted an ethnology that appeared to distance the civilised from the savage and was ultimately hostile to the plight of indigenous peo-ples. An outstanding trait of Crawfurd's ethnological writing from the 1860s was his utter rejection of the idea of the 'noble savage'. Citing Crawfurd's writing from this time, Ter Ellingson identifies Crawfurd as the first person to misattribute the phrase the 'noble savage' to Jean Jacques Rousseau as part of a process of creating a new ethnology that blended barbarians and savages into one group. The powerful conclusion that Ellingson draws is that Crawfurd created a mindset within ethnology and later anthropology in which the:

> opposition now was simply between "civilised white" society and all others, while the extension of the scorn generated by the original hyper-bolically absurd juxtaposition of "noble" with "savage" translated logically—but with great emotional intensity—into a denial of the pos-sibility of attribution of good qualities to any people who were not white.[17]

The irony with Ellingson's position is that Crawfurd believed in equality of all peoples and that all people had good and bad qualities—an argument that was compounded in the campaigns against British colonial expansion in Asia. Crawfurd's rejection of 'noble savage' metaphors derives from his desire to stop aggressive colonial practices in their name. He saw the romanticism in the writings of James Brooke and his supporters as a source of legitimising colonial conquests in the name of protection and civilisation.

Crawfurd's harsh view of indigenous societies evolved out of his attempts to prevent colonial escapades being portrayed as an historical duty to civilise the savage. Crawfurd's goal at this stage was to create an ethnology separate from narrative history that did not make sentimental historical claims that he believed wrongly connected Europeans to Asians and therefore legitimised actions that were destructive to both. His position was that the historical narrative too easily supported sentimental connections between the savage, the barbarian and the civilised. Instead, he wanted to focus the new science of ethnology on the material forces of geography and race to understand the causes of difference.

The impoverishment of savages was a theme that Crawfurd emphasised in all surviving versions of the lecture. Impoverishment, however, did not merely extend to the material products of the savage, such as clothes, food and accommodation. Savagery, Crawfurd came to realise, was produced by a hostile environment that was inherently unfair and inhumane. The much-vaunted freedom of the savage, he realised, was the freedom to fall victim to one's fellows or pitiless nature:

> I cannot set much value on the freedom of the being who was liable to be knocked on the head by the first stronger man he met, for the sake of the possession of a dead rat or a cocoa-nut; nor can I conceive anything noble in the poor naked, crouching creature, trembling with cold and starving from hunger.[18]

In this above comment and others, Crawfurd severed the idea of freedom from that of the savage and the barbarian. His disapproval of the sentimental and romantic fog that had obscured a clear view of the savage was enlarged to include a critique of savage freedom. In doing so, Crawfurd was adopting a position that was in stark contrast to the position that he had held 40 years earlier, when he had promoted the Enlightenment ideas of savage and barbarian freedom as creative forces, impelling the development of identity and culture.

For the older Crawfurd, freedom was no longer a product of barbarian savagery that needed to be romanticised, with ideas of barbarian hordes or savages with natural nobility. According to his revised reasoning, savagery did not produce culture and civilisation, as Enlightenment philosophy had held. Human ingenuity produced culture and civilisation.

By 1858, Crawfurd began proposing that civilisation needed to be defended against savagery, or else the civilised could easily revert to savagery, as Brooke had done in Sarawak. The origins of civilisation was still the key theme. But now, he wanted to demonstrate the huge gulf that existed between savage society and civilised society. He emphasised the fragility of modern civilisation. In each version of the lecture, he concluded by congratulating his audience for being civilised:

> I think I may safely congratulate you that you are not the red men of Terra del Fuego, but civilized white men and accomplished women, the humblest amongst your having the power of enjoying more of the comforts and pleasures, physical and intellectual, of life, than the proud lords of a horde of ten thousand barbarians.[19]

By the 1850s, he came to the view that all people were naturally savage and colonialism brought out savagery in the civilised as well as in the savage. It is easy to view Crawfurd's work as presenting the civilised world in dichotomous opposition to the savage world. In a recent paper on Crawfurd, Martin Muller argues that the idea of civilisation was at the core of Crawfurd's work.[20] Muller's argument appears to support Ellingson's conclusions, which proposed that Crawfurd's work contributed to a nineteenth-century attitude, in which 'opposition now was simply between "civilised white" society and all others'.[21] Crawfurd's views on civilisation and savagery are more complex than a simple dichotomous opposition. His views on the savage were forever changed by the politics of colonisation in Sarawak.

Crawfurd's rejection of savage society as being barbaric evolved over the course of his writings on Sarawak and Borneo and was a response to colonialism rather than an endorsement of it. In the case of Sarawak, his sanguine writings on the barbaric habits of the Dayaks were a product of his argument that these Dayaks had not committed the crime of piracy, but rather, were practising inter-tribal warfare. This argument he used to further his political agenda of halting the colonisation of the Dayaks and their lands.

Although his lectures and articles *On Conditions Which Favour, Retard, or Obstruct the Early Civilization of Man* may now appear as a defence of civilisation, the opposite was actually the case. Crawfurd's newspaper columns documented how savages suffered more from violence from the civilised than the harm that savages inflicted on the civilised. He claimed that Brooke had 'diffused the light of civilization by the flash of the cannon cutting to pieces hundreds of unresisting wretches with canister shot'.[22] Sarcastically, he likened Brooke to a lion, which was also the symbol of British imperialism, writing:

> Woe to those who cannot believe in the virtues of a fashionable lion,— who cannot think that his growls are music, or his homicides the best means of taming the savage and the barbarian. At every attempt to enunciate a truth about him, we have honourable and right honourable gentlemen vociferating their painful oh! oh![23]

Crawfurd's concerns were not limited to South-East Asia. In early 1860, he campaigned within the Geographical Society to not use the exploration of Africa as a means of colonising the interior of Africa and trying to build a European enclave within the territory of African savages.[24] In his 'Conditions' lecture, he made veiled criticisms of his 'friends', such as the then Governor of New Zealand George Grey, for being too close to savages and interfering in the lives of the savages.[25] Crawfurd was critical of humanitarian desires to civilise the savage, and thereby remove the savage from his natural path of development and potentially interfering with the savages' rights to choose their way of life.[26]

Crawfurd's polygenic vision of separate races on a shared path to development meant that each race had its own journey. Although critical of the savage's conditions for living a harsh life, Crawfurd was repeatedly relativist in defending the savages' way of life as best suiting their environment. Quoting Charles Darwin, Crawfurd wrote of the inhabitants of Tierra del Fuego, 'we must suppose that they enjoy a sufficient share of happiness (of whatever kind it may be) to render life worth having'. Similarly, Crawfurd commented on the Esquimaux (Inuit), 'notwithstanding the severity of their climate, a more comfortable people than many other races, living in more genial regions'.[27] His paper is full of examples of other races being developed to best suit their environment.

Crawfurd was increasingly concerned that Brooke's approach was symptomatic of a wider paternalistic approach to indigenous peoples throughout the British Empire. In 1861, Crawfurd reviewed James Money's *How to Manage a Colony*, which argued, like Wallace, that the British empire should adopt the Dutch colonial system of paternalism. In rejecting Money's proposal, Crawfurd maintained that the Dutch 'reduced the natives to the condition of serfs' and concluded by stating, 'We must have none of a scheme which sets against economic science, sound legislation, and the natural rights of man, whatever be his race or colour, at utter defiance'.[28] This was the Crawfurd, who 44 years earlier, in his seminal *History of the Indian Archipelago*, had argued for social and political equality inside the colonies in 1820.

In 1864, Crawfurd argued with Alfred Russell Wallace at the British Association for the Advancement of Science after hearing his paper on Dutch colonial reforms. Wallace had proposed that Britain should follow the Dutch example of transforming savage people from a 'state of barbarism'.[29] Wallace had described how people under Dutch rule had progressed from their previous state of constant war and now were living with their huts 'raised upon lofty posts, to guard against attacks, and decorated them with the heads of their enemies. Their clothing was strips of bark, and their religion was a degrading demon-worship'. Wallace argued that the Dutch government had transformed the natives:

> The country is now becoming a garden; the villages are almost all like
> model villages; and the cottages as neat and pretty as those one sees

upon the stage. The streets are bordered with hedges of roses in perpetual bloom; near every village are the most beautifully cultivated and productive coffee plantations, while hill rice fields, and fruit and vegetable grounds, supply an abundance of food to the inhabitants.[30]

Wallace's picture of social transformation ascribed very much to the idea of civilisation that James Brooke was propagating in Sarawak. Crawfurd had always been cautious of Wallace, believing he was too close to the Brooke regime. In 1856, Crawfurd commented on a paper of Wallace's being read in absentia as 'the only thing remarkable in it was an high-wrought, sanguine, and therefore somewhat indiscreet eulogy of the administration of the little district of Sarawak'.[31] In his address, Wallace advocated that the Dutch method be used to solve the New Zealand Wars and that British policy should be to civilise the Maori.[32] He characterised the conflict in New Zealand as 'the deplorable result of the free competition of antagonistic races in New Zealand, which can only end in the extermination of a people (Maori)'.[33] He advocated ruling 'an uncivilized race' with the same attitude as that of a 'parent to child, or generally of adults to infants' and advised that a 'certain amount of despotic rule and guidance is essential in the one case as it is in the other'.[34] This, he believed, would end the free competition between races. Rather than a bloody free-for-all, the interracial competition would become a gesture of compassion by the civilised European races.

Crawfurd, however, was shocked to the core by Wallace's ideas of a civilising 'paternal despotism'.[35] He responded to Wallace's address by stating that:

> he had neither expected to have an apology for monopoly nor despotism from Mr. Wallace. The system which Mr. Wallace had lauded was simply the enforced coffee labour of Java. It was a system that treated the people as children, but the people were not children; and something better than flogging them to make them work hard.[36]

Here we see Crawfurd's true colours: it was equality of people that concerned Crawfurd as much as, if not more than civilisation. Crawfurd was calling Wallace and others like him, who believed they were advocating civilisation, advocates of slavery. Wallace's paternalistic logic was unmasked as supporting the suppression of people's natural rights. Crawfurd's ethnology led him to believe in equality between the races, not inequality between the races. All the learning and experience he had accumulated in his long life led him to this conclusion. His ethnology was about how to achieve equality between the races.

Equality and Polygenic Thought

Crawfurd's arguments over equality in the early 1860s also occurred in the context of the American Civil War. The war began in 1861, when Crawfurd was 78 years old. All observers knew that the slavery of African Americans by the White plantation owners in the Southern States was at the core of the conflict. The future of African American slavery gave ethnological theorising a new currency and importance in the 1860s. Ethnologists knew that their arguments on race had a moral dimension. Just prior to the war in 1859, Charles Darwin released his *Origin of Species*. One of the driving reasons Darwin released his book was to demonstrate that all races of men were one species and should be treated as equals.[37] In 1862, Crawfurd surmised how Americans saw race: 'The nigger, they will say perhaps, may be a man, but most certainly he is not a man and a brother'.[38] The choice of words deliberately referenced the British anti-slavery medallion by Josiah Wedgwood that depicted a kneeling slave in chains, asking, 'Am I not a man and a brother?'.[39] Unlike many of his contemporaries, Crawfurd was just old enough to remember when the Wedgwood medallions were new. In 1807, when he was 24 years old, the Atlantic slave trade was abolished, and, in 1833, slavery was abolished throughout the British Empire. Crawfurd had born witness to, as well as fought for, the slow death of slavery. The war in America forced British ethnologists to consider the question of equality of races and what equality meant for their discipline and for the British Empire.

In 1861, the United States of America was divided. The Southern states formed the confederacy and chose to secede from the United States of America. The Northern states waged war on the South to force them back into the United States of America. In summarising the Northern states' initial approach to the war, Crawfurd correctly concluded:

> The black man is not the stake for which the game of war is played, except for a small part of earnest and enthusiastic men; he is but as a reserved card in a gambler's hand. When, how, and with what effect he will be played depends upon the fortune of the game. At best the black man in America is accepted as the white man's poor distant relation, not his brother.[40]

Crawfurd's 1861 analysis was prophetic. It was not until January 1863 that President Abraham Lincoln made his Proclamation of Emancipation, partly as a 'gambler's hand' to stop British intervention in support of the cotton supplying the Southern states' Confederacy, which Crawfurd had predicted. Before the Civil War, British industry was dependent on the supply of cotton from the Southern states, and in 1862, the British government considered intervening diplomatically to preserve the South's independence, which would end the war and allow trade to continue.[41] With Lincoln transforming the war into a war to end slavery, it became politically impossible for Britain to support the Confederacy. Crawfurd's prediction, however, supported a claim he was making about how the anti-slavery northern states saw the African American population as the 'white man's poor distant relation, not his brother'.

Although, Crawfurd's statement that the African American was the 'white man's poor distant relation, not his brother' was a pun on the Wedgwood medallion, the analogy had a deeper basis in Crawfurd's thinking. The majority of abolitionists were Christians who believed in monogenesis, universal history and the paramountcy of the Bible. Therefore, they claimed that Black Africans and White Europeans were part of the broader Abrahamic family descending from Adam and Eve. Crawfurd, however, held that all races were separate species and not related to each other—and was trying to use the political actions of the Northern state abolitionists as evidence that there was no familial connection. Crawfurd's analysis demonstrates the politically expedient view of nineteenth-century people towards racial equality and that it was for them not simply a matter of declaring all people were equal. Equality could mean many things.

Colonialism and African American slavery were both moral problems of injustice that were at the heart of attempts by philosophers in the nineteenth century to develop racial theories. James Cowles Prichard and Darwin developed their respective theories with a view to demonstrating the scientific truth of monogenesis and thereby demonstrating that all races were equal and part of a broad family.[42] Some individuals used polygenesis to argue that non-Europeans were unrelated to Europeans, and therefore, the same moral rules did not apply.

Crawfurd believed in racial equality. As an advocate of polygenesis, he believed that all races were distinct and unrelated to each other. He believed that polygenesis was an observable fact determined by scientific enquiry. However, for many humanitarian activists in the nineteenth century, polygenesis was evil, because it rejected the idea that all humans are related and derived from one source. Crawfurd recognised all humans as part of the collective species of 'man'. The monogenesis argument, that all humans derived from the one source, indicated family and a genealogical connection. As an advocate for polygenesis, Crawfurd believed there was no familial connection between Europeans and Africans. However, he also understood that advocacy of polygenesis could be misused by advocates of slavery and colonial abuses. In an anonymously written article published in 1862, Crawfurd talked about himself in the third person and acknowledged the potential for his views to be misinterpreted:

> Mr Crawfurd agrees with Agassiz and others in considering that the same order shown in the creation of families of plants must have been followed also in the peopling of the earth with families of men. By the Europeans settled in America, such doctrine has been misapplied sometimes into a justification of injustice between race and race.[43]

In the above passage, Crawfurd acknowledged that polygenesis could be misused to justify what he saw as the morally reprehensible injustice of slavery. By claiming people were a different species, dubious moral claims could be made to justify treating people inhumanely. Despite recognising the morally ambiguous problems with his theoretical beliefs, Crawfurd stuck to them and believed there was no contradiction. For him, it was a misapplication of a doctrine of polygenesis.

The British Association for the Advancement of Science conference in 1863 became a battleground over the humanity of the Negro. A delegation from the Anthropological Society led by James Hunt, who also supported polygenesis, attended the meeting. Hunt argued the inherent racial inequality of Africans to Europeans. Hunt supported the racial and political ideas of the Confederacy and concluded that Africans should be either returned to Africa or held in bondage.[44] As believers in polygenesis, Crawfurd and Hunt initially saw each other as allies; however, Crawfurd despised Hunt's political views and made it his objective to fight Hunt at every occasion.[45]

Although Crawfurd argued that Africans were a separate race and unrelated to Europeans, he defended their rights as humans to be treated equally. Crawfurd certainly believed slavery was a 'mighty evil': throughout his life he expressed his disgust and condemnation at slavery.[46] When it came to slavery and race relations in America, he understood that the war was not being fought purely to liberate the African American slaves. Crawfurd readily castigated the Southern states of America as the practitioners of evil, but he also characterised the Northern *free* states as practicing hypocrisy when it came to race relations.

> Let us see to the actual state of this mighty evil. Out of a population of thirty millions, four millions and a half are Africans, planted side by side with the rest of the population, consisting of free Europeans of the highest grade of civilisation. Four millions of the Africans are slaves confined to the Southern States, while the remaining half-million are nominally free men, but in reality pariahs living chiefly among the Brahmins of the Northern States. Where is the remedy for this great wrong?[47]

In his castigation of the Northern states, Crawfurd was demonstrating his notion of equality. The Northern states, he argued, did not allow people to be free, but rather treated African Americans as 'pariahs', and consequently, any liberation by the Northern states was no 'remedy for this great wrong'. Through his critiques in *The Examiner* and at the British Association for the Advancement of Science, Crawfurd argued that democracy should not be limited to one race. All peoples should be entitled to freedom because they are human.

Despite his belief in the equality between races, Crawfurd also argued about positions, which modern readers and some from the nineteenth century could misinterpret as inherently unequal, discriminatory and ignorant. In 1866, when Crawfurd was 83 years old, he presented a lecture comparing European and Asiatic nations.[48] In the lecture, he argued that all races were originally created with equality, with a reporter noting that 'Mr Crawfurd assumed that all the races of man are of equal antiquity, and that so far as length of time is concerned, they have enjoyed equal opportunities of social advancement'.[49] He maintained that the Asiatic races developed civilisation first, but had been surpassed by the European races. Crawfurd then explained why he believed the European nations were physically, morally and intellectually superior by the time of the nineteenth century. With European political and increasingly scientific mastery in the nineteenth century, Crawfurd's view must have appeared as a natural reality from a European perspective.

Professor Dadabhai Naoroji, a 41-year-old Parsee from India, attended the lecture and was incensed at Crawfurd's blatant expressions of inequality, discrimination and Eurocentrism. For Naoroji, the attitudes of a clearly aging Crawfurd were symptomatic of wider discrimination in Britain that for him was antediluvian and unjust. A reporter recorded Naoroji's initial indignation at Crawfurd's lecture:

The unfavourable opinions of Asiatics entertained in England were founded on the misrepresentations of persons ignorant of their language and of their manners, and he contended that the morality of the Persians is equal to that of Europeans. He stated that a Persian man had lived eight years in England had recently returned to his country and given as unfavourable a report of the English as had been given that evening of the Asiatics, for it described them as the most hypocritical and most unprincipled people on the face of the earth.[50]

The following month, Crawfurd arranged for Naoroji to make a right of reply.[51] In his reply, Naoroji first demonstrated that Indians were as intelligent as Europeans. He then attacked Crawfurd's polygenic positions and used Max Muller's Aryan thesis (which proposed the Aryan language as the protolanguage linking European languages with Asian languages) to demonstrate that Europeans and Asians are related. Naoroji objected to Crawfurd's assumptions of European racial superiority and saw the lecture as demonstrating a presumption of inequality of peoples on Crawfurd's part.

Crawfurd had long held that Europeans were superior to all other peoples: similar statements are found in his *History of the Indian Archipelago*. Crawfurd was not alone: statements of European superiority are common throughout the nineteenth century. Charles Darwin called the Fuegians from Tierra Del Fuego the 'most subject and miserable creatures I anywhere beheld' and 'viewing such men, one can hardly make oneself believe that they are fellow-creatures, and inhabitants of the same world'.[52] Precursing his ideas of evolution, Darwin wrote in his *Voyage of the Beagle* diary, 'there appears to be some more mysterious agency generally at work. Wherever the European has trod, death seems to pursue the aboriginal . . . The variants of man seem to act on each other in the same way as different species of animals—the stronger always extirpating the weaker'.[53] Later, when writing the *Descent of Man*, Darwin wrote, '[T]he races differ also in constitution, in acclimatisation and in liability to certain diseases. Their mental characteristics are likewise very distinct; chiefly as it would appear in their emotional, but partly in their intellectual faculties'.[54] Darwin was being intentionally derogatory, but his words are symptomatic of the wider derogatory ideas present in British society, in which the British people could talk about equality whilst still believing in their own superiority. It was this assumption of moral and intellectual superiority that Naoroji objected to in Crawfurd's lecture.

The debate between Naoroji and Crawfurd demonstrates that equality could be understood in multiple ways. Crawfurd believed in political equality and advocated a position that would see all people as having equal political and social rights. In 1820, Crawfurd argued that anybody who was eligible to pay taxes and had lived in a city for an extended period of time should have equal political rights to representation. Crawfurd's argument is steeped in British liberal philosophy of individuals competing in a free commercial environment—who all have the same rights to own property and participate in politics, over the distribution of common goods—however, he reserved the right to declare Europeans as morally superior. Naoroji, however, saw the limitations of Crawfurd's equality before the law approach, noting that it did not allow for respecting another person's culture as equal to your own.

Naoroji revealed the limitations of Crawfurd's vision of equality. Rather than political equality limited to commercial exchanges and social rights, Naoroji was more concerned with what appeared to him as cultural chauvinism: the assumption by liberal-minded British intellectuals of their own innate superiority. Naoroji was demanding what could be termed cultural equality, a recognition that all cultures were equal—no matter how technologically advanced one race appeared at any given moment in time.

Unfortunately, Crawfurd's response to Naoroji has not been recorded.[55] Despite Crawfurd's idea of European superiority, after 1859, he increasingly became concerned with changes in the idea of evolution and its implication for the recognition of individual rights for peoples throughout the British Empire.

Darwinism and Crawfurd's Final Rejection of Hierarchy of Peoples

In the 1850s, Crawfurd was at the forefront of ethnographic thought and took on the presidency of the London Ethnological Society in 1859. His ideas were at the cutting edge of science. His research supported an evidence-based analysis as opposed to ideas deriving from biblical scripture. Nevertheless, after the publication of Darwin's *Origin of Species*, Crawfurd faced problems. Evolution advocated the unity of human races and therefore undermined the theoretical ideas he had advocated throughout his career. It also undermined Crawfurd's idea of equality.

All advocates of evolution maintained that humans were equal, in the sense that they had the same origins and therefore were familial obligations to other humans. However, many advocates of evolution in the nineteenth century also maintained that evolution supported a racial hierarchy, with some races being less evolved than other races. Alfred Russell Wallace made such an argument in relation to South-East Asia when he advocated protecting peoples as children at the British Association for the Advancement of Science. Wallace's ideas were against Crawfurd's idea of human equality, but Wallace was probably more in line with public opinion than Crawfurd was. After hearing Crawfurd's response, a member of the audience, the linguist and traveller Ármin Vambery, stood up and supported Wallace's argument, stating 'that savages were children, and we must educate them as we do our own children, not because they desired it, but because they needed it'. Wallace also retorted to Crawfurd that 'Mr. Crawfurd had enunciated a doctrine with which he would find but few sympathisers in that room'.[56]

On 24 November 1859, Charles Darwin's *Origin of Species* went on sale and sold out on the first day. As a review editor for *The Examiner*, Crawfurd received one of the first copies of *Origin*.[57] By early December, Crawfurd had written his review and wrote to Darwin before publishing it. Crawfurd's letter does not survive, but Darwin complained to geologist Charles Lyle that 'Crawfurd writes to me that his notice will be hostile, but that "he will not calumniate the author": he says he has read my book "at least such parts as he could understand"'.[58] Crawfurd was one of Darwin's circle of friends. Both men were members of many of the intellectual societies and knew each other from at least the 1840s onwards. At Darwin's request, Crawfurd had supported Thomas Huxley's candidature to the Royal Society in 1856—Huxley was known by his contemporaries as Darwin's bulldog for his dogged defense of evolutionary theory.[59] After their close relationship, Darwin's ego was certainly insulted when he read Crawfurd's neutral review. Crawfurd's review also raised questions that Darwin believed were trivial and ill-informed. Nevertheless, Crawfurd's review was actually positive.

Crawfurd called *Origin*, a 'remarkable book', and he realised it would be a landmark in contemporary thought, maintaining that *Origin* was 'sure to make a mighty stir among the philosphers—perhaps even among the theologians'.[60] Crawfurd, however, summarised his approach to Darwin's theory as one of reservation:

> The doctrine he adopts to account for the present condition of the living world is, in fact, a revival of the old one of the transmutation of species; but he illustrates it with an amount of knowledge and ingenious appliances never befor brough to its support. We are ourselves by no means convinced by his reasoning, nor do we think that it overthrows the existing theory of philosophers, founded on the evidences of geological

discoveries, that the organic world, as we see it, is the result of a succession of creations and destructions.[61]

Instinctively, Crawfurd knew that Darwin was such an important figure and that people had been experimenting with theories of 'transmutation' (the earler word for evolution) for such a long time that the idea of evolution was not about to disappear. After publishing *Origin*, Darwin and his supporters must have continued to discuss the issue of evolution with Crawfurd with the aim of persuading him. In April 1861, Crawfurd sent a letter to Darwin apparently on the role of Genesis and metempsychosis (or transmutation of the soul) in Darwin's thought. Darwin's response was catogoric: 'I do not believe', Darwin stated, 'in metempsychosis nor in Genesis—& you are growing so orthodox, that you will end your days, I believe, in believing in the Tower of Babel'.[62] It is clear from Crawfurd's polygenesism and his early writings on Java that he did not believe in the standard orthodox form of Genesis or in the Tower of Babel. Crawfurd's staunchest opposition had always derived from his rejection of biblical creation, and religious complaints to Crawfurd were made throughout his life. In 1862, the religious journal *English Churchman* compared Crawfurd to Darwin at the annual meeting of the British Association for the Advancement of Science, complaining, '[W]e regret to observe that Messrs Crauford [sic] and Darwin's essentially antiscriptural notions with regard to the origin of Man have been again brought forward'.[63] Darwin's reference to Crawfurd believing in the Tower of Babel was a joke on Crawfurd's rejection of the mosaic narrative and the belief that all language connected back to one source language. Darwin was probably expecting more acceptance from Crawfurd, who must have been asking questions that Darwin believed verged on the irritating.

In 1863, Lyell came out in support of Darwin, publishing his *Geological Evidence of the Antiquity of Man, with Remarks on the Theories of the Origin of Species by Variation*. Crawfurd gave Lyell's publication pride of place in *The Examiner*, devoting two consecutive editions of the *Literary Examiner* to Lyell, with both articles consuming one and a half pages of newsprint each.[64] Crawfurd and Lyell shared a belief in deep time. Crawfurd's review was overwhelmingly supportive of Lyell's argument that human history was ancient, but still not as ancient as the Earth. In both of these articles, Crawfurd avoided the issue of evolution, concluding the second on 7 March 1863, with

> Thus far in his book Sir Charles Lyell speaks with authority as a geologist. But having given his evidence in the nineteen chapters of which we have now shown the purport, he closes with five chapters upon the Theories of Progression and Transmutation, which are rather an appendix to his work than a true part of it. Into this topic we do not follow him to-day, as we intend in a few weeks to discuss generally the recent books upon the subject.[65]

Crawfurd never did discuss the point further in *The Examiner*. Instead, the following month, on 14 April 1863, he gave a lecture to a packed audience at the Ethnological Society that was widely reported in the newspapers.[66] Lyell had some forewarning of Crawfurd's response. He wrote to Darwin that Crawfurd was coming around to the idea, as he had written to Lyell that 'You have put the case with such moderation that one cannot complain'. However, Crawfurd then 'read Huxley' and according to Lyell, 'was up in arms again'.[67]

Although Crawfurd overwhelmingly supported the idea that humans had a deep pre-history extending back thousands of years before recorded history, he was incensed that Lyell used Max Muller's Aryan hypothesis that there was one original language for the Eurasian region. Crawfurd had long held linguistic diversity was a sign of savagery, with civilisation leading to the reduction in languages. In his lecture, Crawfurd retorted to Lyell by stating:

> As a general rule, languages are numerous in proportion as men are barbarous; that is, in proportion as we get nearer to the time when each primordial horde, or tribe, framed its own independent tongue. As we advance in society, they become fewer.

For evidence, Crawfurd cited:

> France and England have each three languages, and, in both cases, two of these are in progress of extinction. China is said to have eighteen languages. Not many for a population of 400,000,000. Considering the uniformity of manners, customs, and laws which prevails over that vast country, it is probable that by this time the eighteen would have been reduced to one, had not the accident of a language which is one of the eye and not of the tongue interposed to arrest this uniformity. Java, with twelve millions of inhabitants, has but two languages; while in rude and barbarous Borneo, with probably not a tithe of its population, fifty have been counted.[68]

Although Crawfurd claimed authority on languages and therefore attacked Lyell for being a geologist meddling in linguistics, when it came to discounting Huxley, Crawfurd was on more difficult ground.

> The Professor compares man with the apes, placing them anatomically and physiologically in the same category; and here I must premise that the views which I have to offer are more of a popular than scientific character.[69]

The subsequent analysis of Huxley demonstrated an extreme lack of technical comprehension on Crawfurd's part and consisted mainly of trite comments such as: 'The natural abode of man is the level earth—that of the monkeys, the forest. If there were no forests, there would be no monkeys: their whole frame is calculated for this mode of life'.[70] He finally concluded by acknowledging that monkeys 'have an outward and even a structural resemblance to man beyond all other animals, and that is all; but why Nature has bestowed upon them this similarity is a mystery beyond our understanding'. Huxley never bothered replying to Crawfurd's buffoonery and his lack of comprehension spoke for itself.

Throughout the 1860s, Crawfurd maintained ambiguity when it came to the issue of evolution. He always demonstrated problems with the theory where he could, but would avoid stating that he was against the theory. On 21 January 1868, four months before Crawfurd died, at 85 years of age, he finally decided to make his position known and read a speech at the Ethnological Society. He concluded his speech by declaring, 'The theory itself will vanish, but the invaluable assemblage of facts and reasoning, adduced in illustration of it, will be a lasting record of the knowledge, skill, and ingenuity of its accomplished author'.[71] Unlike his speech in 1863, Crawfurd's condemnation of Darwin's theory of evolution was not reported in the wider press—Crawfurd's influence was certainly waning.

Crawfurd's condemnation of evolution made him appear as an anachronism. Darwin's supporters referred to him as 'Old Crawfurd' and his obituary called him the 'evergreen veteran'.[72] Crawfurd's ethnographic presumptions had been based on the belief that there were multiple original languages corresponding to multiple original creations of humans. Accepting evolution meant the unravelling of his key intellectual idea—that all races were separate creations. Crawfurd had been arguing for the inherent individuality of races since at least 1814, with the publications in the *Edinburgh Review*. He was not about to accept defeat in the last months of his life.

Crawfurd's insistence on the separate creation of races was interconnected with his belief in indigenous civilisation and his rejection of colonialism. In 1866, Crawfurd reviewed Samuel Laing's *Pre-historic Remains of Caithness* in the *Examiner* and used the review to reject the colonising implications of evolutionary theory and monogenesis. Crawfurd used the evidence in the book to declare that 'wherever in the same region two distinct races of man have existed they still continue to exist', thereby in his mind refuting the idea of extinction of lesser races by superior races which was at the heart of the monogenesis view of universal history.[73] Crawfurd went further in his rejection of the colonising narrative and its connection to evolutionary theory stating:

> There is no ground for believing that Europe was first inhabited by an inferior race of man, superseded by a superior, and consequently no argument to support the wild theory of progressive development, or that which, due time given, would turn gorillas into Australians, and Australians into Britons.[74]

Crawfurd linked evolution with the legitimisation of one group of people supplanting another group of people. He had always maintained that all peoples should be treated equally and was against the monogenesis arguments, which maintained that equality could only be recognised if people accepted that all races originated from the same source. Crawfurd disputed the way James Cowles Prichard and his followers had framed ethnology, around the assumption that believers of polygenesis were arguing against racial equality. He expressed this frustration with Prichard and his followers when reviewing the writings of Samuel Morton: 'the valuable contribution that this book makes to the science of which it treats, may be expected to meet with bitter opposition from the mere use that will be made of its arguments against the moral and intellectual equality of the negro'.[75]

In the 1820s, Crawfurd proposed the idea of 'indigenous civilisation' as a means of arguing against the idea pursued by Raffles that peoples in South-East Asia were passive and that one could impose on them foreign ideas. He argued that colonial policy needed to respond to local traditions. In the 1840s and 1850s, Crawfurd rejected Brooke's civilising impulses for the same reason. Politically, he argued that foreign intervention leads to death and destruction. Therefore, Crawfurd's belief in racial separateness was connected to his political beliefs in 'indigenous civilisation'.

Crawfurd's idea of equality was not based on a shared history and origin, but rather, a recognition of all races as human. As he demonstrated in his argument with Alfred Russell Wallace over the plight of the Maoris and the peoples of South-East Asia, any system of government that treated some peoples as children needing guidance was morally wrong. All people needed to be treated as equal citizens.

When it came to the issue of evolution, Crawfurd maintained the same concerns he had with Mosaic history—that the argument of unity of races supported the legitimising of colonial interventions. Crawfurd understood that Darwin developed his theories based on a moral belief. In his initial review of *Origin*, Crawfurd noted, '[W]e cannot help observing in conclusion, that his piety must be fastidious indeed, who objects to a theory the tendency of which is to show that all organic being, man included, are in a perpetual progress of amelioration'.[76] But it was the idea of perpetual progress that Crawfurd was concerned with, for it emphasised a race to 'perfection' without any idea what that perfection meant, with Crawfurd asking the rhetorical question to his readers and listeners, '[W]hat, then, does absolute perfection consist in?' Although Crawfurd's reasoning demonstrates a lack of comprehension of the theory of evolution, with Crawfurd misunderstanding the idea of perfection (or fitness) as a final state rather than a shifting condition based on the environment at any one time, Crawfurd's concerns are with the implications that perfection had towards his idea of equality.

The criticism that Crawfurd continually made was that evolution implied a hierarchy of races. In his final word on the subject, he exclaimed, '[I]t was incumbent, therefore, on the theory, to show that such differences were brought about by "natural selection in the struggle for life", and to indicate within which of the many races the mutation began; or, in other words, which of the races it is that stands nearest to the apes'.[77] Crawfurd's concern was that rather than demonstrating equality through showing a family relationship between the races, evolution was giving some races a greater moral status than others. He believed that evolution meant declaring that some races were closer to apes than other races. Crawfurd's concern therefore was that evolution, like monogenesis and Mosaic history, was that these ideas made the case for equality harder and not easier.

Crawfurd's opposition to evolution can easily appear as little more than a footnote in the history of ideas. His opposition was misguided and demonstrated a total lack of comprehension of evolutionary theory. However, his opposition also demonstrates that in the nineteenth century, ideas of equality were at the heart of moral deliberation over scientific theory and debates on colonisation. Crawfurd's ideas demonstrate that the theories of monogenesis did not have a monopoly on moral virtue. Crawfurd's position of polygenesis made a legitimate critique of colonialism.

Since the time of Raffles, Crawfurd had argued against colonialism as a means of explaining civilisational development. He had always maintained that indigenous development and local conditions explained the adoption of culture or civilisation—civilisation could not be imposed. His writings after the Sarawak controversy were no different. Crawfurd's papers in the 1860s represented a plea to leave savages where they were and let them develop (or not) according to their own resources. Civilisation should not be forced upon the savage, for in forcing civilisation onto people, Crawfurd believed the savages' natural rights were being trampled on. Equality of people was the most important principle that Crawfurd upheld all his life.

Crawfurd's political and scholarly positions on colonial expansion were interrelated. Crawfurd realised that Brooke presented a romantic story of colonisation that connected to a deep historical narrative of advancing civilisation in South-East Asia. Crawfurd used ethnology to challenge these romantic ideals. This meant he had to present what he saw as a realistic view of the savage, in which the savage was not an empty vessel waiting to be filled by civilised thought, but rather, an individual shaped by their environment. Crawfurd concluded that savages were not noble and that they should be left alone.

Underpinning his politics and his ethnology was Crawfurd's belief in the separate creation of humans. His argument was that every society was a product of its environment. Savage environments did not lend themselves to advanced civilisations. All societies were ultimately developed through indigenous development or through the multi-racial mingling of people. Civilising missions resulted in destruction of all involved. In defending his vision of anti-imperialism, Crawfurd worked to destroy the romantic ideal of the 'noble savage' in South-East Asia and in anthropology more generally.

In doing so, Crawfurd disconnected the savage and the barbarian from the ideal of freedom.

Crawfurd's idea of a polygenesis that also supported equality died with his death in 1868. Even before Crawfurd's death, evolutionary theory was becoming mainstream. After Crawfurd's death, Darwinism dominated anthropological thinking. However, Crawfurd's concerns with the implicit hierarchical impacts of evolution were prophetic. From the 1870s until the end of World War Two, evolutionary metaphors such as 'survival of the fittest' would be used by Europeans to justify the political inequality between people based on the colour of their skin. This use of race to justify inequality would have appalled Crawfurd—it was what he was fighting against.

Notes

1 John Crawfurd*, 'The Lion-Worshipers', *The Examiner*, (19 July, 1851).
2 Ibid.
3 John Crawfurd*, 'Rajah Brooke and his Claims', *The Examiner*, (16 October, 1858).
4 John Crawfurd*, 'The Brooke Testimonial', *The Examiner*, (12 July, 1851).
5 In arguing that Crawfurd rejected the use of conjectural history by the 1850s, my argument differs from a recent thesis by Martin Müller on Crawfurd's ideas of conjectural history. In his thesis on Crawfurd, Müller stresses the importance of civilisation to Crawfurd's intellectual framework. However, Müller sees Crawfurd's position as emanating out of conjectural history, and moves back and forward through time comparing Crawfurd's writing from 1820 with his writings from the 1834 and more particularly from the 1860s. Müller states, 'Crawfurd . . . wanted to provide a set of universally valid explanations of the dynamic aspects present in the theories of conjectural history and socio-evolutionary inclined anthropology'. Muller, 'Civilization, Culture, and Race in John Crawfurd's Discourses on Southeast Asia: Continuities and Changes, c.1814–1868', Ph.D. Thesis, (Florence: European University Institute, 2013), p. 88. In making this argument, Müller is trying to compare Crawfurd's work post 1857 with his writings from 1820 without addressing the life-changing political battles Crawfurd fought over Brooke's colonialism in Sarawak. Crawfurd's intellectual positions cannot be separated from his political positions. Müller's position, albeit more comprehensive than previous analysis of Crawfurd, follows mainstream thinking about Crawfurd that does not recognise how disruptive polygenesis thinking is to conjectural history. In rejecting universal history, Crawfurd could not follow a traditional conjectural history approach, and instead began looking for what common material forces shaped social development towards civilisation.
6 Crawfurd, *HIA.*, vol. 1, p. 13.
7 Crawfurd, 'On the Conditions Which Favour, Retard, or Obstruct the Early Civilization of Man', p. 159 the summaries of the earlier version published in Anonymous, 'Leeds Philosphical & Literary Society Lectures by Mr. J. Crawfurd, F.R.S.', (18 November, 1858). Also suggest that Crawfurd made similar statements in 1858.
8 Crawfurd*, 'On the Projected Colonization of Borneo', (24 October, 1846).
9 Crawfurd*, 'Rajah Brooke and his Claims', (16 October, 1858). See also the related first part of the article ibid.
10 Ibid.

11 The lecture went through a variety of forms between its first delivery in Leeds Philosophical Society and its final delivery as Crawfurd's first presidential lecture at the London Ethnological Society on 20 May 1859. Crawfurd, 'Crawfurd to Richard Cobden 16 October'; Anonymous, 'Leeds Philosphical & Literary Society Lectures by Mr. J. Crawfurd, F.R.S.', (18 November, 1858); Crawfurd, 'On the Conditions which Favour, Retard, or Obstruct the Early Civilization of Man'.

12 For life expectancy, see Adrian Gallop, 'Mortality Improvements and Evolution of Life Expectancies', <http://www.osfi-bsif.gc.ca/Eng/Docs/DEIP_Gallop.pdf> date accessed 11 January, 2016.

13 Crawfurd, 'Crawfurd to Richard Cobden 16 October'.

14 Crawfurd, 'On the Conditions which Favour, Retard, or Obstruct the Early Civilization of Man'.

15 Anonymous, 'Leeds Philosphical & Literary Society Lectures by Mr. J. Crawfurd, F.R.S.', (18 November, 1858).

16 Anonymous, 'Mr John Crawfurd', *The Examiner*, (16 May, 1868).

17 Ellingson, *The Myth of the Noble Savage*, p. 296.

18 Crawfurd, 'On the Conditions which Favour, Retard, or Obstruct the Early Civilization of Man', p. 159.

19 Ibid. p. 177. original was, 'They might safely congratulate themselves' for not being 'Red Men of Terra-del-Fuego, but the civilised white men and accomplished women of leads, the humblest of their townsmen having the power of enjoying more of the comforts and pleasures of life, physical and intellectual, than the proud lord of a horde of 10,000 barbarians'. Anonymous, 'Leeds Philosphical & Literary Society Lectures by Mr. J. Crawfurd, F.R.S.', (18 November, 1858).

20 Müller,'Manufacturing Malayness'.

21 Ellingson, *The Myth of the Noble Savage*, p. 296.

22 Crawfurd*, 'The Brooke Testimonial', (12 July, 1851).

23 Crawfurd*, 'The Lion-Worshipers', (19 July, 1851).

24 In 1860, Crawfurd was also critical of Dr Livingston's ideas of colonisation in Africa. Crawfurd, 'Crawfurd to Norton Shaw, 29 February', and John Crawfurd*, 'The Recent African Discovers', *The Examiner*, (3 December, 1859).

25 Crawfurd, 'On the Conditions which Favour, Retard, or Obstruct the Early Civilization of Man', p. 157.

26 Ibid.

27 Ibid. pp. 175, 77.

28 John Crawfurd*, 'Java, or How to Manage a Colony; Showing a Practical Solution of the Questions Now Affecting British India: By J.W.B. Money, Barrister-at-Law: Hurst and Blackett', *The Examiner*, (1 June, 1861).

29 Anonymous, 'Anthropology at the British Association, A.D. 1864', *Anthropological Review*, 2 7 (1864), p. 332.

30 Ibid.

31 John Crawfurd*, 'Geographical Society Meeting', *The Examiner*, (15 November, 1856).

32 In New Zealand, British settlers had been involved in a brutal confrontation with indigenous Maori inhabitants.

33 Anonymous, 'Anthropology at the British Association, A.D. 1864', p. 333.

34 Ibid.

35 Ibid.

36 Ibid. p. 334.

37 Desmond and Moore, *Darwin's Sacred Cause*.

38 John Crawfurd*, 'Black and White', *The Examiner*, (13 September, 1862).

39 Adam Hochschild, *Bury the Chains: The British Struggle to Abolish Slavery*, (London: Macmillian, 2005), p. 128.
40 Crawfurd*, 'Black and White', (13 September, 1862).
41 H. Jones, *Union in Peril: The Crisis Over British Intervention in the Civil War*, (Chapel Hill: University of North Carolina Press, 1992).
42 Desmond and Moore, *Darwin's Sacred Cause*.
43 Crawfurd*, 'Black and White', (13 September, 1862).
44 Desmond and Moore, *Darwin's Sacred Cause*, p. 333.
45 Burrow, *Evolution and Society*; Stocking, *Victorian Anthropology*; Ellingson, *The Myth of the Noble Savage*.
46 John Crawfurd*, 'The Slave Trade and West Indies', *The Examiner*, (22 January, 1848); John Crawfurd*, 'The Negro and Slavery', *The Examiner*, (26 September, 1863). Also John Crawfurd and T. Perronet Thompson, 'Sugar without Slavery', *The Westminster Review, 1824–1900*, (19 July, 1833).
47 Crawfurd*, 'The Negro and Slavery', (26 September, 1863).
48 Anonymous, 'The Ethnological Society', *The Morning Post* (15 February, 1866); Crawfurd, 'On the Physical and Mental Characteristics of the European and Asiatic Races of Man'.
49 Anonymous, 'The Ethnological Society', (15 February, 1866).
50 Ibid.
51 Dadabhai Naoroji, 'Observations on Mr. John Crawfurd's Paper on the European and Asiatic Races', *Transactions of the Ethnological Society of London*, 5 (1867); Anonymous, 'Ethnological Society', *The Morning*, (29 March, 1866).
52 Charles Darwin, *Journal of Researches into the Natural History and Geology of the Countries Visited During the Voyage of H.M.S. "Beagle" Round the World, under the Command of Capt. Fitz Roy, R.A.*, (London: Ward, Lock, & Co., Limited, 1897), p. 213.
53 Ibid. p. 411.
54 Charles Darwin, 'The Descent of Man, and Selection in Relation to Sex', in *Charles Darwin, The Descent of Man*, ed. by James Moore and Adrian Desmond (London: Penguin, 2004 [1879]), p. 196.
55 Anonymous, 'Ethnological Society', (29 March, 1866).
56 Anonymous, 'Anthropology at the British Association, A.D. 1864', p. 334.
57 Charles R Darwin, 'Darwin to Thomas Huxley, 5 December', Darwin Correspondence Database, The Darwin Project, (1859), <http://www.darwinproject.ac.uk/entry-2572>.
58 Charles R Darwin, 'Darwin to Charles Lyell, 2 December', Darwin Correspondence Database, Darwin Project, (1859), <http://www.darwinproject.ac.uk/entry-2565>.
59 Charles R Darwin, 'Darwin to Joseph Hooker, 9 May', Darwin Correspondence Database, (1856), <http://www.darwinproject.ac.uk/entry-1870>.
60 John Crawfurd*, 'On the Origin of Species by Means of Natural Selectin, or the Preservation of Favoured Races in the Struggle for Life: By Charles Darwin', *The Examiner* (3 December, 1859).
61 Ibid.
62 Charles R Darwin, 'Darwin to John Crawfurd, 7 April', Darwin Correspondence Database, Darwin Project, (1861), <http://www.darwinproject.ac.uk/entry-3114>.
63 A. Ellegård, *Darwin and the General Reader: The Reception of Darwin's Theory of Evolution in the British Periodical Press, 1859–1872*, (Chicago: University of Chicago Press, 1958), p. 73.
64 John Crawfurd*, 'The Geologicl Evidences of the Antiquity of Man, with Remarks on Theories of the Origin of Species by Variation: By Sir Sharles Lyell',

The Examiner, (28 February, 1863); John Crawfurd*, 'The Geologicl Evidences of the Antiquity of Man, with Remarks on Theories of the Origin of Species by Variation: By Sir Sharles Lyell [Second Notice]', *The Examiner*, (21 March, 1863).

65　Crawfurd*, 'The Geologicl Evidences of the Antiquity of Man, with Remarks on Theories of the Origin of Species by Variation: By Sir Sharles Lyell [Second Notice]', (21 March, 1863).

66　Anonymous, 'The Antiquity of Man', *The Morning Post*, (15 April, 1863). The article was also republished in the *Daily News, The Leeds Mercury, The Hampshire Advertiser, The Leeds Times, The Belfast Morning News, The Bradford Observer, Manchester Courier and Lancashire General Advertiser. The Leeds Intelligencer and Yorkshire General Advertiser*, and *The Yorkshire Gazette*. The paper was later published in full. Crawfurd, 'On Sir Charles Lyell's "Antiquity of Man", and on Professor Huxley's "Evidence as to Man's Place in Nature"'.

67　Charles Lyell, ' Lyell to Charles Darwin, 11 March', Darwin Correspondence Database, Darwin Project, (1863), <http://www.darwinproject.ac.uk/entry-4035>.

68　Crawfurd, 'On Sir Charles Lyell's "Antiquity of Man", and on Professor Huxley's "Evidence as to Man's Place in Nature"', p. 66.

69　Ibid. p. 70.

70　Ibid.

71　Crawfurd, 'On the Theory of the Origin of Species by Natural Selection in the Struggle for Life', p. 38.

72　Anonymous, 'Death of Mr. John Crawfurd', (13 May, 1868).

73　John Crawfurd*, 'Pre-historic Remains of Caithness: By Samuel Laing M.P, with Notes by Thomas H. Huxley', *The Examiner*, (24 February, 1866).

74　Ibid.

75　Crawfurd*, 'Types of Mankind; or Ethnological Researches, Based upon the Ancient Monuments, Paintings, Sculptures, and Crania of Races, and upon the Natural, Geographical, Philological, and Biblical History: Illustrated by Selections from the Indeited Papers of Samuel George Morton, M.D., and by Additional Contributions from Prof. L. Agassiz L.L.D.; W. Usher M.D.; Prof H.S. Patterson, MD. By J. C Nott, M.D. and Geo. R. Gliddon. Philadelphia: Lippincott, Grambo, and Co.', (Saturday, 20 January, 1855).

76　Crawfurd*, 'On the Origin of Species by Means of Natural Selectin, or the Preservation of Favoured Races in the Struggle for Life. By Charles Darwin.', (3 December, 1859).

77　Crawfurd, 'On the Theory of the Origin of Species by Natural Selection in the Struggle for Life'.

Conclusion

John Crawfurd died on 11 May 1868, aged 85. His last intellectual act was to reject Darwin's idea of evolution as a fallacy and castigate *Origin of Species* as little more than a 'collection of facts'. Such hyperbole probably sealed Crawfurd's fate to his nineteenth-century contemporaries as a cantankerous old man with quaint ideas. Yet, as this book has argued, Crawfurd's ideas were revolutionary in their time. He grappled with the problem of equality, colonialism and the colonising implications of a universal history within liberal thought.

Crawfurd's criticism of colonialism, universal history and his advocacy of democracy and equality for all races demonstrates that the colonial experience could produce Radical liberal ideals in the early nineteenth century. He addressed questions of race, identity and democracy in multi-racial societies which people are still grappling with in the twenty-first century. His vision of equality, although limited, was still contested in 1968–100 years after his death—with many people in English-speaking democracies denied the equality Crawfurd espoused in 1820.

This book has charted the development of Crawfurd's critique of colonialism and interconnections with his ideas of equality, race and history. Since his time in Java, Crawfurd had worked to prevent colonial expansion in South-East Asia. His firm hand in curtailing James Brooke's advances in Sarawak suggests it is no coincidence that British imperial expansion in South-East Asia did not occur whilst Crawfurd was alive. It was not until the 1870s that a new generation of colonial officials—that did not have to contend with Crawfurd's strategic lobbying—were able to push British power out of Singapore and take possession of the Malay peninsula and the remains of North Borneo. Crawfurd, therefore, was a dominating figure of British South-East Asian colonial policy in the nineteenth century.

Throughout his long life, Crawfurd debated the origins of human racial diversity—rejecting universal history for a polygenic view of human history. Behind these debates between Crawfurd and his adversaries was a deeper debate on the ethnics of colonisation. His adversaries all shared a monogenic vision of human history. Some of them supported colonisation and others, such as Darwin, did not. But Crawfurd argued that all of them

shared a belief in a form of history that supported the legitimacy of colonisation and the supplanting of one culture by another.

At the source of Crawfurd's interconnected views on colonialism, history
and race were his experiences in Java. In his search for the customs of landownership, Crawfurd rejected Raffles' belief that Javanese civilization was
a product of Indian colonisation. Crawfurd saw no evidence of an Indian
colonisation of Java. Instead, his theory of Javanese history was that the
Javanese adopted aspects of Hindu culture in the same way as people in
South-East Asia had adopted Islam—peacefully, through individual conver-
sions. He saw these religious changes as being superficial—underneath the
Javanese adoption of Hinduism, Buddhism and Islam, Crawfurd believed,
lay an inherent Javanese indigenous civilisation. He interpreted South-East
Asians as having an inherent cultural core, which absorbed foreign influ-
ences whilst maintaining an indigenous character to their civilisation.

Crawfurd's and Raffles's competing views of Javanese history were a
direct product of their administrative responsibilities. Both men used these
views of history to support their ideas of economic and legal reform in Java.
Believing that Java was an extension of Indian history, Raffles concluded
that the Ryotwari system of land tenure—that collected taxes directly
from the peasants—was closest to the ancient laws and customs of Java.
Crawfurd, on the other hand, looked at finding the organic and indigenous
sources of Javanese law and found it in the villages. He argued that the village community was the basis of Javanese social-political life and that the
village, through the Bekel or village chief, should pay the taxes.

In implementing reform of the land tax in Java, both men argued over the
source of history and civilisation. Raffles maintained a view that all civilisation spread to Java through successive waves of migration and invasions.
Crawfurd, however, believed that migrations and invasions were superficial
and that Javanese civilisation was a product of Javanese achievement and
not the product of foreigners. In rejecting the role of foreign interventions,
Crawfurd was building his critique of European colonialism and intercon-
necting it with a theory of historical agency. Raffles and Crawfurd developed
two competing visions of colonial empire in South-East Asia. Raffles advocated colonial territorial control to improve the native condition through
the direct introduction of laws to help people. On the other hand, Crawfurd
argued for a minimalist intervention, maintaining that colonisation was violent and destructive for all concerned.

In 1820, Crawfurd provided two views of colonisation. On one hand, he
used the 'decline and fall' understanding of universal history to argue that
European colonialism of the sixteenth and seventeenth century represented
a wave of barbarians bringing primordial liberty to South-East Asia—in the
1850s, Crawfurd would drop the 'decline and fall' argument and reject the
idea that European barbarism was a source of liberty in Asia.

Crawfurd's second minimalist view of colonisation had greater resonance
in the 1820s and 1830s. He found it hard to see much that was positive

with colonialism in Asia. In his own time, Crawfurd argued that colonialism was destructive, violent and rapacious for the indigenous civilisations—to the detriment of all concerned, but, at the same time, he saw it as a painful necessity that made foreign trade possible.

Crawfurd's approach to colonialism was to encourage European settlement, but to limit it to island colonies that would have minimum effect on the indigenous course of civilisation. In these small island colonies, Crawfurd wanted to encourage racial mixing politically, culturally and sexually. He argued that this union produced a better race of people than either of the original races. Crawfurd would later label this process of racial blending as 'commimixture'. He argued that colonies produced a cultural improvement, with new ideas being introduced to the region where the colony was established. But this cultural improvement did not supplant the existing culture. Identity formation was inherently indigenous for Crawfurd, and colonialism only had a transient effect on people. In these colonies, Crawfurd proposed radical democratic reforms such as universal suffrage and total racial equality. His notion of equality was shaped around the ideas of legal equality, wherein all races were treated as being legal equals.

The historian-administrators all pushed the boundaries of historical explanations for social and racial structures in South-East Asia. Crawfurd also realised that history was probably much older than recorded chronologies suggested. Early in his career, Crawfurd demonstrated an interest in the idea of deep time. He saw that humans had a long history, and much of his work was an attempt to discover a pre-history to South-East Asia.

Race and polygenesis were one manifestation of his search for pre-history; however, Crawfurd also considered geography as another force shaping human development. Crawfurd wanted to explain why some societies developed and changed from the savage condition more than others. Throughout his career, he juxtaposed the ideas of race with geography. Sometimes he argued that geography determined development. A naturally irrigated environment, he concluded, created civilisation—but there were examples where geography appeared to offer no explanation. At this point, Crawfurd focused on race as an explanation of difference—not because race was an effective explanation—but rather because he had no other explanation. Race, for Crawfurd, became a label for what was unexplainable.

Crawfurd's idea of race focused on the act of original creation—he saw each of the races as distinct with no familial connection. He rejected the Mosaic narrative of human unity based on biblical ideas of the Tower of Babel or other accounts of the separation of the different races, such as those of Noah and his sons. Crawfurd's argument relied on linguistic assumptions that in the least developed (or savage) societies there were a multitude of languages. Consequently, he pointed to the Island of Papua, Borneo and Australia, where there were innumerable languages spoken by the people encountered there. Whilst in the highly civilised areas, Crawfurd saw an extinction of separate languages, pointing to China and parts of

Europe as examples. From this pattern of languages, Crawfurd concluded that there were originally many different aboriginal people, who represented distinct races. Each of these races, he argued, had their own distinct path to civilisation.

In developing an idea of race based on polygenesis, Crawfurd was arguing against the idea of universal history, which meant that all people shared a common origin. It also contained implicit moral arguments that supported colonial rule and imperialism as a legitimate human process, which was historically necessary. The universal history narrative told story after story of one group of humans displacing another group of humans through conquest and settlement. Those who believed in the universal history narrative could look to the displacement of aboriginal populations within British and European history as indicative of a natural order whereby new, invading peoples supplanted aboriginal groups. This process of one culture supplanting another had, according to universal history, occurred for time immemorial. It implied that colonisation was not only legitimate, but also ubiquitous.

Crawfurd's ideas were influential throughout the 1820s and 1830s, but would come under challenge by James Brooke in the 1840s. Brooke was inspired by Raffles's ideas of protecting and civilising the peoples of South-East Asia by territorial control. Brooke connected with the humanitarian ethos (post-1835) and argued that colonialism needed to occur for the benefit of the savage aborigine in Borneo. In presenting his case, Brooke made his private colonial endeavour appear like a noble humanitarian cause. Like Raffles, Brooke presented South-East Asian peoples as passive actors who could consume European civilisation.

Brooke was careful in his use of language in describing savages and barbarians in Borneo. He and his followers depicted indigenous sources of resistance as foreign to Borneo. Borneo became in the British imagination a passive land of aborigines who remained noble and resolute, but suggested that these savages needed protection or they would degenerate into pirates under the sinister influences of the Malays and Arabs. Brooke used the imagery of aborigines as innocents who needed protection or discipline. He wanted to offer both.

Crawfurd was quick to see how Brooke's civilising claims could lead to territorial expansion in South-East Asia. Throughout the 1840s, Crawfurd tried to direct government policy away from directly supporting Brooke. It was Crawfurd who proposed that the British government create a colony on the island of Labuan rather than absorb Sarawak, and Crawfurd used his anonymous newspaper articles in *The Examiner* to caution against colonial acquisitions in Borneo. The Battle of Beting Marau was a turning point in public perceptions of Brooke. The parliamentarian Richard Cobden had already been receiving advice from Crawfurd on how to challenge Brooke. With news of the Beting Marau massacres, Cobden rallied the Aborigines Protection Society and the Peace Society against James Brooke. Crawfurd was instrumental in providing informed commentary and evidence. From surviving evidence in the Cobden papers, it is clear that Crawfurd also designed much of the strategy in challenging Brooke.

The campaign against Brooke was a contest of ideas on how colonial policy should deal with savages. Brooke may have used the language of protection, but his protection was paternalistic and involved the British Empire massacring wayward peoples. In challenging Brooke's ideas, Crawfurd also challenged a paternalistic colonialism, and throughout the 1850s and 1860s, his newspaper articles reiterated his arguments on equality. In the writings of James Brooke and his followers, Crawfurd saw a tendency to treat savages as children and needing protection. This went against his basic beliefs in individual equality.

Crawfurd used his knowledge of ethnology throughout his campaign against Brooke. However, in lobbying against Brooke, Crawfurd was forced to reconsider his ideas of the savage, the barbarian and the pathway to civilisation. He became strident in portraying what he saw as a realistic view of the savage. Savages were not noble. They were human and their brutal lifestyle meant that savages lead brutal lives. This did not mean they were any more brutal than civilized people. Crawfurd was quick to point out that the crimes of the civilised were far more brutal than those of the savage, because the civilised had more resources at their disposal.

In the 1850s, Crawfurd's writing changed focus away from a discussion on the barbarian and became focused on the savage and the civilised. The change was also reflected in the language of his peers who also conflated the barbarian with the savage, but for Crawfurd, it also reflected a personal shift in ideas. This change in language demonstrated a move away from the stadial history of the Enlightenment and Crawfurd's youth and, in doing so, he jettisoned the last vestiges of a universal narrative of history. Stadial history held that people advanced along a staged pathway to civilisation. By moving away from stadial history, Crawfurd began arguing that savagery and civilisation were relative states of existence and that the transition was dependent on local conditions.

Crawfurd was not attempting to place an insurmountable gulf between the savage and the civilised. He believed that savages should be treated with equality. His arguments were designed to refute a paternalistic impulse towards protection of aborigines through conquest. His writings in the 1860s constituted a plea to leave the savages alone. Colonialism, in the guise of protection, meant that this impinged on the savage's natural rights to their independence and freedom to develop their culture through indigenous means.

In the 1850s, Crawfurd's polygenic ideas of race were gaining traction. As Philip Sclater argued in his paper on the distribution of birds, the majority of naturalists in Britain were of the opinion that the different races constituted different species of humans.[1] The monogenesis position, with its origins in Mosaic history and advocacy of a universal history, was increasingly rejected during the 1850s. Some advocates of polygenesis, such as

James Hunt from the Anthropological Society, argued that as separate species, the different races had very little moral obligations towards each other. Charles Darwin and many advocates of universal history saw polygenesis as an immoral belief that legitimised the servitude of dark-skinned people by white skinned people. It was in this cauldron of competing ideas that Darwin published *Origin of Species* and thereby changed the focus away from monogenesis verses polygenesis to a mechanism of universal history, whereby people evolve differently, but were still related.

Yet, to view mid-nineteenth-century ethnology as a moral division between monogenesis and polygenesis is simplistic. Crawfurd's ideas demonstrate that it was possible to advocate polygenesis and also believe in the equality of all peoples, regardless of race. His rejection of monogenesis also derived from a moral position.

Beginning with his advocacy of a Javanese history that emphasised local sources of change, Crawfurd developed his ideas of polygenesis as part of his overall critique of colonialism as a force for civilisation. Crawfurd saw colonialism as destructive and continually rejected arguments supporting universal history for their colonial assumptions.

Crawfurd's final rejection of evolution in the last months of his life was a reaffirmation of his longstanding opposition to universal historical narratives. Crawfurd rejected evolution because he believed it meant determining that one race was closer to apes and animals than another. Crawfurd was against understanding race through the lens of hierarchy. He always argued that each race was equal, but some had developed superior attributes. Crawfurd saw his ideas as distinctly different to those related to hierarchy. For Crawfurd, evolution was another form of universal history that legitimised colonial servitude and meant that colonised peoples would be treated as children rather than as equals or adults.

From his experience in South-East Asia, Crawfurd developed two ideas: a belief in equality and a belief in polygenesis. His belief in polygenesis meant that each race had a unique history driven by indigenous factors. Colonial interventions had little impact on the course of civilization. Each race, however, was equal—and should be treated as equal.

Unlike the monogenesis advocates, who argued that equality needed to be grounded in a familial relationship of descent, Crawfurd was asking his readers to extend their ideas of equality to all people, even to those who, he argued, had no familial connection. When commenting on the American Civil War, Crawfurd outlined this as a central problem of the Northern states attitude to slavery: 'The nigger, they will say perhaps, may be a man, but most certainly he is not a man and a brother'.[2] This comment went to the heart of Crawfurd's criticism of Mosaic history, monogenesis and universal history. All three ideas were based on the belief that humanity and equality could only be extended to 'brothers' or people that had a familial relationship—no matter how distant. Crawfurd's ideas appear idiosyncratic; however, they were offering a polygenic idea of equality. Crawfurd was arguing that races were separate creations and therefore separate species—but they were all still entitled to fully enjoy equal rights.

The widespread support amongst many liberal thinkers for James Brooke's civilising mission in Sarawak was one example of how nineteenth-century British liberalism favoured imposing civilisation on the savage and the barbarian. The support for a civilising mission amongst liberal thinkers was a 'turn to empire' in which liberal thinkers abandoned the enlightenment's disdain for empire. The nineteenth-century civilising mission was a contradiction whereby savages could be 'reclaimed' and taught 'the arts of civilised life'. These mechanisms, however, were paternalistic at best and murderous at their worst. Edward Said argued that nineteenth-century orientalists (or historian-administrators) like Crawfurd provided the intellectual justifications behind such contradictions by presenting the colonised peoples as an 'other' who could be civilised by the process of colonialism. Yet, as this book has demonstrated, the turn towards empire was not universal. Leading thinkers and activists bitterly contested the idea of imposing civilisation on savages and barbarians. In these debates over British expansion, all sides depicted Asian peoples as an 'other'—with Crawfurd even considering Asians as a separate species to Europeans. Nevertheless, being an 'other' did not mean that leading liberal thinkers could not envision Asian peoples as being the legal equals to Europeans. Some liberal thinkers believed in, and fought for, the rights of Asian peoples. These thinkers argued Asians had natural rights like all peoples and an identity that demanded respect.

Notes

1 Sclater, 'On the general Geographical Distribution of the Members of the Class Aves', *Journal of the Proceedings of the Linnean Society of London*, 2 7 (1858), 130–6.
2 Crawfurd*, 'Black and White', (13 September, 1862).

Appendix
Identifying John Crawfurd's Writings in *The Examiner*

For more than 30 years, from the mid-1830s until his death in 1868,[1] John Crawfurd was a leading contributor to *The Examiner*, a London weekly newspaper that espoused Radical liberal views. For most of this time, the paper was edited by Albany Fonblanque, who commissioned work from other leading nineteenth-century figures, including John Stuart Mill, John Forster, William Makepeace Thackeray, Henry Morley and Charles Dickens, as columnists and writers.[2] Similar most nineteen-century newspapers and review journals, *The Examiner*, published articles without author attribution. In consequence, very few articles have actually been attributed to Crawfurd and his contribution to nineteenth-century thought has thus gone largely unnoticed.

In exploring Crawfurd's role in the contest of ideas on South-East Asia, this book has newly attributed a number of articles to Crawfurd. In identifying articles to John Crawfurd, I have applied a methodology with four levels of attribution. The first level of attribution uses Crawfurd's own letters to make a positive attribution of articles. The second level relies on Crawfurd's contemporaries who identified him as the author. The final two levels of attribution look to the internal evidence within the articles.

Crawfurd wrote five books and published 38 articles which he acknowledged with a by-line. All of the books focused on South-East Asia, whilst his articles mainly addressed ethnographic theory and racial science. In addition to these acknowledged works, Crawfurd wrote many more articles anonymously: first in the review journals, such as the *Edinburgh Review* and the *Westminster Review*, and later in life, with *The Examiner*. Anonymous writing was a common part of nineteenth-century authorship and therefore Crawfurd was not unique. Yet, even Crawfurd's friends at times found the extent of Crawfurd's writing and what he acknowledged confusing. Even Charles Darwin felt the need for clarification, writing to Crawfurd, 'I felt sure the one I asked about, was by you: but I did not know whether you acknowledged it'.[3] Some of Crawfurd's friends even felt a reluctance to write against some anonymous articles because they suspected Crawfurd was the author.[4] Crawfurd himself believed that political activism was often best conducted anonymously, explaining his desire for anonymity to Richard Cobden: 'such things are most biting when anonymous'.[5]

After his death, three different obituaries were written for Crawfurd. Together, these obituaries address the scale and extent of his anonymous writing. The obituary in *The Examiner* is the most useful, for it identifies Crawfurd as one of the newspaper's regular columnists:

> He was an indefatigable contributor to the press on matters relating to the East, and herein we ourselves shall feel his loss, as he has been for many years a contributor to the columns of the Examiner, the pages of which he enriched by his articles on Eastern, Colonial, and other subjects.[6]

The second obituary from *The Times* newspaper stated:

> An inclination to study and capacity for work enabled him to keep up and perfect his stores of Indian and Eastern information. He was an indefatigable contributor to the Press on matters relating to the East, and indeed on many other subjects.[7]

The final obituary was written by Roderick Murchison and published in the *Journal of the Royal Geographical Society*, in which Murchison references Crawfurd's literary contribution that included: 'his frequent contributions to reviews and weekly newspapers, particularly the "Examiner", Mr. Crawfurd has perhaps written more than it has been given to any one author of this century to accomplish'.[8]

Crawfurd's contributions were so frequent that he even had a following of people purchasing *The Examiner* purely to read his anonymous articles. Thomas Carlyle recounted to his brother John in 1853 the 'dulness' he found in many 'books and pamphlets', and how he had 'given up the *Leader* News-paper, it had got so utterly washy and frothy', preferring instead *The Examiner*, although he claimed it 'is not a lively or inspired production'. Carlyle bought *The Examiner* purely because 'one finds old Crawfurd &c in it'.[9]

The obituaries list three areas of focus. 'Eastern affairs', 'colonial matters' and 'other matters'. Using Crawfurd's acknowledged publications as a guide, 'eastern affairs' refers to India, South-East Asia and China. Colonialism was a common topic in his the *Edinburgh Review* and later in the *Westminster Review*, where he wrote about India, Australia and colonisation more broadly.[10] In his review, Murchison states that Crawfurd wrote two types of articles: 'reviews and weekly newspapers'. Crawfurd was probably a regular contributor to the '*Political Examiner*', where he commented on social and political issues. His writing for the *Edinburgh Review* and *Westminster Review* appears to have largely ended in the mid-1830s. However, Crawfurd is attributed with reviewing two important scientific works in *The Examiner*; therefore, his review work probably continued in the *Literary Examiner*.

The obituaries all list Crawfurd as one of Britain's leading intellects. *The Times* made reference to his extensive involvement in the Ethnological Society and Geographical Society, of which he was President and Vice President, and whilst a member, he 'scarcely ever failed to take part in their discussions'.[11] Murchison also noted Crawfurd possessed a 'strong mind and untiring energy' and that Crawfurd was 'devoted almost exclusively to his favourite topics of philology, ethnology, geography and statistics' and summarised Crawfurd's contribution to ethnological field:

> First presiding over the Ethnological Society in 1861, he continued to be the life and soul of it to the day of his death. In fact, he gave to this body quite a new impetus, and astonished even his most intimate friends by his unceasing contributions on the prodigious variety of subjects, which he skilfully connected with his favourite science.

Most of Crawfurd's acknowledged articles were published in either the *Transactions of the Ethnological Society*, the *Journal of the Anthropological Society* or the *Journal of the Geographical Society*. His topics of choice were ethnology, anthropology and racial science and therefore, he probably reviewed works on ethnology for the *Literary Examiner*. The two reviews that we can positively identity as by Crawfurd are Charles Darwin's *Origin of Species* and Charles Lyell's *Antiquity of Man*. Crawfurd's analysis of both books focused on their ethnological implications rather than the broader scientific implications. Crawfurd probably wrote other reviews on topics that interested him, such as new writings on South-East Asia and ethnographic theory.

The first level of attribution consists of articles of which Crawfurd positively identified himself as the author. A number of letters survive in which Crawfurd refers to himself as the author. In some instances, his contemporaries have identified Crawfurd as the author. I consider his contemporaries' identification of Crawfurd as a second level of attribution. Both first- and second-level attributions are positive identifications; these include the following articles:

'On the Projected Colonization of Borneo', *The Examiner*, October 24 1846[12]

'The Slave Trade and West Indies', *The Examiner*, 22 January 1848[13]

'Piracy in the Eastern Archipelago', *The Examiner*, October 21 1848[14]

'The Edinburgh Review and the Examiner', *The Examiner*, December 16 1848[15]

'The Government of India', *The Examiner*, 4 January 1851[16]

'What do we gain from India', *The Examiner*, 18 January, 1851[17]

'The future of India', *The Examiner*, 15 February, 1851[18]

'How Wars Are Got up in India. The Origin of the Burmese War. By Richard Cobden, Esq., M.P.', *The Examiner*, 20 August 1853[19]

'On the Origin of Species by Means of Natural Selectin, or the Preservation of Favoured Races in the Struggle for Life. By Charles Darwin', *The Examiner*, 3 December 1859[20]

'Rajah Brook and His Claims', *The Examiner*, 9 October 1858[21]

'Rajah Brooke and His Claims', *The Examiner*, 16 October 1858[22]

'The Geological Evidences of the Antiquity of Man, with Remarks on Theories of the Origin of Species by Variation. By Sir Charles Lyell', *The Examiner*, 28 February 1863[23]

'The Geological Evidences of the Antiquity of Man, with Remarks on Theories of the Origin of Species by Variation. By Sir Charles Lyell [Second Notice]', *The Examiner*, 21 March 1863[24]

The final two levels of attribution look to the internal evidence within the articles. The first part of this approach looks to identifying a continuity of argument between *The Examiner* articles and other known writings by Crawfurd. For example, most of Crawfurd's writings on ethnology or racial science made either a statement supporting polygenesis or assumed the factuality of polygenesis and used that assumption as the basis for a greater claim. Unlike most of his contemporaries, Crawfurd held liberal attitudes to racial equality. Polygenesis coupled with an affirmation of racial equality provides a unique ideological marker within Crawfurd's writing. Another example pertinent to this book is Crawfurd's argument against colonising Borneo. In his letters to Richard Cobden, Crawfurd regularly makes reference to his campaigning against Brooke.[25] In his *Descriptive Dictionary of the Indian Archipelago* and the articles that can be positively identified as being written by Crawfurd, he makes the following consistent claims: one, that the people in Borneo were practicing inter-tribal, war not piracy. Secondly, that Borneo was an unprofitable swamp. Thirdly, that the Dayak tribes in Borneo were frightened of firearms and that his ethnological evidence is heavily reliant on John Dalton's and Robert Burns's evidence of the Kayan Dayaks.[26]

The final level of attribution addresses the structural formulation of the articles. When developing an argument, Crawfurd would use a combination of evidence to support his claims. He would usually make some broad argument based on geography, which was supported by extensive statistical evidence, some reflection based on his previous experience in Singapore or Java and finally, some reference to ethnology and languages. When writing anonymously, Crawfurd would also make grand statements on the psychology of individuals in question that were often belittling to the person, although such an approach was not unique to Crawfurd.

In the 1840s, *The Examiner* published reviews of the travel writings published by James Brooke's supporters. These reviews were:

'The Expedition to Borneo of H.M.S. Dido, for the Suppression of Piracy: With Extracts from the Journal of James Brooke, Esq., of Sarawak (Now Agent for the British Government in Borneo). By Captain the Hon. Henry Keppel, R.N. Two Vols. Capman and Hall', *The Examiner*, February 21, 1846.

'Narrative of the Voyage of H.M.S Samarang, During the Years 1843–46; Employed Surveying the Islands of the Eastern Archipelago; Accompanied by a Brief Vocabulary of the Principal Languages. By Captain Sir Edward Belcher, R.N. Commander of the Expedition. With Notes on the Natural History of the Islands, by Arthur Adams, Assistant Surgeon, R.N. Reeve and Co.', *The Examiner*, March 18 1848.

Both of these accounts required somebody with extensive knowledge of Borneo to assess the books, and in his 1848 letter to Cobden, Crawfurd mentioned he had been the sole campaigner in *The Examiner*.[27] The reviews also suggest that the reviewer had personal knowledge of South-East Asia. Keppel's book included a chapter written by Crawfurd. A common feature of Crawfurd's anonymous writings was to highlight his own writings on the topic and then use his anonymous voice to praise his work wherever possible.[28] In quoting Crawfurd's own writings in Keppel's work, Keppel was drawing attention to the Crawfurd's continuing relevance. Crawfurd was also trying to change the focus away from colonising Sarawak and focusing instead on the island of Labuan. The review of Belcher's *Voyage of H.M.S Samarang* demonstrates such a knowledge of South-East Asia. In this passage, we see Crawfurd's grasp of the literature and also his ideological differences over the prospective returns from colonising Sarawak and Borneo, which he had previously made clear in the article 'On the Projected Colonization of Borneo' (which we can positively identify through Crawfurd's letters to Richard Cobden):

> Sir E Belcher much resembles his colleagues, and the portions of his book to which we are now advertising much resemble most of their recent publications. They also have a strong family resemblance to many of the publication respecting Labuan and the Rajah of Sarawak (such as that of Mr Low—Sarawak, its Inhabitants and Productions, a very clever and interesting book), with which we have recently been inundated. The only novel feature about them is their greater conscientiousness and apparent veracity, in recapitulating the trading capabilities of Borneo and the natural advantages of Labuan. Sir E. Belcher describes these as he found them, without any over-anxiety of laudation; and such of our merchants as contemplate enterprises to that new El Dorado, will do well to consult his pages beforehand.

Throughout the 1850s, *The Examiner* published a continual stream of articles taking issue with the colonisation of Borneo and also Brooke's actions in attacking pirates in Borneo. Some of these include:

'Borneo and Its Resources', *The Examiner*, January 12 1850
'Modest Merit', *The Examiner*, May 31 1851.

'Bornean Piracy', *The Examiner*, June 28 1851.

'The Brooke Testimonial', *The Examiner*, 12 July 1851.

'The Lion-Worshipers', *The Examiner*, 19 July 1851.

"Robert Burns' and Sir James Brooke', *The Examiner*, 4 October 1851.

'A Visit to the Indian Archipelago in H.M.S. Maeander, with Portions of the Private Journal of Sir James Brooke, K.C.B. By Captain the Hon. Henry Keppel, R.N. Two Vols. Bentley', *The Examiner*, 19 February 1853, p. 117.

'The Borneo Inquiry', *The Examiner*, 20 May 1854.

'The Rajah Brooke', *The Examiner*, 27 July 1850.

'Results of the Brooke Inquiry', *The Examiner*, 25 August 1855.

'The Brooke and Borneo Inquiry', *The Examiner*, 1 September 1855.

'Sarawak and Canton Affairs', *The Examiner*, 2 May 1857.

'Chinese Settlers', *The Examiner*, 29 October 1859.

We know from Crawfurd's letters to Richard Cobden that he was regularly writing about Borneo and Brooke in *The Examiner*. The first of these articles, 'Borneo and Its Resources', is an enlarged version of an 1846 article 'On the Projected Colonization of Borneo' that Crawfurd acknowledged writing to Cobden.[29] These articles constitute a consistent campaign of ideas concluding with the positivity identified articles 'Rajah Brooke and His Claims' published in 1858. The Borneo articles all share an ideological focus and a similar construction of argument using geography, ethnographic details and statistics. The arguments listed are shared with Crawfurd's *Descriptive Dictionary of the Indian Archipelago*. For example, consider the two passages below, the first from *The Examiner*, the second from Crawfurd *Descriptive Dictionary*. Both extracts share the same argument, that the Dayaks were frightened of firearms, the same use of analogy to Cortez in Mexico and the same quotation from John Dalton as evidence.

How is it within the power of possibility for miserable men, without fire-arms, and who take to their heels at the sound of a pistol shot, to attack men of war and armed merchantmen, or even the armed craft of the Chinese of civilised natives . . . Four and twenty years ago Mr. J. Dalton, an English trader and traveler, visited the most powerful and warlike tribe of Dayaks in the island of Borneo, the Kyans [sic], and lived among and was most hospitably entertained by them for several months. "What these people" says he, "mostly dread is the musket; it is inconceivable what a sensation of fear comes over the bravest of the Diaks [sic] when they have the idea a few muskets may possibly be brought against theme" . . . This beats hollow the Mexican and Peruvian fear of the arquebuses of the followers of Cortes and Pizarro.[30]

Compare with the following from Crawfurd's *Descriptive Dictionary of the Indian Archipelago*:

> it is strange enough that with a long and almost daily familiarity with inter-tribal warfare, conducted in their own ruthless manner, the Day-aks should, down to the present day, have as great a dread of fire-arms as the Aztec nations on the invasion of Cortes. Such, however, is the case, for the fact is attested by several independent witnesses, of whom Mr. Dalton is the best. "What these people most dread," says he, "is the musket. It is inconceivable what a sensation of fear comes over the bravest of the Dyaks [sic] when they have an idea that a few muskets may possibly be brought against them".[31]

In addition to the articles on Brooke and Borneo, I have also attributed other articles to Crawfurd from *The Examiner*. These include:

> 'Types of Mankind; or Ethnological Researches, Based Upon the Ancient Monuments, Paintings, Sculptures, and Crania of Races, and Upon the Natural, Geographical, Philological, and Biblical History: Illustrated by Selections from the Inedited Papers of Samuel George Morton, M.D., and by Additional Contributions from Prof. L. Agassiz L.L.D.; W. Usher M.D.; Prof H.S. Patterson, Md. By J. C Nott, M.D. And Geo. R. Gliddon. Philadelphia: Lippincott, Grambo, and Co.', *The Examiner*, Saturday 20 January 1855.

and

> 'Pre-Historic Remains of Caithness. By Samuel Laing M.P, with Notes by Thomas H. Huxley', *The Examiner*, 24 February 1866.

Both articles focused on recent research into ethnology and were written by a person who supported polygenesis. In the review of Gliddon, the writer is a liberal-minded thinker who is against slavery and against racial inequality. The writer is trying to demonstrate the scientific fact of polygenesis, but rejects any political arguments of inequality that could emanate from a belief in polygenesis. The second review of the 'Pre-historic Remains of Caithness' also expresses a belief in polygenesis and a rejection of evolution and is consistent with Crawfurd's writing. As president of the Ethnological Society and as a leading correspondent at *The Examiner*, Crawfurd, who had reviewed Darwin and Lyle, would also take the opportunity of promoting his own ideas by reviewing other works that he believed could support his intellectual opinion.

In 1861, *The Examiner* published a review of the book:

> 'Java, or How to Manage a Colony; Showing a Practical Solution of the Questions Now Affecting British India. By J. W. B. Money, Barrister-at-Law. Hurst and Blackett', *The Examiner*, 1 June 1861.

As the foremost living expert on Java in Britain, any new publication on Java would spark Crawfurd's interest. This review is notable for a command of economic detail within Java and India and an ability to challenge the Lawrence Money's own use of evidence. The reviewer had an extensive knowledge of Java. He quoted revenues from time the British occupied Java and matched them with Money's evidence to demonstrate that free trade was much better than Money's advocacy of the Dutch Cultivation System, and the reviewer also demonstrated his knowledge of commercial crops and the price of food in Java, quoting information absent from Money's account. All these details Crawfurd would have had at his fingertips.

Crawfurd was a committed free trader who found abhorrent the Dutch Cultivation System of land management which replaced the reforms that he and Raffles established. In a public lecture responding to Alfred Russell Wallace's advocacy of the cultivation system, Crawfurd called it 'an apology for monopoly nor despotism from Mr. Wallace. The system which Mr. Wallace had landed was simply the enforced coffee labour of Java'.[32] In his 1857 *Descriptive Dictionary*, Crawfurd was also disparaging of the Cultivation System, stating:

> By this impolitic measure, the Dutch government has become, once more, a cultivator, a trader, and necessarily, from its position to a certain extent, a monopolist trader, the evil effects of which on that wealth, which is the only source of public revenue, must be obvious to every enlightened modern statesman.[33]

The reviewer expressed an ideological repugnance to Money's proposals, stating that if it applied to the British in India,

> It would exhibit the Government as the sole landlord—make it a huge agriculturist and trader on the borrowed capital of the mother country—reduce the natives to the condition of serfs—dishonor our national character, and produce an universal rebellion which would very properly and justly drive us headlong out of the country. We must have none of a scheme which sets economic science, sound legislation and the natural rights of man, whatever be his race or colour, at utter defiance.

Since the publication of his *History of the Indian Archipelago*, Crawfurd had repudiated the mercantilist system of colonies. He had argued for the commercial and political equality of all races within the British Empire. He continually argued for the rights of people to command their own economic affairs and for free trade. These views were all expressed in review of Money's book. Based on this analysis of ideological viewpoints and knowledge of Java, Crawfurd is most likely author.

The following five articles all demonstrate a focus on promoting Crawfurd's intellectual importance. The first was a review of Crawfurd's own *Descriptive Dictionary*.

'A Descriptive Dictionary of the Indian Islands and Adjacent Countries', *The Examiner*, 16 August 1856.

The review finds no faults with Crawfurd's book and discusses at length his importance. As the leading expert on South-East Asia and one of the lead reviewers and columnists at *The Examiner*, Crawfurd would not let somebody with lesser experience review his book. There are numerous articles and reviews in *The Examiner* that emphasise Crawfurd's intellectual importance. Other newspapers do not use Crawfurd's writings to the same extent.

I have attributed an account of the 'Geographical Society Meeting', published in *The Examiner* on 15 November 1856, to Crawfurd's hand. Crawfurd was a longstanding member of the Geographical Society and the account appeared to give an inordinate amount of space to expressing what Crawfurd said at the meeting and rejecting Alfred Russell Wallace's paper for being inconsequential and too close to James Brooke. During the Geographical Society meeting in question, Crawfurd was not delivering a paper; his role was merely as a commentator. The writer of *The Examiner* article devoted most of the column to expanding upon Crawfurd's ideas of Borneo and failed to report anything stated by Wallace. Crawfurd was probably the author.

The obituaries all point to Crawfurd writing on other colonial topics. One article I have attributed to him—in keeping with the broad focus of the obituaries—is the 'The Recent African Discovers', published in *The Examiner* on 3 December 1859. This article outlined debates at the Geographical Society over a letter received from David Livingston from Africa. In the article, the writer presents an ideological view that rejects colonial expansion and argues that Central Africa does not possess a geography suitable for colonisation. The argument relies on geographical arguments, statistics and also some ethnology. *The Examiner* article urged the Society to not support colonisation. Crawfurd also wrote a letter to the society also arguing the Geographical Society should not support the colonisation of Africa.[34]

The final three articles that this book has attributed to Crawfurd are on slavery and the American Civil War. The first article, 'Black and White', published in *The Examiner* on 13 September 1862, addresses the role of race in the American Civil War. The only ethnologist or expert whose views are referenced in the article is John Crawfurd, and most of the article is devoted to exploring the war through Crawfurd's ideas. Most of these ideas had not been previously published, and therefore it was either based on an interview with Crawfurd or written by Crawfurd himself, the latter more likely the case.

The final article, 'The Negro and Slavery', published in *The Examiner* on 26 September 1863, is a continuation of the ideas outlined in 'Black and White' published the year before. The article is listed directly under another article that was most likely written by Crawfurd called 'Man and Beast'. Both 'Man and Beast' and 'The Negro and Slavery' appear to be responding to issues and arguments emanating from the British Association for the Advancement of Science (BAAS) meeting that occurred a few weeks prior. The article 'Man and Beast' begins by stating the article was a response to the BAAS conference:

> The man and beast question, which interests some people as much as the bird and fruit question interests others, is always especially popular with the philosopher. The anthropoid ape is a regular attendant at the meetings of the British Association, and it must soon become an open question whether it was not he who spoke the ancient Aryan language, which nobody ever saw a word in or heard a word of, but about which everything is known in Germany.[35]

Crawfurd was an active delegate at the BAAS meeting and the supercilious and arrogant writing style was a common aspect of his articles. The writer's desire to belittle the Aryan thesis was also consistent with Crawfurd's writing style. The rest of the article is an elaboration of Crawfurd's views on the subject making reference to his experience in Singapore and what he had to say at the BAAS meeting. The article makes no reference to anybody else's opinions.

The article following the 'Man and Beast' article was 'The Negro and Slavery'. This also opened by stating that 'the subject of the Negro and Slavery has of late been a prominent one, for it has been a favorite topic at the British Association among philosophers, and at public meetings among the working classes and their leaders'. The style of opening with reference to philosophers and the British Association is much the same as the first article; nevertheless, the seriousness of the topic required a more respectful use of language. The article expresses the author's opinion of slavery: 'we utterly detest and loathe slavery as the greatest crime that can be committed between man and man'. This view is consistent with Crawfurd's views. The article assumes polygenesis but maintains Crawfurd's view of human equality races, despite his view of intellectual and physical superiority of some races over others:[36]

> The black African is just as much a man as the fairest European, but of the many various races of man he is among the inferior. With the stature and strength of the European, in mental capacity he is not only inferior to the European but to the Asiatic. Coeval in origin with the rest of mankind, and having the greater part of a continent to themselves, no negro people has ever surpassed the civilisation of which we have examples in Dahomey and Ashantee.[37]

The article makes consistent use of statistics and economic theory. The article also speaks with loathing of the slave-owning Confederacy in the

Southern American states, but also disparagingly of the Northern free states, calling them 'Brahmins' and hypocrites. Crawfurd often likes to insult the hypocrisy of Europeans by linking them to Brahmins and Hindus. The article also maintains an ideological consistency with the article published the previous year in 'Black and White', with both articles arguing that the Northern states are fighting for conquest and not emancipation. Consider this passage 'The black man is not the take for which the game of war is played . . . he is but a reserved card in a gambler's hand' from the article 'Black and White' with the passage: 'As for the combatants of the North—with whom, except as combatants in this vain struggle, our sympathies are stronger than they can be with the South—even by their own admission, it is not for the emancipation of the Negro, but for conquest' from 'The Negro and Slavery'.[38] The writer of both articles has the view that the North is not serious about emancipation, but using it as a tool. Together, the articles 'Black and White', 'Man and Beast' and 'The Negro and Slavery' provide internal evidence in argument and structure that supports attribution to Crawfurd.

Crawfurd was certainly a prolific writer. This book has attributed 33 articles to Crawfurd from *The Examiner*. Of these articles, 13 are positively identified by either Crawfurd's own correspondence or the correspondence of others, with the remaining articles being attributed from the internal evidence of the articles in accompaniment with Crawfurd's letters to Richard Cobden and comparative analysis with his other writings. However, there were are probably hundreds more articles that Crawfurd wrote for *The Examiner* on matters relating to India, China, South-East Asia, colonisation, economics and slavery. Crawfurd's contribution to *The Examiner* was probably monthly and at times maybe even weekly.

Notes

1 The *Wellesley Index to Victorian Periodicals* <wellesley.chadwyck.co.uk> lists Crawfurd as a regular contributor to the *Edinburgh Review*, *Quarterly Review* and the *Westminster Review* until 1836. After this time, Crawfurd is listed as only publishing one more review article in 1853. Therefore, Crawfurd's time at *The Examiner* probably started somewhere in the late 1830.

2 Albany the Elder Fonblanque and Edward Barrington De Fonblanque, *The Life and Labours of Albany Fonblanque: Edited by his Nephew E. B. De Fonblanque*, (London: Richard Bentley and Son, 1874), pp. 38–39.

3 Darwin, 'Darwin to John Crawford, 7 April'.

4 A note in *The Wellesley Index* for the article 'The colonial expenditure', WR-666, attributed to Crawfurd states, 'Thompson to John Bowring, 21 December, 1835, Thompson Papers, mentions the German commercial league and says he has kept out of Westminster Review all attacks on it "as were intended, I think, in one of Crawfurd's articles"'.

5 Crawfurd, 'Crawfurd to Richard Cobden, 24 December'.

6 Anonymous, 'Mr John Crawfurd', (16 May, 1868).

7 Anonymous, 'Death of Mr. John Crawfurd', (13 May, 1868).

8 Murchison, 'Address to the Royal Geographical Society', p. cli.

9 Thomas Carlyle, 'Thomas Carlyle to John Carlyle', *CARLYLE LETTERS*, 28 1 (1853).

10 Crawfurd to John McCulloch, 28 September, 1844, Private Collection.

11 Anonymous, 'Death of Mr. John Crawfurd', (13 May, 1868).

12 Crawfurd, 'Crawfurd to Richard Cobden 10 February'.

13 Ibid.

14 Crawfurd is identified as the author in John, 'To the editor of the "Examiner", Piracy in the Indian Archipelago', (16 December, 1848).

15 John Crawfurd*, 'The Edinburgh Review and the Examiner', ibid.

16 Crawfurd, 'Crawfurd to Richard Cobden 24 December'.

17 Ibid.

18 Ibid.

19 John Crawfurd, 'Crawfurd to Richard Cobden, 12 August with Memoranda on Burmah', Ibid. West Sussex Record Office, Cobden M, 3/4 (MF 3) (1853).

20 Darwin, 'Darwin to Charles Lyell, 2 December'.

21 Crawfurd, 'Crawfurd to Richard Cobden 16 October'.

22 Ibid.

23 Lyell, 'Lyell to Charles Darwin, 11 March'.

24 Ibid.

25 All the following correspondence was marked 'private' and makes reference to Crawfurd's work in *The Examiner* relating to Borneo and Brooke: Crawfurd, 'Crawfurd to Richard Cobden 10 February', Crawfurd, 'Crawfurd to Richard Cobden, 24 December'; Crawfurd, 'Crawfurd to Richard Cobden, 31 December'; Crawfurd, 'Crawfurd to Richard Cobden, 22 March'; John Crawfurd, 'Crawfurd to Richard Cobden, 22 September', Cobden Papers, West Sussex Record Office, Cobden MS 5/103 (1858). There were other letters not marked private that Crawfurd wrote that also relate to Sarawak.

26 Crawfurd, *Descriptive Dictionary*, pp. 127–134.

27 Crawfurd, 'Crawfurd to Richard Cobden, 10 February'.

28 'Beside several important memoranda by himself on the opening of the Indian Archipelago, a document embodying the opinions of the late Governor of Singapore, Mr Crawfurd, on the subject of a settlement on the Borneo coast. Mr Crawfurd recommends the Island of Labuan, lately ceded to the British Government, with regard both to military and commercial advantage; and strongly confirms what is said on that subject by Mr Brooke'. See Crawfurd*, 'The Expedition to Borneo of H.M.S. Dido, for the Suppression of Piracy: with Extracts from the Journal of James Brooke, Esq., of Sarawak (now Agent for the British Government in Borneo). By Captain the Hon. Henry Keppel, R.N. Two vols. Capman and Hall', (21 February, 1846).

29 Crawfurd, 'Crawfurd to Richard Cobden, 10 February', Crawfurd*, 'On the Projected Colonization of Borneo', (24 October, 1846); Crawfurd*, 'Borneo and its Resources', (12 January, 1850).

30 Crawfurd*, 'Bornean Piracy', (28 June, 1851).

31 Crawfurd, *Descriptive Dictionary*, p. 130.

32 Anonymous, 'Anthropology at the British Association, A.D. 1864'.

33 Crawfurd, *Descriptive Dictionary*, p. 189.

34 Crawfurd, 'Crawfurd to Norton Shaw, 29 February'.

35 John Crawfurd*, 'Man and Beast', *The Examiner*, (26 September, 1863).

36 Crawfurd, 'On the Physical and Mental Characteristics of the Negro'.

37 Crawfurd*, 'The Negro and Slavery', (26 September, 1863).

38 Crawfurd*, 'Black and White', (13 September, 1862); Crawfurd*, 'The Negro and Slavery', (26 September, 1863).

Bibliography

Adas, Michael, *Machines as the Measure of Men: Science, Technology, and Ideologies of Western Dominance*. (Ithaca: Cornell University Press, 1989).

Agassiz, L., *An Essay on Classification*. (London: Longman, Brown, Green, Longmans & Roberts & Trübner, 1859).

Aljunied, Syed Muhd Khairudin, *Rethinking Raffles: A Study of Stamford Raffles' Discourse on Religions amongst Malays*. (Singapore: Marshall Cavendish Academic, 2005).

Allbrook, M., *Henry Prinsep's Empire: Framing a Distant Colony*. (Canberra: ANU Press, 2014).

Andaya, B.W., and L.Y. Andaya, *A History of Malaysia*. (Basingstoke: Palgrave, 2001).

Anderson, G.W., and James Cook, *A New, Authentic, and Complete Collection of Voyages Round the World, Undertaken and Performed by Royal Authority: Containing an Authentic, Entertaining, Full, and Complete History of Captain Cook's First, Second, Third and Last Voyages, Undertaken by Order of his Present Majesty, for Making Discoveries in Geography, Navigation, Astronomy, &c. in the Southern and Northern Hemispheres &c. &c. &c. . . . the Whole Comprehending a Full Account, from the Earliest Period to the Present Time*. (London: Printed for the proprietors).

Anderson, John, *Political and Commercial Considerations Relative to the Malayan Peninsula and the British Settlements in the Straits of Malacca*. (Prince of Wales Island: William Cox, 1824).

Anderson, John, 'Memorandum Respecting a British Settlement on Borneo', *Foreign Office*, National Archives, CO 144/1 (1844).

Anderson, Kay, *Race and the Crisis of Humanism*. (Milton Park, Abingdon, Oxon; New York: UCL Press, 2007).

Anderson, Perry, *Lineages of the Absolutist State*. (New York: New Left Books, 1974).

Anonymous, 'Borneo 1844 to 1846', *Colonial Office*, National Archives United Kingdom, CO 144/1 (1845).

Anonymous, 'Letter from Captain Forrest to Bengal, 8th June 1784', Striats Settlemetns Factory Records, *National Library of Australia*, Vol. 1. (Prince of Wales Island: Consultations).

Anonymous, *The Present System of Our East India Government and Commerce Considered: In which are Exposed the Fallacy, the Incompatibility, and the Injustice of a Political and Despotic Power Possessing a Commercial Situation*

Also, Within the Countries Subject to Its Dominion. (London: J. Gillet, and sold by Sherwood, Neely, and Jones, 1813).

Anonymous, 'The Stamp Tax', *The Asiatic Journal and Monthly Miscellany*, 27 May (1829), 614–5.

Anonymous, 'Radical Club', *Phoenix; or, The Christian Advocate of Equal Knowledge*, 26 February (1837), 2.

Anonymous, 'Exploring Expedition to the Asiatic Archipelago', *The Athenaeum*, 572 (1838), 774.

Anonymous, 'Colonial Land and Emigration Commission: General Report of the Colonial Land and Emigration Commissioners', *House of Commons Papers; Reports of Commissioners*, no. 621 (London: 1843).

Anonymous, 'Evidence of William Napia (Former Governor of Labuan and at the Time Law Agent in Singapore Court House) 29 September', *Foreign Office*, National Archives (UK), FO12/20 (1854).

Anonymous, 'Commission of Inquiry into James Brooke', *Foreign Office*, National Archives UK, FO 881/482 (1855).

Anonymous, 'The Graphic Letter of Sir James Brooke', *The Times*, 29 April (1857).

Anonymous, 'The Sultan of Johore', *Journal of the Indian Archipelago and Eastern Seas (New Series)*, 2 (1858), 46–67.

Anonymous, 'Royal Geographical Society', *The Examiner*, 15 December (1860).

Anonymous, 'Anthropology at the British Association, A.D. 1864', *Anthropological Review*, 2 7 (1864), 294–335.

Anonymous, 'Ethnological Society', *The Morning*, 29 March (1866), 2.

Anonymous, *Thirty-Fifth Meeting; Held at Birmingham in September 1865: 34.* (London: Murray, 1866).

Anonymous, 'Death of Mr. John Crawfurd', *The Times*, 13 May (1868), 5.

Anonymous, 'Mr John Crawfurd', *Examiner*, 16 May (1868).

Anonymous, *Java Gazette*, 29 February (1812).

Anonymous, 'History of Java by Sir Thomas Stamford Raffles', *The Asiatic Journal and Monthly Miscellany*, 4 August (1817), 141–53.

Anonymous, 'History of Java by Sir Thomas Stamford Raffles', *The Asiatic Journal and Monthly Miscellany*, 4 September (1817), 245–60.

Anonymous, 'History of Java by Sir Thomas Stamford Raffles', *The Asiatic Journal and Monthly Miscellany*, 4 October (1817), 375–72.

Anonymous, 'History of Java by Sir Thomas Stamford Raffles', *The Asiatic Journal and Monthly Miscellany*, 4 December (1817), 572–91.

Anonymous, 'History of Java by Sir Thomas Stamford Raffles', *The Asiatic Journal and Monthly Miscellany*, 4 November (1817), 372–485.

Anonymous, 'Raffles History of Java', *The British Review*, 11 21 (1818).

Anonymous, 'History of the Indian Archipelago; Containing an Account of the Manners, Arts, Languages, Religions, Institutions and Comerce of its Inhabitants: By John Crawfurd, FRS.', *The British Review*, 32 (1820), 318–46.

Anonymous, 'Mr Crawfurd's History of the Indian Archipelago', *Asiatic Journal*, 10 56 (1820).

Anonymous, 'Mr Crawfurd's Mision to Siam and Cochin China', *The Asiatic Journal and Monthly Miscellany*, 13 (1822).

Anonymous, 'Singapore', *Singapore Chronicle and Commercial Register*, 9 January (1836).

Anonymous, *The Singapore Free Press and Mercantile Advertiser*, 15 April (1847), 3.

Anonymous, 'News', *The Singapore Free Press and Mercantile Advertiser*, 21 October (1847), 3.

Anonymous, 'The Expedition against the Sakarran and Sarebas Pirates', *The Morning Chronicle*, 21 November (1849).

Anonymous, 'Foreign Gleanings', *Examiner*, 3 November (1849).

Anonymous, 'Singapore', *Daily News*, 27 October (1849).

Anonymous, 'Sir James Brooke and the Pirates of the Indian Ocean', *The Times*, 23 November (1849).

Anonymous, 'Meeting of the Aboriginal Protection Society Over Borneo', *The Examiner*, 2 February (1850).

Anonymous, 'Leeds Philosphical & Literary Society Lectures by Mr. J. Crawfurd, F.R.S.', *The Leeds Mercury*, 18 November (1858).

Anonymous, 'The Antiquity of Man', *The Morning Post*, 15 April (1863), 3.

Anonymous, 'The Ethnological Society', *The Morning Post*, 15 February (1866), 2.

Anonymous, 'Mr John Crawfurd', *The Examiner*, 16 May (1868).

Armitage, David, *The Ideological Origins of the British Empire*. (Cambridge: Cambridge University Press, 2000).

Assey, Charles, *Review of the Administration, Value and State of the Colony of Java, with its Dependencies, etc.* (London: Black, Parbury & Allen, 1816).

Attwood, Bain, *The Making of the Aborigines*. 1st edition. (London: Allen & Unwin, 1989).

Bailey, Anne M., and Joseph R. Llobera, eds., *The Asiatic Mode of Production: Science and Politics*. (London, Boston and Henley: Routledge & Kegan Paul, 1981).

Bain, Alexander, *James Mill: A Biography*. (New York: Henry Holt and Company, 1882).

Ballard, Chris, "Oceanic Negroes': British Anthropology of Papuans, 1820–1869', in *Foreign Bodies: Oceania and the Science of Race 1750–1940*, ed. by Bronwen Douglas and Chris Ballard (Canberra, A.C.T.: ANU E Press, 2008), pp. 157–201.

Barrow, John, '653 Article 5: Crawfurd, History of the Indian Archipelago: With Maps and Engravings; Proceedings of the Agricultural Society, Established in Sumatra: Vol. I; Malayan Miscellanies: Vol. I, 111–38: Author: John Barrow, Probably with Sir Thomas Stamford Raffles', in *Quarterly Review Archive*, ed. by Jonathan Cutmore (1822).

Bartra, Roger, *Wild Men in the Looking Glass: The Mythic Origins of European Otherness*. (Ann Arbor: University of Michigan Press, 1994).

Bastin, John, 'Sir Stamford Raffles's and John Crawfurd's Idea of Colonizing the Malay Archipelago', *Journal of the Malayan Branch of the Royal Asiatic Society*, 26 1 (1953), 81–5.

Bastin, John, 'Malayan Portraits: John Crawfurd', *Malaya*, 3 December (1954), 697–98.

Bastin, John, *Raffles' Ideas on the Land Rent System in Java and the Mackenzie Land Tenure Commission*. ('s-Gravenhage: Nijhoff, 1954).

Bastin, John, *The Native Policies of Sir Stamford Raffles in Java and Sumatra: An Economic Interpretation*. (Oxford: Oxford University Press, 1957).

Bastin, John, 'English Sources for the Modern Period of Indonesian History', in *An Introduction to Indonesian Historiography*, ed. by Soedjatmoko and Cornell University, Modern Indonesia Project. (Ithaca, NY: Cornell University Press, 1965), pp. 252–72.

Bastin, John, *Raffles and Hastings: Private Exchanges behind the Founding of Singapore.* (Singapore: Marshall Cavendish Editions, 2014).

Bayly, C.A., *Indian Society and the Making of the British Empire.* (Cambridge: Cambridge University Press, 1988).

Bayly, C.A., *Recovering Liberties: Indian Thought in the Age of Liberalism and Empire.* (Cambridge: Cambridge University Press, 2011).

Beasley, Edward, *The Victorian Reinvention of Race: New Racisms and the Problem of Grouping in the Human Sciences.* (London: Routledge, 2010).

Bellwood, Peter, *Man's Conquest of the Pacific: The Prehistory of Southeast Asia and Oceania.* (Auckland; London: Collins, 1978).

Bellwood, Peter, 'Southeast Asia before History', in *The Cambridge History of Southeast Asia*, ed. by Nicholas Tarling (Cambridge: Cambridge University Press, 1999).

Bentham, Jeremy, *Emancipate Your Colonies!* (London: Robert Heward, 1830).

Berlin, Isaiah, *Liberty*, ed. by Henry Hardy. (Oxford: Oxford University Press, 2002 [1969]).

Bhabha, Homi K., *The Location of Culture.* (London: Routledge, 2004).

Bindman, David, *Ape to Apollo: Aesthetics and the Idea of Race in the 18th Century.* (London: Reaktion Books, 2002).

Blackstone, William, *Commentaries on the Laws of England in Four Books: Notes Selected from the Editions of Archibold, Christian, Coleridge, Chitty, Stewart, Kerr, and Others, Barron Field's Analysis, and Additional Notes, and a Life of the Author by George Sharswood: In Two Volumes.* (Philadelphia: J.B. Lippincott Co., 1893 [1753]).

Bolt, Christine, *Victorian Attitudes towards Race.* (London: Routledge, 2013).

Boon, James A., *Affinities and Extremes.* (Chicago: Univeristy of Chicago Press, 1990).

Brooke, Greville, 'New Markets for British Trade in the East', *The Sunday Times*, 11 October (1846), 2.

Brooke, Greville, 'The Peace Agitators', *The Sunday Times*, 8 December (1850), 2.

Brooke, Greville, 'Trade and Piracy', *The Sunday Times*, 28 July (1850), 2.

Brooke, James, 'On the Malayan Archipelago: A Proposed Exploration', *Journal Mss South East Asia, Royal Geographical Society*, Royal Geographical Society, JMS/8/2 1838 (1838).

Brooke, James, 'Proposed Exploring Expedition to the Asiatic Archipelago', *Journal of the Royal Geographical Society of London*, 8 (1838), 443–48.

Brooke, James, *A Letter from Borneo with Notices of the Country and its Inhabitants Addressed to James Gardner esq.* (London: L & G Shelley, 1842).

Brooke, James, 'Memorandum', Borneo 1844 to 1846, *Colonial Office*, National Archives United Kingdom, CO 144/1 (1845).

Brooke, James, 'Brooke to Earl of Aberdeen 10 March', *Colonial Office*, National Archives United Kingdom, CO 144/1 (1846).

Brooke, James, and John C. Templer, *The Private Letters of Sir James Brooke, K.C. B Rajah of Sarawak.* (London: Richard Bentley, 1853).

Buchan, James, *Capital of the Mind: How Edinburgh Changed the World.* (London: John Murray, 2004).

Buchan, James, *Adam Smith and the Pursute of Perfect Liberty.* (London: Profile Books, 2006).

Buckley, Charles Burton, *An Anecdotal History of Old Times in Singapore.* (Singapore: Malaya University Press, 1965 [1902]).

Burgess, G., and M. Festenstein, *English Radicalism, 1550–1850*. (Cambridge: Cambridge University Press, 2007).

Burrow, J.W., *Evolution and Society: A Study in Victorian Social Theory*. (London: Cambridge University Press, 1966).

Burrow, J.W., *A History of Histories: Epics, Chronicles, Romances and Inquiries from Herodotus and Thucydides to the Twentieth Century*. (London: Penguin, 2009).

Buyers, Christopher, 'Royal Ark—Johor' (2000–2012) <http://www.royalark.net/Malaysia/johor.htm> [Accessed 27 November 2014].

Campbell, A., *The Grampians Desolate: A Poem*. (Edinburgh: J. Moir, 1804).

Campbell, Enid, 'The Quit Rent System in Colonial New South Wales', *Monash University Law Review*, 35 4 (2009).

Carey, Peter, *The Power of Prophecy: Prince Dipanagara and the End of an Old Order in Java, 1785–1855*. (Leiden: KITLV Press, 2007).

Carlyle, Thomas, 'Thomas Carlyle to Margaret Carlyle', *Carlyle Letters*, 9 1 (1837), 205–08.

Carlyle, Thomas, 'Thomas Carlyle to John Carlyle', *Carlyle Letters*, 28 1 (1853), 109–12.

Carroll, Diana, 'Savages and Barbarians: The British Enlightenment and William Marsden's Contribution to a Malayo-Polynesian Discourse', *Signatures*, 5 (2002), 44.

Carroll, Diana, 'William Marsden and his Malayo-Polynesian Legacy' (Ph.D. Thesis, Australian National University, 2005), p. 2 v.

Chambers, Robert, *Vestiges of the Natural History of Creation*, 12 edition. (London: W. & R. Chambers, 1884).

Claeys, G., *Imperial Sceptics: British Critics of Empire, 1850–1920*. (Cambridge: Cambridge University Press, 2010).

Clarendon, Earl of, 'Earl of Clarendon to Sir Charles Wood, 21 June', *Foreign Office*, National Archives (UK), FO 12/21 (1853).

Cobbett, William, 'Glasgow Election', *Cobbett's Weekly Political Register*, 27 October (1832).

Cobden, R., A. Howe, S. Morgan, and G. Bannerman, *The Letters of Richard Cobden: Volume III: 1854–1859*. (Oxford: Oxford University Press, 2012).

Cobden, Richard, 'Rajah Brooke and the Bornean Massacre', *Manchester Times*, 8 December (1849).

Cook, James, *Captain Cook's Voyages of Discovery*, ed. by John Barrow. (Switzerland: Heron Books, c.1975).

Crawfurd, John, 'Papers Relating to Java and Other Areas of East Asia, ca. 1811–1823', British Library, MS 30353.

Crawfurd, John, 'History and Languages of the Indian Islands', *Edinburgh Review*, 23 (1814).

Crawfurd, John, 'Of the Eastern Penisular of India', *Edinburgh Review*, 22 44 (1814).

Crawfurd, John, 'Publications respecting the Eastern Peninsula of India', *Edinburgh Review*, 22 44 (1814), 331–63.

Crawfurd, John, 'Raffles's History of Java', *Edinburgh Review*, 31 March (1819), 395–413.

Crawfurd, John, *History of the Indian Archipelago: Containing an Account of the Manners, Arts, Languages, Religions, Institutions, and Commerce of its Inhabitants*. (Edinburgh: Archibald Constable and Co., 1820).

Crawfurd, John, *Journal of an Embassy from the Governor-General of India to the Court of Ava in the Year 1827*. (London: Henry Colburn, 1829).

Crawfurd, John, 'Description of India', India Office Library, *British Library*, British Library, Mss eur d 457/a (1832–3).

Crawfurd, John, *Notes on the Settlement or Colonization of British Subjects in India*. (London: J. Ridgway, 1833).

Crawfurd, John, *To the Inhabitants of the Borough of Marylebone, Transcribed by Terr Ellingson* (London: Royal Anthropolgical Institute, 1834).<https://www.therai.org.uk/archives-and-manuscripts/archive-contents/ethnological-society-of-london-council-a1>.

Crawfurd, John, 'Thomas Carlisle's Lectures', *The Spectator*, 6 May (1837).

Crawfurd, John, 'Land Regulations', *The Singapore Free Press and Mercantile Advertiser*, 11 October (1838).

Crawfurd, John, 'Letter to G. Sinton, Secretary to the Government, 3 August 1824', in *'Singapore notices' Journal of the Indian Archipelago*, ed. by J.R. Logan (Singapore: 1853).

Crawfurd, John, 'Notes for a British Settlement on the North-West Coat of Borneo', *Foreign Office*, National Archives, CO 144/1 (1844).

Crawfurd, John, 'Crawfurd to Richard Cobden February 10', Cobden Papers, *West Sussex Record Office*, MS 89, 90, 91 (1848).

Crawfurd, John, 'Crawfurd to Richard Cobden December 24', Cobden Papers, *West Sussex Record Office*, MS 3/11 (1850).

Crawfurd, John, 'Crawfurd to Richard Cobden, December 31', West Sussex Record Office, Cobden Mss 3/12 (1850).

Crawfurd, John, 'John Crawfurd Letters', *Royal Geographic Society*, CB4/Crawfurd (1850–61).

Crawfurd, John, 'Crawfurd to Richard Cobden, March 22 ', Cobden Papers, *West Sussex Record Office*, MS 3/17 (1851).

Crawfurd, John, 'Crawfurd to Richard Cobden, 12 August with Memoranda on Burmah', Cobden Papers, *West Sussex Record Office*, Cobden M, 3/4 (MF 3) (1853).

Crawfurd, John, 'Crawfurd to Cobden, 30 September', Cobden Papers, *West Sussex Record Office*, Cobden MSS 5/109, 5/110 (1858).

Crawfurd, John, 'Crawfurd to Richard Cobden October 16', Cobden Papers, *West Sussex Record Office*, Cobden s/111 (1858).

Crawfurd, John, 'Crawfurd to Richard Cobden September 20', Cobden Papers, *West Sussex Record Office*, Cobden s/114 (1858).

Crawfurd, John, 'Crawfurd to Richard Cobden, 22 September', Cobden Papers, *West Sussex Record Office*, Cobden MS 5/103 (1858).

Crawfurd, John, 'Crawfurd to F Rogers, 12 November', *Foreign Office*, National Archives (UK), FO 12/28 (1860).

Crawfurd, John, 'Crawfurd to Norton Shaw, 3 May', *Royal Geographical Society*, Royal Geographical Society, CB4/Crawfurd (1860).

Crawfurd, John, 'Crawfurd to Norton Shaw, 29 February', *Royal Geographical Society*, Royal Geographical Society, CB4/Crawfurd (1860).

Crawfurd, John, 'Crawrud to Norton Shaw June 8', *Royal Geographical Society*, Royal Geographical Society, RGS/CB4/Crawfurd (1860).

Crawfurd, John, 'On the Conditions which Favour, Retard, or Obstruct the Early Civilization of Man', *Transactions of the Ethnological Society of London*, 1 (1861), 154–77.

Crawfurd, John, 'On the Commixture of the Races of Man as Affecting the Progress of Civilization (Europe)', *Transactions of the Ethnological Society of London*, 2 (1863), 201–13.

Crawfurd, John, 'On Sir Charles Lyell's "Antiquity of Man", and on Professor Huxley's "Evidence as to Man's Place in Nature"', *Transactions of the Ethnological Society of London*, 3 (1865), 58–70.

Crawfurd, John, 'On the Physical and Mental Characteristics of the Negro', *Transactions of the Ethnological Society of London*, 4 (1866), 212–39.

Crawfurd, John, 'On the Physical and Mental Characteristics of the European and Asiatic Races of Man', *Transactions of the Ethnological Society of London*, 5 (1867), 58–81.

Crawfurd, John, 'On the Theory of the Origin of Species by Natural Selection in the Struggle for Life', *Transactions of the Ethnological Society of London*, 7 (1869), 27–38.

Crawfurd, John, *A Descriptive Dictionary of the Indian Islands & Adjacent Countries*. (Kuala Lumpur; New York: Oxford University Press, 1971 [1856]).

Crawfurd, John, *Journal of an Embassy to the Courts of Siam and Cochin China*. (New Gupta Colony: Isha Boks, 2013 [1830]).

Crawfurd, John, and T. Perronet Thompson, 'Sugar without Slavery', *The Westminster Review, 1824–1900*, 19 July (1833), 247–62.

Crawfurd*, John, 'New South Australian Colony', *The Westminster Review*, 21 42 (1834).

Crawfurd*, John, 'The Opium Debate', *The Examiner*, 15 April (1843).

Crawfurd*, John, 'The Expedition to Borneo of H.M.S. Dido, for the Suppression of Piracy: With Extracts from the Journal of James Brooke, Esq., of Sarawak (now Agent for the British Government in Borneo): By Captain the Hon. Henry Keppel, R.N. Two vols. Capman and Hall', *The Examiner*, 21 February (1846).

Crawfurd*, John, 'On the Projected Colonization of Borneo', *The Examiner*, 24 October (1846).

Crawfurd*, John, 'The Edinburgh Review and the Examiner', *The Examiner*, 16 December (1848).

Crawfurd*, John, 'Narrative of the Voyage of H.M.S Samarang, During the Years 1843–46; Employed Sureving the Islands of the Eastern Archipelago; Accompanied by a Brief Vocabulary of the Pincipal Languages: By Captain Sir Edward Belcher, R.N. Commander of the Expedition: With Notes on the Natural History of the Islands, by Arthur Adams, Assistant Surgon, R.N. Reeve and Co.', *The Examiner*, 18 March (1848).

Crawfurd*, John, 'Piracy in the Eastern Archipelago', *The Examiner*, 21 October (1848).

Crawfurd*, John, 'The Slave trade and West Indies', *The Examiner*, 22 January (1848).

Crawfurd*, John, 'Borneo and its resources', *The Examiner*, 12 January (1850).

Crawfurd*, John, 'The Rajah Brooke', *The Examiner*, 27 July (1850).

Crawfurd*, John, 'Bornean Piracy', *The Examiner*, 28 June (1851).

Crawfurd*, John, 'The Brooke Testimonial', *The Examiner* 12 July (1851).

Crawfurd*, John, 'The Lion-Worshipers', *The Examiner*, 19 July (1851).

Crawfurd*, John, 'Modest Merit', *The Examiner*, 31 May (1851).

Crawfurd*, John, "Robert Burns' and Sir James Brooke', *The Examiner*, 4 October (1851).

Crawfurd*, John, 'How Wars are got up in India: The Origin of the Burmese War: By Richard Cobden, Esq., M.P.', *The Examiner*, 20 August (1853).

Crawfurd*, John, 'A Vist to the Indian Archipelago in H.M.S. Maeander, with Portions of the Private Journal of Sir James Brooke, K.C.B.: By Captain the Hon. Henry Keppel, R.N. Two Vols. Bentley', *The Examiner*, 19 February (1853), p. 117.

Crawfurd*, John, 'The Borneo Inquiry', *The Examiner*, 20 May (1854).

Crawfurd*, John, 'The Brooke and Borneo Inquiry', *The Examiner*, 1 September (1855).

Crawfurd*, John, 'Results of the Brooke Inquiry', *The Examiner*, 25 August (1855).

Crawfurd*, John, 'Types of Mankind; or Ethnological Researches, Based upon the Ancient Monuments, Paintings, Sculptures, and Crania of Races, and upon the Natural, Geographical, Philological, and Biblical History: Illustrated by Selections from the Indeited Papers of Samuel George Morton, M.D., and by Additional Contributions from Prof. L. Agassiz L.L.D.; W. Usher M.D.; Prof H.S. Patterson, MD. By J. C Nott, M.D. and Geo. R. Gliddon:Philadelphia: Lippincott, Grambo, and Co.', *The Examiner*, Saturday 20 January (1855).

Crawfurd*, John, 'A Descriptive Dictionary of the Indian Islands and Adjacent Countries', *The Examiner*, 16 August (1856).

Crawfurd*, John, 'Geographical Society Meeting', *The Examiner*, 15 November (1856).

Crawfurd*, John, 'Sarawak and Canton Affairs', *The Examiner*, 2 May (1857).

Crawfurd*, John, 'Rajah Brook and his Claims', *The Examiner*, 9 October (1858).

Crawfurd*, John, 'Rajah Brooke and his Claims', *The Examiner*, 16 October (1858).

Crawfurd*, John, 'Chinese Settlers', *The Examiner*, 29 October (1859).

Crawfurd*, John, 'On the Origin of Species by Means of Natural Selectin, or the Preservation of Favoured Races in the Struggle for Life: By Charles Darwin', *The Examiner*, 3 December (1859).

Crawfurd*, John, 'The Recent African Discovers', *The Examiner*, 3 December (1859).

Crawfurd*, John, 'Java, or How to Manage a Colony; showing a Practical Solution of the Questions now affecting British India: By J. W. B. Money, Barrister-at-Law: Hurst and Blackett', *The Examiner*, 1 June (1861).

Crawfurd*, John, 'Black and White', *The Examiner*, 13 September (1862).

Crawfurd*, John, 'The Geologicl Evidences of the Antiquity of Man, with Remarks on Theories of the Origin of Species by Variation: By Sir Sharles Lyell', *The Examiner*, 28 February (1863).

Crawfurd*, John, 'The Geologicl Evidences of the Antiquity of Man, with Remarks on Theories of the Origin of Species by Variation: By Sir Sharles Lyell [Second Notice]', *The Examiner*, 21 March (1863).

Crawfurd*, John, 'Man and Beast', *The Examiner*, 26 September (1863).

Crawfurd*, John, 'The Negro and Slavery', *The Examiner*, 26 September (1863).

Crawfurd*, John, 'Pre-historic Remains of Caithness: By Samuel Laing M.P, with Notes by Thomas H. Huxley', *The Examiner*, 24 February (1866).

Cribb, R.B., H. Gilbert, and H. Tiffin, *Wild Man from Borneo: A Cultural History of the Orangutan*. (Honolulu: University of Hawaii Press, 2014).

Cutmore, Jonathan, 'Quarterly Review Archive' <http://www.rc.umd.edu/reference/qr/index.html> [Accessed 21 February 2015].

Darwin, Charles, *Journal of Researches into the Natural History and Geology of the countries Visited during the Voyage of H.M.S. "Beagle" Round the World, under the Command of Capt. Fitz Roy, R.A.* (London: Ward, Lock, & Co., Limited, 1897).

Darwin, Charles, 'On the Origin of Species by Means of Natural Selection', in *Charles Darwin, On the Origin of Species*, ed. by Joseph Carroll (Peterborough: Broadview Texts, 2003 [1859]).

Darwin, Charles, 'The Descent of Man, and Selection in Relation to Sex', in *Charles Darwin, the Descent of Man*, ed. by James Moore and Adrian Desmond (London: Penguin, 2004 [1879]).

Darwin, Charles R., 'Darwin to Joseph Hooker, 9 May', Darwin Correspondence Database, (1856), <http://www.darwinproject.ac.uk/entry-1870>

Darwin, Charles R., 'Darwin to Charles Lyell, 2 December', Darwin Correspondence Database, Darwin Project, (1859), <http://www.darwinproject.ac.uk/entry-2565>

Darwin, Charles R., 'Darwin to Thomas Huxley, 5 December', Darwin Correspondence Database, The Darwin Project, (1859), <http://www.darwinproject.ac.uk/entry-2572>

Darwin, Charles R., 'Darwin to John Crawfurd, 7 April', Darwin Correspondence Database, Darwin Project, (1861), <http://www.darwinproject.ac.uk/entry-3114>

Darwin, Charles R., and Alfred Russell Wallace, 'On the Tendency of Species to Form Varietiesl and on the Pepetuation of Varieties and Species by Natural Means of Selection [Read 1 July]', *Journal of the Proceedings of the Linnean Society of London: Zoology*, 2, 20 (1858), 45–50.

Davis, David Brion, *The Problem of Slavery in Western Culture.* (Harmondsworth: Penguin, 1970).

Desmond, Adrian, *The Politics of Evolution: Morphology, Medicine, and Reform in Radical London.* (Chicago: University of Chicago Press, 1989).

Desmond, Adrian, and James Moore, *Darwin's Sacred Cause: How a Hatred of Slavery Shaped Darwin's Views on Human Evolution.* (New York: Houghton Mifflin Harcourt Publishing Comapany, 2009).

Dirks, Nicholas B., 'Colin Mackenzie: Autobiography of an Archive', in *The Madrass School of Orientalism: Producing Knowledge in Colonial South India*, ed. by Thomas R. Trautmann (New Delhi: Oxford University Press, 2009), pp. 29–47.

Douglas, B., and C. Ballard, *Foreign Bodies: Oceania and the Science of Race 1750–1940.* (Canberra, A.C.T.: ANU E Press, 2008).

Earl, G.W., *A Correspondence Relating to the Discovery of Gold in Australia.* (London: Pelham Richardson, 1853).

Earl, George Windsor, *The Eastern Seas, or, Voyages and Adventures in the Indian Archipelago in 1832–33–34: Comprising a Tour of the Island of Java, Visits to Borneo, the Malay Peninsula, Siam, etc.; Also an Account of the Present State of Singapore.* (London: W.H. Allen, 1837).

Earl, George Windsor, 'On the Physical Structure and Arrangement of the Islands in the Indian Archipelago', *Journal of the Geographical Society*, 15 (1845), 358–65.

Echols, John M., Hassan Shadily, John U. Wolff, and James T. Collins, *An Indonesian-English Dictionary.* 3rd edition. (Ithaca: Cornell University Press, 1989).

Editorial, 'Death of Mr. John Crawfurd', *The Times*, 13 May (1868), 5.

Egerton, Hugh Edward, *Sir Stamford Raffles: England in the Far East*. ([S.l.]: T. Fisher Unwin, 1900).

Ellegård, A., *Darwin and the General Reader: The Reception of Darwin's Theory of Evolution in the British Periodical Press, 1859–1872*. (Chicago: University of Chicago Press, 1958).

Ellingson, Ter, *The Myth of the Noble Savage*. (Berkeley: University of California, 2001).

Endersby, Jim, *Imperial Nature: Joseph Hooker and the Practices of Victorian Science*. (Chicago: Universtiy of Chicago Press, 2008).

Farquar, William, 'Report upon the Company's affairs at Prince of Wales Island, and on the General Interests of the British Government in the Eastern Seas', Straits Settlements, *East India Compay Library*, National Library of Australia, vol. 9 (1806).

Farquhar, William, 'Memorial of Lt. Col. Farquar', Java, *East India Company*, British Library, MS 542 (1824).

Federspiel, H.M., *Sultans, Shamans, and Saints: Islam and Muslims in Southeast Asia*. (Honolulu: University of Hawaii Press, 2007).

Fieldhouse, D.K., *The Colonial Empires: A Comparative Survey from the Eighteenth Century*. 2nd edition. (London: Macmillan, 1982, 1966).

Filmer, Robert, and Peter Laslett, *Patriarcha and other Political Works*. (New Brunswick, NJ: Transaction Publishers, 2009).

Finn, Margot, 'Slaves Out of Context: Domestic Slavery and the Anglo-Inidan Family, c. 1780–1830', *Transactions of the Royal Historical Society*, 19 (2009), 181–203.

Fisher, Michael H., *Indirect Rule in India: Residents and the Residency System, 1764–1858*. (Delhi; New York: Oxford University Press, 1991).

Fitzmaurice, Henry Thomas Petty th marquess of Lansdowne, *Report—Relative to the Trade with the East Indies and China- from the Select Committee of the House of Lords, Together with the Minutes of Evidence Taken in Sessions 1820 and 1821, before the Said Committee: 11 April 1821*. ([S.l.]: [s.n.], 1821).

Fleischacker, Samuel, *On Adam Smith's Wealth of Nations: A Philsophical Companion*. (Princeton: Princeton University Press, 2005).

Fonblanque, Albany the Elder, and Edward Barrington De Fonblanque, *The Life and Labours of Albany Fonblanque: Edited by his Nephew E.B. De Fonblanque*. (London: Richard Bentley and Son, 1874).

Forge, Anthony, 'Raffles and Daniell: Making the Image Fit', in *Recovering the Orient: Artists, Scholars, Appropriations*, ed. by C. Andrew Gerstle and Anthony Crothers Milner (Chur, Switzerland: Harwood Academic Publishers, 1994).

Forrest, Thomas, '2 July 1784 letter from Capt Forrest, Extract of Bengal General Consultations', Factory Records: Straits Settlements, *East India Company*, National Library of Australia, (1782).

Forrest, Thomas, 'Report on Pulo Penang', Warren Hastings Papers, *East India Office Records*, British Library, Add 29210 (c.1784).

Forrest, Thomas, and David K. Bassett, *A Voyage to New Guinea and the Moluccas, 1774–1776 . . . With an Introduction by D.K. Bassett*. (Kuala Lumpur, etc.: Oxford University Press, 1969).

Forth, G., *Images of the Wildman in Southeast Asia: An Anthropological Perspective*. (London: Routledge, 2008).

Fredrickson, George M., *Racism: A Short History*. (Princeton: Princeton University Press, 2003).

Gallop, Adrian, 'Mortality Improvements and Evolution of Life Expectancies' <http://www.osfi-bsif.gc.ca/Eng/Docs/DEIP_Gallop.pdf > [Accessed 11 January 2016].

Gerlich, Bianca Maria, 'Marudu 1845: The Destruction and Reconstruction of a Coastal State in Borneo', (Doctoral Thesis, Abera Universität Hamburg, 2003).

Gibbon, Edward, *The History of the Decline and Fall of the Roman Empire*. (London: The Folio Society, 1997 [1788]).

Glat, Mark, 'John Locke's Historical Sense', *The Review of Politics*, 43 01 (1981), 3–21.

Glendinning, V., *Raffles: And the Golden Opportunity*. (London: Profile Books, 2012).

Google, 'Ngram Viewer for the words 'savage', 'barbarian', 'aboriginal', 'indigneous' date range 1700–1850'.

Gould, Stephen Jay, *The Mismeasure of Man*. (New York: W W Norton & Company, 1981).

Grant, Charles, *Mr. Grant's Observations on the State of Society Among the Asiatic Subjects of Great Britain, Particularly with Respect to Morals; and on the Means of Improving it*. (London, 1813).

Guha, Ranajit, *A Rule of Property for Bengal: An Essay on the Idea of Permanent Settlement*. 2nd edition. (New Delhi: Orient Longman, 1982).

Hall, B., *Fragments of Voyages and Travels by Captain Basil Hall, 3: Second Series*. (Edinburgh: Robert Cadell, 1832).

Hall, Basil, 'Memoir of the Life and Public Servies of Sir Stamford Raffles, F.R.S., Partiqulary in the Government of Java in 1811–6; and of Bencoolen and its Dependencies, 1817–24: With Details of the Commerce and Resources of the Eastern Archipelago; and Selections from the Correspondence: By his Widow', *Edinburgh Review*, 51, 111 (1830), 396–418.

Hall, Catherine, *Civilising Subjects: Metropole and Colony in the English Imagination, 1830–1867*. (Oxford: Polity, 2002).

Hannigan, Tim, *Raffles and the British invasion of Java*. (Singapore: Monsoon, 2012).

Harrington, Jack, *Sir John Malcolm and the Creation of British India*. 1st edition. (New York, NY: Palgrave Macmillan, 2010).

Ho, E., *The Graves of Tarim: Genealogy and Mobility Across the Indian Ocean*. (Berkeley, CA: University of California Press, 2006).

Hochschild, Adam, *Bury the Chains: The British Struggle to Abolish Slavery*. (London: Macmillian, 2005).

Horsfield, T., *Zoological Researches in Java, and the Neighbouring Islands*. (London: Kingsbury, Parbury, & Allen, 1824).

Houghton, W.E., J.H. Slingerland, and Wellesley College, *The Wellesley Index to Victorian Periodicals, 1824–1900*. (Toronto: University of Toronto Press, 1989).

Howe, Anthony, Simon Morgan, and Gordon Bannerman, eds., *The Letters of Richard Cobden Volume II 1848–1853* (Oxford: Oxford University Press, 2010).

Huch, R.K., and P.R. Ziegler, *Joseph Hume, the People's M.P.* (Philadelphia: American Philosophical Society, 1985).

Hume, David, *History of England*. (Indianapolis: Liberty Fund, 1983 [1778]).

Hume, Joseph, 'Piracy and Murder', *The Times*, (1852), 6.

Hume, Joseph, 'Mr Hume, M.P., to the Right Honorable the Earl of Clarendon, Her Majesty's Secretary of State for Foreign Affairs, 30 April', *Foreign Office*, National Archives (UK), FO 12/21 (1853).

Ingleson, John, 'Britain's Annexation of Labuan in 1846', *University Studies in History*, 5 4 (1970), 33–71.

Ingleson, John, *Expanding the Empire: James Brooke and the Sarawak Lobby, 1839–1868*. (Nedlands, WA: Centre for South and Southeast Asian Studies, University of Western Australia, 1979).

Irwin, Graham, 'Nineteenth-Century Borneo: A Study in Diplomatic Rivalry', (Martinus Nijhoff: 's-Gravenhage, 1955), pp. xi. 251. pl. 4.

John, James Augusts St., 'To the Editor of the 'Examiner', Piracy in the Indian Archipelago', *The Examiner*, 16 December (1848).

Johnson, Samuel, *A Dictionary of the English Language: In which the Words are Deduced from their Originals, and Illustrated in their Different Significations by Examples from the Best Writers: To which are Prefixed, a History of the Language, and an English Grammar*. (London: W. Strahan, 1755).

Johnson, Samuel, *A Journey to the Western Islands of Scotland*. (London: Everyman Publishers, 2002 [1775]).

Jones, H., *Union in Peril: The Crisis over British Intervention in the Civil War*. (Chapel Hill: University of North Carolina Press, 1992).

Jupp, Clifford N., *The History of Islay, from Earliest Times to 1848*. (Port Charlotte: The Museum of Islay Life, 1994).

Kadir, Abdullah bin Abdul, *The Hikayat Abdullah: An Annotated Translation by A.H. Hill*. (Kuala Lumpur; Singapore: Oxford University Press, 1970).

Kames, Lord, *Six Sketches on the History of Man*. (Philadelphia: R. Bell, 1774).

Kaye, J.W., *The Life and Correspondence of Major-General Sir John Malcolm, G.C.B.: Late Envoy to Persia, and Governor of Bombay; From Unpublished Letters and Journals*. (London: Smith, Elder, 1856).

Keith, Arthur, 'How Can the Institute Best Serve the Needs of Anthropology?', *The Journal of the Royal Anthropolgical Institute of Great Britain and Ireland*, 47 January-June (1917), 12–30.

Ken, Wong Lin, 'The Trade of Singapore, 1819–69', *Journal of the Malaysian Branch of the Royal Asiatic Society*, 33 4 (1960), 5–302.

Keppel, Henry, *The Expedition to Borneo of H.M.S. Dido for the Suppression of Piracy: With Extracts from the Journal of James Brooke*. 2nd edition. (London: Chapman and Hall, 1846).

Knapman, Gareth, 'The Pacificator: Discovering the Lost Bust of George Augustus Robinson', *La Trobe Journal*, 86 (2010), 37–52.

Knapman, Gareth, 'Museum Anthropology and Imperial Networks as Cultural Status: The Colonial Ethnology Museum in Nineteenth Century Melbourne', *History of Anthropology Newsletter*, 31 (2011).

Knapman, Gareth, 'Curiosities or Science in the Natinal Museum of Victoria: Procurement Networks and the Purpose of a Museum', in *Curating Empire: Museums and the British Imperial Experience*, ed. by Sarah editor Longair and John editor McAleer (Manchester: Manchester University Press, 2012), pp. 82–103.

Koditschek, Theodore, *Liberalism, Imperialism and the Historical Imagination: Nineteenth Century Visions of Great Britain*. (Cambridge: Cambridge University Press, 2011).

Krishnan, Sanjay, *Reading the Global: Troubling Perspectives on Britain's Empire in Asia*. (New York; Chichester: Columbia University Press, 2007).

Kyd, Alexander, 'Report into Island of Penang', Straits Settlements, *East India Compay*, National Library of Australia, vol. 9 (1787).

Laffan, Michael Francis, *Islamic Nationhood and Colonial Indonesia: The umma Below the Winds*. (London: RoutledgeCurzon, 2003).

Laidlaw, Zoë, *Colonial Connections, 1815–45: Patronage, the Information Revolution and Colonial Government*. (Manchester: Manchester University Press, 2005).

Larsen, Ib, 'The First Sultan of Sarawak and His Links to Brunei and the Sambas Dynasty, 1599–1826: A Little-known Pre-Brooke History', *Journal of the Malaysian Branch of the Royal Asiatic Society*, 85 303 (2012), 1–16.

Laslett, Peter, 'Introduction', in *Locke: Two Treaties of Government*, ed. by Peter Laslett (Cambridge: Cambridge University Press, 2004).

Latour, Bruno, *Science in Action: How to Follow Scientists and Engineers through Society*. (Cambridge, MA: Harvard University Press, 1987).

Leyden, John, 'On the Languages and Literature of the Indo-Chinese Nations', *Asiatick Researches; Or, Transactions of the Asiatic Society of Bengal*, 10 v. 10 (1811), 158–290.

Light, Frances, 'Report on Junk Ceylon [Phuket]', Warren Hastings Papers, *East India Office Records*, British Library, Ms 29210 (c.1784).

Light, Francis, 'A List of the Inhabitants of Prince of Wales's Island', Straits Settlements, *East India Compay*, National Library, vol. 9 (1788).

Lockard, Craig A., *Southeast Asia in World History*. (New York; Oxford: Oxford University Press, 2009).

Locke, John, *Two Treatieses of Goverenment*, ed. by Peter Laslett. (Cambridge: Cambridge University Press, 2004 [1698]).

Logan, James Richardson, 'The Present Condition of the Indian Archipelago', *The Journal of The Indian Archipelago and Eastern Asia*, 1 (1847), 1–21.

Lovejoy, Arthur O., *The Great Chain of Being: A Study of the History of an Idea*. (Cambridge, MA: Harvard University Press, 1957).

Lyell, Charles, 'Lyell to Charles Darwin, 11 March', Darwin Correspondence Database, Darwin Project, (1863), <http://www.darwinproject.ac.uk/entry-4035>

MacDonald, James, *General View of the Agriculture of the Hebrides, or Western Isles of Scotland: With Observations on the Means of their Improvement, Together with a Separate Account of the Principal Islands; Comprehending their Resources, Fisheries, Manufactures, Manners, and Agriculture*. (Edinburgh: Sir R. Phillips, 1811).

Mackenzie, William Cook, and Colin Surveyor-General of India Mackenzie, *Colonel Colin Mackenzie: First Surveyor-General of India, etc. [With a portrait.]*. (W. & R. Chambers: Edinburgh & London, 1952), pp. ix. 230.

MacQueen, J., and Z. Macaulay, *The Colonial Controversy: Containing a Refutation of the Calumnies of the Anticolonists, the State of Hayti, Sierra Leone, India, China, Cochin China, Java, &c., &c., the Production of Sugar, &c., and the State of the Free and Slave Labourers in those Countries, Fully Considered in a Series of Letters Addressed to the Earl of Liverpool, with a Supplementary Letter to Mr. Macaulay*. (Printed by Khull, Blackie, 1825).

Manickam, Sandra Khor, 'Taming Race: The Construction of Aborigines in ColonialMalaya, 1783–1937', (Ph.D. Thesis, Australian National University, 2010).

Marsden, William, 'Remarks on the Sumatran Languages, by Mr Marsden: In a Letter to Sir Joseph Banks, Bart: President of the Royal Society', *Archaeologia or Miscellaneous Tracts Relating to Antiquity*, 6 (1782), 154–8.

Marsden, William, *The History of Sumatra, Containing an Account of the Government, Laws, Customs, and Manners of the Native Inhabitants, with a Description of the Natural Productions and a Relation of the Ancient Political State*. (London: The Author, 1783).

Marsden, William, *The History of Sumatra, Containing an Account of the Government, Laws, Customs, and Manners of the Native Inhabitants, with a Description of the Natural Productions, and a Relation of the Ancient Political State of that Island*. 2nd edition. (London, The Author, 1784).

Marsden, William, *The History of Sumatra: Containing an Account of the Government, Laws, Customs and Manners of the Native Inhabitants, with a Description of the Natural Productions, and a Relation of the Ancient Political State of that Island*. 3rd edition. (London: Printed for the author by J. McCreery and sold by Longman, Hurst, Rees, Orme and Brown, 1811).

Marsden, William, *The History of Sumatra*. (Kuala Lumpur: Oxford University Press, 1966 [1811]).

McCarthy, Thomas, *Race, Empire, and the Idea of Human Development*. (Cambridge, UK; New York: Cambridge University Press, 2009).

McGilvary, George K., *East India Patronage and the British State: The Scottish Elite and Politics in the Eighteenth Century*. (London: Tauris Academic Studies, 2008).

McNiven, Ian J., and Lynette Russell, *Appropriated Pasts: Indigenous Peoples and the Colonial Culture of Archaeology*. (Lanham, MD: AltaMira Press, 2005).

Meek, R.L., *Social Science and the Ignoble Savage*. (Cambridge: Cambridge University Press, 1976).

Mehta, Uday Sing, *Liberalism and Empire: A Study in Nineteenth-Century British Liberal Thought*. (Chicago: University of Chicago Press, 1999).

Mill, James, 'Bruce's Report on the East-India Negotiation', *The Monthly Review*, LXX January (1813).

Mill, James, 'Colony', in *Supplement to the Encyclopedia Britannica* (London: J. Iinnes, 1825).

Mill, James, *The History of British India*. (London: Baldwin, Cradock, and Joy, 1820 [1817]).

Milner, Anthony, *Kerajaan: Malay Political Culture on the Eve of Colonial Rule*. (Tucson: University of Arizona Press, 1982).

Milner, Anthony, *The Invention of Politics in Colonial Malaya*. (Cambridge: Cambridge University Press, 2002).

Milner, Anthony Crothers, 'Islam and the Muslim State', in *Islam in South-East Asia*, ed. by M.B. Hooker (Leiden: E.J. Bril, 1983).

Milner, Anthony Crothers, *The Malays*. (Oxford: Wiley-Blackwell, 2008).

Milner, Anthony Crothers, *The Malays*. 1st edition. (Chichester: Wiley-Blackwell, 2011).

Minto, Gilbert Elliot, and Emma Eleanor Elizabeth Elliot-Murray-Kynynmound Minto, *Lord Minto in India*. (London,: Longmans, Green, and co., 1880).

Morley, John, *The Life of Richard Cobden*. (London: T. Fisher Unwin, 1903).

Müller, Martin, 'Manufacturing Malayness', *Indonesia and the Malay World*, 42 123 (2014), 170–96.

Müller, Martin, 'Civilization, Culture, and Race in John Crawfurd's Discourses on Southeast Asia: Continuities and Changes, c.1814–1868', (Ph.D. Thesis, Florence: European University Institute, 2013).

Murchison, Roderick, 'Address to the Royal Geographical Society', *Journal of the Royal Geographical Society of London*, 38 (1868), cxxxiii-cxcviii.

Murray, H., J. Crawfurd, P. Gordon, T. Lynn, W. Wallace, and G.T. Burnett, *An Historical and Descriptive Account of China: Its Ancient and Modern History, Language, Literature, Religion, Government, Industry, Manners, and Social State; Intercourse with Europe from the Earliest Ages; Missions and Embassies to the Imperial Court; British and Foreign Commerce; Directions to Navigators; State of Mathematics and Astronomy; Survey of Its Geography, Geology, Botany, and Zoology*. (Edinburgh: Oliver & Boyd, 1836).

Muthu, Sankar, *Enlightenment against Empire*. (Princeton, NJ; Oxford: Princeton University Press, 2003).

Naoroji, Dadabhai, 'Observations on Mr. John Crawfurd's Paper on the European and Asiatic Races', *Transactions of the Ethnological Society of London*, 5 (1867), 127–49.

Nisbet, Robert, 'Vico and the Idea of Progress', *Social Research*, 43 3 (1976), 625.

Noor, Farish A.'Know our People', S. Rajaratnam School of International Relations, Nanyang Technological University, < https://www.rsis.edu.sg/profile/farish-badrol-hisham-ahmad-noor/#.Vpgsmvl97IV> [Accessed 15 January 2016].

Pagden, A.R., *The Fall of Natural Man: The American Indian and the Origins of Comparative Ethnology*. (Cambridge: Cambridge University Press, 1982).

Paley, William, *Natural Theology*. (Oxford: Oxford University Press, 2008 [1802]).

Panular, P.B.R. Carey, British Library., and British Academy., *The British in Java, 1811–1816: A Javanese Account : A Text Edition, English Synopsis, and Commentary on British Library Additional Manuscript 12330 (Babad bdhah ing Ngayogyakarta)*. (Oxford; New York: Published for the British Academy by Oxford University Press, 1992).

Parekh, Bhikhu, 'Liberalism and Colonialism: A Critique of Locke and Mill', in *The Decolonization of Imagination: Culture, Knowledge and Power*, ed. by Jan Nederveen Pieterse and Bhikhu Parekh (London: Zed Books, 1995), pp. 81–98.

Pitts, Jennifer, *A Turn to Empire: The Rise of Imperial Liberalism in Britain and France*. (Princeton: Princeton Unversity Press, 2005).

Pocock, J.G.A., *The Ancient Constituion and the Feudal Law: A Study of English Historical Though in the Seventeenth Century*. (Cambridge: Cambridge University Press, 1987).

Pocock, J.G.A., *Barbarism and Religion II: Narratives of Civil Government*. (Cambridge: Cambridge University Press, 1999).

Pocock, J.G.A., *Barbarism and Religion IV: Barbarians, Savages and Empires*. (Cambridge: Cambridge Universtiy Press, 2005).

Porter, B., *Critics of Empire: British Radical Attitudes to Colonialism in Africa*. (London: Macmillan, 1968).

Porter, Roy, *Enlightenment: Britain and the Creation of the Modern World*. (London: Penguin, 2001).

Porter, Roy, *Flesh in the Age of Reason*. (London: Penguin, 2004).

Prichard, James Cowles, *The Natural History of Man*. (London: H. Bailliere, 1855).

Pringle, Robert, *Rajahs and Rebels: The Ibans of Sarawak under Brooke rule, 1841–1941*. (London: Macmillan, 1970).

Prinsep, Charles, 'Mr Prinsep to the Governor-General of India in Council, Opinion', *Foreign Office*, National Archives UK, FO 881/482 (1855).

Pryor, Francis, *Britain AD: A Quest for Arthur, England and the Anglo-Saxons*. (London: Harper Perennial, 2005).

Quilty, Mary, *Textual Empires: A Reading of Early British Histories of Southeast Asia*. (Melbourne: Monash Asia Institute, 1998).

Quilty, Mary, 'British Economic Thought and Colonization in Southeat Asia, 1776–1850', (Ph.D. Thesis, Sydney: University of Sydney, 2001).

Raby, Peter, *Alfred Russel Wallace*. (London: Chatto & Windus, 2001).

Raffles, Sophia, ed., *Memoir of the Life and Public Services of Sir Thomas Stamford Raffles* (London: James Duncan, 1835).

Raffles, Thomas Stamford, *Substance of a Minute Recorded by the Honourable Thomas Stamford Raffles . . . on the 11th February 1814; on the Introduction of an Imprived System of Internal Management and the Establishment of a Land Rental on the Island of Java: to which are Added Several of the Most Interesting Documents therein Referred to*. (London: Printed for Black, Parry, and Co., 1814).

Raffles, Thomas Stamford, *The History of Java*. (Kuala Lumpur: Oxford University Press, 1965 [1817]).

Raffles, Thomas Stamford, William Marsden, and John Barrow, 'Crawfurd's History of the Indian Archipelago', *Quarterly Review*, 28 55 (1822), 111–38.

Raffles, Thomas Stamford Sir, 'Minute on Land Tenure', Factory Records: Java, *British Library*, India Office Records and Private Papers, IOR/G/21/60 vol. 69. British Library.

Raffles, Thomas Stamford, 'Arrangements with the Sultan and Toomoongong.' 7 June (1823), in *'Singapore notices' Journal of the Indian Archipelago*, ed. by Logan (Singapore: 1853).

Raynal, Guillaume Thomas Franc ois, *A Philosophical and Political History of the British Settlements and Trade in North America*. (Edinburgh: printed by C. MacFarquhar. Sold by the booksellers, 1776).

Reid, Anthony, 'Islamization and Christianization in Southeast Asia: The Critical Phase, 1550–1650', in *Southeast Asian in the Early Modern Era*, ed. by Anthony Reid (Ithaca: Cornell University Press, 1993), pp. 151–79.

Rendall, Jane, 'Scottish Orientalism: From Robertson to James Mill', *The Historical Journal*, 25 1 (1982), 43–69.

Reynolds, Henry, *Fate of a Free People*. (Ringwood, VIC: Penguin, 1995).

Robertson, William, *The History of America*. (London: Printed for W. Strahan; T. Cadell . . . ; and J. Balfour, at Edinburgh, 1777).

Rothschild, Emma, *Economic Sentiments: Adam Smith, Condorcet, and the Enlightenment*. (Cambridge: Harvard University Press, 2001).

Rowley-Conwy, P., *From Genesis to Prehistory: The Archaeological Three Age System and Its Contested Reception in Denmark, Britain, and Ireland*. (Oxford: Oxford University Press, 2007).

Rudwick, Martin J.S., *Bursting the Limits of Time: The Reconstructionof Geohistory in the Age of Revolution*. (Chicago: University of Chicago Press, 2005).

Runciman, S., *The White Rajah: A History of Sarawak from 1841 to 1946*. (Cambridge: Cambridge University Press, 2011).

Runciman, Steven, *The White Rajahs: A History of Sarawak from 1841 to 1946*. (London: Cambridge University Press, 1960).

Russell, Lynette, *Savage Imaginings: Historical and Contemporary Constructions of Australian Aboriginalities*. (Melbourne: Australian Scholarly Publishing, 2001).

Ryder, Dudley nd E. Harrowby, 'Report from the Select Committee on Commercial Relations with China; Together with the Minutes of Evidence, Appendix, and Index', *House of Commons Papers; Reports Of Committees*, No. 654, (London: 1847).

Said, Edward W., *Orientalism: Western Conceptions of the Orient*. (London: Penguin, 1995).

Sarich, Vincent, and Frank Miele, *Race: The Reality of Human Differences*. (Boulder, CO: Westview Press, 2004).

Schama, Simon, *Landscape and Memory*. (London: Fontana, 1996).

Schnapp, Alain, *The Discovery of the Past*. (London: British Museum Press, 1993).

Sclater, Philip Lutley, 'On the General Geographical Distribution of the Members of the Class Aves', *Journal of the Proceedings of the Linnean Society of London*, 2 7 (1858), 130–6.

Scott, James C., *Weapons of the Weak: Everyday Forms of Peasant Resistance*. (New Haven; London: Yale University Press, 1985).

Scott, James C., 'Hill and Valley in Southeast Asia . . . or Why the State is the Enemy of People who Move Around . . . or . . . Why Civilizations Can't Climb Hills', in *The Concept of Indigenous Peoples in Asia : A Resource Book*, ed. by Christian Erni (Copenhagen: International Work Group for Indegenous Affairs, 2008).

Secord, J.A., *Victorian Sensation: The Extraordinary Publication, Reception, and Secret Authorship of Vestiges of the Natural History of Creation*. (Chicago: University of Chicago Press, 2000).

Sellato, Bernard, *Nomads of the Borneo Rainforest: The Economics, Politics, and Ideology of Settling Down*. (Honolulu: University of Hawaii Press, 1994).

Sen, Sudipta, *Distant Sovereignty: National Imperialism and the Origins of British India*. (New York; London: Routledge, 2002).

Shermer, Michael, *In Darwin's Shadow: The Life and Science of Alfred Russel Wallace: A Biographical Study on the Psychology of History*. (Oxford: Oxford University Press, 2002).

Slotten, Ross A., *The Heretic in Darwin's Court: The Life of Alfred Russel Wallace*. (New York: Columbia University Press, 2004).

Smith, A., W.P.D. Wightman, J.C. Bryce, I.S. Ross, R.H. Campbell, D.D. Raphael, and A.S. Skinner, *The Glasgow Edition of the Works and Correspondence of Adam Smith: III: Essays on Philosophical Subjects : With Dugald Stewart's 'Account of Adam Smith': With Dugald Stewart's 'Account of Adam Smith'*. (Oxford: Oxford University Press, 1980).

Smith, Adam, *The Wealth of Nations*. (London: Everyman's Library, 1981 [1776]).

Smith, Samuel, *An Essay on the Causes of the Variety of Complexion and Figure in the Human Species, to which are Added Strictures on Lord Kames's Discourses on the Origninal Diversity of Mankind*. (Edinburgh: C.Elliot, 1778).

Smith, Thomas, 'To the Radical Reformers of Preston', *Preston Chronicle*, 24 December (1836).

St. John, Horace Stebbing Roscoe, *The Indian Archipelago; Its History and Present State*. (London: Longman, Brown, Green and Longmans, 1853).

St. John, James, 'Piracy in the Oriental Archipelago', *The Edinburgh Review: Or Critical Journal*, 88 177 (1848), 63–94.

St. John, Spencer, *The Life of Sir James Brooke, Rajah of Srarwak from his Persoanal Papers and Correspondance.* (Edinburgh: W. Blackwood, 1879).

Stockdale, John Joseph, *Sketches, Civil and Military, of the Island of Java . . . Second edition, with Additions.* (London: J.J. Stockdale, 1812).

Stocking, George W., *Victorian Anthropology.* (New York: Free Press, 1987).

Tarling, Nicholas, *Piracy and Politics in the Malay World: A Study of British Imperialism in Nineteenth-Century South-East Asia.* (Melbourne: F.W. Cheshire, 1963).

Tarling, Nicholas, *British Policy in the Malay Peninsula And Archipelago: 1824–1871.* (Kuala Lumpur: Oxford University Press, 1969).

Tarling, Nicholas, *Imperial Britian in South-East Asia.* (Kuala Lumpur: Oxford Univeristy Press, 1975).

Tarling, Nicholas, *The Burthen, the Risk, and the Glory: A Biography of Sir James Brooke.* (Kuala Lumpur; Oxford: Oxford University Press, 1982).

Tarling, Nicholas, 'Brooke Rule in Sarawak and its Principles', *Journal of the Malaysian Branch of the Royal Asiatic Society*, 65 1 (1992), 15–27.

Tarling, Nicholas, 'The British Empire in South-East Asia', in *The Oxford History of the British Empire: Historiography*, ed. by Robin W. Winks (Oxford: Oxford University Press, 1999).

Teignmouth, Charles John Shore, Baron, *Sketches of the Coasts and Islands of Scotland and of the Isle of Man, Descriptive of the Scenery and Illustrative of the Progressive Revolution in the Economical, Moral, and Social Condition of the Inhabitants of those Regions.* (London: J.W. Parker, 1836).

Thomson, John Turnbull, *Glimpses Into Life in Malayan Lands.* (Singapore: Oxford University Press, 1984 [1864]).

Tomkins, Stephen, *The Clapham Sect: How Wilberforce's Circle Transformed Britain.* (Oxford: Lion, 2010).

Torrens, R., *Colonization of South Australia.* (London: Longman, Rees, Orme, Brown, Green, and Longman, 1835).

Trumpener, Katie, *Bardic Nationalism: The Romantic Novel and the British Empire.* (Princeton: Princeton University Press, 1997).

Turnbull, C.M., 'Introduction', in *G.W. Earl, The Eastern Seas* (Singapore: Oxford University Press, 1971), pp. v–xviii.

Turnbull, C.M., *The Straits Settlements, 1826–1867: Indian Presidency to Crown Colony.* (London: Athlone Press, 1972).

Turnbull, C.M., *A History of Modern Singapore, 1819–2005.* (Singapore: NUS Press, 2009).

van 't Veer, P., *Daendels: maarschalk van Holland.* (Bussum: Fibula-Van Dishoeck, 1983).

Van Niel, Robert, *Java's Northeast Coast, 1740–1840: A Study in Colonial Encroachment and Dominance.* (Leiden: Research School CNWS, Leiden University, 2005).

Victoria, Museum, 'Albertus Seba's Depiction of the Southern Common Opossum Didelphis Marsupialis in the 18th Century Thesaurus held by the Museum Victoria Library', (2009).

Villiers, Hyde, 'Report from the Select Committee on the Affairs of the East India Company; with Minutes of Evidence in Six Parts, and an Appendix and Index to Each', *House Of Commons Papers; Reports Of Committees*, No. 734, 735-I, 735-II, 735-III, 735-IV, 735-V, 735-VI (London: 1831).

von Humboldt, A., A. Bonpland, and T. Ross, *Personal Narrative of Travels to the Equinoctial Regions of America: During the Years 1799–1804*. (London: Henry G. Bohn, 1853).

Wake, C.H., 'Raffles and the Rajas: The Founding of Singapore in Malayan and British colonial history', *Journal of the Malaysian Branch of the Royal Asiatic Society*, 48 1 (1975), 47–73.

Walker, J.H., *Power and Prowess: The Origins of Brooke Kingship in Sarawak*. (Crows Nest, N.S.W. Australia: Asian Studies Association of Australia in association with Allen & Unwin, 2002).

Wallace, Alfred Russell, 'Letter from Mr. Wallace Concerning the Geographical Distribution of Birds (S52: 1859)', in *Alfred Russell Wallace Page* (1859).

Wallace, Alfred Russell, 'On the Physical Geography of the Malay Archipelago', *Proceedings of the Royal Geographical Society of London*, 75 (1863), 206–13.

Wallace, Alfred Russell, *The Malay Archipelago*. 10th edition. (New York: Dover Publications, 1962 [1869]).

Wallace, Thomas st Bn Wallace, 'First Report from the Select Committee on the Affairs of the East India Company (China Trade)', *House Of Commons Papers; Reports Of Committees*, No. 644. (London: 1830).

Warren, James F., *The Sulu Zone, 1768–1898: The Dynamics of External Trade, Slavery and Ethnicity in the Transformation of a Southeast Asian Maritime State*. 2nd edition. (Singapore: Singapore University Press, 2007).

Watson, Frederick, ed., *Historical Records of Australia*. (Sydney: The Library Committee of the Commonwealth Parliament, 1914–1926).

White, Charles, *An Account of the Regular Gradation in Man*. (London: Printed for C. Dilly 1799).

Wilson, Jon E., *The Domination of Strangers: Modern Governance in Eastern India, 1780–1835*. (Basingstoke: Palgrave Macmillan, 2010).

Wise, Henry, 'Wise to Lord John Russell, 26 November', *Foreign Office*, National Archives (UK), FO 12/7 (1849).

Wolfe, Patrick, *Settler Colonialism and the Transformation of Anthropology: The Politics and Poetics of an Ethnographic Event*. (London: Cassell, 1999).

Wright, Nadia, *Image is All: Lt-Colonel William Farquhar, Sir Stamford Raffles, and the Founding and Early Development of Colonial Singapore*. (Australia: University of Melbourne, 2012).

Wurtzburg, Charles Edward, and Clifford Witting, *Raffles of the Eastern Isles*. (London: Hodder and Stoughton, 1954).

Z., A., 'To the Editor of the Singapore Free Press', *The Singapore Free Press and Mercantile Advertiser*, 21 June (1850), 2–3.

Index

abolitionists 219
Aboriginal Protection Society 163, 184, 188
aboriginal 71, 73–4, 75–6, 78–80, 84–6, 88, 92, 172, 236
Adas, Michael 98
Agassiz, Louis 87
Ali of Brunei, Sultan Omar 157, 158–9
America 72–3
American Civil War 217–20, 294
Anderson, John 180
anonymous writing 241
anthropology 116, 228
antiquarian 46–7
Apanage 53–4
Arabs 171–2
Arrow War (Second Opium War) 201–202
Arthur, Lieutenant Governor 164
Aryan language 221, 250
Assey, Charles 33
Australia 164
Austronesian 88–9, 112
autochthony 79, 86, 91

Banks, Joseph 81
barbarians/barbarism 2, 12, 23, 27, 49, 75, 76, 210–16, 229; colonial history 24; freedom 13, 16, 24, 211
Bastin, John 46, 125
Bekel 54, 63, 65
Belcher, Edward 1, 187
Bentham, Jeremy 6
Bible 50, 78
Blumenbach, Johann 101
Bonham, Samuel George (Governor of Singapore) 161
Boon, James 99
Bright, John 186

British Association for the Advancement of Science 98, 220
Brooke, James 1, 114, 154–73, 236; aboriginal protection 165; Commission of Inquiry into 196–200; defines piracy 166; influence of Stamford Raffles 156; life 158; offered government of Sarawak 160–1; opinions of 158; status as an independent sovereign 198; supporters 180
Brunei 157–9, 168
Bupati 53–4
Burns, Robert 192
Burrow, John 116
Buxton, Thomas Foxwell 164

Caesar, Julius 47–8
chain of being 87, 106
Chambers, Robert 114
Chinese 75, 128–30, 200–2
Cirebon 53
civilisation 43, 75, 76, 77, 101, 103, 104, 109, 125, 155, 190, 211, 214, 217, 228; decay of 169–70, 190, 191, 211, 221; Indic 43, 61, 64; Indigenous 9n43, 65, 89, 109, 111, 182, 226–7, 234–5
civilising mission 32–3, 154, 163, 182, 190, 209, 211, 214, 217, 223, 227, 228, 239
Cobden, Richard 182, 184–6, 192–3; on Arrow War 201–2; on Brooke 189; on massacre of the Saribas and Sekrang Dayaks 186, 192–3, 236–7; relationship with Crawfurd 188, 193–4
colonial intervention in native states 125, 138–40, 187

colonialism 5, 13, 28, 71, 125, 154, 187, 209, 216, 233–4; conquest 76, 236; criticism 2, 12, 17–19, 28, 187; expansion 35; migration 75; multicultural centres 30; strategic position 30, 138–9; trade 30
commerce 24
Commission of Inquiry into James Brooke and Piracy in Sarawak 196–200
Cook, James 102
Crawfurd, John 65, 85, 86, 89, 98, 125, 185, 201–2; advocates Labuan as a colony 180; American Civil War 218–20; and Richard Cobden 188, 193–4, 246; anonymous writing 241; as lobbyist 132, 179–80; Asian independence 26, 187; barbarians 23; campaigns against Brooke 181, 185; Thomas Carlyle 242; civilization 212, 215; colonialism 18, 28–9, 34, 163–4, 182, 187; critical of Marsden 101; critical of Stamford Raffles 127; death of 233; descriptive dictionary of the Indian Archipelago 109, 195, 211, 244; Edinburgh Review 23, 35, 44, 191, 226; environmental determinism 109–10, 213, 228; fair trade 26, 29; History of the Indian Archipelago 23, 27, 33, 34–5, 43–4; House of Commons 139; ideas on language 83; importance of geography 213; interpretations of 44, 99, 111, 233; Java 42, 60, 63–4; Javanese 84; life 7–9, 20–22, 35, 139, 179, 220; obituaries 242; on James Brooke 157, 162, 180, 194, 215; on Charles Darwin 224; on Charles Lyell 224–5; on Chinese 128, 136; on Christianity 224; on commission of inquiry into Sarawak 199; on history 51, 86, 88–9, 210; on massacre of the Saribas and Sekrang Dayaks 186; on Roderick Murchinson 242; on piracy 191–6; on savages 209, 213–5; on Thomas Huxley 223, 225; polygenesis 88, 112, 227, 229; race 104–5, 108, 110, 112; radicalism 4, 27, 179; rejected colonisation of Borneo 181–2, 187, 212; relationship with Alfred Russel Wallace 114, 216–7, 248; resident of Singapore 131, 134–8; resident 23, response to evolution

224–5; reviews *Origin of the Species* 223; self-promoting 249 stadial/ conjectural development 90–2, 210, 212, 237; The Examiner 35, 179, 181, 185, 191, 209, 220, 224–5, 241–51; the Spectator 35, views on Opium 132–3; Westminster Review 35, writing style 244–5, 250
custom 47, 48, 101
Cuvier, George 87

Daendels, General Herman Willem 54–5
Darwin, Charles 114, 117, 218, 221–5, 233; on John Crawfurd 224, 243
Dayaks 170–1
degeneration 107–8
Desmond, Adrian and James Moore 117
despotism 57
Devereux, Humphrey 197–200
'Dick', 104
Dutch 53, 57

Earl, George Windsor 116, 157
East India Company 1; attitude to Asians 25; critics 18–19, 33; diplomatic office 22; India Act 1874 18; patronage networks 19, 45; Scotts in 19; sovereignty 25; treaties 25–6
economic improvement 56
Egerton, Hugh 44
Ellingson, Terr 98
Elphinstone, Mountstuart 48–9
Enlightenment 3, 43, 75
equality *see* racial equality
ethnology 8, 23, 99, 111, 114, 117, 118, 157, 166, 179, 189, 190, 192–3, 196, 209–10, 213–14, 217–18, 222, 247
Ethnology Society of London 96n 98, 112, 116, 222, 225, 226, 243
Eurocentric 221–2
evolution 114, 222–5, 227; and colonialism 226

Farquhar, Colonel Robert 75, 127, 134
Farquhar, Commander Arthur 183–4
Ferguson, Adam 90
Forrest, Thomas 29, 32, 47–8, 72, 81, 102
freedom 5, 12–13, 15, 58, 76, 130–1, 132–3, 172, 209, 214, 222, 234
free trade 131

Genesis 49
geographic determinism 107, 108, 215–16
Gibbon, Edward 24, 48
Gladstone, William 164
Gliddon, George 116, 247
Gliddon, William 188, 205n

Hall, Basil 60
Hassim, Pangeran Muda (Rajah of Sarawak) 158–9
Hastings, Warren 18
historian-administrators 1, 2, 4, 12, 13, 35, 71
history 3, 42, 43, 46–7, 72, 86, 105, 107; circular history 210–12; civil history 106–7; Conjectural/Stadial History 2, 46, 48–9, 51, 52, 74, 210; global history 17, 42; great man thesis 60; Javanese Chronicle tradition 50; mosaic history 49–51, 61, 71–2, 78–80, 81, 87, 106–7, 227, 228, 235; national 75; natural history 105–6; race in history 105, 108; universal history 2, 15, 210, 233, 236
Hobbes, Thomas 51
humanitarianism, evangelical 155, 162–3, 184, 187
Humboldt, Alexander von 79
Hume, David 48, 75–6, 90
Hume, Joseph 158, 184–5, 189, 196–7
Hunt, James 220
Hussein, Sultan Mahomet Shah 134–5

Ibans, Sekrang and Saribas 161, 183, 192–3; massacre of 186
Indian 75
Irwin, Graham 184
Islam, interpretations of 62, 64, 108, 190–1, 234
Islay 20–2

Java 42; corvée labour 54, 55; British expedition to 13; Indic culture 61, 62, 234; land ownership 51–2, 63, 234; returns to Dutch control 126
Javanese culture 43, 64
Johnson, Samuel 79
Johor 134
Jones, William 80–1, 89
Junk Ceylon (Phuket) 32

Kadir, Abdullah bin Abdul 135
Kames, Lord (Henry Home) 79, 87

Kant, Immanuel 101
Keppel, Henry 1, 154, 161, 162
Knox, Robert 87

land 42–43; as equality 134–5, 138, 233; as source of civil history 51; hereditary 61; improvement 134; India 55; Java 53, 55–6, 59, 63; ownership 43, 58, 134; Roytwari system 42, 56, 234; tenure 42, 47, 49; Zamindari system 42, 56
Leyden, John 1, 77, 80, 82–4
liberalism 2, 5–7, 9, 13–16, 27, 29, 31–2, 35, 39n 52, 179, 222–3, 239, 241; *liberal imperialism* 2, 14
Light, Francis 32, 74
Locke, John 6, 51–2, 72
Logan, James 116
Lyell, Charles 224–5, 243

Mackenzie, Colonel Colin 59
Macqueen, James 27
Mahkota, Pengiran Indera 159, 161
Majapahit 61
Majeed, Javed 6
Malacca 128
Malay 75, 76–7, 81, 103, 115, 170–1
Marsden, William 1, 72–3, 74–8, 81, 82, 84, 88, 99; race 103–4, 108
Matram 53
Max Muller 221, 225
mercantilism 25
Metha, Uday Singh 6, 15
migration 80, 85, 113; Chinese 130
Mill, James 6, 57–8
Milner, Anthony 90
Minto, Lord 13–14, 22, 45, 55, 56–7, 58, 82
Monboddo, Lord (James Burnett) 90
monogenesis 87, 117, 210, 219, 226, 227
monopoly 25
Morton, Samuel 117, 227
Mundy, Rodney 1, 154
Muthu, Sankar 6
mythology 50

Naoroji, Dadabhai 221–2
national character 43, 48, 61, 90–2
nature, state of 51
Negro 77, 84, 103, 104, 111
New Zealand 164
New Zealand Association 164
Nott, Josiah 116

occupation 30; unoccupied
    territory 29
opium 132–3, 201
Orang Lut 75
Orang Utan 73, 78
Orientalism 4
origins, idea of 78–9, 82

Papuans 77, 104, 111
Peace Society 184, 188
Penang (Prince of Wales Island)
    29, 47
Peranakan 130
philology 80
piracy 154, 161, 166–9, 181, 187,
    189–91, 198–9; as inter-tribal war
    198–199; law against 168, 191–6
Pitt, William 18
Pitts, Jenifer 6
Pocock, J. G. A. 24
polygenesis 4, 79, 81, 87, 88, 91, 101,
    108, 112, 114, 116–18, 210–11,
    219–20, 226, 229, 233, 236
Polynesian 81, 89
Prichard, James Cowles 117, 219, 227
Prinsep, Charles 197–200
property 129

race 77, 81, 85, 91, 92, 98–103, 113,
    218, 233; brown 105, 111; climatic
    theory 107; environment 108, 216
race illustrations 102–4
racial equality 30–2, 99, 131, 133,
    138, 209–10, 213, 216–17, 220–2,
    226–7, 235, 239
racial mixing/commixture/
    miscegenation 112–13, 133, 235
racial purity 31, 113
racial superiority 98, 111, 221
radicalism 7
radicals 163, 179, 182, 184–5,
    188–9, 196
Raffles, Lady Sophia 44, 155
Raffles, Thomas Stamford 1, 33, 34,
    42, 58, 65, 83, 99, 125, 126, 140;
    criticism of John Crawfurd 34, 62,
    85; 'Dick' 104–5; History of Java
    43, 44, 61; Islam 62; race 104, 108;
    relationship with John Crawfurd 44,
    45; review into land tenure in Java
    58–61; Singapore 127, 135
residents, role of 140
Robertson, William 17, 48
Robinson, George Augustus 164

Rothschild, Emma 6
Rousseau, Jean-Jacques 98
Royal Geographical Society 114,
    242–3, 249
Royal Navy 183, 187–8; head money
    184, 188

Said, Edward 5, 239
Saints / Clapham Sect 164–5
Sanskrit 80, 85, 89
Sarawak 158–73; antimony 160;
    Chinese rebellion 200–1
savages 72–4, 77–8, 162, 191, 209–15,
    214, 228, 235; rights 209
Sclater, Philip 116
Scotland 20; Scottish Highlands 16, 82
Scott, James 90
Scott, Walter 12
Singapore 126; Chinese in 129–30;
    economy 131; land grants 134,
    137–8 migration to 128; multi-racial
    society 127, 133; sovereignty 134–6;
    strategic position 126; taxation 132
slavery 33, 111, 116, 131, 217,
    218–19, 249, 251
Smith, Adam 6, 48, 90, 100
sovereignty 25, 134–136
spices 16
St. John, Horace 1
St. John, James Augustus 1, 154,
    191–2; on John Crawfurd 194; on
    piracy 190
St. John, Spencer 1, 156, 200
stages of society 74
Stocking, George 116, 118
Stokes, Eric 6
Sumatra 126
survival of the fittest 222
suzerainty 159

Templer, John 154
Tierra Del Fuego 221
travel writing 101–2

universal suffrage/voting 5, 27, 31–2,
    130, 235

village republic 63, 234
VOC (Vereenigde Oostindische
    Compagnie) 53

Wallace Line 115–16, 123n
Wallace, Alfred Russell 99, 100,
    113–14, 118, 112n 223; evolution

115, 226; influence of Phillip Sclater 118; racial ideas 115; relationship with James Brooke 114; relationship with John Crawfurd 114, 216–17, 223, 226

Washington, Captain John 156
White, Charles 87
Wise, Henry Herman 180, 184–5

Yogyakarta 55